Chapterwise
DPP
for
JEE Advanced

disha
Nurturing Ambitions

PHYSICS

AF380141

Collection of 540+ MCQs based on NCERT

Improves your Score by at least 20%

25 Chapters based on NCERT

Scoring Grid	DAILY PRACTICE PROBLEM DPP CHAPTERWISE CP07 - PHYSICS			
	Total Questions	20	Total Marks	74
	Attempted		Correct	
	Incorrect		Net Score	
	Cut-off Score	24	Qualifying Score	35
	Success Gap = Net Score – Qualifying Score			
	Net Score = (Correct × 4) – (Incorrect × 1)			

- **Corporate Office** : 45, 2nd Floor, Maharishi Dayanand Marg, Corner Market, Malviya Nagar, New Delhi-110017

  Tel. : 011-49842349 / 49842350

Typeset by Disha DTP Team

Printed at : Repro Knowledgecast Limited, Thane

DISHA PUBLICATION

For further information about books from DISHA,

Log on to www.dishapublication.com or email to info@dishapublication.com

DPP - Daily Practice Problems

Chapter-wise Sheets

Date : [ ] Start Time : [ ] End Time : [ ]

PHYSICS 

SYLLABUS : Units and Measurements

Max. Marks : 74 **Time : 60 min.**

GENERAL INSTRUCTIONS

- The Daily Practice Problem Sheet contains 20 Questions divided into 5 sections.

Section I has **5** MCQs with ONLY 1 Correct Option, **3** marks for each correct answer and **−1** for each incorrect answer.

Section II has **4** MCQs with ONE or MORE THAN ONE Correct options.

For each question, marks will be awarded in one of the following categories:

Full marks: **+4** If only the bubble(s) corresponding to all the correct option(s) is (are) darkened.

Partial marks: **+1** For darkening a bubble corresponding to each correct option provided NO INCORRECT option is darkened.

Zero marks: If none of the bubbles is darkened.

Negative marks: **−2** In all other cases.

Section III has **4** Single Digit Integer Answer Type Questions, **3** marks for each Correct Answer and 0 marks in all other cases.

Section IV has Comprehension/Matching Cum-Comprehension Type Questions having **5** MCQs with ONLY ONE correct option, **3** marks for each Correct Answer and 0 marks in all other cases.

Section V has **2** Matching Type Questions, **2** mark for the correct matching of each row and 0 marks in all other cases.

- You have to evaluate your Response Grids yourself with the help of Solutions.

Section I - Straight Objective Type

This section contains 5 multiple choice questions. Each question has 4 choices (a), (b), (c) and (d), out of which **ONLY ONE** is correct.

1. A student measured the length of a rod and wrote it as 3.50 cm. Which instrument did he use to measure it?
   (a) A meter scale.
   (b) A vernier calliper where the 10 divisions in vernier scale matches with 9 division in main scale and main scale has 10 divisions in 1 cm.
   (c) A screw gauge having 100 divisions in the circular scale and pitch as 1 mm.
   (d) A screw gauge having 50 divisions in the circular scale and pitch as 1 mm.

RESPONSE GRID 1. ⓐⓑⓒⓓ

Space for Rough Work

2. If the constant of gravitational constant (G) and Planck's constant (h) and the velocity of light (c) be chosen as fundamental units then the dimensions of the radius of gyration is :

(a) $h^{1/2}\, c^{-3/2} G^{1/2}$ (b) $h^{1/2} c^{3/2} G^{1/2}$

(c) $h^{1/2}\, c^{-3/2} G^{-1/2}$ (d) $h^{-1/2}\, c^{-3/2} G^{1/2}$

3. Intensity observed in an interference pattern is $I = I_0 \sin^2 \theta$. At $\theta = 30°$ intensity $I = 5 \pm 0.0020$ W/m^2. Find percentage error in angle if $I_0 = 20$ W/m^2.

(a) $\dfrac{4}{\pi}\sqrt{3}\times 10^{-2}\%$ (b) $\dfrac{2}{\pi}\sqrt{3}\times 10^{-2}\%$

(c) $\dfrac{1}{\pi}\sqrt{3}\times 10^{-2}\%$ (d) $\dfrac{3}{\pi}\sqrt{3}\times 10^{-2}\%$

4. Two masses M_A and M_B ($M_A < M_B$) are weighed using same weighing machine. Absolute error and relative error in two measurements are (Assume only systematic errors are involved)

(a) absolute error same for both, relative error greater for M_A and lesser for M_B

(b) absolute error same for both, relative error greater for M_B and lesser for M_A

(c) relative error same for both, absolute error greater for M_A and lesser for M_B

(d) relative error same for both, absolute error greater for M_B and lesser for M_A

5. Students I, II and III perform an experiment for measuring the acceleration due to gravity (g) using a simple pendulum. They use different lengths of the pendulum and /or record time for different number of oscillations. The observations are shown in the table.

Least count for length = 0.1 cm
Least count for time = 0.1 s

Student	Length of the pendulum (cm)	No. of oscillat- ions (n)	Total time for (n) oscillations (s)	Time period (s)
I	64.0	8	128.0	16.0
II	64.0	4	64.0	16.0
III	20.0	4	36.0	9.0

If E_I, E_{II} and E_{III} are the percentage errors in g, i.e., $\left(\dfrac{\Delta g}{g}\times 100\right)$ for students I, II and III, respectively, then

(a) $E_I = 0$ (b) E_I is minimum

(c) $E_I = E_{II}$ (d) E_{II} is maximum

Section II - Multiple Correct Answer Type

This section contains 4 multiple correct answer(s) type questions. Each question has 4 choices (a), (b), (c) and (d), out of which **ONE OR MORE** is/are correct.

6. The quantity/quantities that does/do not have mass in its/ their dimensions is/are

(a) specific heat

(b) latent heat

(c) electric potential difference

(d) electrical resistance

7. A student uses a simple pendulum of exactly 1m length to determine g, the acceleration due to gravity. He uses a stop watch with the least count of 1 sec for this and records 40 seconds for 20 oscillations. For this observation, which of the following statement(s) is (are) true?

(a) Error ΔT in measuring T, the time period, is 0.05 seconds

(b) Error ΔT in measuring T, the time period, is 1 second

(c) Percentage error in the determination of g is 5%

(d) Percentage error in the determination of g is 2.5%

8. If velocity of light in vacuum (3×10^8 m/s), acceleration due to gravity (9.81 m/s^2) and density of mercury (13600 kgm^{-3}) be adopted as the fundamental units, choose the correct option(s)

(a) unit of mass is 1.05×10^{52} kg

(b) unit of length is 9.17×10^{15} m

(c) unit of time is 3.06×10^{7} s

(d) unit of time is 3.06×10^{4} s

9. Which of the following are dimensionless quantities?

(a) $\dfrac{L}{CR^2}$ (b) $\dfrac{\varepsilon_0 \mu_0 E^2}{B^2}$ (c) $\dfrac{E^2}{B^2}$ (d) mLI^2

(Here symbols have their usual meanings)

Section III - Integer Type

This section contains 4 questions. The answer to each of the questions is a single digit integer ranging from 0 to 9.

10. If the time period t of a drop of liquid of density d, radius r, vibrating under surface tension s is given by the formula $t = \sqrt{d^a r^b s^c}$ and if $a = 1$, $c = -1$, then b is

11. To find the distance d over which a signal can be seen clearly in foggy conditions, a railways-engineer uses dimensions and assumes that the distance depends on the mass density ρ of the fog, intensity (power/area) S of the light from the signal and its frequency f. The engineer finds that d is proportional to $S^{1/n}$. The value of n is

12. Density of a substance is $\rho = \dfrac{M}{V}$ where $M = (20 \pm 0.2)$ kg and $V = (10 \pm 0.1)$ m^3. Calculate the percentage error in ρ.

13. In Searle's experiment, which is used to find Young's Modulus of elasticity, the diameter of experimental wire is $D = 0.05$ cm (measured by a scale of least count 0.001 cm) and length is $L = 110$ cm (measured by a scale of least count 0.1 cm). A weight of 50 N causes an extension of $X = 0.125$ cm (measured by a micrometer of least count 0.001cm). The maximum possible error in the values of Young's modulus is $x \times 10^{10}$ N/m^2. Find the value of x. Screw gauge and meter scale are free from error.

Section IV - Comprehension/Matching Cum-Comprehension Type

Directions (Qs. 14 and 15) : Based upon the given paragraph, 2 multiple choice questions have to be answered. Each question has 4 choices (a), (b), (c) and (d), out of which **ONLY ONE** is correct.

PARAGRAPH

In an experiment to determine the charge to mass ratio e/m of the electron using a cylindrical diode, the following equation is derived: $\dfrac{e}{m} = \dfrac{8V}{r^2 B^2}$, where V is the potential difference across the diode of radius r at the critical magnetic field B. The latter is supplied by passing a current I through a solenoid of diameter D and length L, and is given by

$$B = \frac{\mu_0 nI}{(1 + D^2 / L^2)^{1/2}} ,$$

where n is the number of turns per unit length. The appropriate experimental quantities are determined as follows:

$n = 3920$ m^{-1}; $D = 0.035 \pm 0.001$ m; $L = 0.120 \pm 0.001$ m; $r = (3.4 \pm 0.1) \times 10^{-3}$ m; $I = 1.92 \pm 0.02$ A; $V = 20 \pm 1$ V.

14. Error in B is
    (a) ± 0.9 T
    (b) ± 0.09 mT
    (c) ± 0.9 mT
    (d) ± 0.09 T

15. Error in e/m is
    (a) $\pm 0.01 \times 10^{11}$ c/kg
    (b) $\pm 1 \times 10^{11}$ c/kg
    (c) $\pm 0.1 \times 10^{11}$ c/kg
    (d) $\pm 0.001 \times 10^{11}$ c/kg

Directions (Qs. 16-18) : This passage contains a table having 3 columns and 4 rows. Based on the table, there are three questions. Each question has four options (a), (b), (c) and (d) **ONLY ONE** of these four options is correct.

If dimensions are given, physical quantity may not be unique as two different physical quantities may have same dimensional formula. Column I and III shows physical quantities while column II gives dimensional formula with respect to M, L and T (fundamental physical quantities mass, length and time respectively).

Column I		Column II		Column III	
I.	Torque	(i)	$M^0L^0T^0$	(P)	Wave number
II.	Power of lens	(ii)	$M^0L^{-1}T^0$	(Q)	Moment of force
III.	Plane angle	(iii)	$M^0L^0T^{-1}$	(R)	π
IV.	Angular frequency	(iv)	$M^1L^2T^{-2}$	(s)	Angular velocity

16. Which of the following shows the correct matching in terms of dimensionally simillar quantity as x in e^x.
    (a) (I)(i)(R)
    (b) (II)(iii)(S)
    (c) (III)(i)(R)
    (d) (IV)(iii)(S)

17. Which of the follwoing will remain unaffected if mass and length of the body changes?
    (a) III (i) R
    (b) IV (iii) S
    (c) I (iv) Q
    (d) Both (a) and (b)

18. The dimensions of physical quantity 'X' in the equation
$$\frac{1}{\text{Angular frequency}} = \frac{\text{'X'}}{\text{Angular velocity}} \text{ is same as:}$$
    (a) II (i) R
    (b) IV (i) R
    (c) III (i) R
    (d) I (i) P

RESPONSE GRID	**12.** ⓪①②③④⑤⑥⑦⑧⑨ **13.** ⓪①②③④⑤⑥⑦⑧⑨	
	14. ⓐⓑⓒⓓ **15.** ⓐⓑⓒⓓ **16.** ⓐⓑⓒⓓ **17.** ⓐⓑⓒⓓ **18.** ⓐⓑⓒⓓ	

Section V - Matrix-Match Type

This section contains 2 questions. It contains statements given in two columns, which have to be matched. Statements in column I are labelled as A, B, C and D whereas statements in column II are labelled as p, q, r and s. The answers to these questions have to be appropriately bubbled as illustrated in the following example. If the correct matches are A-p, A-r, B-p, B-s, C-r, C-s and D-q, then the correctly bubbled matrix will look like the following:

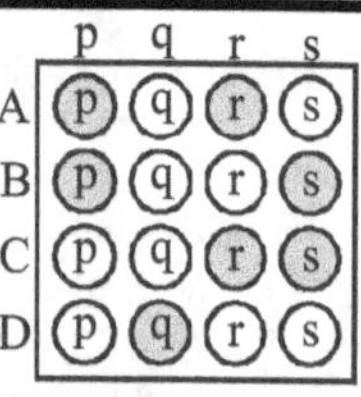

19. Some of the quantities in Column I have the same dimension as the quantities in Column II. Match the two columns.

Column I

(A) $\dfrac{ms\ell}{KA}$

m = mass
s = specific heat capacity; ℓ = length;
K = thermal conductivity; A = area

(B) E/B
E = strength of electric field
B = strength of magnetic field

(C) $\dfrac{1}{2}\varepsilon_0 E^2$
E = electric field
ε_0 = permittivity of free space

(D) $\dfrac{1}{2}\rho v^2$
ρ = density of fluid; v = speed of flow

Column II

(p) $\dfrac{1}{\sqrt{\mu_0 \varepsilon_0}}$
μ_0 = permeability of free space
ϵ_0 = permittivity of free space

(q) $\rho g h$
ρ = density of fluid
g = acceleration due to gravity; h = height of column

(r) $\sqrt{\dfrac{GM}{r}}$
G = Newton's gravitational constant
M = mass; r = radius

(s) $\sqrt{LC}$
L = inductance; C = capacitance.

20. Column-I gives four physical quantities. Select the appropriate units for the choices given in Column-II. Some of the physical quantities may have more than one choice correct :

Column I
(A) Capacitance
(B) Inductance
(C) Magnetic Induction
(D) Magnetic flux density

Column II
(p) ohm-second
(q) coulomb^2–joule^{-1}
(r) coulomb (volt)$^{-1}$
(s) newton (amp-metre)$^{-1}$

RESPONSE GRID	
19. A - (p)(q)(r)(s); B - (p)(q)(r)(s); C - (p)(q)(r)(s); D - (p)(q)(r)(s)	
20. A - (p)(q)(r)(s); B - (p)(q)(r)(s); C - (p)(q)(r)(s); D - (p)(q)(r)(s)	

DAILY PRACTICE PROBLEM DPP CP01 - PHYSICS

Total Questions	20	Total Marks	74
Attempted		Correct	
Incorrect		Net Score	
Cut-off Score	24	Qualifying Score	35

$$\text{Net Score} = \sum_{i=\mathrm{I}}^{\mathrm{V}} \left[\left(\text{correct}_i \times MM_i \right) - \left(In_i - NM_i \right) \right]$$

Space for Rough Work

DPP - Daily Practice Problems

Chapter-wise Sheets

Date : [ ]   Start Time : [ ]   End Time : [ ]

PHYSICS $\boxed{\text{CP02}}$

SYLLABUS : Motion in a Plane

Max. Marks : 74   **Time : 60 min.**

GENERAL INSTRUCTIONS

- The Daily Practice Problem Sheet contains 20 Questions divided into 5 sections.
- **Section I** has **5** MCQs with ONLY 1 Correct Option, **3** marks for each correct answer and **−1** for each incorrect answer.
- **Section II** has **4** MCQs with ONE or MORE THAN ONE Correct options.
- For each question, marks will be awarded in one of the following categories:
- Full marks: **+4** If only the bubble(s) corresponding to all the correct option(s) is (are) darkened.
- Partial marks: **+1** For darkening a bubble corresponding to each correct option provided NO INCORRECT option is darkened.
- Zero marks: If none of the bubbles is darkened.
- Negative marks: **−2** In all other cases.
- **Section III** has **4** Single Digit Integer Answer Type Questions, **3** marks for each Correct Answer and 0 marks in all other cases.
- **Section IV** has Comprehension/Matching Cum-Comprehension Type Questions having **5** MCQs with ONLY ONE correct option, **3** marks for each Correct Answer and 0 marks in all other cases.
- **Section V** has **2** Matching Type Questions, **2** mark for the correct matching of each row and 0 marks in all other cases.
- You have to evaluate your Response Grids yourself with the help of Solutions.

Section I - Straight Objective Type

This section contains 5 multiple choice questions. Each question has 4 choices (a), (b), (c) and (d), out of which **ONLY ONE** is correct.

1. A particle is ejected from the tube at A with a velocity v at an angle θ with the vertical y-axis. A strong horizontal wind gives the particle a constant horizontal acceleration a in the x-direction. If the particle strikes the ground at a point directly under its released position and the downward y -acceleration is taken as g then

(a) $h = \dfrac{2v^2 \sin\theta \cos\theta}{a}$

(b) $h = \dfrac{2v^2 \sin\theta \cos\theta}{g}$

(c) $h = \dfrac{2v^2}{g} \sin\theta \left(\cos\theta + \dfrac{a}{g}\sin\theta \right)$

(d) $h = \dfrac{2v^2}{a} \sin\theta \left(\cos\theta + \dfrac{g}{a}\sin\theta \right)$

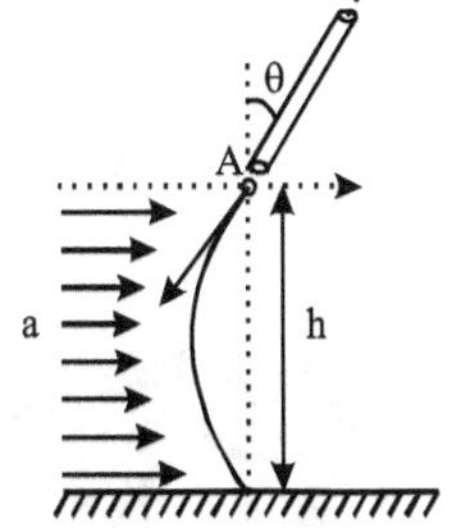

RESPONSE GRID   **1.** ⓐⓑⓒⓓ

Space for Rough Work

2. Rain, pouring down at an angle α with the vertical has a speed of 10 ms^{-1}. A girl runs against the rain with a speed of 8 ms^{-1} and sees that the rain makes an angle β with the vertical, then relation between α and β is

(a) $\tan\alpha = \dfrac{8+10\sin\beta}{10\cos\beta}$ (b) $\tan\beta = \dfrac{8+10\sin\alpha}{10\cos\alpha}$

(c) $\tan\alpha = \tan\beta$ (d) $\tan\alpha = \cot\beta$

3. A vector $\vec{A}$ is rotated by a small angle $\Delta\theta$ radian ($\Delta\theta \ll 1$) to get a new vector $\vec{B}$. In that case $\left|\vec{B}-\vec{A}\right|$ is :

(a) $\left|\vec{A}\right|\Delta\theta$ (b) $\left|\vec{B}\right|\Delta\theta - \left|\vec{A}\right|$

(c) $\left|\vec{A}\right|\left(1-\dfrac{\Delta\theta^2}{2}\right)$ (d) 0

4. For an observer on trolley direction of projection of particle is shown in the figure, while for observer on ground ball rise vertically. The maximum height reached by ball from trolley is

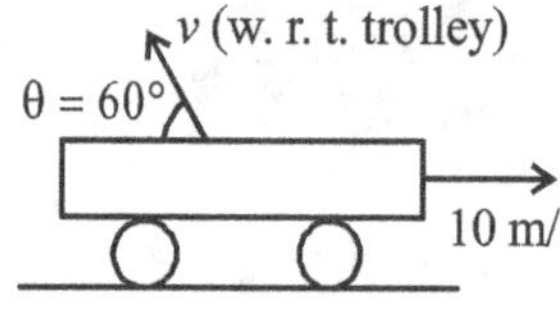

(a) 10 m   (b) 15 m   (c) 20 m   (d) 5 m

5. Two particles A and B separated by a distance $2R$ are moving counter clockwise along the same circular path of radius R each with uniform speed v. At time $t=0$, A is given a tangential acceleration of magnitude $a = \dfrac{72v^2}{25\pi R}$. Then

(a) the time lapse for the two bodies to collide is $\dfrac{6\pi R}{5v}$

(b) the angle covered by A is $11\pi/6$

(c) the angular velocity of A is $\dfrac{11v}{5R}$

(d) the radial acceleration of A is $289v^2/5R$

Section II - Multiple Correct Answer Type

This section contains 4 multiple correct answer(s) type questions. Each question has 4 choices (a), (b), (c) and (d), out of which **ONE OR MORE** is/are correct.

6. A helicopter is trying to land on a submarine deck which is moving south at 17 m/s. A 12 m/s wind is blowing into the west. If to the submarine crew the helicopter is descending vertically at 5 m/s, then

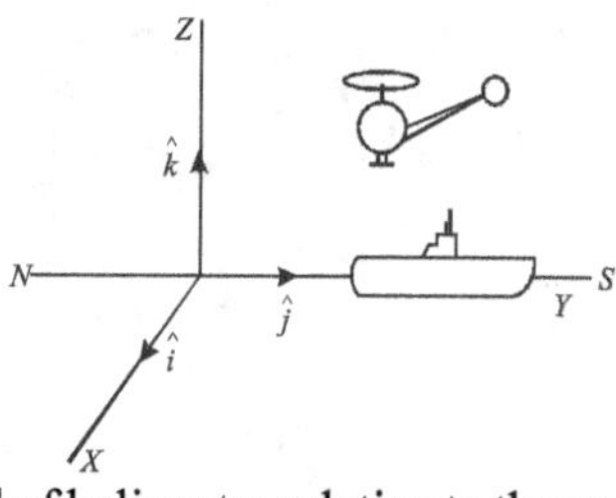

(a) Speed of helicopter relative to the water is $(17\hat{j}-5\hat{k})$ m/s

(b) Speed of helicopter relative to the air is $(-12\hat{i}+17\hat{j}-5\hat{k})$ m/s

(c) Speed of helicopter relative to the water is $(-12\hat{i}+17\hat{j}-5\hat{k})$ m/s

(d) Speed of helicopter relative to the air is $(17\hat{j}-5\hat{k})$ m/s

7. A man can swim with a velocity v relative to water. He has to cross a river of width d flowing with a velocity u ($u > v$). The distance through which he is carried downstream by the river is x. Which of the following statements are correct?

(a) If he crosses the river in minimum time, $x = du/v$

(b) x cannot be less than du/v

(c) For x to be minimum, he has to swim in a direction making an angle of $\pi/2 + \sin^{-1}(v/u)$ with the direction of the flow of water.

(d) x will be maximum if he swims in a direction making an angle of $\pi/2 - \sin^{-1}(v/u)$ with the direction of the flow of water.

8. A particle is projected from a point P with a velocity v at an angle θ with horizontal. At a certain point Q it moves at right angles to its initial direction. Then:

(a) velocity of particle at Q is $v\sin\theta$

(b) velocity of particle at Q is $v\cot\theta$

(c) time of flight from P to Q is $(v/g)\,\mathrm{cosec}\,\theta$

(d) time of flight from P to Q is $(v/g)\sec\theta$

9. The upper end of the string of a simple pendulum is fixed to a vertical z-axis, and set in motion such that the bob moves along a horizontal circular path of radius 2m, parallel to the x-y plane, 5m above the origin. The bob has a speed of 3m/s. The string breaks when the bob is vertically above the x-axis, and it lands on the xy plane at a point (x, y). Then

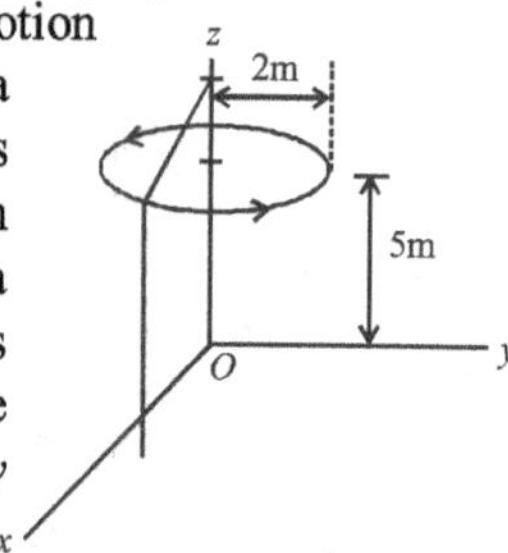

(a) $x = 2$m   (b) $x > 2$m   (c) $y = 3$m   (d) $y = 5$m

RESPONSE GRID					
2. ⓐⓑⓒⓓ	**3.** ⓐⓑⓒⓓ	**4.** ⓐⓑⓒⓓ	**5.** ⓐⓑⓒⓓ	**6.** ⓐⓑⓒⓓ	
7. ⓐⓑⓒⓓ	**8.** ⓐⓑⓒⓓ	**9.** ⓐⓑⓒⓓ			

Section III - Integer Type

This section contains 4 questions. The answer to each of the questions is a single digit Integer ranging from 0 to 9.

10. A train is moving with a constant acceleration 'a'. A boy standing in the train throws a ball forward with a speed of 10 m/s, at an angle of 60° to the horizontal. The boy has to move forward by 1.15 m inside the train to catch the ball back at the initial height. The acceleration of the train, in m/s², is

11. Two guns, situated on the top of a hill of height 10 m, fire one shot each with the same speed $5\sqrt{3}$ m s^{-1} at some interval of time. One gun fires horizontally and other fires upwards at an angle of 60° with the horizontal. The shots collide in air at a point P. Find the time-interval between the firings.

12. Two swimmers leave point A on one bank of the river to reach point B lying right across on the other bank. One of them crosses the river along the straight line AB while the other swims at right angles to the stream and then walks the distance that he has been carried away by the stream to get to point B. What was the velocity u (in km/hr) of her walking if both swimmers reached the destination simultaneously ? The stream velocity is 2km/hr and the velocity of each swimmer with respect to water is 2.5 km/hr.

13. Airplanes A and B are flying with constant velocity in the same vertical plane at angles 30° and 60° with respect to the horizontal respectively as shown in figure. 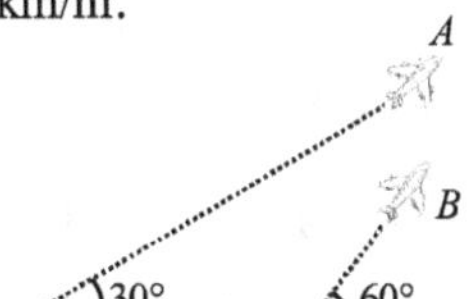

The speed of A is $100\sqrt{3}$ m/s. At time $t = 0$ s, an observer in A finds B at a distance of 500 m. The observer sees B moving with a constant velocity perpendicular to the line of motion of A. If at $t = t_0$, A just escapes being hit by B, t_0 in seconds is

Section IV - Comprehension/Matching Cum-Comprehension Type

Directions (Qs. 14 and 15) : Based upon the given paragraph, 2 multiple choice questions have to be answered. Each question has 4 choices (a), (b), (c) and (d), out of which **ONLY ONE** is correct.

PARAGRAPH

A particle moves in the plane xy with velocity $\vec{v} = a\hat{i} + bx\hat{j}$, where $\hat{i}$ and $\hat{j}$ are the unit vectors of the x and y axes, and a and b are constants. At the initial moment of time the particle was located at the point $x = y = 0$.

14. The equation of the particle trajectory is

(a) $y = \dfrac{ax^2}{b}$ (b) $y = \dfrac{bx^2}{2a}$ (c) $y = \dfrac{ax^2}{2b}$ (d) $y = \dfrac{2ax^2}{b}$

15. The curvature radius of trajectory is

(a) $R = \left[1 + \left(\dfrac{bx}{a}\right)^2\right]^{3/2}$

(b) $R = \dfrac{b}{a}\left[1 + \left(\dfrac{bx}{a}\right)^2\right]^{3/2}$

(c) $R = \dfrac{a}{b}\left[1 + \left(\dfrac{bx}{a}\right)^2\right]^{3/2}$

(d) $R = \dfrac{a}{b}\left[1 + \left(\dfrac{bx}{a}\right)^{1/2}\right]^2$

Directions (Qs. 16-18) : This passage contains a table having 3 columns and 4 rows. Based on the table, there are three questions. Each question has four options (a), (b), (c) and (d) **ONLY ONE** of these four options is correct.

Displacement time graphs are given in column I and their, corresponding velocity–time graphs and acceleration –time graphs are given in column II and III respectively.

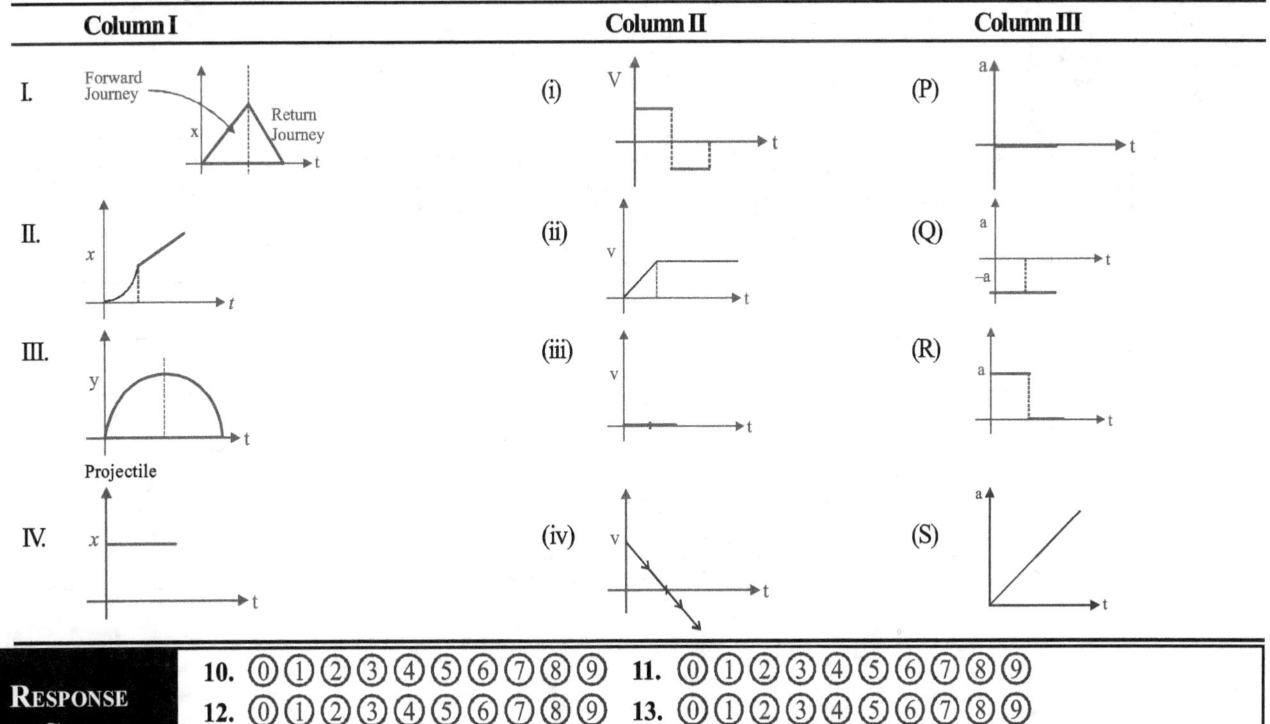

16. A body of mass m projected at an angle θ with horizontal. Which of the following shows the correct matching for the position, velocity and acceleration of the body with respect to time?

   (a) I (i) P   (b) II (ii) R   (c) III (iv) Q   (d) I (i) S

17. Which of the following matching represents the body moving with constant acceleration?

   (a) I (i) P   (b) III (iv) Q   (c) IV (iii) P   (d) All correct

18. Which is wrongly matched?

   (a) IV (iv) R   (b) III (iv) Q   (c) II (ii) R   (d) IV (iii) P

Section V - Matrix-Match Type

This section contains 2 questions. It contains statements given in two columns, which have to be matched. Statements in column I are labelled as A, B, C and D whereas statements in column II are labelled as p, q, r and s. The answers to these questions have to be appropriately bubbled as illustrated in the following example. If the correct matches are A-p, A-r, B-p, B-s, C-r, C-s and D-q, then the correctly bubbled matrix will look like the following:

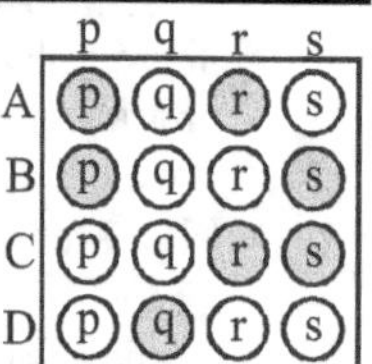

19. For a particle moving in x-y plane, initial velocity of particle is $\vec{u} = u_1\hat{i} + u_2\hat{j}$ and acceleration of particle is always $\vec{a} = a_1\hat{i} + a_2\hat{j}$ where u_1, u_2, a_1, a_2 are constants. Some parameters of motion is given in column I, match the corresponding path given in column II.

Column I

(A) If $u_1 \neq 0, u_2 = 0, a_1 \neq 0, a_2 \neq 0$
(B) If $u_1 = 0, u_2 \neq 0, a_1 \neq 0, a_2 \neq 0$
(C) If $u_1 = 0, u_2 = 0, a_1 \neq 0, a_2 \neq 0$
(D) If $u_1 \neq 0, u_2 \neq 0, a_1 \neq 0, a_2 \neq 0$

Column II

(p) path of particle must be parabolic
(q) path of particle must be straight line
(r) path of particle may be parabolic
(s) path of particle may be straight line

20.

Column I

(A) Particles are projected at same speed from same point on level ground such that their ranges are same
(B) Particles are projected from same point on ground such that maximum heights reached are same.
(C) Particles are projected horizontally from same point at a height with different initial velocities
(D) Particles are projected from the same point at a height with same initial speed, direction of velocity makes equal angle with horizontal one below and the other above horizontal

Column II

(p) Time of flight will be same
(q) Speed just before reaching ground will be same
(r) Vertical component of velocity just before reaching ground will be same
(s) Minimum kinetic energy during the flight will be equal.

<table>
<tr><td rowspan="3">RESPONSE GRID</td><td>16. (a)(b)(c)(d)   17. (a)(b)(c)(d)   18. (a)(b)(c)(d)</td></tr>
<tr><td>19. A - (p)(q)(r)(s); B - (p)(q)(r)(s); C - (p)(q)(r)(s); D - (p)(q)(r)(s)</td></tr>
<tr><td>20. A - (p)(q)(r)(s); B - (p)(q)(r)(s); C - (p)(q)(r)(s); D - (p)(q)(r)(s)</td></tr>
</table>

DAILY PRACTICE PROBLEM DPP CP02 - PHYSICS

Total Questions	20	Total Marks	74
Attempted		Correct	
Incorrect		Net Score	
Cut-off Score	20	Qualifying Score	35

$$\text{Net Score} = \sum_{i=I}^{V} \left[\left(\text{correct}_i \times MM_i\right) - \left(In_i - NM_i\right)\right]$$

Space for Rough Work

DPP - Daily Practice Problems

Chapter-wise Sheets

Date : | Start Time : | End Time :

PHYSICS $\boxed{\text{CP03}}$

SYLLABUS : Laws of Motion

Max. Marks : 74 **Time : 60 min.**

GENERAL INSTRUCTIONS

- The Daily Practice Problem Sheet contains 20 Questions divided into 5 sections.
- **Section I** has **5** MCQs with ONLY 1 Correct Option, **3** marks for each correct answer and **−1** for each incorrect answer.
- **Section II** has **4** MCQs with ONE or MORE THAN ONE Correct options.
- For each question, marks will be awarded in one of the following categories:
- Full marks: **+4** If only the bubble(s) corresponding to all the correct option(s) is (are) darkened.
- Partial marks: **+1** For darkening a bubble corresponding to each correct option provided NO INCORRECT option is darkened.
- Zero marks: If none of the bubbles is darkened.
- Negative marks: **−2** In all other cases.
- **Section III** has **4** Single Digit Integer Answer Type Questions, **3** marks for each Correct Answer and 0 marks in all other cases.
- **Section IV** has Comprehension/Matching Cum-Comprehension Type Questions having **5** MCQs with ONLY ONE correct option, **3** marks for each Correct Answer and 0 marks in all other cases.
- **Section V** has **2** Matching Type Questions, **2** mark for the correct matching of each row and 0 marks in all other cases.
- You have to evaluate your Response Grids yourself with the help of Solutions.

Section I - Straight Objective Type

This section contains 5 multiple choice questions. Each question has 4 choices (a), (b), (c) and (d), out of which **ONLY ONE** is correct.

1. Three blocks A, B, C of weights 40N, 30N, 80N respectively are at rest on an inclined plane as shown in figure. Determine the smallest value of coefficient of limiting friction (μ_s) for which equilibrium of system is maintained.

(a) 0.1757

(b) 0.2757

(c) 0.5757

(d) 0.8757

RESPONSE GRID 1. (a)(b)(c)(d)

Space for Rough Work

2. A bob is hanging over a pulley inside a car through a string. The second end of the string is in the hand of a person standing in the car. The car is moving with constant acceleration a directed horizontally as shown in figure. Other end of the string is pulled with constant acceleration a vertically. The tension in the string is equal to

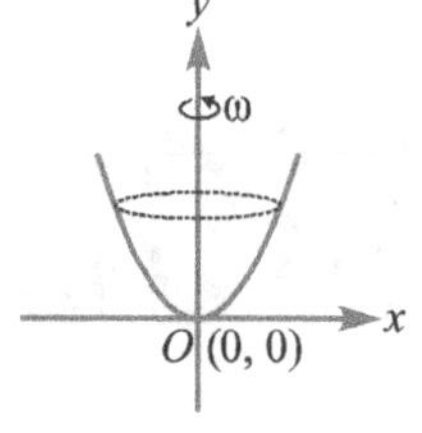

(a) $m\sqrt{g^2 + a^2}$

(b) $m\sqrt{g^2 + a^2} - ma$

(c) $m\sqrt{g^2 + a^2} + ma$

(d) $m(g + a)$

3. In the given figure, a smooth parabolic wire track lies in the xy-plane (vertical). The shape of track is defined by the equation $y = x^2$. A ring of mass m which can slide freely on the wire track, is placed at the position $A(1,1)$. The track is rotated with constant angular speed ω such that there is no relative slipping between the ring and the track. The value of ω is

(a) $\sqrt{g/2}$ (b) $\sqrt{g}$ (c) $\sqrt{2g}$ (d) $2\sqrt{g}$

4. A block of mass m is placed on a surface with a vertical cross section given by $y = \dfrac{x^3}{6}$. If the coefficient of friction is 0.5, the maximum height above the ground at which the block can be placed without slipping is:

(a) $\dfrac{1}{6}$m   (b) $\dfrac{2}{3}$m   (c) $\dfrac{1}{3}$m   (d) $\dfrac{1}{2}$m

5. A plank of mass $M_1 = 8$ kg with a bar of mass $M_2 = 2$ kg placed on its rough surface, lie on a smooth floor of elevator ascending with an acceleration g/4. The coefficient of friction is $\mu = 1/5$ between m_1 and m_2. A horizontal force $F = 30$ N is applied to the plank. Then the acceleration of bar and the plank in the reference frame of elevator are

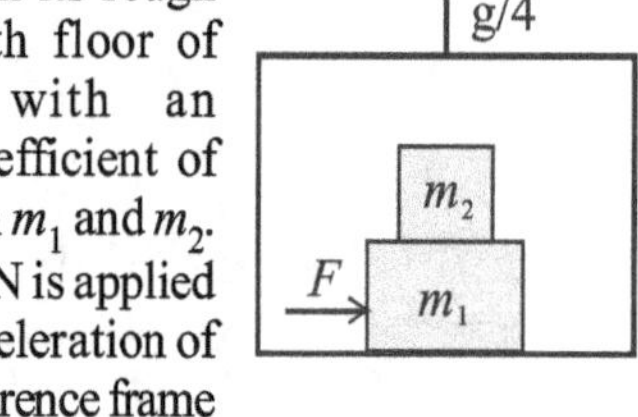

(a) 3.5 m/s^2, 5 m/s^2 (b) 5 m/s^2, $50/8$ m/s^2

(c) 2.5 m/s^2, $25/8$ m/s^2 (d) 4.5 m/s^2, 4.5 m/s^2

7. The system in figure is given an acceleration. Weight of the ball is W.

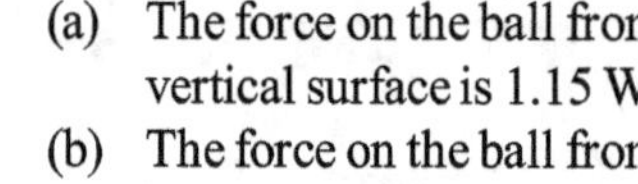
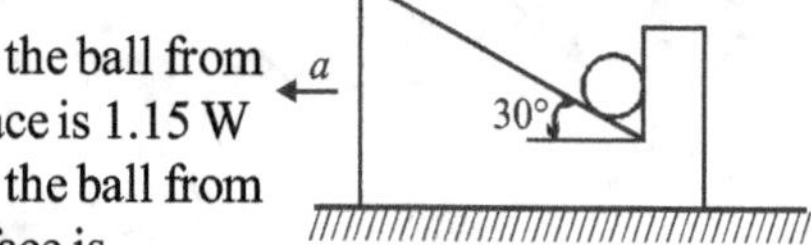

(a) The force on the ball from vertical surface is 1.15 W

(b) The force on the ball from inclined surface is
$$W\left(0.58 + \frac{a}{g}\right)$$

(c) The force on the ball from vertical surface is
$$W\left(0.58 + \frac{a}{g}\right)$$

(d) The forces on the ball from inclined surface is 1.15 W

8. A car C of mass m_1 rests on a plank P of mass m_2. The plank rests on a smooth floor. The string and pulley are ideal. The car starts and moves towards the pulley with acceleration.

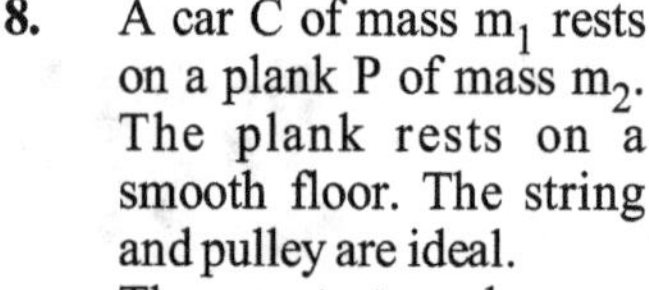
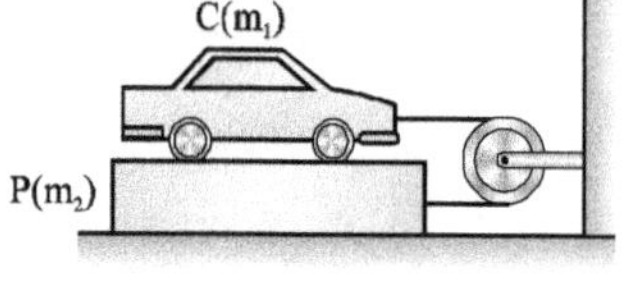

(a) If $m_1 > m_2$, the string will remain under tension

(b) If $m_1 < m_2$, the string will become slack

(c) If $m_1 = m_2$, the string will have no tension, and C and P will have accelerations of equal magnitude

(d) C and P will have acceleration of equal magnitude if $m_1 \geq m_2$

9. A machine, in an amusement park, consists of a cage at the end of one arm, hinged at O. The cage revolves along a vertical circle of radius r (ABCOEFGH) about its hinge O, at constant linear speed $v = \sqrt{gr}$.

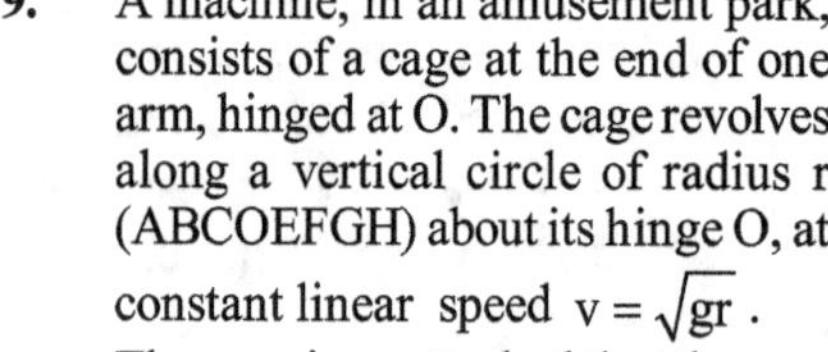
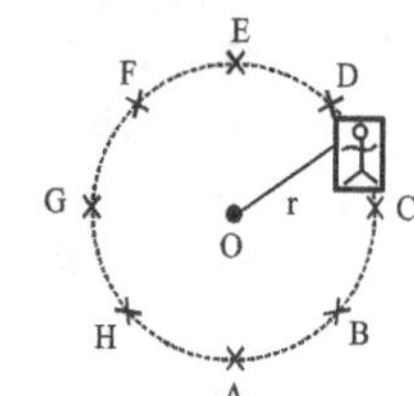

The cage is so attached that the man of weight 'w' standing on a weighing machine, inside the cage, is always vertical. Then which of the following is correct?

(a) The reading of his weight on the machine is the same at all positions

(b) The weight reading at A is greater than the weight reading at E by 2 w.

(c) The weight reading at G = w

(d) The ratio of the weight reading at E to that at A = 0

Section II - Multiple Correct Answer Type

This section contains 4 multiple correct answer(s) type questions. Each question has 4 choices (a), (b), (c) and (d), out of which **ONE OR MORE** is/are correct.

6. A horizontal force P is exerted on a 20 kg box in order to slide it up a 30° incline. The friction force retarding the motion is 80N. If the acceleration of the moving box is to be

(a) zero then P is 223N   (b) 0.75 m/s^2 then P is 206 N

(c) zero then P is 206 N   (d) 0.75 m/s^2 then P is 223 N

Section III - Integer Type

This section contains 4 questions. The answer to each of the questions is a single digit integer ranging from 0 to 9.

10. A block slides down a smooth inclined plane to the ground when released from the top, in time t seconds. Another block is dropped vertically from the same point, in the absence of the inclined plane and reaches the ground in $t/2$ second. Then find the angle (in degree in multiple of 10) of inclination of the plane with the vertical.

11. Find the mass of the hanging block which will prevent the smaller block from slipping over the triangular block. All the surfaces are frictionless and the strings and the pulleys are light. Given $m = M = 1$ kg; $\cot\theta = 2$.

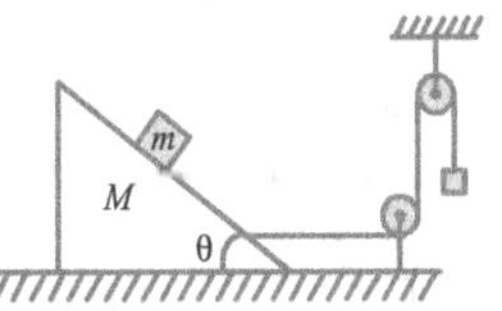

12. A uniform rod of length 2ℓ and mass m is suspended from one end by inextensible string and other end lies on smooth ground. The angle made by rod with vertical is $\theta = \sin^{-1}(1/\sqrt{3})$. If N_1 and N_2 represents the contact force from ground on rod just before and just after cutting string then find the ratio of N_1/N_2.

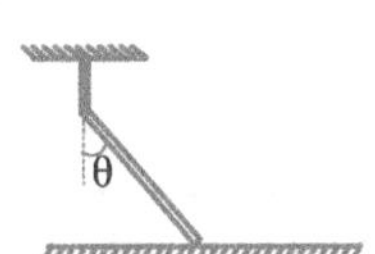

13. In the arrangement shown in figure $m_A = 1$ kg and $m_B = 2$ kg, while all the pulleys and strings are massless and frictionless. At $t = 0$, a force $F = 10\,t$ starts acting over central pulley in vertically upward direction. Find the velocity of A (in deca m/s) when B loses contact with floor.

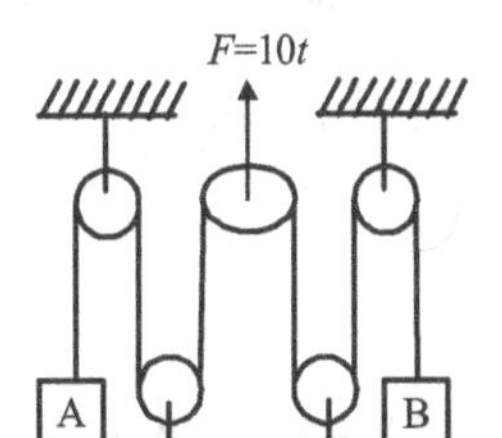

Section IV - Comprehension/Matching Cum-Comprehension Type

Directions (Qs. 14 and 15) : Based upon the given paragraph, 2 multiple choice questions have to be answered. Each question has 4 choices (a), (b), (c) and (d), out of which **ONLY ONE** is correct.

PARAGRAPH

Two bodies A and B of masses 10 kg and 5 kg are placed very slightly separated as shown in figure. The coefficients of friction between the floor and the blocks are as $\mu_s = \mu_k = 0.4$. Block A is pushed by an external force F.

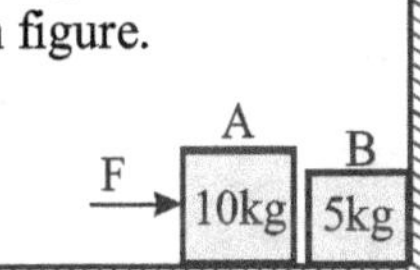

The value of F can be changed. When the welding between block A and ground breaks, block A will start pressing block B and when welding of B also breaks, block B will start pressing the vertical wall.

14. If $F = 50$ N, the friction force acting between block B and ground will be –

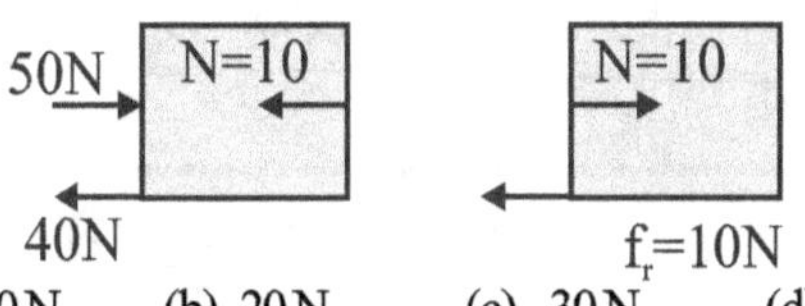

   (a) 10 N   (b) 20 N   (c) 30 N   (d) 15 N

15. The force of friction acting on B varies with the applied force F according to curve –

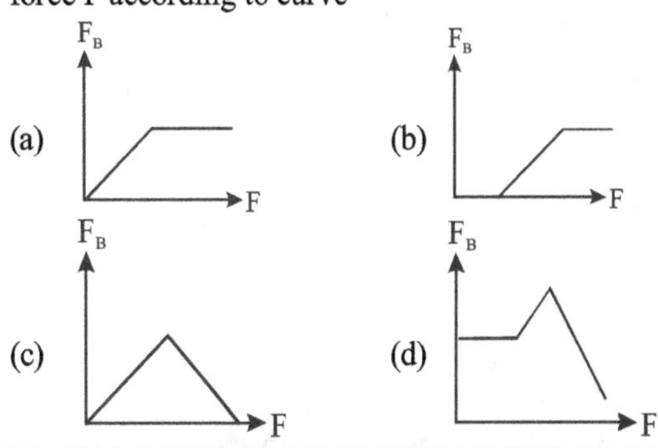

Directions (Qs. 16-18) : This passage contains a table having 3 columns and 4 rows. Based on the table, there are three questions. Each question has four options (a), (b), (c) and (d) **ONLY ONE** of these four options is correct.

The acceleration of a particle as measured from an inertial frame is given by the vector sum of all the forces acting on the particle divided by its mass. Column I shows the motion of blocks (m_1, m_2, m_3) in contact/connected by massless string on a smooth horizontal surface. If f_1 is the contact force between body m_1 and m_2, f_2 between body m_2 and m_3, T_1 be the tension in the string between body m_1 and m_2, T_2 between body m_2 and m_3. Column II and III shows different values of f_1, f_2, T_1 and T_2 in different situations shown in column I.

Column I	Column II	Column III
I. $\xrightarrow{F}$ m_1 m_2 m_3	(i) $\quad T_1 = \dfrac{(m_2 + m_3)F}{m_1 + m_2 + m_3}$	(P) $\quad f_2 = \dfrac{(m_1 + m_2)F}{m_1 + m_2 + m_3}$
II. m_1 m_2 m_3 $\xleftarrow{F}$	(ii) $\quad T_1 = \dfrac{m_1 F}{m_1 + m_2 + m_3}$	(Q) $\quad f_2 = \dfrac{m_3 F}{m_1 + m_2 + m_3}$
III. m_1 $\overset{T_1}{\rightarrowtail}$ m_2 $\overset{T_2}{\rightarrowtail}$ m_3 $\xleftarrow{F}$	(iii) $\quad f_1 = \dfrac{m_1 F}{m_1 + m_2 + m_3}$	(R) $\quad T_2 = \dfrac{(m_1 + m_2)F}{m_1 + m_2 + m_3}$
IV. $\xleftarrow{F}$ m_1 $\overset{T_1}{\rightarrowtail}$ m_2 $\overset{T_2}{\rightarrowtail}$ m_3	(iv) $\quad f_1 = \dfrac{(m_2 + m_3)F}{m_1 + m_2 + m_3}$	(S) $\quad T_2 = \dfrac{m_3 F}{m_1 + m_2 + m_3}$

Space for Rough Work

16. If the acceleration of body m_1, m_2 and m_3 respectively shown in situation Column I (I) are (2, 2, 2) then the correct matching is [Take $m_1 = 1$ kg, $m_2 = 2$ kg, $m_3 = 3$ kg, F = 12 N]

  (a) I (iv) Q   (b) IV (iv) P   (c) III (ii) P   (d) I (iii) Q

17. If the value of T_1 and T_2 shown in the situation column I (IV) are 10N and 6N respectively then find the correct matching. [Take $m_1 = 1$ kg, $m_2 = 2$ kg, $m_3 = 3$ kg, F = 12 N].

  (a) II (i) R   (b) IV (i) S   (c) IV (iii) S   (d) III (ii) S

18. Which of the following does not show the correct matching?

  (a) II (iii) P   (b) III (ii) R   (c) I (iv) Q   (d) IV (i) R

Section V - Matrix-Match Type

This section contains 2 questions. It contains statements given in two columns, which have to be matched. Statements in column I are labelled as A, B, C and D whereas statements in column II are labelled as p, q, r and s. The answers to these questions have to be appropriately bubbled as illustrated in the following example. If the correct matches are A-p, A-r, B-p, B-s, C-r, C-s and D-q, then the correctly bubbled matrix will look like the following:

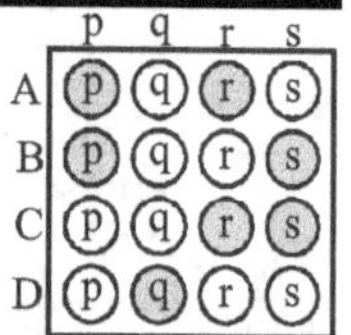

19. The block is placed at different position of earth from A to B as shown. Then the following parameters for different positions from A to B will vary as follows. Consider the effect of rotation of earth about its own axis. Neglect the effect of rotation of earth around the sun and assume earth as a perfect sphere, (F = centrifugal force; f = frictional force; $\theta < 45°$) Match the two columns.

Column I	Column II
(A) Gravity force	(p) first increases and then decreases
(B) Normal force	(q) first decreases and then increases
(C) Centrifugal force	(r) remains constant
(D) Frictional force	(s) increases only

20. Match the columns ($g = 10$ m/s^2)

Column I	Column II
(A) Block of mass 2 kg on a rough horizontal surface pulled by a horizontal force of 20N, $\mu_s = 0.5$	(p) Tension at the mid point of block is 10N
(B) Block of mass 2 kg pulled with constant speed up an incline of inclination 30° and coefficient of friction $1/\sqrt{3}$	(q) Acceleration of block is 5 m/s^2
(C) Block of mass 0.75kg pulled by a constant force of 7.5N upon incline of inclination 30° and coefficient of friction $1/\sqrt{3}$	(r) Force of friction acting is 5N
(D) Block of mass 2 kg pulled vertically by a force of 20N	(s) Resultant force on the block is zero

<table>
<tr><td rowspan="3">RESPONSE GRID</td><td>16. ⓐⓑⓒⓓ   17. ⓐⓑⓒⓓ   18. ⓐⓑⓒⓓ</td></tr>
<tr><td>19. A - ⓟⓠⓡⓢ ; B - ⓟⓠⓡⓢ ; C - ⓟⓠⓡⓢ ; D - ⓟⓠⓡⓢ</td></tr>
<tr><td>20. A - ⓟⓠⓡⓢ ; B - ⓟⓠⓡⓢ ; C - ⓟⓠⓡⓢ ; D - ⓟⓠⓡⓢ</td></tr>
</table>

DAILY PRACTICE PROBLEM DPP CP03 - PHYSICS

Total Questions	20	Total Marks	74
Attempted		Correct	
Incorrect		Net Score	
Cut-off Score	24	Qualifying Score	35

$$\text{Net Score} = \sum_{i=1}^{V} \left[\left(correct_i \times MM_i \right) - \left(In_i - NM_i \right) \right]$$

DPP - Daily Practice Problems

Chapter-wise Sheets

Date :   Start Time :   End Time :

PHYSICS $\boxed{\text{CP04}}$

SYLLABUS : Work, Energy and Power

Max. Marks : 74   **Time : 60 min.**

GENERAL INSTRUCTIONS

- The Daily Practice Problem Sheet contains 20 Questions divided into 5 sections.
  Section I has **5** MCQs with ONLY 1 Correct Option, **3** marks for each correct answer and **−1** for each incorrect answer.
  Section II has **4** MCQs with ONE or MORE THAN ONE Correct options.
  For each question, marks will be awarded in one of the following categories:
  Full marks: **+4** If only the bubble(s) corresponding to all the correct option(s) is (are) darkened.
  Partial marks: **+1** For darkening a bubble corresponding to each correct option provided NO INCORRECT option is darkened.
  Zero marks: If none of the bubbles is darkened.
  Negative marks: **−2** In all other cases.
  Section III has **4** Single Digit Integer Answer Type Questions, **3** marks for each Correct Answer and 0 marks in all other cases.
  Section IV has Comprehension/Matching Cum-Comprehension Type Questions having **5** MCQs with ONLY ONE correct option, **3** marks for each Correct Answer and 0 marks in all other cases.
  Section V has **2** Matching Type Questions, **2** mark for the correct matching of each row and 0 marks in all other cases.
- You have to evaluate your Response Grids yourself with the help of Solutions.

Section I - Straight Objective Type

This section contains 5 multiple choice questions. Each question has 4 choices (a), (b), (c) and (d), out of which **ONLY ONE** is correct.

1. A variable force P is maintained tangent to a frictionless cylindrical surface of radius a as shown in figure. By slowly varying this force, a block of weight W is moved and the spring to which it is stretched from position 1 to position 2. The work done by the force P is

(a) $W\, a \sin \theta$

(b) $\dfrac{1}{2}\, ka^2\, \theta^2$

(c) $W\, a \sin \theta + k\, a^2\, \theta^2$

(d) $W\, a \sin \theta + \dfrac{1}{2}\, k\, a^2\, \theta^2$

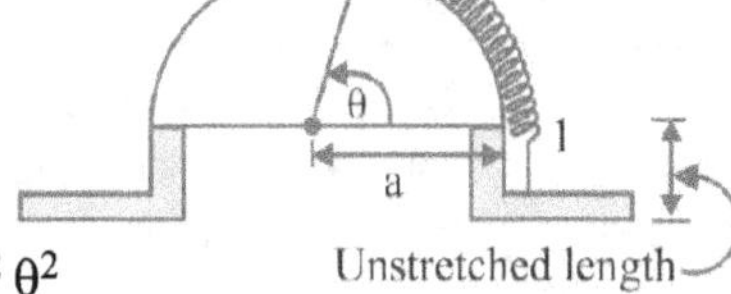

RESPONSE GRID	1. ⓐⓑⓒⓓ

Space for Rough Work

2. A particle falls from a height h on a fixed horizontal plane and rebounds. If e is the coefficient of restitution, the total distance travelled by the particle before it stops rebounding is

(a) $\dfrac{h}{2}\dfrac{[1-e^2]}{[1+e^2]}$ (b) $\dfrac{h[1-e^2]}{[1+e^2]}$ (c) $\dfrac{h}{2}\dfrac{[1+e^2]}{[1-e^2]}$ (d) $\dfrac{h[1+e^2]}{[1-e^2]}$

3. A tennis ball is dropped on a horizontal smooth surface. It bounces back to its original position after hitting the surface. The force on the ball during the collision is proportional to the length of compression of the ball. Which one of the following sketches describes the variation of its kinetic energy K with time t most appropriately? The figure are only illustrative and not to scale.

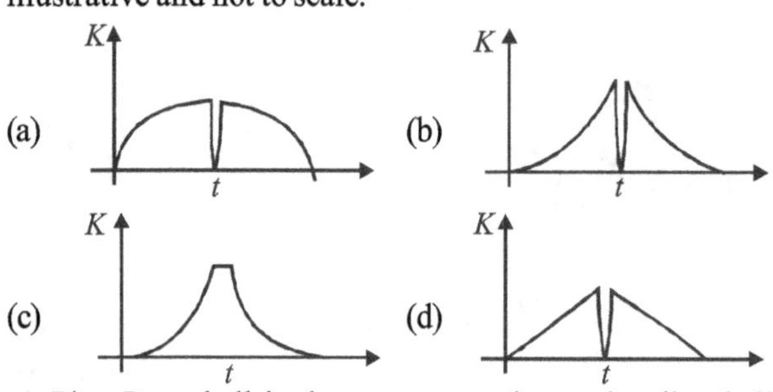

4. A Ping-Pong ball is thrown at a stationary bowling ball hanging from a wire. The Ping-Pong ball makes a one-dimensional elastic collision and bounces back along the same line. After the collision, the Ping-Pong ball has, compared with the bowling ball
(a) a larger magnitude of momentum and more kinetic energy
(b) a smaller magnitude of momentum and more kinetic energy
(c) a larger magnitude of momentum and less kinetic energy
(d) a smaller magnitude of momentum and less kinetic energy

5. An iron ball of mass m, suspended by a light inextensible string of length ℓ from a fixed point O, is shifted by an angle θ_0 as shown so as to strike the vertical wall perpendicularly. The maximum angle made by the string with vertical after the first collision, if e is the coefficient of restitution, is

(a) $\sin^{-1}\{1-e^2(1-\cos\theta_0)\}$

(b) $\cos^{-1}\{1-e^2(1-\cos\theta_0)\}$

(c) $\tan^{-1}\{1-e^2(1-\cos\theta_0)\}$

(d) zero

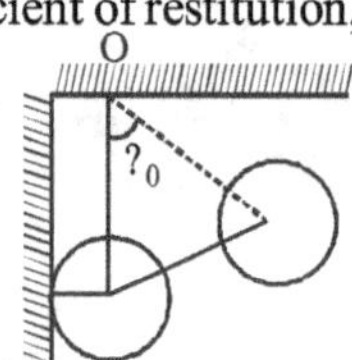

Section II - Multiple Correct Answer Type

This section contains 4 multiple correct answer(s) type questions. Each question has 4 choices (a), (b), (c) and (d), out of which **ONE OR MORE** is/are correct.

6. Among the following choose the correct statement(s)
(a) Work done by a centripetal force is zero
(b) Work done by a conservative force is independent of the path
(c) The area under the force-displacement curve gives work
(d) The product of pressure and volume has same dimensions as that of force

7. A force $\vec{F} = x^2 y^2 \hat{i} + x^2 y^2 \hat{j}\ (N)$ acts on a particle which moves in the XY plane. Choose the correct option(s)

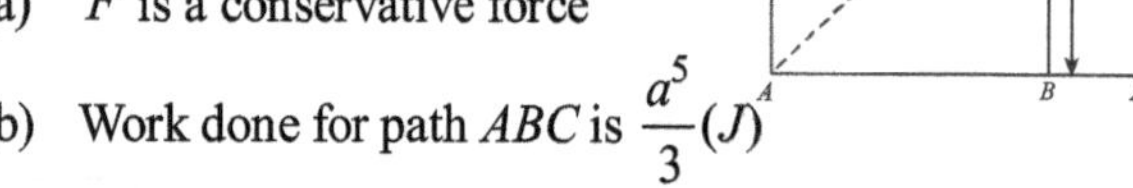

(a) $\vec{F}$ is a conservative force

(b) Work done for path ABC is $\dfrac{a^5}{3}(J)$

(c) Work done for path ADC is $\dfrac{a^5}{3}(J)$

(d) Work done for path AC is $\dfrac{2a^5}{3}(J)$

8. As shown in figure, a smooth rod is mounted horizontally just above a tabletop. A 10 kg collar, which is able to slide on the rod with negligible friction is fastened to a spring whose other end is attached to a pivot at O. The spring has negligible mass, a relaxed length of 10cm, and a spring constant of 500 N/m. The collar is released from rest at point S. Velocity as collar passes point

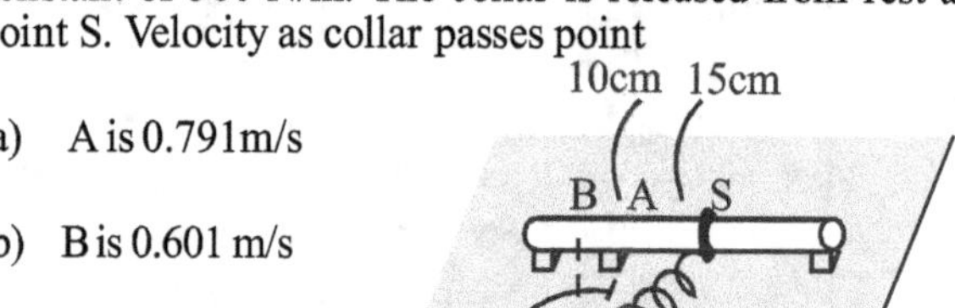

(a) A is 0.791 m/s

(b) B is 0.601 m/s

(c) A is 0.601 m/s

(d) B is 0.791 m/s

9. Two blocks, of masses M and 2M, are connected to a light spring of spring constant K that one end fixed, as shown in figure. The horizontal surface and the pulley are frictionless. The blocks are released from rest when the spring is deformed. The string is light

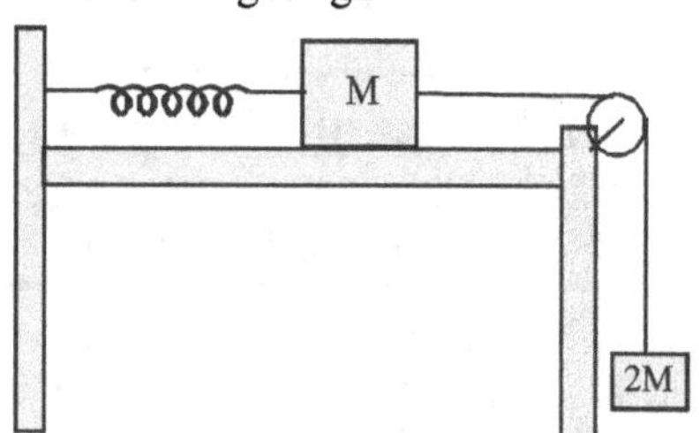

Which of the following are correct?

(a) Maximum extension in the spring is $\dfrac{4Mg}{K}$

(b) Maximum kinetic energy of the system is $\dfrac{2M^2g^2}{K}$

(c) When kinetic energy of the system is maximum, energy stored in the spring is $\dfrac{4M^2g^2}{K}$

(d) Maximum energy stored in the spring is four times that of maximum kinetic energy of the system

Section III - Integer Type

This section contains 4 questions. The answer to each of the questions is a single digit integer ranging from 0 to 9.

10. An object is dropped from a height h from the ground. Every time it hits the ground it looses 50% of its kinetic energy. The total distance covered as $t \to \infty$ is how much times of h ?

11. A particle of mass 0.2 kg is moving in one dimension under a force that delivers a constant power 0.5 W to the particle. If the initial speed of the particle is zero, the speed (in ms^{-1}) after 5 s is

12. A person is pulling a mass $m = 2kg$ from ground on a fixed rough hemispherical surface upto the top of the hemisphere with the help of a light inextensible string. Calculate the work done by the person, if $R = 1/5\ m$ and $m = 0.1$. ($g = 10m/s^2$)

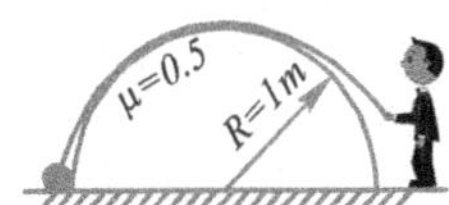

13. A block is initially at rest on a horizontal frictionless surface when a horizontal force in the positive direction of an axis is applied to the block. The force is given by $\vec{F} = (1 - x^2)\hat{i}\ N$, when x is in meters and the initial position of the block is $x = 0$. The maximum kinetic energy of the block is $\dfrac{2}{n}J$ in between $x = 0$ and $x = 2\ m$. Find the value of n.

Section IV - Comprehension/Matching Cum-Comprehension Type

Directions (Qs. 14 and 15) : Based upon the given paragraph, 2 multiple choice questions have to be answered. Each question has 4 choices (a), (b), (c) and (d), out of which **ONLY ONE** is correct.

PARAGRAPH

A ball with mass m is attached to the end of a rod of mass M and length l. The other end of the rod is pivoted so that the ball can move in a vertical circle. The rod is held in the horizontal position shown in figure and then given just enough a downward push so that the ball swings down and around and just reaches the vertical upward position, having zero speed there.

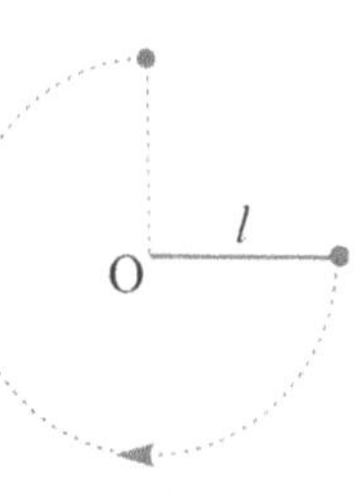

14. The change in potential energy of the system (ball + rod) is

(a) $mg\,l$

(b) $(M + m)\,gl$

(c) $\left(\dfrac{M}{2} + m\right)gl$

(d) $\dfrac{(M + m)}{2}\,gl$

15. The initial speed was given to the ball is

(a) $\sqrt{\dfrac{Mgl + 2mgl}{m}}$

(b) $\sqrt{2gl}$

(c) $\sqrt{\dfrac{2Mgl + mgl}{m}}$

(d) $\sqrt{gl}$

Directions (Qs. 16-18) : This passage contains a table having 3 columns and 4 rows. Based on the table, there are three questions. Each question has four options (a), (b), (c) and (d) **ONLY ONE** of these four options is correct.

Potential energy of spring is given by $\dfrac{1}{2}kx^2$ and for a projectile it is mgh. Column II and III shows increase and decrease of potential and Kinetic energy of the system respectively in different situations of spring/projectile. (Assume air resistance negligible and surfaces are smooth)

	Column I		Column II		Column III
I.	Projectile during upward journey	(i)	Potential energy increases by $\dfrac{1}{2}kx^2$	(P)	Kinetic energy increases by mgh
II.	Projectile during downward journey	(ii)	Potential energy decreases by $\dfrac{1}{2}kx^2$	(Q)	Kinetic energy decreases by mgh
III.	Spring compressed to length x	(iii)	Potential energy decreases by mgh	(R)	Kinetic energy increases by $\dfrac{1}{2}kx^2$
IV.	Spring elongated upto length x	(iv)	Potential energy increases by mgh	(S)	Kinetic energy decreases by $\dfrac{1}{2}kx^2$

16. Which of the following options is correct for the projectile during the upward journey?
    (a) I (iv) Q   (b) I (iii) Q   (c) I (iii) P   (d) Both (a) and (c)

17. Which of the following is the correct matching for the spring compressed to length x?
    (a) III (i) Q   (b) I (ii) P   (c) III (i) S   (d) III (ii) R

18. Which of the following is matched wrongly?
    (a) I (iii) P   (b) II (iii) P   (c) IV (i) S   (d) I (iv) Q

Section V - Matrix-Match Type

This section contains 2 questions. It contains statements given in two columns, which have to be matched. Statements in column I are labelled as A, B, C and D whereas statements in column II are labelled as p, q, r and s. The answers to these questions have to be appropriately bubbled as illustrated in the following example. If the correct matches are A-p, A-r, B-p, B-s, C-r, C-s and D-q, then the correctly bubbled matrix will look like the following:

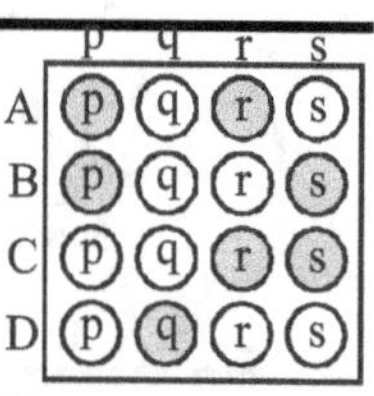

19. A block suspended from a spring is released from rest when spring is unstretched. 'x' represents stretch in spring. Select the appropriate graph taking quantities in column I as y-axis.

Column-I	Column-II
(A) The KE of block	(p) 1
(B) The work done on the block by gravity	(q) 2
(C) The magnitude of work done on the block by spring	(r) 3
(D) The total mechanical energy of block-earth-spring system	(s) 4

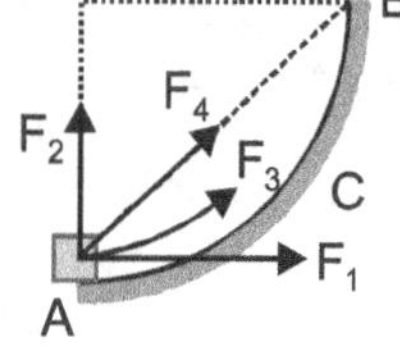

20. ACB is a smooth quarter circular path of radius R. Four forces are acting at a particle placed at A. F_1 is always horizontal, F_2 is always vertical, F_3 is always tangential to path, F_4 is always directed from particle's position to point B. Magnitude of all forces are equal to F.

Column-I	Column-II
(A) Work done by F_1 is	(p) F.R
(B) Work done by F_2 is	(q) $F.R\sqrt{2}$
(C) Work done by F_3 is	(r) $\dfrac{\pi FR}{2}$
(D) Work done by F_4 is	(s) $\dfrac{F.R}{\sqrt{2}}$

DAILY PRACTICE PROBLEM DPP CP04 - PHYSICS

Total Questions	20	Total Marks	74
Attempted		Correct	
Incorrect		Net Score	
Cut-off Score	24	Qualifying Score	35

$$\text{Net Score} = \sum_{i=1}^{V}\left[\left(correct_i \times MM_i\right) - \left(In_i - NM_i\right)\right]$$

DPP - Daily Practice Problems

Chapter-wise Sheets

Date : [ ]   Start Time : [ ]   End Time : [ ]

PHYSICS 

SYLLABUS : System of Particles and Rotational Motion

Max. Marks : 74   **Time : 60 min.**

GENERAL INSTRUCTIONS

- The Daily Practice Problem Sheet contains 20 Questions divided into 5 sections.
  Section I has **5** MCQs with ONLY 1 Correct Option, **3** marks for each correct answer and **–1** for each incorrect answer.
  Section II has **4** MCQs with ONE or MORE THAN ONE Correct options.
  For each question, marks will be awarded in one of the following categories:
  Full marks: **+4** If only the bubble(s) corresponding to all the correct option(s) is (are) darkened.
  Partial marks: **+1** For darkening a bubble corresponding to each correct option provided NO INCORRECT option is darkened.
  Zero marks: If none of the bubbles is darkened.
  Negative marks: **–2** In all other cases.
  Section III has **4** Single Digit Integer Answer Type Questions, **3** marks for each Correct Answer and 0 marks in all other cases.
  Section IV has Comprehension/Matching Cum-Comprehension Type Questions having **5** MCQs with ONLY ONE correct option, **3** marks for each Correct Answer and 0 marks in all other cases.
  Section V has **2** Matching Type Questions, **2** mark for the correct matching of each row and 0 marks in all other cases.
- You have to evaluate your Response Grids yourself with the help of Solutions.

Section I - Straight Objective Type

This section contains 5 multiple choice questions. Each question has 4 choices (a), (b), (c) and (d), out of which **ONLY ONE** is correct.

1. A uniform thin rod AB of length L has linear mass density
   $$\mu(x) = a + \frac{bx}{L},$$
   where x is measured from A. If the CM of the rod lies at a distance of $\left(\frac{7}{12}\right)L$ from A, then a and b are related as :
   (a) $a = 2b$ (b) $2a = b$ (c) $a = b$ (d) $3a = 2b$

2. A particle is confined to rotate in a circular path decreasing linear speed, then which of the following is correct?
   (a) $\vec{L}$ (angular momentum) is conserved about the centre
   (b) Only direction of angular momentum $\vec{L}$ is conserved
   (c) It spirals towards the centre
   (d) Its acceleration is towards the centre.

RESPONSE GRID	1. ⓐⓑⓒⓓ	2. ⓐⓑⓒⓓ

Space for Rough Work

3. A thin uniform rod, pivoted at O, is rotating in the horizontal plane with constant angular speed ω, as shown in the figure. At time $t = 0$, a small insect starts from O and moves with constant speed v, with respect to the rod towards the other end. It reaches the end of the rod at $t = T$ and stops. The angular speed of the system remains ω throughout. The magnitude of the torque $(|\vec{\tau}|)$ about O, as a function of time is best represented by plot

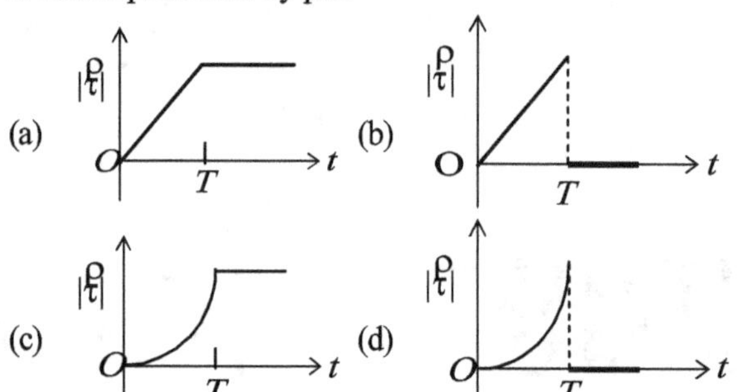

(a)

(b)

(c)

(d)

4. A small object of uniform density rolls up a curved surface with an initial velocity v. It reaches up to a maximum height of $\dfrac{3v^2}{4g}$ with respect to the initial position. The object is

(a) a ring
(b) a solid sphere
(c) a hollow sphere
(d) a disc

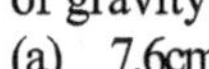

5. A frustum of a solid right circular cone has a base diameter of 20cm, top diameter of 10cm and height 20cm. It has an axial cylindrical hole of diameter 5cm. Determine the position of centre of gravity of this body

(a) 7.6cm   (b) 4.3cm
(c) 12.6cm   (d) 15.3 cm

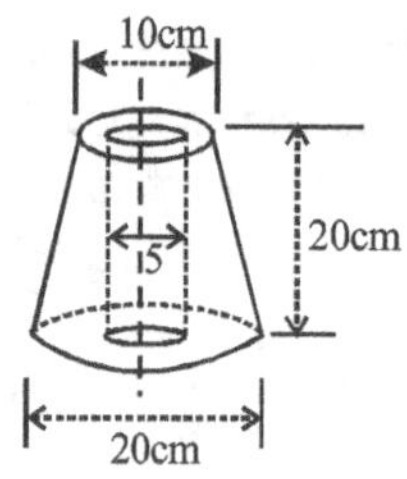

Section II - Multiple Correct Answer Type

This section contains 4 multiple correct answer(s) type questions. Each question has 4 choices (a), (b), (c) and (d), out of which **ONE OR MORE** is/are correct.

6. A horizontal disc rotates freely about a vertical axis through it centre. A ring, having the same mass and radius as the disc, is now gently placed on the disc. After some time, the two rotate with a common angular velocity. Select the correct statements from the following.
(a) Some friction exists between the disc and the ring
(b) The angular momentum of the 'disc plus ring' is conserved.

(c) The final common angular velocity is (2/3) rd of the initial angular velocity of the disc
(d) (2/3) rd of the initial kinetic energy changes to heat.

7. As shown in figure, a planner assembly, having six rods, each of mass m is lying in x-y plane with O at origin, lengths of AD and BC are ℓ. If I_z denotes the moment of inertia of the assembly about z-axis and I_y denotes moment of inertia about y-axis then

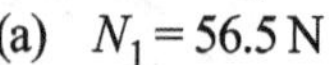

(a) I_z will have its highest value for $\theta = 45°$
(b) I_z will have its highest value for $\theta = 90°$
(c) I_z will have its highest value for $\theta = 0°$
(d) I_y will have its highest value for $\theta = 90°$

8. The torque τ on a body about a given point is found to be equal to $A \times L$ where A is a constant vector, and L is the angular momentum of the body about that point. From this it follows that

(a) $\dfrac{dL}{dt}$ is perpendicular to L at all instants of time.
(b) the component of L in the direction of A does not change with time.
(c) the magnitude of L does not change with time.
(d) L does not change with time

9. A sphere of radius 0.10m and mass 10 kg rests in the corner formed by a 30° inclined plane and a smooth vertical wall. Choose the correct options
(a) $N_1 = 56.5$ N
(b) $N_2 = 113$ N
(c) $f = 0$
(d) $f \neq 0$

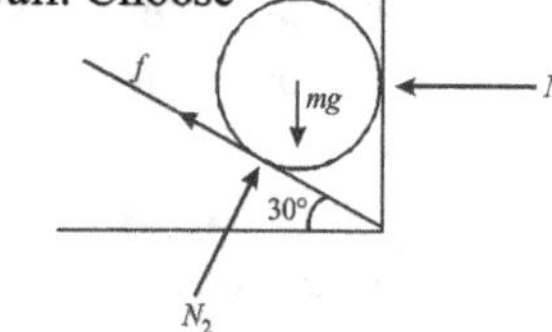

Section III - Integer Type

This section contains 4 questions. The answer to each of the questions is a single digit integer ranging from 0 to 9.

10. A thin uniform rod AB of mass $m = 1.0$ kg moves translationally with acceleration $a = 2.0$ m/s^2 due to two antiparallel forces F_1 and F_2 as shown in figure. The distance between the points at which these forces are applied is equal to $y = 20$ cm. Besides, it is known that $F_2 = 5.0$ N. Find the length of the rod.

11. A circular plate of uniform thickness has a diameter of 56 cm. A circular portion of diameter 42 cm is removed from one edge of the plate as shown. At what distance (in cm) to the left from the centre of the disc is the centre of mass of the remaining portion ?

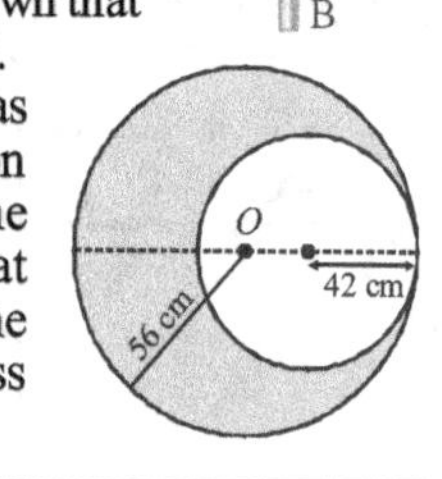

RESPONSE GRID				
3. ⓐⓑⓒⓓ	**4.** ⓐⓑⓒⓓ	**5.** ⓐⓑⓒⓓ	**6.** ⓐⓑⓒⓓ	**7.** ⓐⓑⓒⓓ
8. ⓐⓑⓒⓓ	**9.** ⓐⓑⓒⓓ	**10.** ⓪①②③④⑤⑥⑦⑧⑨		
11. ⓪①②③④⑤⑥⑦⑧⑨				

12. A homogeneous disc with a radius $0.2m$ and mass 5 kg rotates around an axis passing through its centre. The angular velocity of the rotation of the disc as a function of time is given by the formula $\omega = 2 + 6t$ What will be the tangential force applied to the rim of the disc ?

13. The densities of two solid spheres A and B of the same radii R vary with radial distance r as $\rho_A(r) = k\left(\dfrac{r}{R}\right)$ and $\rho_B(r) = k\left(\dfrac{r}{R}\right)^5$, respectively, where k is a constant. The moments of inertia of the individual spheres about axes passing through their centres are I_A and I_B, respectively. If, $\dfrac{I_B}{I_A} = \dfrac{n}{10}$, the value of n is

---

Section IV - Comprehension/Matching Cum-Comprehension Type

Directions (Qs. 14 and 15) : Based upon the given paragraph, 2 multiple choice questions have to be answered. Each question has 4 choices (a), (b), (c) and (d), out of which **ONLY ONE** is correct.

PARAGRAPH

The figure has two disks : one an engine flywheel, and the other a clutch plate attached to a transmission shaft. Their moments of inertia are I_A and I_B; initially, they are rotating with constant angular speeds ω_A and ω_B, respectively. We then push the disks together with forces acting along the axis, so as not to apply any torque on either disk. The disks rub against each other and eventually reach a common final angular speed ω.

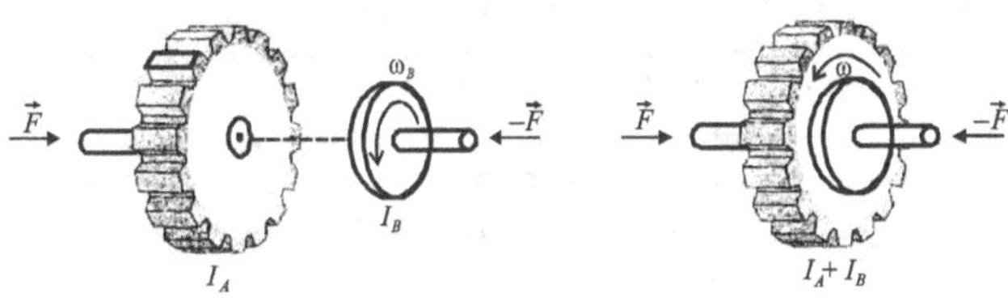

Suppose flywheel A has a mass of 2.0 kg, a radius of 0.20 m and an initial angular speed of 50 rad/sec. (about 500 rpm) and that clutch plate B has a mass of 4.0 kg, a radius of 0.10 m, and an initial angular speed of 200 rad/sec.

14. Find an expression for ω

(a) $\dfrac{I_A\omega_A + I_B\omega_B}{I_A - I_B}$

(b) $\dfrac{I_A\omega_A - I_B\omega_B}{I_A - I_B}$

(c) $\dfrac{I_A\omega_A + I_B\omega_B}{I_A + I_B}$

(d) $\dfrac{I_A\omega_A - I_B\omega_B}{I_A + I_B}$

15. What happens to the final kinetic energy during this process?

(a) 300 J   (b) 3 J   (c) 30 J   (d) 3000 J

Directions (Qs. 16-18) : This passage contains a table having 3 columns and 4 rows. Based on the table, there are three questions. Each question has four options (a), (b), (c) and (d) **ONLY ONE** of these four options is correct.

If moment of inertia of an object about an axis is given by $I = MK^2$, then radius of gyration is given by $K = \left[\dfrac{I}{M}\right]^{1/2}$. Column II and III represents moment of inertia along the tangent (in the plane of the object) and radius of gyration repectively of different objects of Mass M and radius R.

	Column I		Column II		Column III
I.	Solid sphere	(i)	$\dfrac{5}{3}MR^2$	(P)	$\sqrt{\dfrac{3}{2}}R$
II.	Disc	(ii)	$\dfrac{3}{2}MR^2$	(Q)	$\dfrac{\sqrt{5}}{2}R$
III.	Thin spherical shell	(iii)	$\dfrac{7}{5}MR^2$	(R)	$\dfrac{\sqrt{5}}{\sqrt{3}}R$
IV.	Ring	(iv)	$\dfrac{5}{4}MR^2$	(S)	$\dfrac{\sqrt{7}}{\sqrt{5}}R$

16. The correct matching for moment of inertia and radius of gyration of solid sphere of mass M and radius R along the tangent is

(a) I (i) Q(b)   (b) (I) (iii) (S)   (c) (III) (ii) (R)   (d) (I) (iv) (S)

17. What is the correct matching for the disc, if the moment of inertia of the disc about diameter in the plane of the disc is $\dfrac{MR^2}{4}$

(a) II (ii) Q   (b) II (iv) Q   (c) II (i) R   (d) II (iii) S

18. If radius (R) and mass (M) of thin spherical shell are $\sqrt{15}m$ and 2kg respectively, then the moment of inertia and radius of gyration of the shell along the tangent are 50 kg m² and 5m respectively. Which of the following is correct for spherical shell?

(a) III (i) R   (b) I (iii) Q   (c) III (ii) R   (d) IV (iii) S

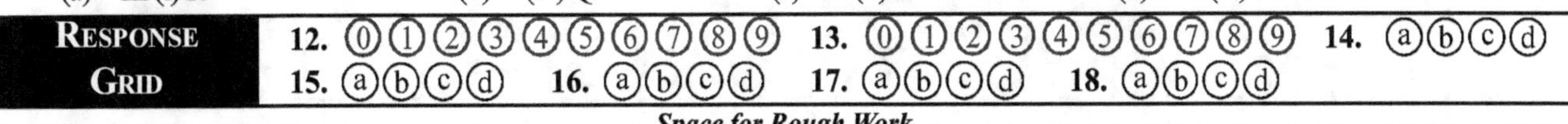

Space for Rough Work

Section V - Matrix-Match Type

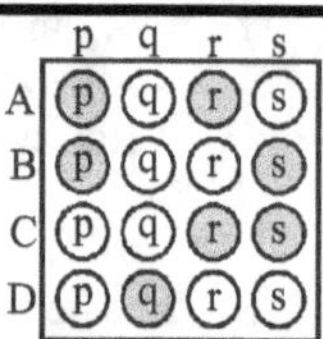

This section contains 2 questions. It contains statements given in two columns, which have to be matched. Statements in column I are labelled as A, B, C and D whereas statements in column II are labelled as p, q, r and s. The answers to these questions have to be appropriately bubbled as illustrated in the following example. If the correct matches are A-p, A-r, B-p, B-s, C-r, C-s and D-q, then the correctly bubbled matrix will look like the following:

19. In each situation of column -I, a uniform disc of mass m and radius R rolls on a rough fixed horizontal surface as shown. At $t = 0$ (initially) the angular velocity of disc is ω_0 and velocity of centre of mass of disc is v_0 (in horizontal direction). The relation between v_0 and ω_0 for each situation and also initial sense of rotation is given for each situation in column-I. Then match the statements in column-I with the corresponding results in column-II.

Column I

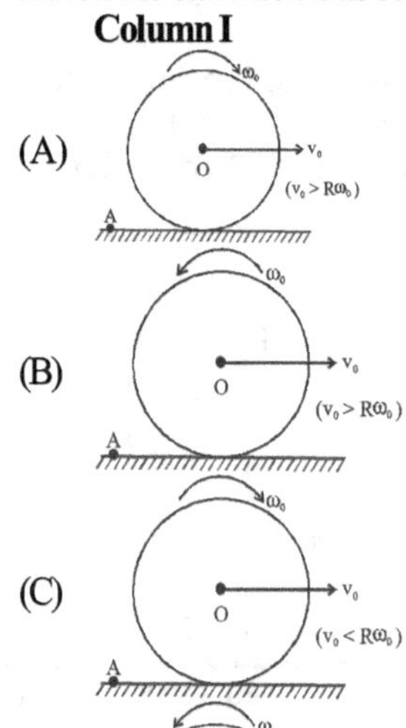

(A) $(v_0 > R\omega_0)$

(B) $(v_0 > R\omega_0)$

(C) $(v_0 < R\omega_0)$

(D) $(v_0 < R\omega_0)$

Column II

(p) The angular momentum of disc about point A remains conserved.

(q) The kinetic energy of disc after it starts rolling without slipping is less than its initial kinetic energy.

(r) In the duration dics rolls with slipping, the friction acts on disc towards left.

(s) In the duration disc rolls with slipping, the friction acts on disc for sometime to right and for sometime to left.

20. A particle moves with position given by $\vec{r} = 3t\hat{i} + 4\hat{j}$. Where $\vec{r}$ is measured in meters and $t\,(>0)$ in seconds

Column I
(A) Rate of change of distance from origin
(B) Magnitude of linear acceleration of particle
(C) Magnitude of angular velocity of particle about origin
(D) Magnitude of angular momentum of particle about origin

Column II
(p) Increasing with time
(q) Decreasing with time
(r) Constant
(s) Zero

RESPONSE GRID	
19. A - p q r s ; B - p q r s ; C - p q r s ; D - p q r s	
20. A - p q r s ; B - p q r s ; C - p q r s ; D - p q r s	

DAILY PRACTICE PROBLEM DPP CP05 - PHYSICS

Total Questions	20	Total Marks	74
Attempted		Correct	
Incorrect		Net Score	
Cut-off Score	24	Qualifying Score	35

$$\text{Net Score} = \sum_{i=I}^{V} \left[\left(\text{correct}_i \times MM_i \right) - \left(In_i - NM_i \right) \right]$$

Space for Rough Work

Date : [   ]   Start Time : [   ]   End Time : [   ]

PHYSICS $\boxed{\text{CP06}}$

SYLLABUS : Gravitation

Max. Marks : 74   **Time : 60 min.**

GENERAL INSTRUCTIONS

- The Daily Practice Problem Sheet contains 20 Questions divided into 5 sections.
  Section I has **5** MCQs with ONLY 1 Correct Option, **3** marks for each correct answer and **−1** for each incorrect answer.
  Section II has **4** MCQs with ONE or MORE THAN ONE Correct options.
  For each question, marks will be awarded in one of the following categories:
  Full marks: **+4** If only the bubble(s) corresponding to all the correct option(s) is (are) darkened.
  Partial marks: **+1** For darkening a bubble corresponding to each correct option provided NO INCORRECT option is darkened.
  Zero marks: If none of the bubbles is darkened.
  Negative marks: **−2** In all other cases.
  Section III has **4** Single Digit Integer Answer Type Questions, **3** marks for each Correct Answer and 0 marks in all other cases.
  Section IV has Comprehension/Matching Cum-Comprehension Type Questions having **5** MCQs with ONLY ONE correct option, **3** marks for each Correct Answer and 0 marks in all other cases.
  Section V has **2** Matching Type Questions, **2** mark for the correct matching of each row and 0 marks in all other cases.
- You have to evaluate your Response Grids yourself with the help of Solutions.

Section I - Straight Objective Type

This section contains 5 multiple choice questions. Each question has 4 choices (a), (b), (c) and (d), out of which **ONLY ONE** is correct.

1. An asteriod of mass m is approaching earth initially at a distance of $10R_e$ with speed v_i. It hits the earth with a speed v_f (R_e and M_e are radius and mass of earth), then

   (a) $v_f^2 = v_i^2 + \dfrac{2Gm}{M_e R}\left(1 - \dfrac{1}{10}\right)$

   (b) $v_f^2 = v_i^2 + \dfrac{2GM_e}{R_e}\left(1 + \dfrac{1}{10}\right)$

   (c) $v_f^2 = v_i^2 + \dfrac{2GM_e}{R_e}\left(1 - \dfrac{1}{10}\right)$

   (d) $v_f^2 = v_i^2 + \dfrac{2Gm}{R_e}\left(1 - \dfrac{1}{10}\right)$

RESPONSE GRID   1. ⓐⓑⓒⓓ

Space for Rough Work

2. Two rings each of radius 'a' are coaxial and the distance between their centres is a. The masses of the rings are M_1 and M_2. The work done in transporting a particle of a small mass m from centre C_1 to C_2 is :

(a) $\dfrac{Gm(M_2 - M_1)}{a}$

(b) $\dfrac{Gm(M_2 - M_1)}{a\sqrt{2}}(\sqrt{2}+1)$

(c) $\dfrac{Gm(M_2 - M_1)}{a\sqrt{2}}(\sqrt{2}-1)$

(d) $\dfrac{Gm(M_2 - M_1)}{\sqrt{2}}a$

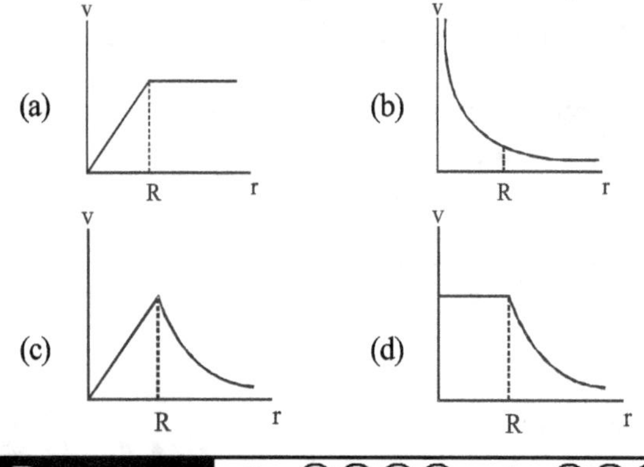

3. Two bodies, each of mass M, are kept fixed with a separation 2L. A particle of mass m is projected from the midpoint of the line joining their centres, perpendicular to the line. The gravitational constant is G. The correct statement is

(a) The minimum initial velocity of the mass m to escape the gravitational field of the two bodies is $4\sqrt{\dfrac{GM}{L}}$

(b) The minimum initial velocity of the mass m to escape the gravitational field of the two bodies is $2\sqrt{\dfrac{GM}{L}}$

(c) The minimum initial velocity of the mass m to escape the gravitational field of the two bodies is $\sqrt{\dfrac{2GM}{L}}$

(d) The energy of the mass m remains constant

4. A spherically symmetric gravitational system of particles has a mass density $\rho = \begin{cases} \rho_0 & \text{for } r \le R \\ 0 & \text{for } r > R \end{cases}$

where ρ_0 is a constant. A test mass can undergo circular motion under the influence of the gravitational field of particles. Its speed v as a function of distance r ($0 < r < \infty$) from the centre of the system is represented by –

(a) [graph]

(b) [graph]

(c) [graph]

(d) [graph]

5. An earth satellite of mass m orbits along a circular orbit C_1 at a height $2R$ from earth's surface. It is to be transferred to a circular orbit C_2, of bigger radius, at a height $5R$ from earth's surface. The transfer is affected by following an elliptical path as shown in figure. Calculate the change in the energy required at points B. [R = radius of earth]

(a) $\dfrac{mgR}{36}$

(b) $\dfrac{mgR}{18}$

(c) $\dfrac{mgR}{2}$

(d) $\dfrac{mgR}{9}$

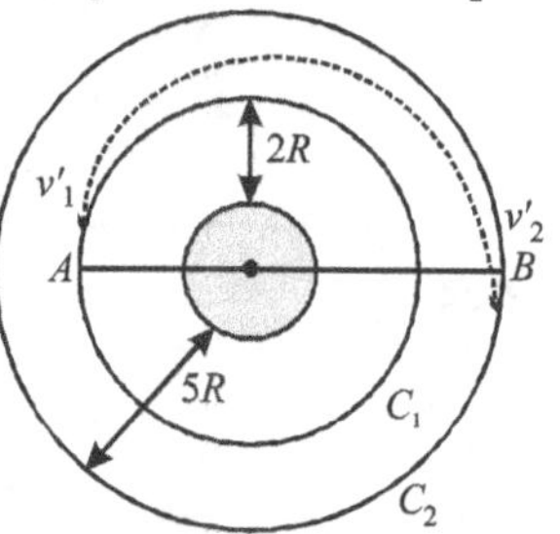

Section II - Multiple Correct Answer Type

This section contains 4 multiple correct answer(s) type questions. Each question has 4 choices (a), (b), (c) and (d), out of which **ONE OR MORE** is/are correct.

6. A satellite is launched and attains a velocity of 30400 km/hr relative to the centre of the earth at a height of 320km from the earth's surface. It has been guided into a path that is parallel to the earth's surface at burnout. Choose the correct options

(a) Satellite moves along an elliptical orbit
(b) Longest distance from the earth's surface is 3550 km.
(c) The period of revolution for the satellite is 2.09 hrs.
(d) The minimum escape velocity for this position of launching is 10930.08 m/s

7. Consider an attractive central force of the form

$F(r) = -\dfrac{k}{r^n}$, k is a constant. For a stable circular orbit to exist

(a) $n = 2$ (b) $n < 3$ (c) $n > 3$ (d) $n = -1$

8. A geostationary satellite is at a height h above the surface of earth. If earth radius is R –

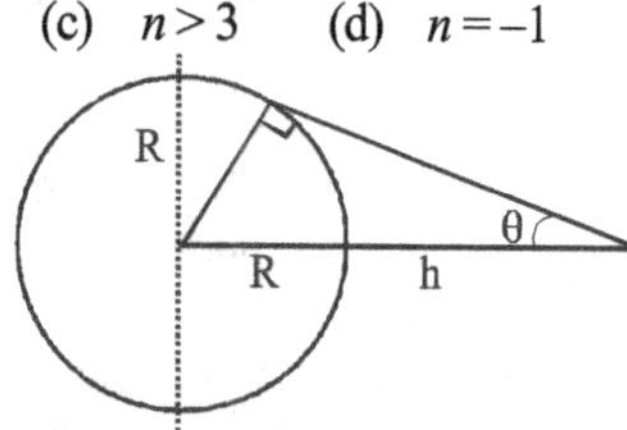

(a) The minimum colatitude on earth upto which the satellite can be used to communicate is $\sin^{-1} R/(R+h)$
(b) The maximum colatitude on earth upto which the satellite can be used to communicate is $\sin^{-1} R/(R+h)$
(c) The area on earth escaped from this satellite is given as $2\pi R^2(1 + \sin\theta)$
(d) The area on earth escaped from this satellite is given as $2\pi R^2(1 + \cos\theta)$

RESPONSE	**2.** ⓐⓑⓒⓓ **3.** ⓐⓑⓒⓓ **4.** ⓐⓑⓒⓓ **5.** ⓐⓑⓒⓓ **6.** ⓐⓑⓒⓓ	
GRID	**7.** ⓐⓑⓒⓓ **8.** ⓐⓑⓒⓓ	

9. A rocket starts vertically upwards with speed v_0. Choose the correct option(s) (R is the radius of the earth).

  (a) Speed v at a height 'h' is given by

  $$v_0^2 - v^2 = \frac{2gh}{1 + \dfrac{h}{R}}$$

  (b) The maximum height reached by the rocket fired with a speed of 90% of escape velocity is 2.26 R

  (c) The maximum height reached by the rocket fired with a speed of 90% of escape velocity is 4.26 R

  (d) Speed v at a height 'h' is given by

  $$v_0^2 - v^2 = \frac{2gh}{1 + \dfrac{h}{2R}}$$

Section III - Integer Type

This section contains 4 questions. The answer to each of the questions is a single digit integer ranging from 0 to 9.

10. If the radius of the earth were to shrink by two per cent, its mass remaining the same, then by how much percentage would the acceleration due to gravity on the earth's surface would increase?

11. The period of revolution of planet A around the sun is 8 times that of B. The distance of A from the sun is how many times greater than that of B from the Sun?

12. An artificial satellite is moving in a circular orbit around the earth with a speed equal to half the magnitude of escape velocity from the earth. If the satellite is stopped suddenly in its orbit and allowed to fall freely onto the earth, find the speed (in km/s) with which it hits the surface of the earth.

13. A bullet is fired vertically upwards with velocity v from the surface of a spherical planet. When it reaches its maximum height, its acceleration due to the planet's gravity is $\frac{1}{4}$ th of its value of the surface of the planet. If the escape velocity from the planet is $v_{esc} = v\sqrt{N}$, then the value of N is (ignore energy loss due to atmosphere)

Section IV - Comprehension/Matching Cum-Comprehension Type

Directions (Qs. 14 and 15): Based upon the given paragraph, 2 multiple choice questions have to be answered. Each question has 4 choices (a), (b), (c) and (d), out of which **ONLY ONE** is correct.

PARAGRAPH

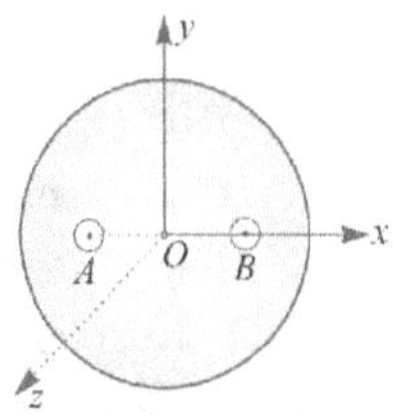

A solid sphere of uniform density and radius 4 m is located with its centre at the origin O of coordinates (0, 0, 0). Two spheres of equal radius 1 m with their cavities at A $(-2, 0, 0)$ and B $(2, 0, 0)$ respectively are taken out, leaving behind spherical cavities (as shown in fig.). The mass of each sphere taken out is M. Calculate

14. The gravitational field at B is

  (a) GM   (b) $\dfrac{21GM}{5}$ (c) $\dfrac{31}{16}GM$ (d) $\dfrac{31}{8}GM$

15. The gravitational potential at any point on circle $y^2 + z^2 = 36$ is

  (a) $-7.90\,GM$ (b) $-10.98\,GM$ (c) $-8.98\,GM$ (d) zero

Directions (Qs. 16-18): This passage contains a table having 3 columns and 4 rows. Based on the table, there are three questions. Each question has four options (a), (b), (c) and (d) **ONLY ONE** of these four options is correct.

A satellite is transferred to a higher orbit r_2 $(r_2 > r_1)$ as shown in figure. Column I shows different physical quantities that may be affected while column III gives the proportionality (or relation) with r (radius).

	Column I		Column II		Column III	
I.	Orbital velocity	(i)	Increases	(P)	$\propto \dfrac{1}{r}$	
II.	Time period	(ii)	Decreases	(Q)	$\propto \dfrac{1}{\sqrt{r}}$	
III.	Angular momentum	(iii)	Remains constant	(R)	$\propto r^{3/2}$	
IV.	Kinetic energy	(iv)	First increases then decreases	(S)	$\propto \sqrt{r}$	

Space for Rough Work

16. When the satellite is transferred from $r_1 = r$ to $r_2 = 2r$ then its time period will increased by $2\sqrt{2}$ times. The correct matching for time period will be

(a) II (iii) R   (b) II (i) R   (c) II (iii) R   (d) II (iv) R

17. What is the correct matching for the kinetic energy of the satellite?

(a) IV (ii) P   (b) IV (ii) R   (c) IV (iii) S   (d) IV (iii) P

18. Which of the following shows the incorrect matching?

(a) I (ii) Q   (b) III (i) S   (c) II (i) R   (d) IV (iii) P

Section V - Matrix-Match Type

This section contains 2 questions. It contains statements given in two columns, which have to be matched. Statements in column I are labelled as A, B, C and D whereas statements in column II are labelled as p, q, r and s. The answers to these questions have to be appropriately bubbled as illustrated in the following example. If the correct matches are A-p, A-r, B-p, B-s, C-r, C-s and D-q, then the correctly bubbled matrix will look like the following:

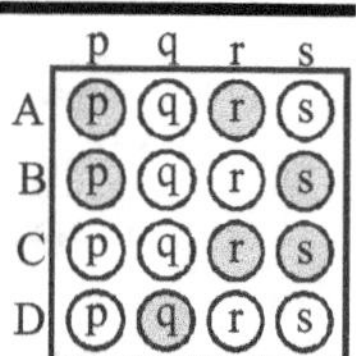

19.

Column I	Column II
(A) Kinetic energy of a body projected from surface of earth, at large distance from surface of earth	(p) must be zero
(B) Gravitational potential energy of a bound system	(q) may be zero
(C) Change in potential energy of a point mass if left free to itself, with time	(r) positive
(D) Change in areal velocity of earth as earth moves from apogee towards perigee	(s) must be negative

20. Considering earth to be a homogeneous sphere but keeping in mind its spin, match the columns I and II correctly.

Column I	Column II
(A) Acceleration due to gravity	(p) May change from point to point
(B) Orbital angular momentum of the earth as seen from a distant star	(q) Does not depend on direction of projection
(C) Escape velocity from the earth	(r) Remains constant
(D) Gravitational potential due to earth at particular point	(s) Depends on earth mass

RESPONSE GRID

16. (a)(b)(c)(d) 17. (a)(b)(c)(d) 18. (a)(b)(c)(d)

19. A - (p)(q)(r)(s); B - (p)(q)(r)(s); C - (p)(q)(r)(s); D - (p)(q)(r)(s)

20. A - (p)(q)(r)(s); B - (p)(q)(r)(s); C - (p)(q)(r)(s); D - (p)(q)(r)(s)

DAILY PRACTICE PROBLEM DPP CP06 - PHYSICS

Total Questions	20	Total Marks	74
Attempted		Correct	
Incorrect		Net Score	
Cut-off Score	24	Qualifying Score	35

$$\text{Net Score} = \sum_{i=1}^{V} \left[\left(\text{correct}_i \times MM_i \right) - \left(In_i - NM_i \right) \right]$$

Space for Rough Work

PHYSICS $\boxed{\text{CP07}}$

SYLLABUS : Mechanical Properties of Solids

Max. Marks : 74   **Time : 60 min.**

GENERAL INSTRUCTIONS

- The Daily Practice Problem Sheet contains 20 Questions divided into 5 sections.
  Section I has **6** MCQs with ONLY 1 Correct Option, **3** marks for each correct answer and **–1** for each incorrect answer.
  Section II has **4** MCQs with ONE or MORE THAN ONE Correct options.
  For each question, marks will be awarded in one of the following categories:
  Full marks: **+4** If only the bubble(s) corresponding to all the correct option(s) is (are) darkened.
  Partial marks: **+1** For darkening a bubble corresponding to each correct option provided NO INCORRECT option is darkened.
  Zero marks: If none of the bubbles is darkened.
  Negative marks: **–2** In all other cases.
  Section III has **4** Single Digit Integer Answer Type Questions, **3** marks for each Correct Answer and 0 marks in all other cases.
  Section IV has Comprehension Type Questions having **4** MCQs with ONLY ONE corect option, 3 marks for each Correct Answer and 0 marks in all other cases.
  Section V has **2** Matching Type Questions, **2** mark for the correct matching of each row and 0 marks in all other cases.
- You have to evaluate your Response Grids yourself with the help of Solutions.

Section I - Straight Objective Type

This section contains 6 multiple choice questions. Each question has 4 choices (a), (b), (c) and (d), out of which **ONLY ONE** is correct.

1. The length of an elastic string is a metre when the longitudinal tension is 7 N and b metre when the longitudinal tension is 9 N. The length of the string in metre when the longitudinal tension is 11 N is

   (a) $a - b$ (b) $2b - a$

   (c) $2b - \dfrac{1}{4}a$ (d) $4a - 3b$

RESPONSE GRID   1. ⓐⓑⓒⓓ

Space for Rough Work

2. A load of 10kN is supported from a pulley which in turn is supported by a rope of sectional area 1×10^3 mm^2 and modulus of elasticity 10^3 N mm^{-2}, as shown in figure. Neglecting the friction at the pulley, determine the deflection of the load.

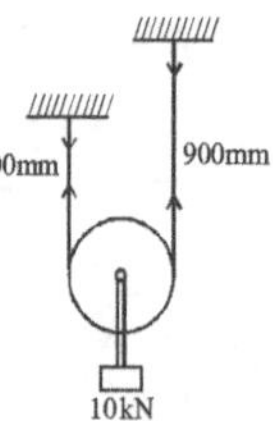

(a) 2.75 mm　　(b) 3.75 mm　　(c) 5.25 mm　　(d) 6.50 mm

3. A platform is suspended by four wires at its corners. The wires are 3m long and have a diameter of 2.0mm. Young's modulus for the material of the wires is $1,80,000\ MPa$. How far will the platform drop (due to elongation of the wires) if a 50 kg load is placed at the centre of the platform?

(a) 0.25 mm　　　　　　　(b) 0.65 mm

(c) 1.65 mm　　　　　　　(d) 0.35 mm

4. Stress vs strain curve for the elastic tissue of the aorta, the large tube (vessel) carrying blood from the heart, will be :
[stress is proportional to square of the strain for the elastic tissue of the aorta]

(a) 　　　　　　　　　　(b)

(c) 　　　　　　　　　　(d)

5. What per cent of length of wire increases by applying a stress of 1 kg weight/mm^2 on it?
($Y = 1 \times 10^{11}$ N/m^2 and 1 kg weight $= 9.8$ newton)

(a) 0.0067%　　　　　　　(b) 0.0098%

(c) 0.0088%　　　　　　　(d) 0.0078%

6. A light rod of length $2m$ suspended from the ceiling horizontally by means of two vertical wires of equal length. A weight W is hung from a light rod as shown in figure. The rod hung by means of a steel wire of cross-sectional area A_1 $= 0.1$ cm^2 and brass wire of cross-sectional area $A_2 = 0.2$ cm^2. To have equal stress in both wires, $T_1/T_2 =$

(a) 1/3

(b) 1/4

(c) 4/3

(d) 1/2

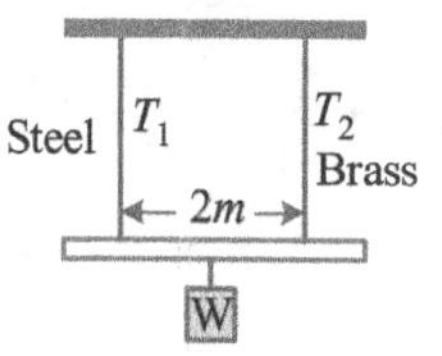

Section II - Multiple Correct Answer Type

This section contains 4 multiple correct answer(s) type questions. Each question has 4 choices (a), (b), (c) and (d), out of which **ONE OR MORE** is/are correct.

---

7. A metal wire of length L, area of cross-section A and Young's modulus Y is stretched by a variable force F such that F is always slightly greater than the elastic forces of resistance in the wire. When the elongation of the wire is ℓ

(a) the work done by F is $\dfrac{YA\ell^2}{L}$

(b) the work done by F is $\dfrac{YA\ell^2}{2L}$

(c) the eleastic potential energy stored in the wire is $\dfrac{YA\ell^2}{2L}$

(d) heat is produced during the elongation.

8. Two identical rods each of cross-sectional area A are placed on smooth horizontal surface. These are acted by forces as shown in figure. The breaking strength of material of each rod is F/A, then :

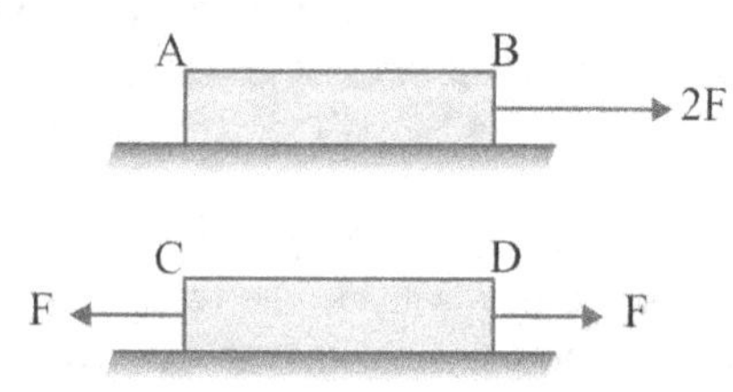

(a) rod AB will break left of the centre

(b) rod AB will break right of the centre

(c) rod CD will break left of the centre

(d) rod CD will break right of the centre

| **RESPONSE** | **2.** ⓐⓑⓒⓓ | **3.** ⓐⓑⓒⓓ | **4.** ⓐⓑⓒⓓ | **5.** ⓐⓑⓒⓓ | **6.** ⓐⓑⓒⓓ |
| **GRID** | **7.** ⓐⓑⓒⓓ | **8.** ⓐⓑⓒⓓ | | | |

---

9. In plotting stress versus strain curves for two materials P and Q, a student by mistake puts strain on the y-axis and stress on the x-axis as shown in the figure. Then the correct statement(s) is (are)

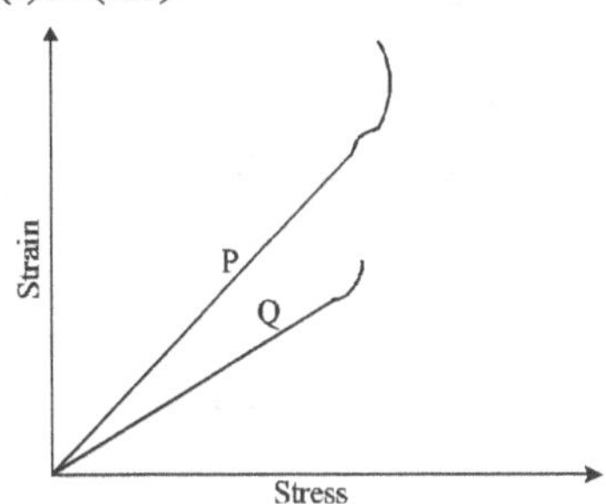

(a) P has more tensile strength than Q

(b) P is more ductile than Q

(c) P is more brittle than Q

(d) Both P and Q have equal tensile strength

10. Two light wires A and B shown in the figure are made of the same material and have radii r_A and r_B respectively. The block between them has a mass m. When the force F is mg/3, one of the wires breaks

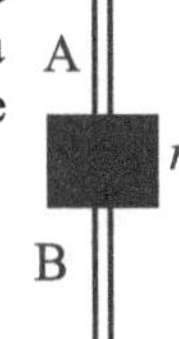

(a) A breaks if $r_A = r_B$

(b) A breaks if $r_A < 2r_B$

(c) either A or B may break if $r_A = 2r_B$

(d) the length of A and B must be known to predict which wire will break.

Section III - Integer Type

This section contains 4 questions. The answer to each of the questions is a single digit integer ranging from 0 to 9.

11. A 5 metre long wire is fixed to the ceiling. A weight of 10 kg is hung at the lower end and is 1 metre above the floor. The wire was elongated by 1 mm. The energy stored in the wire due to stretching is $x \times 10^{-2}$ J. Find the value of x.

12. The breaking stress for a metal is 7.8×10^9 N/m². If $(x \times 10^2)$ km is the maximum length of the wire made of this metal which may be suspended without breaking then find the value of x. The density of the metal = 7.8×10^3 kg/m³. Take g = 10 N/ kg.

13. A body of mass 10 kg is attached to a wire of radius 3 cm. It's breaking stress is 4.8×10^7 Nm⁻², the area of cross-section of the wire is 10^{-6} m². What is the maximum angular velocity with which it can be rotated in the horizontal circle?

14. Two wires are made of the same material and have the same volume. However wire 1 has cross-sectional area A and wire 2 has cross-sectional area $3A$. If the length of wire 1 increases by Δx on applying force F, xF force is needed to stretch wire 2 by the same amount? Find the value of x.

Section IV - Comprehension Type

Directions (Qs. 15-18) : Based upon the given paragraphs, 4 multiple choice questions have to be answered. Each question has 4 choices (a), (b), (c) and (d), out of which **ONLY ONE** is correct.

PARAGRAPH-1

Figure shows qualitatively the relation between the stress and the strain as the deformation gradually increases.

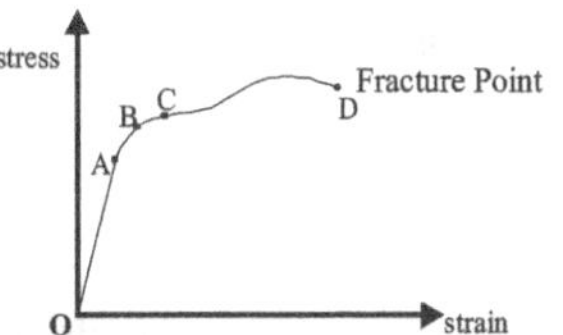

It is observed that for a substantial range of stresses, the stress-strain relation is linear, and the specimen recovers to its original dimensions when the load is removed.

15. For which range, during unloading, the above curve will be retraced?

(a) up to OA only   (b) up to OB

(c) up to OC   (d) never retraced its path

16. In the above question, during loading and unloading the force exerted by the material are conservative up to?

(a) OA only   (b) OB only

(c) OC only   (d) OD

PARAGRAPH-2

A copper rod of length 2 m and cross-sectional area 2.0 cm² is fastened end to end to a steel rod of length L and cross-sectional area 1.0 cm². The compound rod is subjected to equal and opposite pulls of magnitude 3×10^4 N at its ends.

$$Y_{steel} = 2.0 \times 10^{11} \text{ N/m}^2$$
$$Y_{copper} = 1.1 \times 10^{11} \text{ N/m}^2$$

17. The length L of the steel rod if the elongation of the two rods are equal is
(a) 1.82 m
(b) 2.20 m
(c) 3.04 m
(d) 3.84 m

18. The strain in steel rod is
(a) 1.5×10^{-3}
(b) 2.25×10^{-3}
(c) 3.0×10^{-3}
(d) 4.5×10^{-3}

Section V - Matrix-Match Type

This section contains 2 questions. It contains statements given in two columns, which have to be matched. Statements in column I are labelled as A, B, C and D whereas statements in column II are labelled as p, q, r and s. The answers to these questions have to be appropriately bubbled as illustrated in the following example. If the correct matches are A-p, A-r, B-p, B-s, C-r, C-s and D-q, then the correctly bubbled matrix will look like the following:

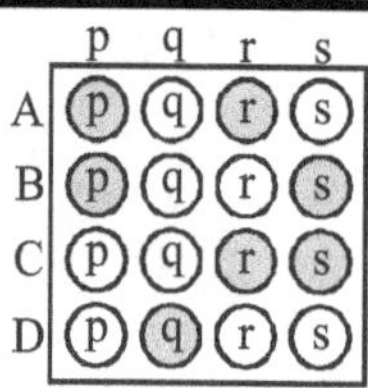

19.

Column I		Column II
(A) Hooke's law	(p)	$\dfrac{1}{2} \times$ stress $\times$ strain $\times$ volume
(B) Elastic potential energy	(q)	stress $\propto$ strain
(C) Young's modulus	(r)	$\dfrac{\text{fractional change in transverse length}}{\text{fractional change in longitudinal length}}$
(D) Poison's ratio	(s)	stress/strain

20.

Column -I		Column-II
(A) Equal force acting perpendicular to each point on a spherical surface	(p)	Balance the net weight to be supported
(B) Cross-sectional area of the rope used in giant structures	(q)	Higher modulus of elasticity
(C) Steel in structural designs	(r)	Reduction in volume without change in shape
(D) Stress-strain curve	(s)	Inversely depends on the yeild strength

RESPONSE GRID	
	17. (a)(b)(c)(d) **18.** (a)(b)(c)(d)
	19. A - (p)(q)(r)(s); B - (p)(q)(r)(s); C - (p)(q)(r)(s); D - (p)(q)(r)(s)
	20. A - (p)(q)(r)(s); B - (p)(q)(r)(s); C - (p)(q)(r)(s); D - (p)(q)(r)(s)

DAILY PRACTICE PROBLEM DPP CP07 - PHYSICS

Total Questions	20	Total Marks	74
Attempted		Correct	
Incorrect		Net Score	
Cut-off Score	24	Qualifying Score	35

$$\text{Net Score} = \sum_{i=\text{I}}^{\text{V}} \left[\left(\text{correct}_i \times MM_i\right) - \left(In_i - NM_i\right) \right]$$

Space for Rough Work

PHYSICS $\boxed{\text{CP08}}$

SYLLABUS : Mechanical Properties of Fluids

Max. Marks : 74　　　　　　　　　　　　　　　　　　　　　**Time : 60 min.**

GENERAL INSTRUCTIONS

- The Daily Practice Problem Sheet contains 20 Questions divided into 5 sections.
- **Section I** has **6** MCQs with ONLY 1 Correct Option, **3** marks for each correct answer and **–1** for each incorrect answer.
- **Section II** has **4** MCQs with ONE or MORE THAN ONE Correct options.
- For each question, marks will be awarded in one of the following categories:
- Full marks: **+4** If only the bubble(s) corresponding to all the correct option(s) is (are) darkened.
- Partial marks: **+1** For darkening a bubble corresponding to each correct option provided NO INCORRECT option is darkened.
- Zero marks:　If none of the bubbles is darkened.
- Negative marks: **–2** In all other cases.
- **Section III** has **4** Single Digit Integer Answer Type Questions, **3** marks for each Correct Answer and 0 marks in all other cases.
- **Section IV** has Comprehension Type Questions having **4** MCQs with ONLY ONE corect option, 3 marks for each Correct Answer and 0 marks in all other cases.
- **Section V** has **2** Matching Type Questions, **2** mark for the correct matching of each row and 0 marks in all other cases.
- You have to evaluate your Response Grids yourself with the help of Solutions.

Section I - Straight Objective Type

This section contains 6 multiple choice questions. Each question has 4 choices (a), (b), (c) and (d), out of which **ONLY ONE** is correct.

1. A spherical body of radius R consists of a fluid of constant density and is in equilibrium under its own gravity. If $P(r)$ is the pressure at $r(r < R)$, then the correct option is

(a)　$P(r=0)=0$

(b)　$\dfrac{P(r=3R/4)}{P(r=2R/3)}=\dfrac{63}{80}$

(c)　$\dfrac{P(r=3R/5)}{P(r=2R/5)}=\dfrac{5}{9}$

(d)　$\dfrac{P(r=R/2)}{P(r=R/3)}=\dfrac{20}{27}$

RESPONSE GRID　　1.　ⓐⓑⓒⓓ

Space for Rough Work

2. A capillary tube with inner cross-section in the form of a square of side 'a' is dipped vertically in a liquid of density ρ and surface tension σ which wet the surface of capillary tube with angle of contact θ. The approximate height to which liquid will be raised in the tube is (Neglect the effect of surface tension at the corners capillary tube)

(a) $\dfrac{2\sigma\cos\theta}{a\rho g}$

(b) $\dfrac{4\sigma\cos\theta}{a\rho g}$

(c) $\dfrac{8\sigma\cos\theta}{a\rho g}$

(d) $\dfrac{4\sigma\sec\theta}{a\rho g}$

3. A hollow wooden cylinder of height h, inner radius R and outer radius $2R$ is placed in a cylindrical container of radius $3R$. When water is poured into the container, the minimum height H of the container for which cylinder can float inside freely is

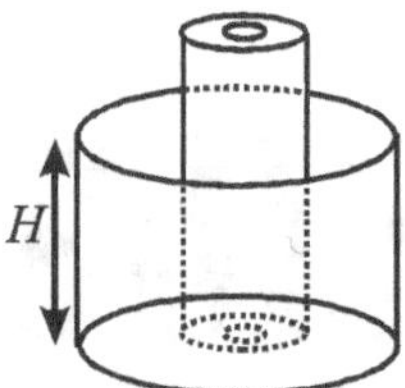

(a) $\dfrac{h\rho_{water}}{\rho_{water}+\rho_{wood}}$

(b) $\dfrac{h\rho_{wood}}{\rho_{water}}$

(c) h

(d) $\dfrac{h^2}{R}$

4. Two solid spherical balls of radii r_1 and r_2 ($< r_1$) and of density σ are tied up with a long string and released in a viscous liquid column of lesser density ρ with the string just taut as shown. The tension in the string when terminal velocity is attained, is

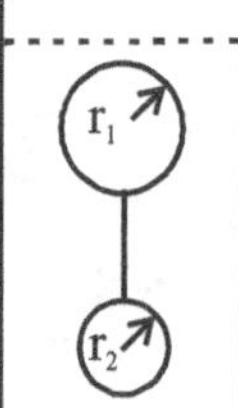

(a) $\dfrac{4}{3}\pi\left(\dfrac{r_2^4-r_1^4}{r_2-r_1}\right)(\sigma-\rho)g$

(b) $\dfrac{2}{3}\pi\left(r_2^3-r_1^3\right)(\rho-\sigma)g$

(c) $\dfrac{4}{3}\pi\left(r_2^3-r_1^3\right)(\sigma-\rho)g$

(d) $\dfrac{4}{3}\pi\left(\dfrac{r_2^4-r_1^4}{r_2+r_1}\right)(\sigma-\rho)g$

5. A narrow tube completely filled with a liquid is lying on a series of cylinders as shown in figure.

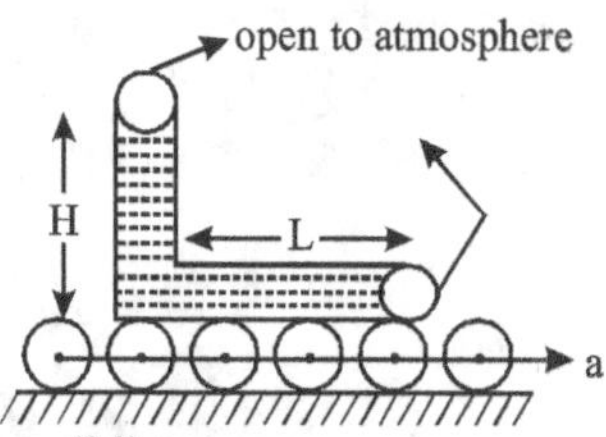

Assuming no sliding between any surfaces, the value of acceleration of the cylinders for which liquid will not come out of the tube from anywhere is given by

(a) $\dfrac{gH}{2L}$ (b) $\dfrac{gH}{L}$ (c) $\dfrac{2gH}{L}$ (d) $\dfrac{gH}{\sqrt{2}L}$

6. Water of density ρ in a clean aquarium forms a meniscus, as illustrated in the figure. Calculate the difference in height h between the centre and the edge of the meniscus. The surface tension of water is γ.

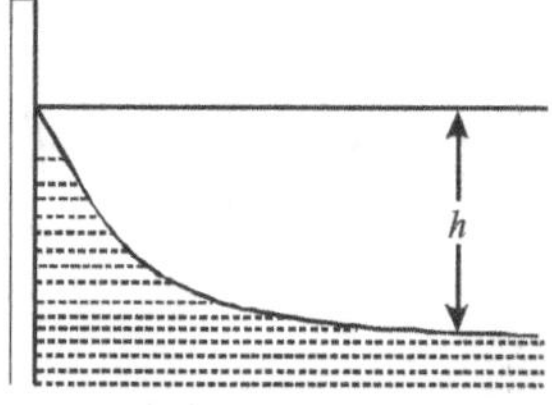

(a) $\sqrt{\dfrac{2\gamma}{\rho g}}$ (b) $\sqrt{\dfrac{\gamma}{\rho g}}$ (c) $\dfrac{1}{2}\sqrt{\dfrac{\gamma}{\rho g}}$ (d) $2\sqrt{\dfrac{\gamma}{\rho g}}$

Section II - Multiple Correct Answer Type

This section contains 4 multiple correct answer(s) type questions. Each question has 4 choices (a), (b), (c) and (d), out of which **ONE OR MORE** is/are correct.

7. An oil drop falls through air with a terminal velocity of 5×10^{-4} m/s. Viscosity of oil is 1.8×10^{-5} N s/m^2 and density of oil is 900 kg/m^3. Neglecting density of air as compared to that of the oil

(a) radius of the drop is 6.20×10^{-2} m

(b) radius of the drop is 2.14×10^{-6} m

(c) terminal velocity of the drop at half of this radius is 1.25×10^{-4} m/s

(d) terminal velocity of the drop at half of this radius is 2.5×10^{-4} m/s

RESPONSE GRID					
2. ⓐⓑⓒⓓ	**3.** ⓐⓑⓒⓓ	**4.** ⓐⓑⓒⓓ	**5.** ⓐⓑⓒⓓ	**6.** ⓐⓑⓒⓓ	
7. ⓐⓑⓒⓓ					

8. Water coming out of a horizontal tube at a speed v strikes normally a vetical wall close to the mouth of the tube and falls down vertically after impact. When the speed of water is increased to $2v$
(a) the thrust exerted by the water on the wall will be doubled
(b) the thrust exerted by the water on the wall will be four times
(c) the energy lost per second by water strike up the wall will also be four times
(d) the energy lost per second by water striking the wall be increased eight times

9. A lawn sprinkler with two nozzles 0.5 cm. diameter each at 20cm. and 15cm. radii is connected across a tap capable of 6 litres/minute discharged. The nozzles discharge water upwards and outwards from the plane of rotation. Choose the correct options.

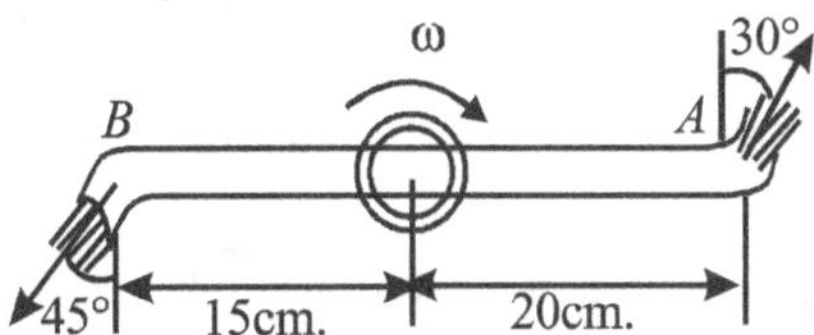

(a) Total torque due to nozzles A and B is 0.355 Nm
(b) If held stationary then angular velocity with which it will rotate freely is 9.72 rad/sec.
(c) If held stationary then angular velocity with which it will rotate freely is 6.14 rad/sec.
(d) Total torque due to nozzles A and B is 0.0355 Nm

10. An air bubble in a water tank rises from the bottom to the top. Which of the following statements are true :
(a) Bubble rises upwards because pressure at the bottom is less than that at the top
(b) Bubble rises upwards because pressure at the bottom is greater than that at the top
(c) As the bubble rises, its size increases
(d) As the bubble rises, its size decreases

Section III - Integer Type

This section contains 4 questions. The answer to each of the questions is a single digit integer ranging from 0 to 9.

11. A wooden plank of length 1m and uniform cross-section is hinged at one end to the bottom of a tank as shown in fig. The tank is filled with water upto a height 0.5 m. The specific gravity of the plank is 0.5. The angle θ (in degree) is 15 x that the plank makes with the vertical in the equilibrium position. (Exclude the case $\theta = 0°$). Find the value of x.

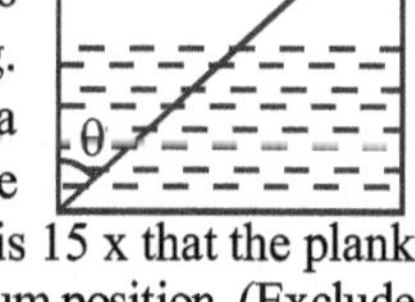

12. Two soap bubbles A and B are kept in a closed chamber where the air is maintained at pressure 8 N/m^2. The radii of bubbles A and B are 2 cm and 4 cm, respectively. Surface tension of the soap-water used to make bubbles is 0.04 N/m. If the ratio P_B/P_A, where P_A and P_B pressure in bubbles A and B, respectively is $\dfrac{x}{3}$. Find the value of x. [Neglect the effect of gravity.]

13. A large tank is filled with water (density $= 10^3$ kg/m^3). A small hole is made at a depth 10 m below water surface. The range of water issuing out of the hole is R on ground. What extra pressure (in atm) must be applied on the water surface so that the range becomes $2R$ (take 1 atm = 10^5 Pa and $g = 10$ m/s^2)

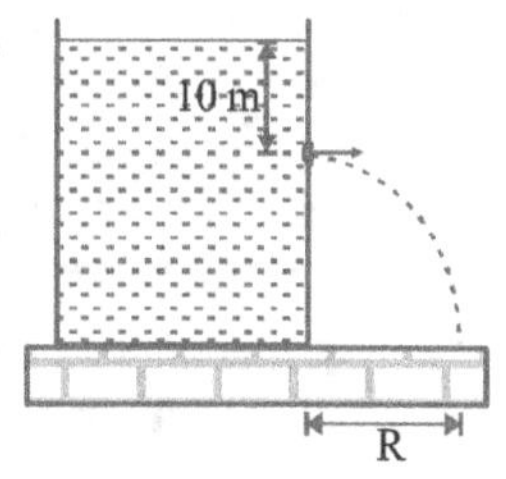

14. A cube of wood supporting 200 g mass just floats in water. When the mass is removed, the cube rises by 2cm. The side of the cube (in cm) is $2x$. Find the value of x.

Section IV - Comprehension Type

Directions (Qs. 15-18) : Based upon the given paragraphs, 4 multiple choice questions have to be answered. Each question has 4 choices (a), (b), (c) and (d), out of which **ONLY ONE** is correct.

PARAGRAPH-1

A cylinder of radius R is kept embedded along the wall of a dam as shown. Take density of water as ρ. Take length as L.

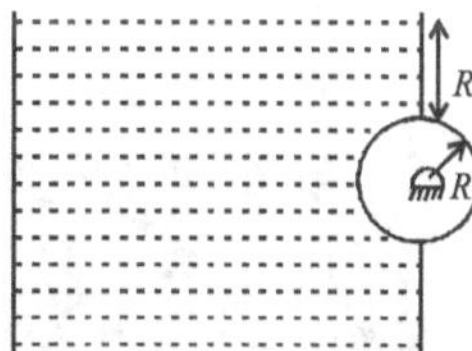

<table>
<tr><td rowspan="3">RESPONSE GRID</td><td colspan="3">8. (a)(b)(c)(d) 9. (a)(b)(c)(d) 10. (a)(b)(c)(d)</td></tr>
<tr><td>11. ⓪①②③④⑤⑥⑦⑧⑨ 12. ⓪①②③④⑤⑥⑦⑧⑨</td></tr>
<tr><td>13. ⓪①②③④⑤⑥⑦⑧⑨ 14. ⓪①②③④⑤⑥⑦⑧⑨</td></tr>
</table>

15. The vertical force exerted by water on the cylinder is
(a) $\rho\pi R^2 Lg$ (b) $\rho\pi R^2 Lg/2$
(c) zero (d) Zero

16. The net torque exerted by liquid on the cylinder is
(a) $\dfrac{2\rho R^3 Lg}{3}$ (b) $\dfrac{\rho R^3 Lg}{3}$
(c) $\dfrac{\rho R^3 Lg}{2}$ (d) Zero

PARAGRAPH-2

A tube of length ℓ and radius R carries a steady flow of fluid whose density is ρ and viscosity η. The velocity v of flow is given by $v = v_0\left(\dfrac{R^2 - r^2}{R^2}\right)$, where r is the distance of the flowing fluid from the axis.

17. Volume of fluid, flowing across the section of the tube, in unit time is
(a) $v_0\pi R^2$ (b) $\dfrac{\pi v_0 R^2}{2}$
(c) $\dfrac{\pi v_0 R^2}{3}$ (d) $\dfrac{\pi v_0 R^2}{4}$

18. Kinetic energy of the fluid within the volume of the tube is
(a) $\dfrac{\pi\ell\rho v_0^2 R^2}{2}$ (b) $\dfrac{\pi\ell\rho v_0^2 R^2}{4}$
(c) $\dfrac{\pi\ell\rho v_0^2 R^2}{6}$ (d) $\dfrac{\pi\ell\rho v_0^2 R^2}{3}$

Section V - Matrix-Match Type

This section contains 2 questions. It contains statements given in two columns, which have to be matched. Statements in column I are labelled as A, B, C and D whereas statements in column II are labelled as p, q, r and s. The answers to these questions have to be appropriately bubbled as illustrated in the following example. If the correct matches are A-p, A-r, B-p, B-s, C-r, C-s and D-q, then the correctly bubbled matrix will look like the following:

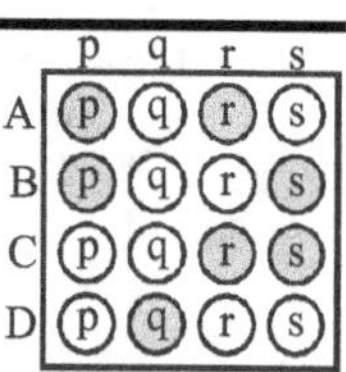

19. Bucket A contains only water, an identical bucket B contains water, but also contains a solid object in the water. Consider the following four situations. Which bucket weighs more

Column I
(A) The object floats in bucket B, and the buckets have the same water level.
(B) The object floats in bucket B, and the buckets have the same volume of water.
(C) The object sinks completely in bucket B, and the buckets have the same water level.
(D) The object sinks completely in bucket B, and the buckets have the same volume of water.

Column II
(p) Bucket A
(q) Bucket B
(r) Both buckets have the same weight
(s) Bucket's weight can't be compaired

20. Figure shows a siphon. It is a long pipe which is used to drain water from the reservoir at higher level to a reservoir at lower level. Regarding the siphon match the following columns :

Column-I
(A) Pressure is more than atmospheric pressure at
(B) Pressure is less than atmospheric pressure at
(C) Pressure is highest of all the five points at
(D) Pressure is least of all the five points

Column-II
(p) 1
(q) 2
(r) 3
(s) 4

RESPONSE GRID

15. (a)(b)(c)(d)	16. (a)(b)(c)(d)	17. (a)(b)(c)(d)	18. (a)(b)(c)(d)
19. A-(p)(q)(r)(s); B-(p)(q)(r)(s); C-(p)(q)(r)(s); D-(p)(q)(r)(s)			
20. A-(p)(q)(r)(s); B-(p)(q)(r)(s); C-(p)(q)(r)(s); D-(p)(q)(r)(s)			

DAILY PRACTICE PROBLEM DPP CP08 - PHYSICS

Total Questions	20	Total Marks		74
Attempted		Correct		
Incorrect		Net Score		
Cut-off Score	24	Qualifying Score		35

$$\text{Net Score} = \sum_{i=1}^{V}\left[(correct_i \times MM_i) - (In_i - NM_i)\right]$$

Space for Rough Work

Date : | **Start Time :** | **End Time :**

PHYSICS $\boxed{\text{CP09}}$

SYLLABUS : Thermal Properties of Matter

Max. Marks : 74   **Time : 60 min.**

GENERAL INSTRUCTIONS

- The Daily Practice Problem Sheet contains 20 Questions divided into 5 sections.
- **Section I** has **6** MCQs with ONLY 1 Correct Option, **3** marks for each correct answer and **−1** for each incorrect answer.
- **Section II** has **4** MCQs with ONE or MORE THAN ONE Correct options.
- For each question, marks will be awarded in one of the following categories:
- Full marks: **+4** If only the bubble(s) corresponding to all the correct option(s) is (are) darkened.
- Partial marks: **+1** For darkening a bubble corresponding to each correct option provided NO INCORRECT option is darkened.
- Zero marks: If none of the bubbles is darkened.
- Negative marks: **−2** In all other cases.
- **Section III** has **4** Single Digit Integer Answer Type Questions, **3** marks for each Correct Answer and 0 marks in all other cases.
- **Section IV** has Comprehension Type Questions having **4** MCQs with ONLY ONE corect option, 3 marks for each Correct Answer and 0 marks in all other cases.
- **Section V** has **2** Matching Type Questions, **2** mark for the correct matching of each row and 0 marks in all other cases.
- You have to evaluate your Response Grids yourself with the help of Solutions.

Section I - Straight Objective Type

This section contains 6 multiple choice questions. Each question has 4 choices (a), (b), (c) and (d), out of which **ONLY ONE** is correct.

1. A glass sinker has a mass M in air. When weighed in a liquid at temperature t_1, the apparent mass is M_1 and when weighed in the same liquid at temperature t_2, the apparent mass is M_2. If the coefficient of cubical expansion of the glass is γ_g, then the real coefficient of expansion of the liquid is :

(a) $\gamma_g + \left(\dfrac{M_2 - M_1}{M - M_2} \right) \cdot \dfrac{1}{(t_2 - t_1)}$

(b) $\gamma_g - \left(\dfrac{M_2 - M_1}{M - M_2} \right) \cdot \dfrac{1}{(t_2 - t_1)}$

(c) $\gamma_g - \left(\dfrac{M - M_2}{M_2 - M_1} \right) \cdot \dfrac{1}{(t_2 - t_1)}$

(d) $\gamma_g + \left(\dfrac{M_2 - M_1}{M_2 + M_1} \right) \cdot \dfrac{1}{(t_2 - t_1)}$

RESPONSE GRID	1. ⓐⓑⓒⓓ

Space for Rough Work

2. The graph, shown in the diagram, represents the variation of temperature (T) of two bodies, x and y having same surface area, with time (t) due to the emission of radiation. Find the correct relation between the emissivity and absorptive power of the two bodies

(a) $E_x > E_y$ & $a_x < a_y$

(b) $E_x < E_y$ & $a_x > a_y$

(c) $E_x > E_y$ & $a_x > a_y$

(d) $E_x < E_y$ & $a_x < a_y$

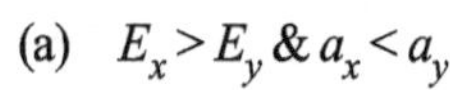

3. A sphere of density ρ, specific heat capacity c and radius r is hung by a thermally insulated thread in an enclosure which is kept at a lower temperature than the sphere. The temperature of the sphere starts to drop at a rate which depends upon the temperature difference between the sphere and the enclosure and the nature of the surface of sphere and is proportional to

(a) $\dfrac{c}{r^3 \rho}$ (b) $\dfrac{1}{r^3 \rho c}$ (c) $3r^3 \rho c$ (d) $\dfrac{1}{r\rho c}$

4. Two elastic rods are joined between fixed supports as shown in figure. Condition for no change in the lengths of individual rods with the increase of temperature. ($\alpha_1, \alpha_2 =$ linear expansion coefficient, $A_1, A_2 =$ area of rods, $y_1, y_2 =$ Youngs modulus)

(a) $\dfrac{A_1}{A_2} = \dfrac{\alpha_1}{\alpha_2}\dfrac{y_1}{y_2}$

(b) $\dfrac{A_1}{A_2} = \dfrac{L_1 \alpha_1 y_1}{L_2 \alpha_2 y_2}$

(c) $\dfrac{A_1}{A_2} = \dfrac{L_2 \alpha_2 y_2}{L_1 \alpha_1 y_1}$ (d) $\dfrac{A_1}{A_2} = \dfrac{\alpha_2 y_2}{\alpha_1 y_1}$

5. A solid copper cube of edges 1 cm each is suspended in an evacuated enclosure. Its temperture is found to fall from $100°C$ to $99°C$ in 100 s. Another solid copper cube of edges 2 cm, with similar surface nature, is suspended in a similar manner. The time required for this cube to cool from $100°C$ to $99°C$ will be approximately

(a) 25 s   (b) 50 s   (c) 200 s   (d) 400 s

6. The temperature of the two outer surfaces of a composite slab, consisting of two materials having coefficients of thermal conductivity K and $2K$ and thickness x and $4x$, respectively, are T_2 and $T_1 (T_2 > T_1)$. The rate of heat transfer through the slab, in a steady state is $\left(\dfrac{A(T_2 - T_1)K}{x}\right)f$, with f equal to

(a) $\dfrac{2}{3}$

(b) $\dfrac{1}{2}$

(c) 1

(d) $\dfrac{1}{3}$

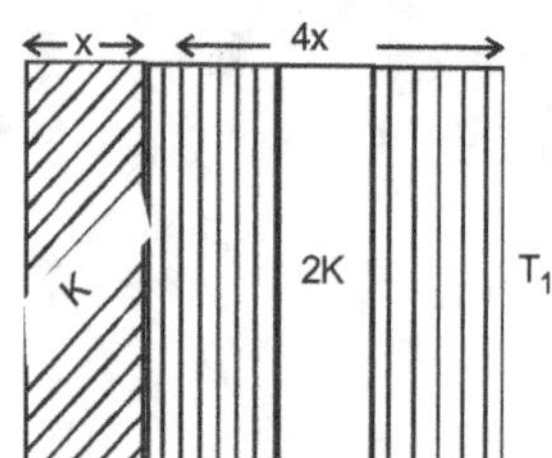

Section II - Multiple Correct Answer Type

This section contains 4 multiple correct answer(s) type questions. Each question has 4 choices (a), (b), (c) and (d), out of which **ONE OR MORE** is/are correct.

7. In a dark room with ambient temperature T_0 a black body is kept at a temperature T. Keeping the temperature of the black body constant (at T) sunrays are allowed to fall on the black body through a hole in the roof of the dark room. Assuming that there is no change in the ambient temperature of the room, which of the following statement(s) is/are correct?

(a) The quantity of radiation absorbed by the black body in unit time will increase.

(b) Since emissivity = absorptivity, hence the quantity of radiation emitted by black body in unit time will increase

(c) Black body radiates more energy in unit time in the visible spectrum

(d) The reflected energy in unit time by the black body remains same

8. A metal sphere of radius R and specific heat C is rotated about an axis passing through its centre at a speed n rotation /second. It is suddenly stopped and 50% of its energy is used in increasing its temperature, then choose the correct statement(s) from the following?

(a) Kinetic energy used to raise the temperature of the sphere is $\dfrac{2\pi^2 n^2}{5}MR^2$

(b) Kinetic energy used to raise the temperature of the sphere is $\dfrac{5\pi^2 n}{3}MR$

(c) The rise in the temperature of the sphere is $\dfrac{4\pi^2 n^2 R^2}{7C}$

(d) The rise in the temperature of the sphere is $\dfrac{2\pi^2 n^2 R^2}{5C}$

9. A uniform cylinder of steel of mass M, radius R is placed on frictionless bearings and set to rotate about its vertical axis with angular velocity ω_0. After the cylinder has reached the specified state of rotation it is heated without any mechanical contact from temperature T_0 to $T_0 + \Delta T$. If $\Delta I/I$ is the fractional change in moment of inertia of the cylinder and $\Delta\omega/\omega_0$ be the fraction change in the angular velocity of the cylinder and α be the coefficient of linear expansion, then

(a) $\dfrac{\Delta I}{I} = \dfrac{2\Delta R}{R}$

(b) $\dfrac{\Delta I}{I} = \dfrac{\Delta\omega}{\omega_0}$

(c) $\dfrac{\Delta\omega}{\omega_0} = -2\alpha\Delta T$

(d) $\dfrac{\Delta I}{I} = -\dfrac{2\Delta R}{R}$

10. A cylindrical metal rod is shaped into a ring with a small gap as shown. On heating the system :

(a) x decreases, r increases
(b) x increase
(c) r increases
(d) x increases, r decreases

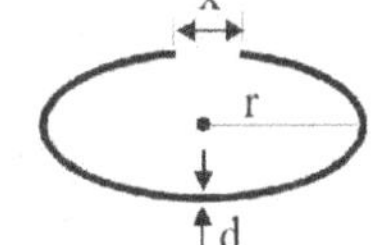

Section III - Integer Type

This section contains 4 questions. The answer to each of the questions is a single digit integer ranging from 0 to 9.

11. Steam at 120°C is continuously passed through a 18 cm long rubber tube of inner and outer radii 1.0 cm and 1.2 cm. The room temperature is 30°C. $x \times 10^2$ is the rate of heat flow through the walls of the tube in J/s. Thermal conductivity of rubber = 0.15 J/m–s–°C. Find the value of x.

12. Two spherical bodies A (radius 6 cm) and B(radius 18 cm) are at temperature T_1 and T_2, respectively. The maximum intensity in the emission spectrum of A is at 500 nm and in that of B is at 1500 nm. Considering them to be black bodies, what will be the ratio of the rate of total energy radiated by A to that of B?

13. A cylindrical rod of length 50 cm and cross–sectional area 1 cm^2 is fitted between a large ice chamber at 0°C and an evacuated chamber maintained at 27°C as shown in figure. Only small portions of the rod are inside the chambers and the rest is thermally insulated from the surrounding. The cross–section going into the evacuated chamber is blackened so that it completely absorbs any radiation falling on it. The temperature of the blackened end is 15.5°C when steady state is reached. Stefan's constant $\sigma = 6 \times 10^{-8}$ W/ m^2–K^4. Find the thermal conductivity of the material of the rod (in W/m – °C).

14. Two spherical stars A and B emit blackbody radiation. The radius of A is 400 times that of B and A emits 10^4 times the power emitted from B. The ratio $\left(\dfrac{\lambda_A}{\lambda_B}\right)$ of their wavelengths λ_A and λ_B at which the peaks occur in their respective radiation curves is

Section IV - Comprehension Type

Directions (Qs. 15-18) : Based upon the given paragraphs, 4 multiple choice questions have to be answered. Each question has 4 choices (a), (b), (c) and (d), out of which **ONLY ONE** is correct.

PARAGRAPH-1

The system shown in figure consists of three springs and two rods as shown. The temperature of the rods is increased by ΔT. The springs are initially relaxed. There is no friction. The coefficient of linear expansion of the material of rods is equal to α.

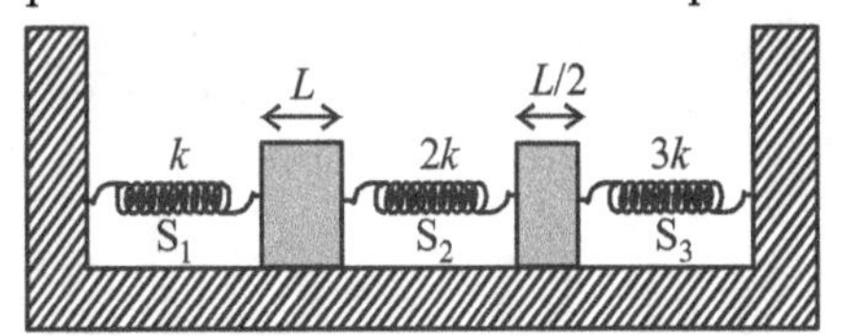

15. The energy stored in spring S_1 is

(a) $\dfrac{81}{484} k L^2\alpha^2(\Delta T)^2$

(b) $\dfrac{27}{242} k L^2\alpha^2(\Delta T)^2$

(c) $\dfrac{81}{242} k L^2\alpha^2(\Delta T)^2$

(d) $\dfrac{49}{484} k L^2\alpha^2(\Delta T)^2$

16. The energy stored in spring S_2 is

(a) $\dfrac{81}{484} k L^2\alpha^2(\Delta T)^2$

(b) $\dfrac{27}{242} k L^2\alpha^2(\Delta T)^2$

(c) $\dfrac{81}{242} k L^2\alpha^2(\Delta T)^2$

(d) $\dfrac{49}{484} k L^2\alpha^2(\Delta T)^2$

PARAGRAPH-2

A brass ball of mass 100g is heated to 100°C and then dropped into 200g of turpentine in a calorimeter at 15°C. The final temperature is found to be 23°C. Determine the specific heat of turpentine. Take specific heat of brass as 0.092 cal/g°C and water equivalent of calorimeter as 4g.

17. Heat lost by the ball is approximately
(a) 810 cal
(b) 610 cal
(c) 710 cal
(d) 510 cal

18. Specific heat of the brass is
(a) 0.62 cal/g°C
(b) 0.52 cal/g°C
(c) 0.42 cal/g°C
(d) 0.32 cal/g°C

<table>
<tr><td rowspan="4">RESPONSE
GRID</td><td>9. ⓐⓑⓒⓓ</td><td>10. ⓐⓑⓒⓓ</td><td>11. ⓪①②③④⑤⑥⑦⑧⑨</td></tr>
<tr><td>12. ⓪①②③④⑤⑥⑦⑧⑨</td><td colspan="2">13. ⓪①②③④⑤⑥⑦⑧⑨</td></tr>
<tr><td>14. ⓪①②③④⑤⑥⑦⑧⑨</td><td>15. ⓐⓑⓒⓓ</td><td>16. ⓐⓑⓒⓓ   17. ⓐⓑⓒⓓ</td></tr>
<tr><td>18. ⓐⓑⓒⓓ</td><td></td><td></td></tr>
</table>

Section V - Matrix-Match Type

This section contains 2 questions. It contains statements given in two columns, which have to be matched. Statements in column I are labelled as A, B, C and D whereas statements in column II are labelled as p, q, r and s. The answers to these questions have to be appropriately bubbled as illustrated in the following example. If the correct matches are A-p, A-r, B-p, B-s, C-r, C-s and D-q, then the correctly bubbled matrix will look like the following:

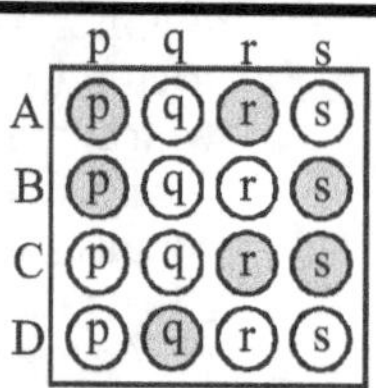

19. A ball has surface temperature T initially at time $t = 0$, that is less than surrounding constant temperature T_0. On the vertical axis of the graph shown has either thermal energy radiated/absorbed per unit time or total energy radiated/absorbed till time t by the ball. Correctly match the curves marked in the graph

Column I		Column II	
(A)	Thermal energy emitted per unit time	(p)	1
(B)	Thermal energy absorbed per unit time	(q)	2
(C)	Total energy emitted till time t	(r)	3
(D)	Total energy absorbed till time t	(s)	4

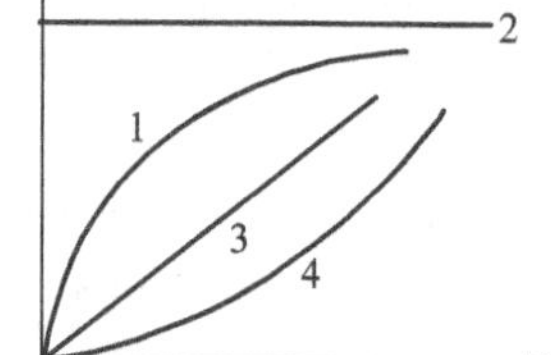

20. Match columns I and II regarding Newton's law of cooling.

Column I

(A) Curve between $\log(\theta - \theta_0)$ and time, plotted on X- and Y - axes respectively

Column II

(p) 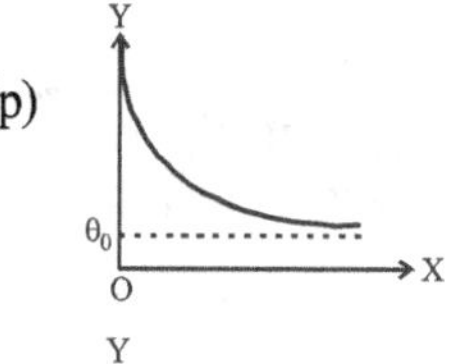

(B) Curve between temperature of body (θ) and time, plotted on X - and Y - axes respectively

(q) 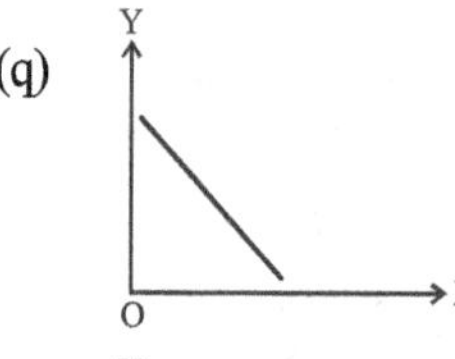

(C) Curve between the rate of cooling (R) and body temperature (θ), plotted on X-and Y-axes respectively

(r) 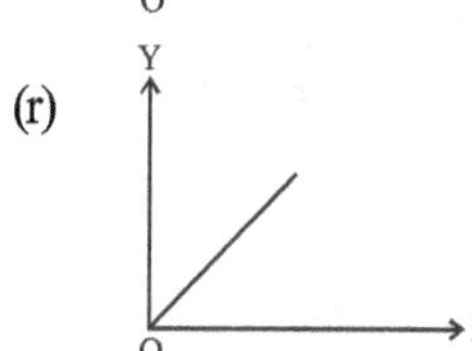

(D) Curve between the rate of cooling (R) and temperature difference between body (θ) and surrounding (θ_0), plotted on X - and Y-axes respectively

(s) 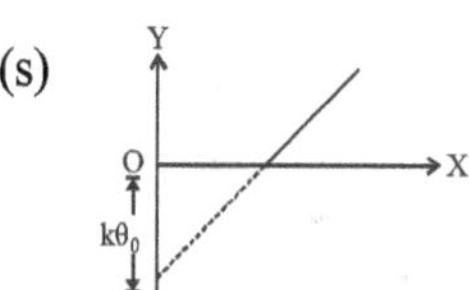

RESPONSE GRID	
19. A - (p)(q)(r)(s); B - (p)(q)(r)(s); C - (p)(q)(r)(s); D - (p)(q)(r)(s)	
20. A - (p)(q)(r)(s); B - (p)(q)(r)(s); C - (p)(q)(r)(s); D - (p)(q)(r)(s)	

DAILY PRACTICE PROBLEM DPP CP09 - PHYSICS

Total Questions	20	Total Marks	74
Attempted		Correct	
Incorrect		Net Score	
Cut-off Score	24	Qualifying Score	35

$$\text{Net Score} = \sum_{i=1}^{V} \left[\left(correct_i \times MM_i \right) - \left(In_i - NM_i \right) \right]$$

Space for Rough Work

DPP - Daily Practice Problems

Chapter-wise Sheets

Date : [ ]　　　Start Time : [ ]　　　End Time : [ ]

PHYSICS　$\boxed{\text{CP10}}$

SYLLABUS : Thermodynamics

Max. Marks : 74　　　　　　　　　　　　　　　**Time : 60 min.**

GENERAL INSTRUCTIONS

- The Daily Practice Problem Sheet contains 20 Questions divided into 5 sections.

Section I has **5** MCQs with ONLY 1 Correct Option, **3** marks for each correct answer and **−1** for each incorrect answer.

Section II has **4** MCQs with ONE or MORE THAN ONE Correct options.

For each question, marks will be awarded in one of the following categories:

Full marks: **+4** If only the bubble(s) corresponding to all the correct option(s) is (are) darkened.

Partial marks: **+1** For darkening a bubble corresponding to each correct option provided NO INCORRECT option is darkened.

Zero marks:　If none of the bubbles is darkened.

Negative marks: **−2** In all other cases.

Section III has **4** Single Digit Integer Answer Type Questions, **3** marks for each Correct Answer and 0 marks in all other cases.

Section IV has Comprehension/Matching Cum-Comprehension Type Questions having **5** MCQs with ONLY ONE correct option, **3** marks for each Correct Answer and 0 marks in all other cases.

Section V has **2** Matching Type Questions, **2** mark for the correct matching of each row and 0 marks in all other cases.

- You have to evaluate your Response Grids yourself with the help of Solutions.

Section I - Straight Objective Type

This section contains 5 multiple choice questions. Each question has 4 choices (a), (b), (c) and (d), out of which **ONLY ONE** is correct.

1. An ideal gas is subjected to cyclic process involving four thermodynamic states, the amounts of heat (Q) and work (W) involved in each of these states

$Q_1 = 6000\,\text{J};\ Q_2 = -5500\,\text{J};\ Q_3 = -3000\,\text{J};\ Q_4 = +3500\,\text{J}$
$W_1 = 2500\,\text{J};\ W_2 = -1000\,\text{J};\ W_3 = -1200\,\text{J};\ W_4 = x\text{J}$

The ratio of the net work done by the gas to the total heat absorbed by the gas is η. The values of x and η respectively are

(a)　500; 7.5%　　　　　　(b)　700; 10.5%

(c)　1000; 21%　　　　　　(d)　1500; 15%

Space for Rough Work

2. Consider the shown diagram where the two chambers separated by piston-spring arrangement contain equal amounts of certain ideal gas. Initially when the temperatures of the gas in both the chambers are kept at 300 K the compression in the spring is $1m$. The temperature of the left and the right chambers are now raised to 400 K and 500 K respectively. If the pistons are free to slide, the compression in the spring is about

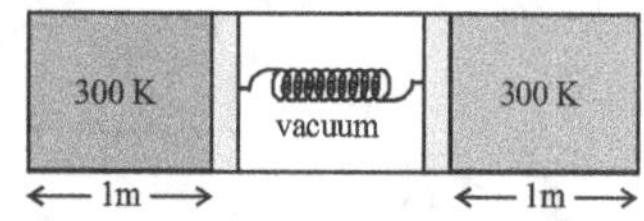

(a) 1.3 m   (b) 1.5 m   (c) 1.1 m   (d) 1.0 m

3. The heat (Q) supplied to a solid, which is otherwise thermally isolated from its surroundings, is plotted as a function of its **absolute temperature**, θ. It is found that they are related by the equation.
$$Q = a\theta^2 + b\theta^{4.} \ (a, b \text{ are constants}).$$
The heat capacity of the solid is given by

(a) $a\dfrac{\theta^3}{3} + b\dfrac{\theta^5}{5}$ (b) $a\theta + b\theta^3$

(c) $a\dfrac{\theta}{3} + b\dfrac{\theta^3}{5}$ (d) $2a\theta + 4b\theta^3$

4. A Carnot engine absorbs 1000 J of heat energy from a reservoir at 127°C and rejects 600 J of heat energy during each cycle. The efficiency of engine and temperature of sink will be:
(a) 20% and – 43°C   (b) 40% and – 33°C
(c) 50% and – 20°C   (d) 70% and – 10°C

5. A cyclic process $ABCD$ is shown in the P-V diagram. Which of the following P-T curves represent the same process?

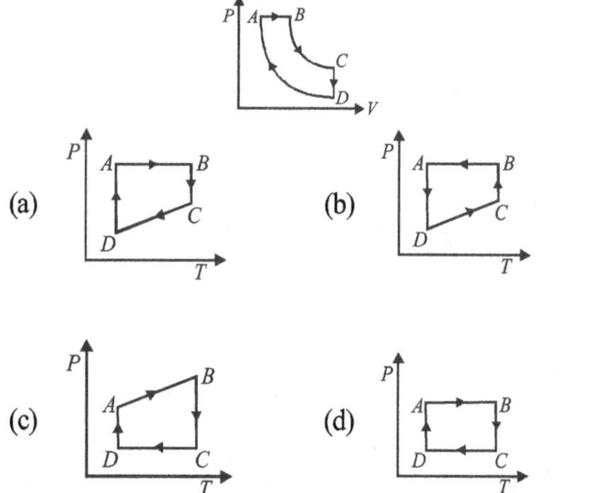

(a)   (b)

(c)   (d)

6. During an experiment, an ideal gas is found to obey a condition $\dfrac{P^2}{\rho} = $ constant [$\rho = $ density of the gas]. The gas is initially at temperature T, pressure P and density ρ. The gas expands such that density changes to $\rho /2$. Then
(a) the pressure of the gas changes to $\sqrt{2}$P
(b) the temperature of the gas changes to $\sqrt{2}$T
(c) the graph of the above process on the P-T diagram is parabola
(d) the graph of the above process on the P-T diagram is hyperbola

7. Four Carnot engines operate between reservoir temperature of (i) 300 K and 400 K (ii) 400 K and 500 K (iii) 500 K and 600 K (iv) 600 K and 800 K. Which engines has/have greatest thermal efficiency?
(a) (i)   (b) (ii)   (c) (iii)   (d) (iv)

8. The figure shows the P-V plot of an ideal gas taken through a cycle $ABCDA$. The part ABC is a semi-circle and CDA is half of an ellipse. Then,

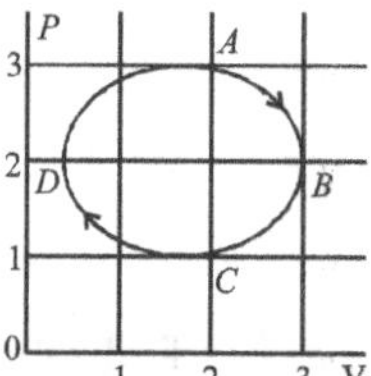

(a) the process during the path $A \rightarrow B$ is isothermal
(b) heat flows out of the gas during the path $B \rightarrow C \rightarrow D$
(c) work done during the path $A \rightarrow B \rightarrow C$ is zero
(d) positive work is done by the gas in the cycle $ABCDA$

9. During the melting of a slab of ice at 273 K at atmospheric pressure,
(a) positive work is done by the ice-water system on the atmosphere
(b) positive work is done on the ice- water system by the atmosphere
(c) the internal energy of the ice-water system increases
(d) the internal energy of the ice-water system decreases

Section III - Integer Type

This section contains 4 questions. The answer to each of the questions is a single digit integer ranging from 0 to 9.

10. A metal rod AB of length $10x$ has its one end A in ice at $0\,°C$, and the other end B in water at $100\,°C$. If a point P on the rod is maintained at $400\,°C$, then it is found that equal amounts of water and ice evaporate and melt per unit time. The latent heat of evaporation of water is 540 cal/g and latent heat of melting of ice is 80 cal/g. If the point P is at a distance of λx from the ice end A, find the value λ.
[Neglect any heat loss to the surrounding.]

11. A thermodynamic system is taken from an initial state i with internal energy $U_i = 100$ J to the final state f along two different paths iaf and ibf, as schematically shown in the figure. The work done by the system along the paths af, ib and bf are $W_{af} = 200$ J, $W_{ib} = 50$ J and $W_{bf} = 100$ J respectively. The heat

Section II - Multiple Correct Answer Type

This section contains 4 multiple correct answer(s) type questions. Each question has 4 choices (a), (b), (c) and (d), out of which **ONE OR MORE** is/are correct.

<table>
<tr><td rowspan="3">RESPONSE
GRID</td><td>2. ⓐⓑⓒⓓ</td><td>2. ⓐⓑⓒⓓ</td><td>4. ⓐⓑⓒⓓ</td><td>4. ⓐⓑⓒⓓ</td><td>5. ⓐⓑⓒⓓ</td></tr>
<tr><td>6. ⓐⓑⓒⓓ</td><td>7. ⓐⓑⓒⓓ</td><td>8. ⓐⓑⓒⓓ</td><td>9. ⓐⓑⓒⓓ</td><td></td></tr>
<tr><td colspan="2">10. ⓪①②③④⑤⑥⑦⑧⑨</td><td colspan="3">11. ⓪①②③④⑤⑥⑦⑧⑨</td></tr>
</table>

supplied to the system along the path iaf, ib and bf are Q_{iaf}, Q_{ib} and Q_{bf} respectively. If the internal energy of the system in the state b is $U_b - 200$ J and $Q_{iaf} - 500$ J, The ratio $\dfrac{Q_{bf}}{Q_{ib}}$ is

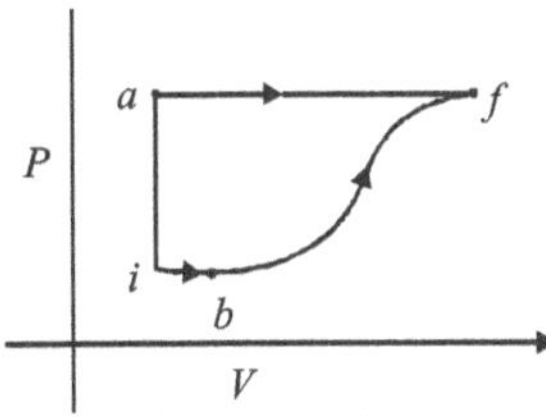

12. The amount of work done to increase the temperature of one mole of an ideal gas by $30°C$ is $10\,x$ cal. Find the value of x, if it is expanding under the condition $V \propto T^{2/3}$. $(R = 2\,\text{cal}/\text{mol–K})$

13. A weightless piston divides a thermally insulated cylinder into two parts of volumes V and $3V$. 2 moles of an ideal gas at pressure $P = 2$ atmosphere are confined to the part with volume $V = 1$ litre. The remainder of the cylinder is evacuated. Initially the gas is at room temperature. The piston is now released and the gas expands to fill the entire space of the cylinder. The piston is then pressed back to the initial position. If the increase of internal energy in the process is $x \times 10^2$ J then find the value of x. The ratio of the specific heat of the gas $\gamma = 1.5$.

Section IV - Comprehension/Matching Cum-Comprehension Type

Directions (Qs. 14 and 15) : Based upon the given paragraph, 2 multiple choice questions have to be answered. Each question has 4 choices (a), (b), (c) and (d), out of which **ONLY ONE** is correct.

PARAGRAPH

Two cylinder A and B having pistons (massless) of cross sectional area $100\,cm^2$ and $200\,cm^2$ respectively. The pistons are connected by massless rod. The pistons can move freely without friction. The cylinder A contains 100 gm of an ideal gas $(\gamma - 1.5)$ at pressure 10^5 N/m² and temperature T_0. The cylinder B contains identical gas at same temperature T_0 but has different mass. The pistons are held at the state such that volume of gas in cylinder A and cylinder B are same and is equal to 10^{-2} m³. The walls and piston of cylinder A are thermally insulated whereas gas in cylinder B is maintained at temperature T_0. Now the temperature T_0. The whole system is in vacuum. Now the piston is slowly released and it moves towards left and mechanical equilibrium is reached at the state when the volume of gas in cylinder A beocmes 25×10^{-4} m³.

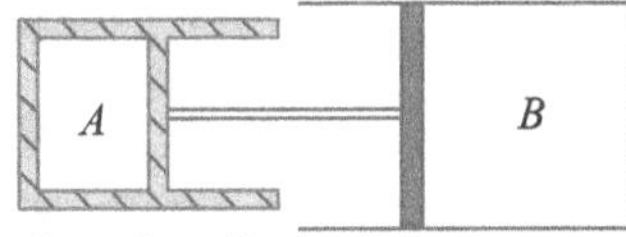

14. The mass of gas in cylinder B is
(a) 200 gm (b) 600 gm (c) 500 gm (d) 1 kg

15. The compressive force in the connecting rod at equilibrium is
(a) 2000 N (b) 4000 N (c) 8000 N (d) 10000 N

Directions (Qs. 16-18) : This passage contains a table having 3 columns and 4 rows. Based on the table, there are three questions. Each question has four options (a), (b), (c) and (d) **ONLY ONE** of these four options is correct.

First Law of Thermodynamics states that, "If certain quantity of heat dQ is added to a system a part of it is used in increasing the internal energy by dU and dW in performing external work i.e dQ = dU + dW." The following columns show (Internal energy/Work done/Heat given or taken out) in the four different thermodynamic processes. Here P = pressure, v = volume. dT = change in temperature.

	Column I		Column II		Column III
I	Isothermal process	(i)	$dU = 0$	(P)	$dQ = 0$
II	Adiabatic process	(ii)	$dU = nC_v\,dT$	(Q)	$dQ = 2.303\,nRT \log_{10}\frac{V_2}{V_1}$
III	Isobaric process	(iii)	$dW = 0$	(R)	$dQ = nC_p\,dT$
IV	Isochoric process	(iv)	$dW = P(V_2 - V_1)$	(S)	$dQ = nC_v\,dT$

16. For the process volume remains constant, which of the following options is corrcet?
(a) IV (iii) S (b) I (iii) Q
(c) III (i) P (d) II (iv) P

17. Which of the following shows the correct match for the process pressure remains constant?
(a) III (iv) R (b) IV (iii) R
(c) I (i) R (d) III (i) S

18. What is the correct match for the process temperature remains constant?
(a) IV (i) R (b) I (i) Q
(c) II (ii) P (d) III (ii) S

Section V - Matrix-Match Type

This section contains 2 questions. It contains statements given in two columns, which have to be matched. Statements in column I are labelled as A, B, C and D whereas statements in column II are labelled as p, q, r and s. The answers to these questions have to be appropriately bubbled as illustrated in the following example. If the correct matches are A-p, A-r, B-p, B-s, C-r, C-s and D-q, then the correctly bubbled matrix will look like the following:

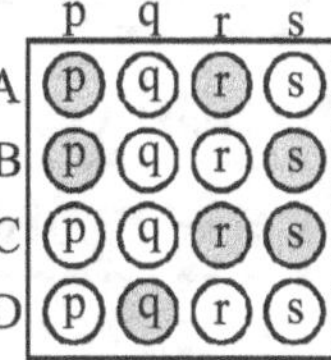

---

19. The figures given below show different processes (relating pressure P and volume V) for a given amount for an ideal gas. ΔW is work done by the gas and ΔQ is heat absorbed by the gas.

Column I	Column II

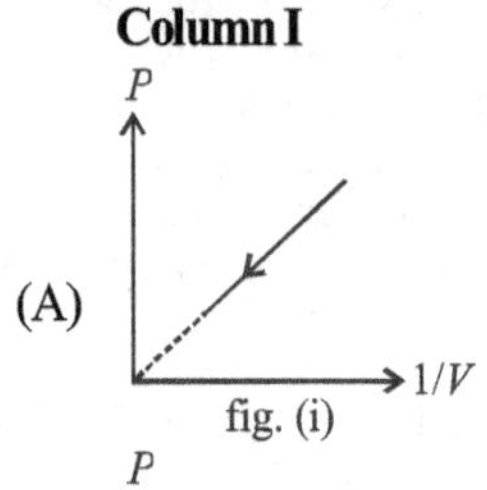

(A) fig. (i)

(p) $\Delta Q > 0$

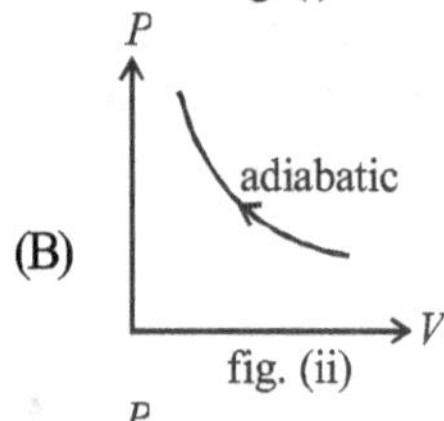

(B) fig. (ii) — adiabatic

(q) $\Delta W < 0$

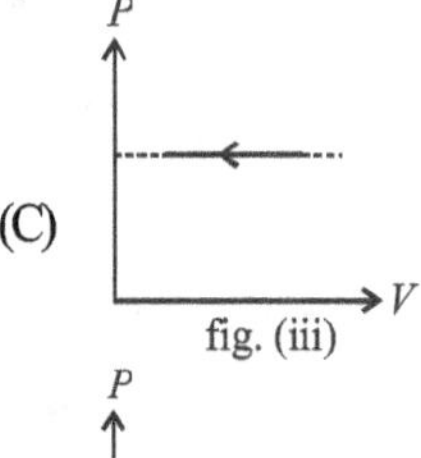

(C) fig. (iii)

(r) $\Delta Q < 0$

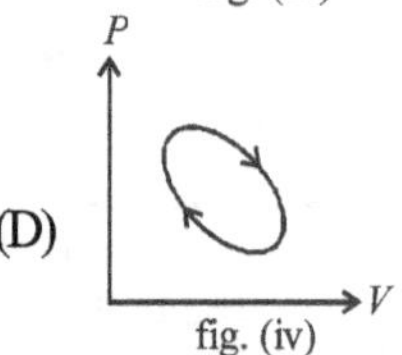

(D) fig. (iv)

(s) $\Delta W > 0$

20. One end of a copper rod is immersed in boiling water at 100°C, the other end in ice water mixture at 0°C. The sides of the rod are insulated. During a certain time interval, 0.5 kg of ice melts. Match the following columns:

Column - I	Column - II
(A) The entropy change of the boiling water	(p) 610 J/K
(B) The entropy change of the ice-water mixture	(q) zero
(C) The entropy change of the copper rod	(r) − 446 J/K
(D) The total entropy change of the entire system	(s) 164 J/K

RESPONSE GRID	
19.	A - ⓟⓠⓡⓢ ; B - ⓟⓠⓡⓢ ; C - ⓟⓠⓡⓢ ; D - ⓟⓠⓡⓢ
20.	A - ⓟⓠⓡⓢ ; B - ⓟⓠⓡⓢ ; C - ⓟⓠⓡⓢ ; D - ⓟⓠⓡⓢ

DAILY PRACTICE PROBLEM DPP CP10 - PHYSICS

Total Questions	20	Total Marks	74
Attempted		Correct	
Incorrect		Net Score	
Cut-off Score	24	Qualifying Score	35

$$\text{Net Score} = \sum_{i=1}^{V} \left[(\text{correct}_i \times MM_i) - (In_i - NM_i) \right]$$

Date : | **Start Time :** | **End Time :**

PHYSICS $\boxed{\text{CP11}}$

SYLLABUS : Kinetic Theory

Max. Marks : 74   **Time : 60 min.**

Section I - Straight Objective Type

This section contains 5 multiple choice questions. Each question has 4 choices (a), (b), (c) and (d), out of which **ONLY ONE** is correct.

1. The maximum attainable temperature of ideal gas in the process
   $$P = P_0 - \alpha V^2 \text{ where } P_0 \text{ and } \alpha \text{ are +ve constants is}$$

(a) $\dfrac{2P_0}{3nR}\left(\dfrac{P_0}{3\alpha}\right)^{1/2}$

(b) $\dfrac{P_0}{2nR}\left(\dfrac{2P_0}{3\alpha}\right)^{1/2}$

(c) $\dfrac{2nR}{P_0}\left(\dfrac{2P_0}{3\alpha}\right)^{1/2}$

(d) $\dfrac{2P_0}{nR}\left(\dfrac{P_0}{2\alpha}\right)^{1/2}$

RESPONSE GRID 1. ⓐ ⓑ ⓒ ⓓ

Space for Rough Work

2. Let V denote the root mean square speed of the molecules in an ideal diatomic gas at absolute temperature T. The mass of a molecule is 'm'. Neglecting vibrational energy terms, which is false?

(a) A molecule can have a speed greater than $\sqrt{2}$ v

(b) V is proportional to $\sqrt{T}$

(c) The average rotational kinetic energy of a molecule is $mv^2/4$

(d) The average kinetic energy of a molecule is $5mv^2/6$

3. Two different masses m and $3m$ of an ideal gas are heated separately in a vessel of constant volume. The pressure P and absolute temperature T, graphs for these two cases are shown in the figure as A and B. The ratio of slopes of curves B to A is

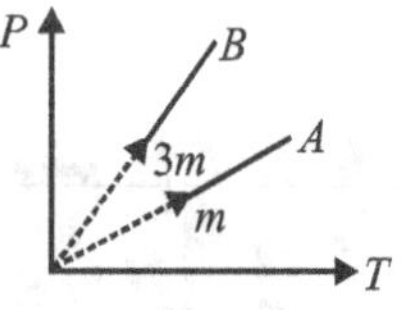

(a) $3:1$ (b) $1:3$ (c) $9:1$ (d) $1:9$

4. A cylinder contains He and O_2 of equal volume. They are separated by massless freely moving piston as shown. If the gas is adiabatically compressed by moving the piston so that volume of He becomes half. Finally:

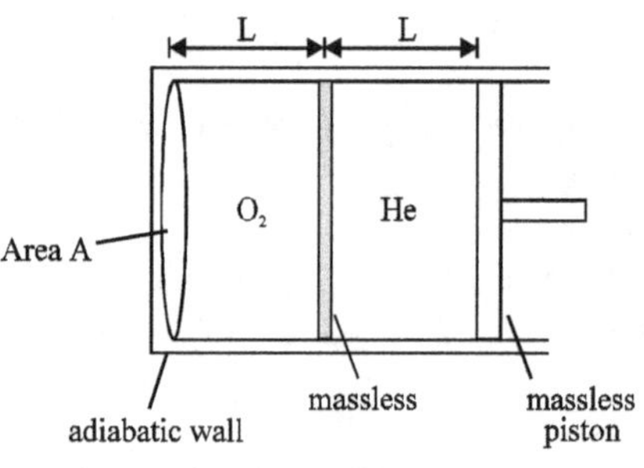

(a) pressure in He chamber will be equal to pressure in O_2 chamber

(b) pressure in He chamber will be less than pressure in O_2 chamber

(c) volume of He chamber will be equal to volume of O_2 chamber

(d) volume of O_2 chamber will be $LA/(2)^{25/21}$

5. Find the value of $\gamma = \dfrac{C_P}{C_V}$ for a mixture consisting of n_1 moles of a monoatomic gas and n_2 moles of a gas of diatomic molecules:

(a) $\dfrac{n_1}{n_2}$

(b) $\dfrac{5n_1 + 7n_2}{3n_1 + 5n_2}$

(c) $\dfrac{3n_1 + 5n_2}{5n_1 + 7n_2}$

(d) $\dfrac{7n_2 + 3n_1}{5n_1 + 3n_2}$

Section II - Multiple Correct Answer Type

This section contains 4 multiple correct answer(s) type questions. Each question has 4 choices (a), (b), (c) and (d), out of which **ONE OR MORE** is/are correct.

6. Hydrogen gas and oxygen gas have volume $1 cm^3$ each at NTP. Then

(a) number of molecules is same in both the gases

(b) the rms velocity of molecules of both the gases is the same

(c) the internal energy of each gas is the same

(d) the average velocity of molecules of each gas is the same

7. The total kinetic energy of translatory motion of all the molecules of 5 litres of nitrogen exerting a pressure P is 3000 J. Then

(a) the total K.E. of 10 litres of N_2 at a pressure of $2P$ is 3000J

(b) the total K.E. of 10 litres of He at a pressure of $2P$ is 3000 J

(c) the total K.E. of 10 litres of O_2 at a pressure of $2P$ is 12000 J

(d) the total K.E. of 10 litres of Ne at a pressure of $2P$ is 12000 J

8. For two different gases X and Y, having degrees of freedom f_1 and f_2 and molar heat capacities at constant volume Cv_1 and Cv_2 respectively, the lnP versus lnV graph is plotted for adiabatic process, as shown. Then

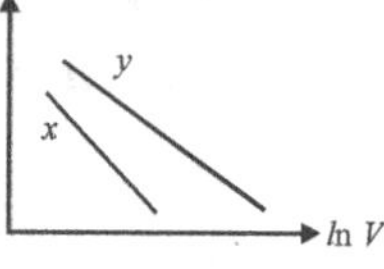

(a) $f_1 > f_2$

(b) $f_2 > f_1$

(c) $Cv_2 > Cv_1$

(d) $Cv_1 > Cv_2$

RESPONSE GRID

2. (a)(b)(c)(d)   3. (a)(b)(c)(d)   4. (a)(b)(c)(d)   5. (a)(b)(c)(d)   6. (a)(b)(c)(d)

7. (a)(b)(c)(d)   8. (a)(b)(c)(d)

9. From the following statements, concerning ideal gas at any given temperature T, select the correct one(s)
  (a) The coefficient of volume expansion at constant pressure is same for all ideal gases
  (b) The average translational kinetic energy per molecule of oxygen gas is $3KT$ (K being Boltzmann constant)
  (c) In a gaseous mixture, the average translational kinetic energy of the molecules of each component is same
  (d) The mean free path of molecules increases with the decrease in pressure

Section III - Integer Type

This section contains 4 questions. The answer to each of the questions is a single digit integer ranging from 0 to 9.

10. The molecules of a given mass of a gas have rms. velocity of 200 ms^{-1} at 300 k and 10^5 Nm^{-2} pressure. When the temperature and pressure of the gas are respectively 400 k and 50×10^3 Nm^{-2}, the rms. velocity of its molecule becomes $x \times 200 / \sqrt{3}$ ms^{-1}. Find the value of x.

11. A jar contains a gas and a few drops of water at TK. The pressure in the jar is 830 mm of mercury. The temperature in the jar is reduced by 3%. The saturated vapour pressure at the two temperatures are 30 mm and 25 mm of mercury. The new pressure in the jar is 100 x mm of Hg. Find the value of x.

12. An ideal gas is kept in a long cylindrical vessel fitted with a frictionless piston of cross–sectional area 10 cm^2 and weight 1 kg. The vessel itself is kept in a big chamber containing air at atmospheric pressure 100 kPa. 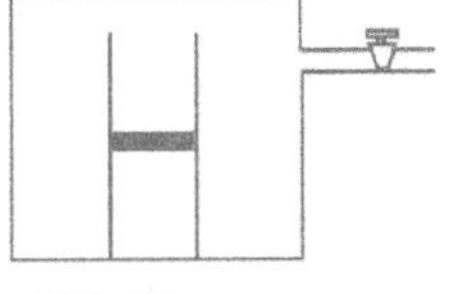
The length of the gas column is 20 cm. If the chamber is now completely evacuated by an exhaust pump, 110 x cm will be the length of the gas column. Assume the temperature remain constant throughout the process. Find the value of x.

13. 0.014 kg of nitrogen is enclosed in a vessel at a temperature of 16°C. How much heat (in kJ) has to be transferred to the gas to double the r.m.s. velocity of its molecules ?

Section IV - Comprehension/Matching Cum-Comprehension Type

Directions (Qs. 14 and 15): Based upon the given paragraph, 2 multiple choice questions have to be answered. Each question has 4 choices (a), (b), (c) and (d), out of which **ONLY ONE** is correct.

PARAGRAPH

A cubical box of side 1 m contains helium gas (atomic weight 4) at a pressure of 100 N/m^2. During an observation time of 1 s , an atom travelling with the root mean square speed parallel to one of its edges of the cube, was found to make 500 collisions with a particular wall, without any collision with other atoms. Taking $R = (25/3)$ J/mol–K and $k = 1.38 \times 10^{-23}$ J/K.

14. The temperature of the gas is
  (a) 160 K   (b) 210 K
  (c) 280 K   (d) 320 K

15. The average kinetic energy per atom is
  (a) 1.612×10^{-21} J   (b) 3.312×10^{-21} J
  (c) 3.521×10^{-21} J   (d) 4.20×10^{-21} J

Directions (Qs. 16-18): This passage contains a table having 3 columns and 4 rows. Based on the table, there are three questions. Each question has four options (a), (b), (c) and (d) **ONLY ONE** of these four options is correct.

According to law of equipartition of energy, if we deal with a large no of particles in thermal equilibrium to which we can apply Newtonion mechanics, the energy associated with each degree of freedom has the same average value (i.e. $\frac{1}{2}KT$) and this value depends on temperature. Column I, II, & III gives relation between degree of freedom (of monoatomic, di & poly atomic gas), C$_v$ and γ.

<table>
<tr><td rowspan="3">**RESPONSE GRID**</td><td>9. ⓐⓑⓒⓓ</td><td>10. ⓪①②③④⑤⑥⑦⑧⑨</td></tr>
<tr><td>11. ⓪①②③④⑤⑥⑦⑧⑨</td><td>12. ⓪①②③④⑤⑥⑦⑧⑨</td></tr>
<tr><td>13. ⓪①②③④⑤⑥⑦⑧⑨</td><td>14. ⓐⓑⓒⓓ   15. ⓐⓑⓒⓓ</td></tr>
</table>

Column I		Column II	Column III
I.	For monoatomic gas f = 3	(i) $\dfrac{7}{2}R$	(P) $\gamma = 1.67$
II.	For diatomic gas (molecule translate and rotate only) f = 5	(ii) $3R$	(Q) $\gamma = 1.33$
III.	For polyatomic gas if, f = 6	(iii) $\dfrac{5}{2}R$	(R) $\gamma = 1.4$
IV.	For diatomic gas (molecule translate, rotate as well as vibrate also) f = 7	(iv) $\dfrac{3}{2}R$	(S) $\gamma = 1.29$

16. If $\dfrac{9R}{2}$ be the value of C_p for diatomic gas when we consider translational, rotational as well as vibrational motion of gas moleclues, the correct matching satisfying the above condition is
(a) IV (ii) R (b) IV (iii) Q (c) IV (i) S (d) IV (iii) P

17. Which of the following shows the correct match for the polyatomic gas?
(a) III (i) P (b) III (ii) Q (c) III (ii) S (d) III (ii) P

18. Which of the following does not show the correct matching?
(a) II (iii) R (b) IV (i) S (c) II (iv) Q (d) I (iv) P

Section V - Matrix-Match Type

This section contains 2 questions. It contains statements given in two columns, which have to be matched. Statements in column I are labelled as A, B, C and D whereas statements in column II are labelled as p, q, r and s. The answers to these questions have to be appropriately bubbled as illustrated in the following example. If the correct matches are A-p, A-r, B-p, B-s, C-r, C-s and D-q, then the correctly bubbled matrix will look like the following:

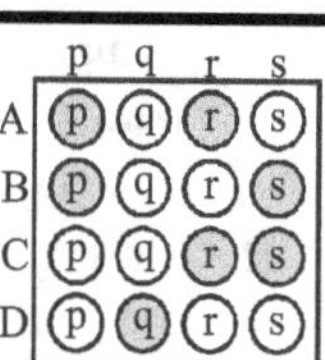

19. Match **Column I** (Physical Variables) with **Column II** (Expressions) (n = number of gas molecules present per unit volume, k = Boltzmann constant, T = absolute temperature, m = mass of the particle) :

Column I	Column II
(A) Most probable velocity	(p) nkT
(B) Energy per degree of freedom	(q) $\sqrt{(3kT/m)}$
(C) Pressure	(r) $\sqrt{(2kT/m)}$
(D) R.M.S. velocity	(s) $kT/2$

20.

Column I	Column II
(A) An ideal gas obeys gas equation	(p) with decrease in pressure
(B) A real gas behaves as an ideal gas at low pressure	(q) at all temperature
(C) Mean free path of molecules increases	(r) at high temperature
(D) Charle's law	(s) pressure constant

RESPONSE GRID

16. (a)(b)(c)(d)   17. (a)(b)(c)(d)   18. (a)(b)(c)(d)
19. A - (p)(q)(r)(s); B - (p)(q)(r)(s); C - (p)(q)(r)(s); D - (p)(q)(r)(s)
20. A - (p)(q)(r)(s); B - (p)(q)(r)(s); C - (p)(q)(r)(s); D - (p)(q)(r)(s)

DAILY PRACTICE PROBLEM DPP CP11 - PHYSICS

Total Questions	20	Total Marks	74
Attempted		Correct	
Incorrect		Net Score	
Cut-off Score	24	Qualifying Score	35

$$\text{Net Score} = \sum_{i=1}^{V}\left[\left(\text{correct}_i \times MM_i\right) - \left(In_i - NM_i\right)\right]$$

DPP - Daily Practice Problems

Chapter-wise Sheets

Date :   Start Time :   End Time :

PHYSICS $\boxed{\text{CP12}}$

SYLLABUS : Oscillations

Max. Marks : 74   **Time : 60 min.**

GENERAL INSTRUCTIONS

- The Daily Practice Problem Sheet contains 20 Questions divided into 5 sections.

  Section I has **5** MCQs with ONLY 1 Correct Option, **3** marks for each correct answer and **−1** for each incorrect answer.

  Section II has **4** MCQs with ONE or MORE THAN ONE Correct options.

  For each question, marks will be awarded in one of the following categories:

  Full marks: **+4** If only the bubble(s) corresponding to all the correct option(s) is (are) darkened.

  Partial marks: **+1** For darkening a bubble corresponding to each correct option provided NO INCORRECT option is darkened.

  Zero marks: If none of the bubbles is darkened.

  Negative marks: **−2** In all other cases.

  Section III has **4** Single Digit Integer Answer Type Questions, **3** marks for each Correct Answer and 0 marks in all other cases.

  Section IV has Comprehension/Matching Cum-Comprehension Type Questions having **5** MCQs with ONLY ONE correct option, **3** marks for each Correct Answer and 0 marks in all other cases.

  Section V has **2** Matching Type Questions, **2** mark for the correct matching of each row and 0 marks in all other cases.

- You have to evaluate your Response Grids yourself with the help of Solutions.

Section I - Straight Objective Type

This section contains 5 multiple choice questions. Each question has 4 choices (a), (b), (c) and (d), out of which **ONLY ONE** is correct.

1. A particle of mass m is executing oscillations about the origin on the x axis. Its potential energy is $V(x) = k\,|\,x\,|^3$ where k is a positive constant. If the amplitude of oscillation is a, then its time period T is
   (a) proportional to $1/\sqrt{a}$ (b) independent of a
   (c) proportional to $\sqrt{a}$ (d) proportional to $a^{3/2}$

2. Two identical balls A and B each of mass 0.1 kg are attached to two identical massless springs. The spring mass system is constrained to move inside a rigid smooth pipe bent in the form of a circle as shown in the figure. The pipe is fixed in a horizontal plane. The centres of the balls can move in a circle of radius 0.06 m. Each spring has a natural length of 0.06πm and force constant 0.1 N/m. Initially both the balls are displaced by an angle $\theta = \pi/6$ radian with respect to the diameter PQ of the circle and released from rest. The frequency of oscillation of the ball B is

   (a) πHz

   (b) $\dfrac{1}{\pi}$Hz

   (c) 2π Hz

   (d) $\dfrac{1}{2\pi}$Hz

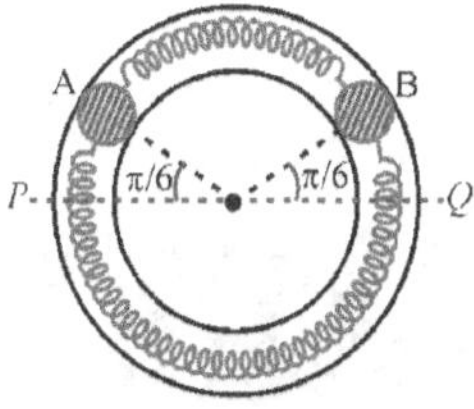

Space for Rough Work

3. A particle free to move along the x-axis has potential energy given by $U(x) = k[1 - \exp(-x^2)]$ for $-\infty \le x \le +\infty$, where k is a positive constant of appropriate dimensions. Then
   (a) at points away from the origin, the particle is in unstable equilibrium
   (b) for any finite nonzero value of x, there is a force directed away from the origin
   (c) if its total mechanical energy is $k/2$, it has its minimum kinetic energy at the origin.
   (d) for small displacements from $x = 0$, the motion is simple harmonic

4. In an experiment for determining the gravitational acceleration g of a place with the help of a simple pendulum, the measured time period square is plotted against the string length of the pendulum in the figure. What is the value of g at the place?

   (a) 9.81 m/s^2

   (b) 9.87 m/s^2

   (c) 9.91 m/s^2

   (d) 10.0 m/s^2

5. A small block is connected to one end of a massless spring of un-stretched length 4.9 m. The other end of the spring (see the figure) is fixed. The system lies on a horizontal frictionless surface. The block is stretched by 0.2 m and released from rest at $t = 0$. It then executes simple harmonic motion with angular frequency $\omega = \pi/3$ rad/s. Simultaneously at $t = 0$, a small pebble is projected with speed v form point P at an angle of $45°$ as shown in the figure. Point P is at a horizontal distance of 10 m from O. If the pebble hits the block at $t = 1$ s, the value of v is (take $g = 10 \text{ m/s}^2$)

   (a) $\sqrt{50} \text{ m/s}$

   (b) $\sqrt{51} \text{ m/s}$

   (c) $\sqrt{52} \text{ m/s}$

   (d) $\sqrt{53} \text{ m/s}$

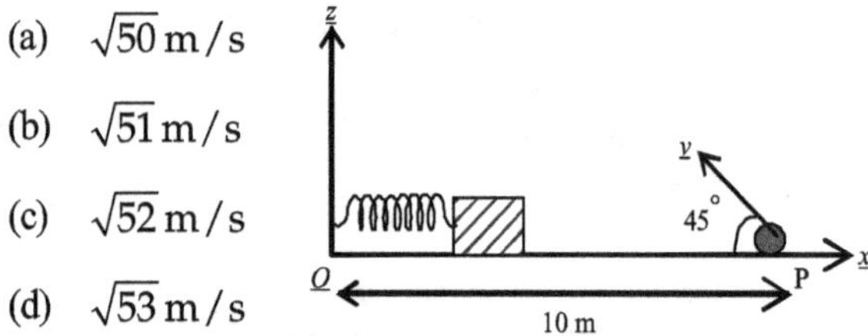

Section II - Multiple Correct Answer Type

This section contains 4 multiple correct answer(s) type questions. Each question has 4 choices (a), (b), (c) and (d), out of which ONE OR MORE is/are correct.

6. A block of mass m is kept on a horizontal platform of mass M. The platform is doing SHM in horizontal plane with angular frequency ω. There is no slipping between the block and the platform due to friction. Then

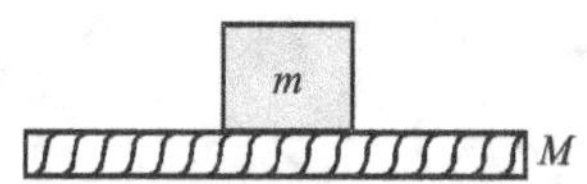

   (a) the friction force on the block is directly proportional to the displacement of the platform from mean position.
   (b) the contact force on the block is directly proportional to the displacement of the platform from mean position.
   (c) the net contact force on the block is directly proportional to mass of block (m)
   (d) the net contact force on the platform due to the block is directly proportional to mass of plank (M)

7. A conservative force has the potential energy function U (x) as shown by the graph. A particle moving in one dimension under the influence of this force has kinetic energy 1.0 J when it is at position x_1. Which of the following is/are correct statement(s) about the motion of the particle?

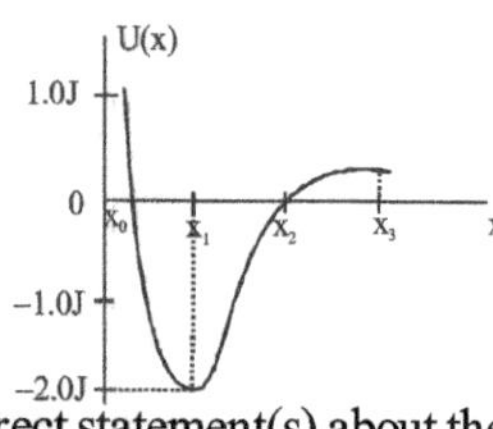

   (a) It oscillates
   (b) It moves to the right of x_3 and never returns
   (c) It comes to rest at either x_0 or x_2
   (d) It cannot reach either x_0 or x_2

8. A horizontal plank has a rectangular block placed on it. The plank starts oscillating vertically and simple harmonically with an amplitude of 40 cm. The block just loses contact with the plank when the latter is at momentary rest. Then
   (a) the period of oscillation is $(2\pi/5)$
   (b) the block weighs double its weight, when the plank is at one of the positions of momentary rest
   (c) the block weighs 0.5 times its weight on the plank halfway up
   (d) the block weighs 1.5 times its weight on the plank halfway down

9. A particle is executing SHM between points $-X_m$ and X_m, as shown in figure-I. The velocity of V (t) of the particle is partially graphed and shown in figure-II. Two points A and B corresponding to time t_1 and time t_2 respectively are marked on the V(t) curve –

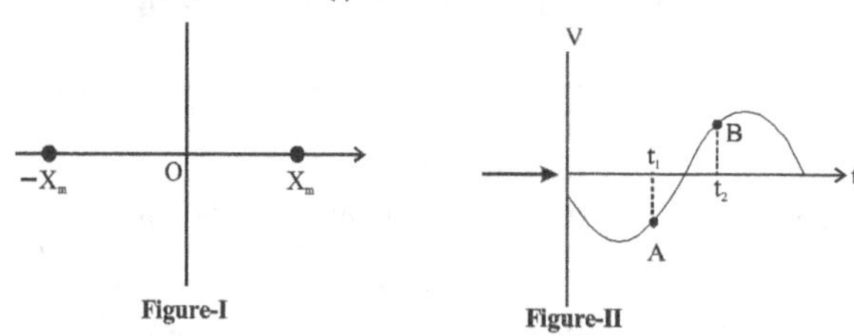

Figure-I · · · · · · · Figure-II

   (a) At time t_2, its position lies in between $-X_m$ and O.
   (b) The phase difference $\Delta\phi$ between points A and B must be expressed as $90° < \Delta\phi < 180°$.
   (c) At time t_1, its speed is decreasing
   (d) At time t_1, it is going towards X_m.

RESPONSE	3. (a)(b)(c)(d)	4. (a)(b)(c)(d)	5. (a)(b)(c)(d)	6. (a)(b)(c)(d)	7. (a)(b)(c)(d)
GRID	8. (a)(b)(c)(d)	9. (a)(b)(c)(d)			

Section III - Integer Type

This section contains 4 questions. The answer to each of the questions is a single digit integer ranging from 0 to 9.

10. A point particle of mass 0.1 kg is executing S.H.M. of amplitude 0.1 m. When the particle passes through the mean position, its kinetic energy is 8×10^{-3} joule. Obtain the positive value of angular frequency (in rad/s).

11. Two particles execute SHM on same straight line with same mean position, same time period 6 second and same amplitude 5cm. Both the particles start SHM from their mean position (in same direction) with a time gap of 1 second. What is the maximum separation (in cm) between the two particles during their motion.

12. A uniform rod is placed on two spinning wheels as shown in figure. The axes of the wheels are separated 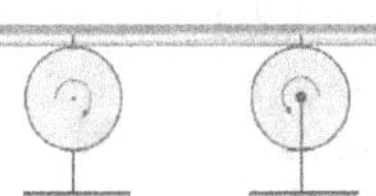 by a distance $\ell = \dfrac{50}{\pi^2} m$, the coefficient of friction between the rod and the wheels is $\mu = 0.1$.
The rod performs harmonic oscillations. The period of these oscillations is $10x$ sec. Find the value of x

13. A mass M attached to a spring oscillates with a period of 2 sec. If the mass is increased by 2 kg, the period increases by 1 second. Find the initial mass M (in kg) assuming that Hooke's law is obeyed.

Section IV - Comprehension/Matching Cum-Comprehension Type

Directions (Qs. 14 and 15) : Based upon the given paragraph, 2 multiple choice questions have to be answered. Each question has 4 choices (a), (b), (c) and (d), out of which **ONLY ONE** is correct.

PARAGRAPH

Two identical blocks P and Q have mass m each lie on a smooth horizontal surface as shown. They are attached to two identical springs (of spring constant k) initially unstretched. Now the left spring (attached with P) is compressed by A/2 and the right spring (attached with Q) is compressed by A. Both the blocks are then released from rest simultaneously.

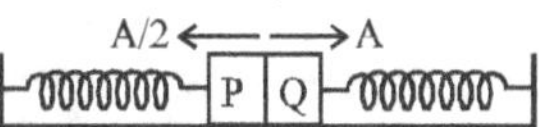

14. The speed of block Q just before P and Q are about to collide for the first time is
    (a) $\sqrt{\dfrac{k}{m}}\dfrac{A}{2}$
    (b) $\sqrt{\dfrac{k}{m}}A$
    (c) $\sqrt{\dfrac{k}{4m}}A$
    (d) None of these

15. After what time when they were released from rest, shall the blocks collide for the first time ?
    (a) $\dfrac{\pi}{2}\sqrt{\dfrac{m}{k}}$
    (b) $\pi\sqrt{\dfrac{m}{k}}$
    (c) $\dfrac{\pi}{3}\sqrt{\dfrac{m}{k}}$
    (d) None of these

Directions (Qs. 16-18) : This passage contains a table having 3 columns and 4 rows. Based on the table, there are three questions. Each question has four options (a), (b), (c) and (d) **ONLY ONE** of these four options is correct.

Time period of spring-mass system executing S.H.M is given by $T = 2\pi\sqrt{\dfrac{M}{K_{eff}}}$ Column I shows the spring-mass system executing S.H.M. column II shows the force constant (spring constant) of the combination, while column III represents the time period of the oscillation.

Column I	Column II	Column III
I.	(i) $K = K_1 + K_2$	(P) $T = 2\pi[M/K_1 + K_2]^{1/2}$
II.	(ii) $K = K_1 + 2K_2$	(Q) $T = 2\pi[M(K_1+K_2)/K_1K_2]^{1/2}$
III.	(iii) $K = \dfrac{K_1K_2}{K_1+K_2}$	(R) $T = 2\pi[M(2K_1+K_2)/2K_1K_2]^{1/2}$

<table>
<tr><td rowspan="2">RESPONSE GRID</td><td>10. ⓪①②③④⑤⑥⑦⑧⑨</td><td>11. ⓪①②③④⑤⑥⑦⑧⑨</td><td></td></tr>
<tr><td>12. ⓪①②③④⑤⑥⑦⑧⑨</td><td>13. ⓪①②③④⑤⑥⑦⑧⑨</td><td>14. ⓐⓑⓒⓓ</td></tr>
<tr><td></td><td>15. ⓐⓑⓒⓓ</td><td></td><td></td></tr>
</table>

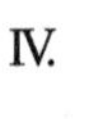

IV.
$\qquad$ (iv) $\quad K = \dfrac{2K_1 K_2}{2K_1 + K_2}$ $\qquad$ (S) $\quad T = 2\pi\left[M/K_1 + 2K_2\right]^{1/2}$

16. If the time period of the combination of spring-mass system shown in column I (III) [if $K_1 = K_2 = K^1$] is $2\pi\sqrt{M/3K^1}$. The correct matching for the system is:
   (a) III (i) P $\qquad$ (b) III (ii) S $\qquad$ (c) III (iv) R $\qquad$ (d) IV (iii) Q
17. The spring constant for the combination shown in the column I (II) becomes twice if K_1 and K_2 becomes twice. Then correct matching shown for this spring-mass system is
   (a) II (iii) Q $\qquad$ (b) I (ii) S $\qquad$ (c) II (i) P $\qquad$ (d) II (iv) R
18. Which of the following shows the wrong matching?
   (a) I (i) P (b) $\qquad$ II (iii) Q $\qquad$ (c) III (ii) R $\qquad$ (d) IV (iv) R

Section V - Matrix-Match Type

This section contains 2 questions. It contains statements given in two columns, which have to be matched. Statements in column I are labelled as A, B, C and D whereas statements in column II are labelled as p, q, r and s. The answers to these questions have to be appropriately bubbled as illustrated in the following example. If the correct matches are A-p, A-r, B-p, B-s, C-r, C-s and D-q, then the correctly bubbled matrix will look like the following:

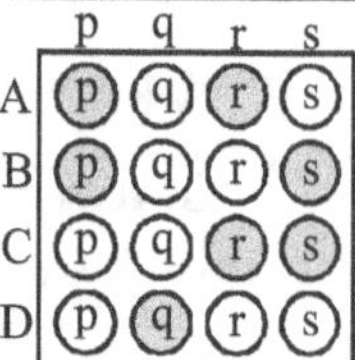

19. For a particle executing SHM along a straight line, match the statements in column I with statement in column II. (Note that displacement given in column I is to be measured from mean position).

Column-I	Column-II
(A) Velocity-time graph will be	(p) straight line
(B) Acceleration-velocity graph may be	(q) circle
(C) Acceleration-displacement graph will be	(r) ellipse
(D) Acceleration-time graph will be	(s) sinusoidal curve

20. In the column I, a system is described in each option and corresponding time period is given in the column II. Suitably match them.

Column-I

(A) A simple pendulum of length 3ℓ oscillating with small amplitude in a lift moving down with retardation g/2.

(B) Two springs of force constants k and 2k are connected to a mass as shown below

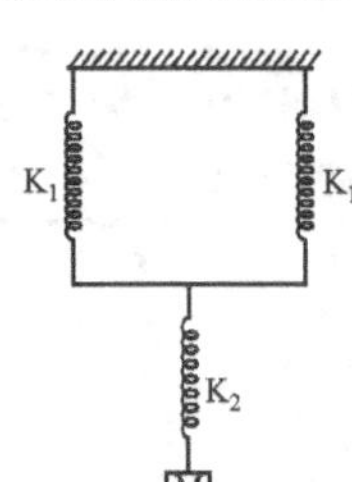

(C) The time period of small oscillation of a uniform rod of length ℓ smoothly hinged at one end. The rod oscillates in vertical plane.

(D) A cubical block of edge 2ℓ and specific density $\rho/2$ is in equilibrium with some volume inside water filled in a large fixed container. Neglect viscous forces and surface tension. The time period of small oscillations of the block in vertical direction.

Column-II

(p) $T = 2\pi\sqrt{\dfrac{2\ell}{3g}}$

(q) $T = 2\pi\sqrt{\dfrac{\ell}{g}}$

(r) $T = 2\pi\sqrt{\dfrac{2\ell}{g}}$

(s) $T = 2\pi\sqrt{\dfrac{m}{3k}}$

DAILY PRACTICE PROBLEM DPP CP12 - PHYSICS

Total Questions	20	Total Marks	74
Attempted		Correct	
Incorrect		Net Score	
Cut-off Score	24	Qualifying Score	35

$$\text{Net Score} = \sum_{i=1}^{V}\left[\left(correct_i \times MM_i\right) - \left(In_i - NM_i\right)\right]$$

Chapter-wise Sheets

Date :   Start Time :   End Time :

PHYSICS $\boxed{\text{CP13}}$

SYLLABUS : Waves

Max. Marks : 74   **Time : 60 min.**

GENERAL INSTRUCTIONS

- The Daily Practice Problem Sheet contains 20 Questions divided into 5 sections.
- **Section I** has **5** MCQs with ONLY 1 Correct Option, **3** marks for each correct answer and **–1** for each incorrect answer.
- **Section II** has **4** MCQs with ONE or MORE THAN ONE Correct options.
- For each question, marks will be awarded in one of the following categories:
- Full marks: **+4** If only the bubble(s) corresponding to all the correct option(s) is (are) darkened.
- Partial marks: **+1** For darkening a bubble corresponding to each correct option provided NO INCORRECT option is darkened.
- Zero marks: If none of the bubbles is darkened.
- Negative marks: **–2** In all other cases.
- **Section III** has **4** Single Digit Integer Answer Type Questions, **3** marks for each Correct Answer and 0 marks in all other cases.
- **Section IV** has Comprehension/Matching Cum-Comprehension Type Questions having **5** MCQs with ONLY ONE correct option, **3** marks for each Correct Answer and 0 marks in all other cases.
- **Section V** has **2** Matching Type Questions, **2** mark for the correct matching of each row and 0 marks in all other cases.
- You have to evaluate your Response Grids yourself with the help of Solutions.

Section I - Straight Objective Type

This section contains 5 multiple choice questions. Each question has 4 choices (a), (b), (c) and (d), out of which **ONLY ONE** is correct.

1. The amplitude of a wave disturbance propagating in the positive x–direction is given by $y = \dfrac{1}{1+x^2}$ at $t = 0$ and $y = \dfrac{1}{2+x^2-2x}$ at $t = 2s$, where x and y are in meter. Assuming that the shape of the wave disturbance does not change during the propagation, the speed of the wave is

   (a)   0.5 m/s   (b)   1 m/s

   (c)   1.5 m/s   (d)   2 m/s

RESPONSE GRID	1. ⓐⓑⓒⓓ

Space for Rough Work

2. An object of specific gravity ρ is hung from a thin steel wire. The fundamental frequency for transverse standing waves in the wire is 300 Hz. The object is immersed in water so that one half of its volume is submerged. The new fundamental frequency in Hz is

(a) $300\left(\dfrac{2\rho-1}{2\rho}\right)^{1/2}$ (b) $300\left(\dfrac{2\rho}{2\rho-1}\right)^{1/2}$

(c) $300\left(\dfrac{2\rho}{2\rho-1}\right)$ (d) $300\left(\dfrac{2\rho-1}{2\rho}\right)$

3. The temperature of a mono-atomic gas in an uniform container of length L varies linearly from T_0 to T_L as shown in the figure. If the molecular weight of the gas is M_0, then the time taken by a wave pulse in travelling from end A to end B is

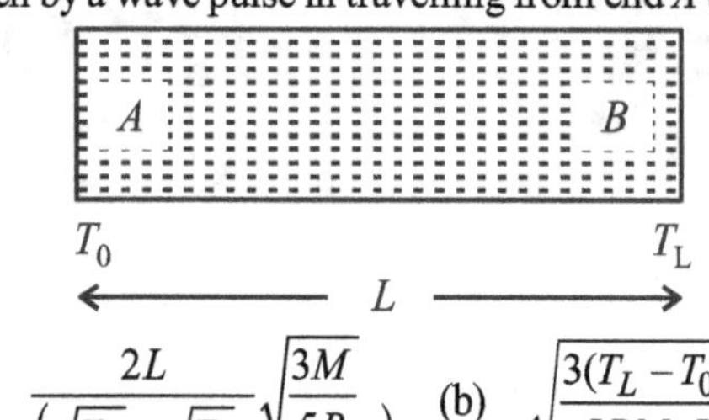

(a) $\dfrac{2L}{\left(\sqrt{T_L}+\sqrt{T_0}\right)}\sqrt{\dfrac{3M}{5R}}$ (b) $\sqrt{\dfrac{3(T_L-T_0)}{5RM_0L}}$

(c) $\dfrac{L}{\left(\sqrt{T_L}-\sqrt{T_0}\right)}\sqrt{\dfrac{3M}{5R}}$ (d) $L\sqrt{\dfrac{M_0}{2R(T_L-T_0)}}$

4. The displacement-time graphs for two sound waves A and B are shown in the figure. Then the ratio of their intensities I_A/I_B is equal to

(a) $1:4$

(b) $1:16$

(c) $1:2$

(d) $1:1$

5. Two identical pulses move in opposite directions with same uniform speeds on a stretched string. The width and kinetic energy of each pulse is L and k respectively. At the instant they completely overlap, the kinetic energy of the width L of the string is

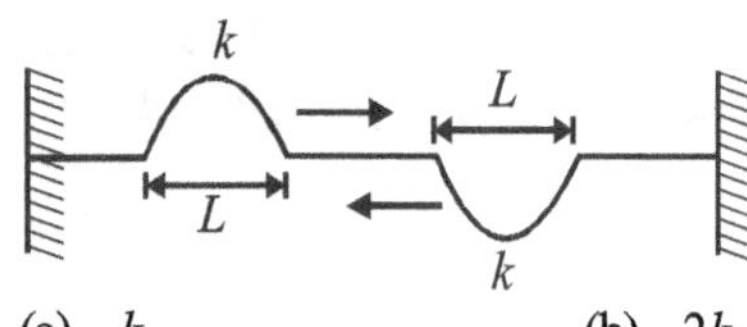

(a) k (b) $2k$
(c) $4k$ (d) $8k$

Section II - Multiple Correct Answer Type

This section contains 4 multiple correct answer(s) type questions. Each question has 4 choices (a), (b), (c) and (d), out of which **ONE OR MORE** is/are correct.

6. A wave pulse moving to the right along the x-axis is represented by the wave function $y(x,t)=\dfrac{2.0}{(x-3.0t)^2+1}$, where x and y are in centimeters and t is in seconds. (The maximum pulse height is defined as maximum displacement along y-axis). Then

(a) the maximum pulse height is decreasing with time
(b) the maximum pulse height is constant with time
(c) the speed of the pulse is 3.0 cm/s
(d) the speed of the pulse is 0.33 cm/s

7. A person blows into open-end of a long pipe. As a result, a high pressure pulse of air travels down the pipe.
When this pulse reaches the other end of the pipe,

(a) a high-pressure pulse starts travelling up the pipe, if the other end of the pipe is open.
(b) a low-pressure pulse starts travelling up the pipe, if the other end of the pipe is open.
(c) a low-pressure pulse starts travelling up the pipe, if the other end of the pipe is closed.
(d) a high-pressure pulse starts travelling up the pipe, if the other end of the pipe is closed.

8. Displacement (y) of air column at position x from its mean position at any instant is given by graph shown in the figure. We can conclude from graph that

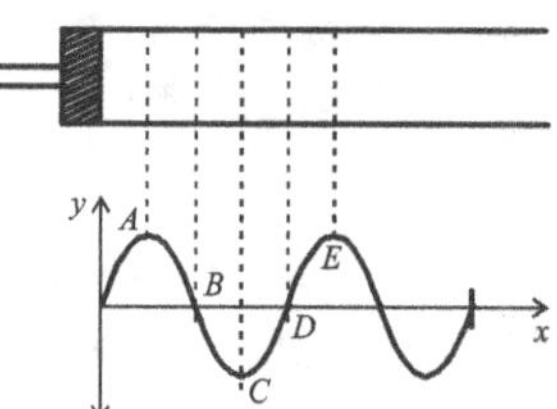

(a) density of air is maximum at B
(b) density of air is minimum at D
(c) density is maximum at D
(d) density is minimum at A

9. Standing waves can be produced
(a) on a string clamped at both the ends.
(b) on a string clamped at one end free at the other
(c) when incident wave gets reflected from a wall
(d) when two identical waves with a phase difference of π are moving in the same direction

RESPONSE	2. ⓐⓑⓒⓓ	3. ⓐⓑⓒⓓ	4. ⓐⓑⓒⓓ	5. ⓐⓑⓒⓓ	6. ⓐⓑⓒⓓ
GRID	7. ⓐⓑⓒⓓ	8. ⓐⓑⓒⓓ	9. ⓐⓑⓒⓓ		

Section III - Integer Type

This section contains 4 questions. The answer to each of the questions is a single digit integer ranging from 0 to 9.

10. Two vibrating strings of the same material but lengths L and $2L$ have radii $2r$ and r respectively. They are stretched under the same tension. Both the strings vibrate in their fundamental nodes, the one of length L with frequency v_1 and the other with frequency v_2. The raio v_1/v_2 is given by

11. Three waves of equal frequency having amplitudes 10 mm, 4 mm and 7 mm arrive at a given point with successive phase difference of $\dfrac{\pi}{2}$. What will be the amplitude of the resulting wave in mm?

12. A whistling train approaches a junction. An observer standing at junction observes the frequency to be 2.2 kHz and 1.8 kHz of the approaching and the receding train respectively. If 10x is the speed (in m/s) of the train . Find the value of x (speed of sound = 300 m/s).

13. A tuning fork of frequency 392 Hz, resonates with 50 cm length of a string under tension (T). If length of the string is decreased by 2 %, keeping the tension constant, the number of beats heard when the string and the tuning fork made to vibrate simultaneously is :

Section IV - Comprehension/Matching Cum-Comprehension Type

Directions (Qs. 14 and 15) : Based upon the given paragraph, 2 multiple choice questions have to be answered. Each question has 4 choices (a), (b), (c) and (d), out of which **ONLY ONE** is correct.

PARAGRAPH

A uniform string of length ℓ is fixed at both ends such that tension T is produced in it. The string is excited to vibrate with maximum displacement amplitude a_0.

14. The maximum kinetic energy of the string for its fundamental tone is

(a) $\dfrac{a_0^2 \pi^2 T}{4\ell}$ (b) $\dfrac{a_0^2 \pi^2 T}{\ell}$

(c) $\dfrac{a_0^2 \pi^2 T}{2\ell}$ (d) $\dfrac{a_0^2 \pi^2 T}{3\ell}$

15. The maximum kinetic energy of the string for its first overtone is

(a) $\dfrac{a_0^2 \pi^2 T}{4\ell}$ (b) $\dfrac{a_0^2 \pi^2 T}{\ell}$

(c) $\dfrac{a_0^2 \pi^2 T}{2\ell}$ (d) $\dfrac{a_0^2 \pi^2 T}{3\ell}$

Directions (Qs. 16-18) : This passage contains a table having 3 columns and 4 rows. Based on the table, there are three questions. Each question has four options (a), (b), (c) and (d) **ONLY ONE** of these four options is correct.

Let us consider an organ pipe (may be open or closed) of length 'l'. V is the velocity of sound. Column I represents the harmonics, Column II represents the frequency while column III represents the corresponding wavelength.

Column I		Column II		Column III
I. First harmonic for open organ pipe	(i)	$v = \dfrac{3V}{4l}$	(P)	$\lambda = 2l$
II. Third harmonic for open organ pipe	(ii)	$v = \dfrac{V}{2l}$	(Q)	$\lambda = \dfrac{4l}{3}$
III. First harmonic for closed organ pipe	(iii)	$v = \dfrac{3V}{2l}$	(R)	$\lambda = \dfrac{2l}{3}$
IV. Third harmonic for closed organ pipe	(iv)	$v = \dfrac{V}{4l}$	(S)	$\lambda = 4l$

16. If velocity of sound in air is 330 m/s and the length of the open organ pipe is 0.30 m then the wavelength and the frequency for the first harmonic or fundamental tone is 0.6m and 550 Hz. The correct matching satisfying the above condition is
(a) I(ii)P   (b) III(iv)Q
(c) III(iv)S   (d) I(ii)S

17. Which of following shows the correct match for the first overtone of a closed organ pipe?
(a) III(ii)R   (b) IV(i)Q
(c) II(iv)S   (d) I(iii)R

18. Which of the following does not show the correct relation?
(a) I(ii)P   (b) II(iii)R
(c) III(iv)Q   (d) IV(i)Q

Section V - Matrix-Match Type

This section contains 2 questions. It contains statements given in two columns, which have to be matched. Statements in column I are labelled as A, B, C and D whereas statements in column II are labelled as p, q, r and s. The answers to these questions have to be appropriately bubbled as illustrated in the following example. If the correct matches are A-p, A-r, B-p, B-s, C-r, C-s and D-q, then the correctly bubbled matrix will look like the following:

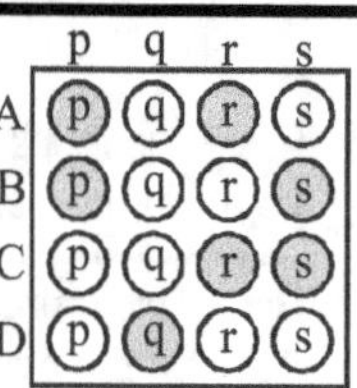

19. Match the columns

Column I

(A) Graphical representation of pressure variation in both end open organ pipe.

(B) Graphical representation of pressure variation in one end closed organ pipe.

(C) Snapshot of string fixed at both ends

(D) Snapshot of a string fixed at one end and connected to a smooth massless ring that is constrained to move vertically.

Column II

(p) Maximum kinetic energy at B

(q) Maximum potential energy at B

(r) Maximum particle velocity at B

(s) Maximum particle acceleration at B

20. Two identical speakers emit sound waves of frequency 660 Hz uniformly in all directions. The audio output of each speaker is 1 mW and the speed of sound in air 330 m/s. A point P is a distance 2m from one speaker and 3m from the other. Match the columns:

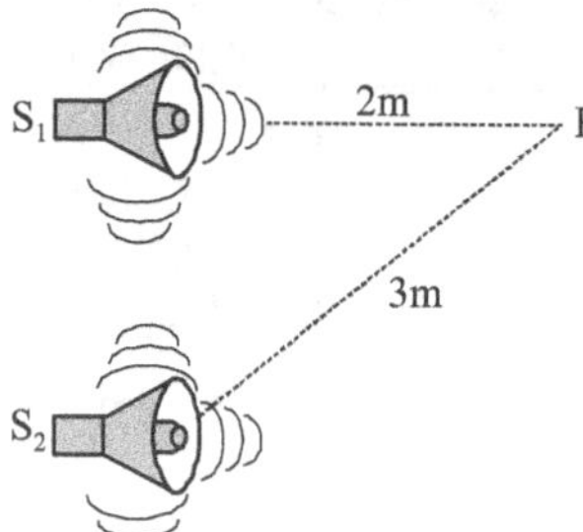

Column I

(A) Intensity of speaker S_1 at P

(B) Intensity of sound at P, if the speakers are driven coherently and in phase

(C) Intensity of sound at P, if speakers are incoherent and out of phase by $180°$

(D) Intensity of sound at P, if speakers are incoherent.

Column II

(p) 55.3×10^{-6} W/m^2

(q) 19.90×10^{-6} W/m^2

(r) 28.7×10^{-6} W/m^2

(s) 2.2×10^{-6} W/m^2

RESPONSE GRID	
19. A- p q r s ; B- p q r s ; C- p q r s ; D- p q r s	
20. A- p q r s ; B- p q r s ; C- p q r s ; D- p q r s	

DAILY PRACTICE PROBLEM DPP CP13 - PHYSICS

Total Questions	20	Total Marks	74
Attempted		Correct	
Incorrect		Net Score	
Cut-off Score	24	Qualifying Score	35

$$\text{Net Score} = \sum_{i=1}^{V} \left[\left(correct_i \times MM_i \right) - \left(In_i - NM_i \right) \right]$$

DPP - Daily Practice Problems

Chapter-wise Sheets

Date :   Start Time :   End Time :

PHYSICS   CP14

SYLLABUS : Electric Charges and Fields

Max. Marks : 74   **Time : 60 min.**

Section I - Straight Objective Type

This section contains 5 multiple choice questions. Each question has 4 choices (a), (b), (c) and (d), out of which **ONLY ONE** is correct.

1. Consider an electric field $\vec{E} = E_0 \hat{x}$ where E_0 is a constant. The flux through the shaded area (as shown in the figure) due to this field is

(a) $2E_0 a_2$

(b) $\sqrt{2}E_0 a^2$

(c) $E_0 a^2$

(d) $\dfrac{E_0 a^2}{\sqrt{2}}$

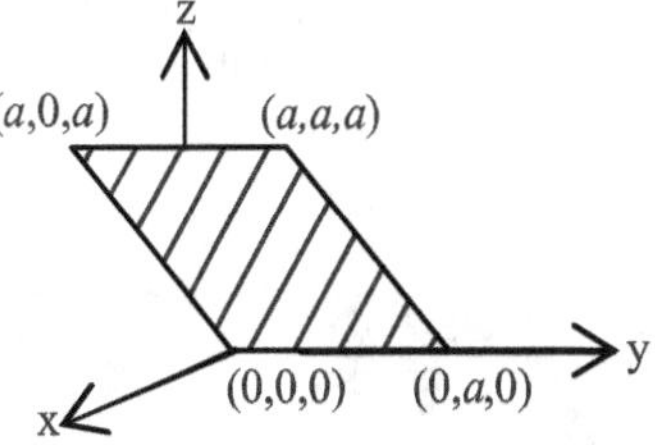

RESPONSE GRID	1. ⓐⓑⓒⓓ

Space for Rough Work

2. Let $E_1(r)$, $E_2(r)$ and $E_3(r)$ be the respective electric field at a distance r from a point charge Q, an infinitely long wire with constant linear charge density λ, and an infinite plane with uniform surface charge density σ. If $E_1(r_0) = E_2(r_0) = E_3(r_0)$ at a given distance r_0, then

(a) $Q = 4\sigma\pi r_0^2$

(b) $r_0 = \dfrac{\lambda}{2\pi\sigma}$

(c) $E_1(r_0/2) = 2E_2(r_0/2)$

(d) $E_2(r_0/2) = 4E_3(r_0/2)$

3. A particle of charge $-q$ and mass m moves in a circle of radius r around an infinitely long line charge of linear charge density $+\lambda$. Then time period will be

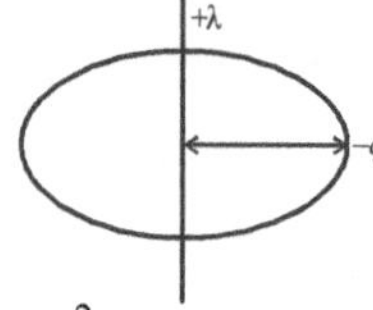

(a) $T = 2\pi r\sqrt{\dfrac{m}{2k\lambda q}}$

(b) $T^2 = \dfrac{4\pi^2 m}{2k\lambda q}r^3$

(c) $T = \dfrac{1}{2\pi r}\sqrt{\dfrac{2k\lambda q}{m}}$

(d) $T = \dfrac{1}{2\pi r}\sqrt{\dfrac{m}{2k\lambda q}}$

4. The electric dipole is situated is an electric field as shown in fig 1. The dipole and electric field are both in the plane of the paper. The dipole is rotated about an axis perpendicular to plane of paper passing through A in anticlockwise direction. If the angle of rotation (θ) is measured with respect to the direction of electric field, then the torque (τ) experienced by the dipole for different values of the angle of rotation θ will be represented in fig. 2, by

(a) curve (1)   (b) curve (2)   (c) curve (3)   (d) curve (4)

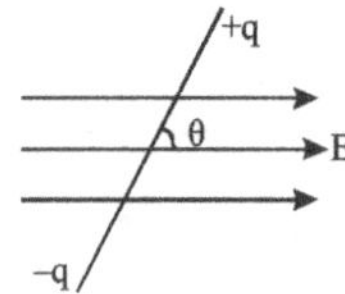

<table>
<tr><td>Fig. 1</td><td>Fig. 2</td></tr>
</table>

5. A spherical conductor A contains two spherical cavities. The total charge on the conductor itself is zero. However, there is a point charge q_b at the centre of one cavity and q_c at the centre of the other.

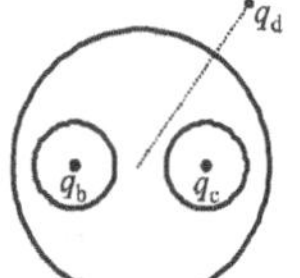

A considerable distance r away from the centre of the spherical conductor, there is another charge q_d. Force acting on q_b, q_c and q_d are F_1, F_2 and F_3 respectively, then (Assume all charges are positive)

(a) $F_1 < F_2 < F_3$

(b) $F_1 = F_2 < F_3$

(c) $F_1 = F_2 > F_3$

(d) $F_1 > F_2 > F_3$

Section II - Multiple Correct Answer Type

This section contains 4 multiple correct answer(s) type questions. Each question has 4 choices (a), (b), (c) and (d), out of which ONE OR MORE is/are correct.

6. An electric dipole is placed at the centre of a sphere
(a) the flux of the electric field through the sphere is zero
(b) the electric field is zero at every point on the sphere
(c) the electric field is not zero anywhere on the sphere
(d) the electric field is zero on a circle on the sphere

7. Figure shows a cross-section of a spherical metal shell of inner radius R and out radius $2R$. A point charge q is located at a distance $R/2$ from the centre of the shell. If the shell is electrically neutral, then :

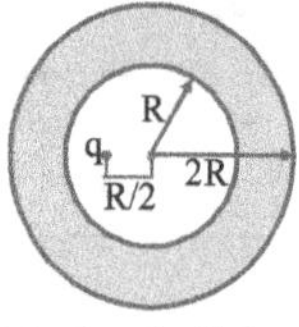

(a) the electrical field at some point inside the shell is zero.
(b) the electrical field at a point inside the shell is non-zero.
(c) the electrical field at the outer surface of the shell is
$$E = \dfrac{1}{4\pi\varepsilon_0}\dfrac{q}{(3R/2)^2}$$
(d) the electrical field at the outer surface is
$$E = \dfrac{1}{4\pi\varepsilon_0}\dfrac{q}{(2R)^2}$$

8. Two balls of charge q_1 and q_2 initially have a velocity (v) of the same magnitude and direction. After a uniform electric field has been applied during a certain time, the direction of the velocity of the first ball changes by 60°, and the velocity magnitude is reduced by half. The direction of the velocity of the second ball changes thereby by 90°. The velocity of the second ball changes to v_2. The magnitude of the charge-to-mass ratio for the second ball is x if it is equal to k for the first ball. The electrostatic interaction between the balls should be neglected. Choose the correct options

(a) $v_2 = \dfrac{v}{\sqrt{3}}$ (b) $x = \dfrac{4}{3}k_1$ (c) $v_2 = \dfrac{v}{\sqrt{2}}$ (d) $x = \dfrac{2}{3}k_1$

9. Two non-conducting spheres of radii R_1 and R_2 and carrying uniform volume charge densities $+\rho$ and $-\rho$, respectively, are placed such that they partially overlap, as shown in

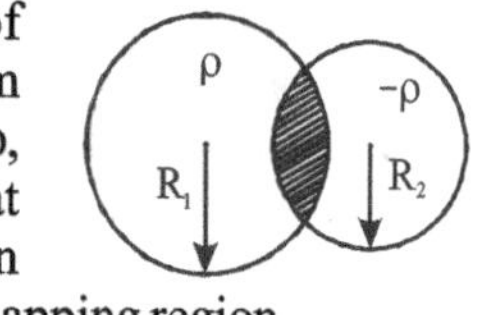

the figure. At all points in the overlapping region
(a) The electrostatic field is zero
(b) The electrostatic potential is constant
(c) The electrostatic field is constant in magnitude
(d) The electrostatic field has same direction

<table>
<tr><td rowspan="2">RESPONSE
GRID</td><td>2. ⓐⓑⓒⓓ</td><td>3. ⓐⓑⓒⓓ</td><td>4. ⓐⓑⓒⓓ</td><td>5. ⓐⓑⓒⓓ</td><td>6. ⓐⓑⓒⓓ</td></tr>
<tr><td>7. ⓐⓑⓒⓓ</td><td>8. ⓐⓑⓒⓓ</td><td>9. ⓐⓑⓒⓓ</td><td></td><td></td></tr>
</table>

Section III - Integer Type

This section contains 4 questions. The answer to each of the questions is a single digit integer ranging from 0 to 9.

10. A ball of mass of mass 10^{-2} kg and having a charge $+3 \times 10^{-6}$C is tied at one end of a 1 m long thread. The other end of the thread is fixed and a charge -3×10^{-6} C is placed at this end. The ball can move in a circular orbit of radius 1 m in the vertical plane. Initially, the ball is at the bottom. Find minimum initial horizontal velocity of the ball so that it will be able to complete the full circle.

11. A charged dust particle of radius 5×10^{-7} m is located in a horizontal electric field having an intensity of 6.28×10^5 V/m. The surrounding medium is air with coefficient of viscosity $\eta = 1.6 \times 10^{-5}$ N-s/m^2. If this particle moves with a uniform horizontal speed 0.02 m/s, $10x$ is the number of electrons on it. Find the value of x.

12. A thin fixed ring of radius 1 metre has a positive charge 1×10^{-5} coulomb uniformly distributed over it. A particle of mass 0.9 gm and having a negative charge of 1×10^{-6} coulomb is placed on the axis at a distance of 1 cm from the centre of the ring. If $(10^{-1})x$ is the time period (in second) of oscillations then find the value of x.

13. A thin half ring of radius $R = 20$ cm is uniformly charged with a total charge $q = 0.70$ millicoloumb (mC). The magnitude of electric field strength is $25\,x$ (in V/m) at the curvature centre of this half ring. Find the value of x.

Section IV - Comprehension/Matching Cum-Comprehension Type

Directions (Qs. 14 and 15) : Based upon the given paragraph, 2 multiple choice questions have to be answered. Each question has 4 choices (a), (b), (c) and (d), out of which **ONLY ONE** is correct.

PARAGRAPH

An electron with initial kinetic energy K_0 is ejected at point A as shown in the figure.

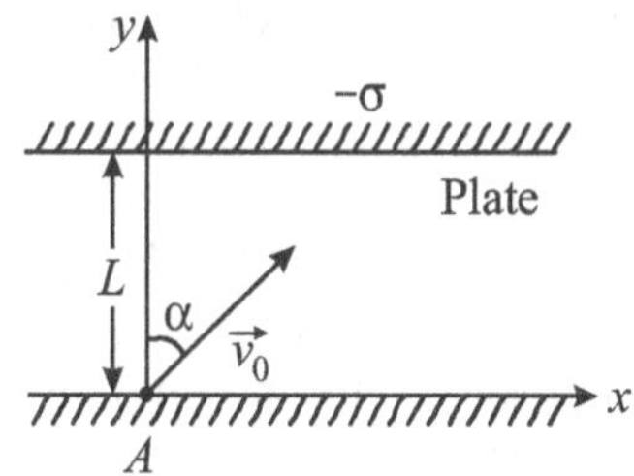

14. The acceleration of the electron (mass $= m_e$) along y-axis is

(a) $\dfrac{4\pi\sigma e^2}{m_e}$ (b) $\dfrac{-4\pi\sigma e}{m_e}$ (c) $\dfrac{-4\pi e\sigma^2}{m_e}$ (d) $\dfrac{-4\pi\sigma}{em_e}$

15. The ejected electron's trajectory for plate $L > L_0$ is

(a) Parabolic (b) Circular (c) Straight (d) Elliptical

Directions (Qs. 16-18) : This passage contains a table having 3 columns and 4 rows. Based on the table, there are three questions. Each question has four options (a), (b), (c) and (d) **ONLY ONE** of these four options is correct.

If the charge distribution is continuous, then the electric field strength at any point may be calculated by dividing the charge into infinitesimal element, and $d\vec{E} = \dfrac{kdq}{r^2}$ then integrate $d\vec{E}$ within certain limit. Column II and column III gives electric field at diffrent points due to various charge. [x = distance from centre along central axis, R = radius, Q = charge on the body]

	Column I		Column II		Column III
I.	Circular ring	(i)	$E_{in} = 0\,(x < R)$	(P)	$E_{out} = \dfrac{KQ}{x^2}$ for $x > R$
II.	Circular disc	(ii)	$E_{centre} = 0$	(Q)	$E = k\dfrac{Qx}{\left(R^2 + x^2\right)^{3/2}}$ for $x \geq 0$
III.	Solid non-conducting sphere	(iii)	$E_{in} = \dfrac{KQx}{R^3}$ for $0 \leq x \leq R$	(R)	$E = \dfrac{2KQ}{R^2}\left[1 - \dfrac{x}{\sqrt{x^2 + +R^2}}\right]$ for $x > 0$
IV.	Spherical shell	(iv)	$E_{in} = \dfrac{2KQ}{R^3}$	(S)	$E = \dfrac{2KQx}{R^4}$

Space for Rough Work

16. Which of the following shows the correct matching for $0 < x$
    (a) (IV)(iii)Q   (b) (IV)(i)P   (c) (III)(iii)P   (d) Both (b) and (c)

17. If $\dfrac{Q}{6\sqrt{3}\pi\varepsilon_0 R^2}$ is the maximum electric field due to the circular ring having uniformly distributed charge Q, then correct matching is:
    (a) I(ii)Q   (b) I(iii)R   (c) IV(iii)Q   (d) I(ii)S

18. The correct matching for the disc is:
    (a) II(i)Q   (b) II(ii)R   (c) II(iii)Q   (d) II(iv)P

Section V - Matrix-Match Type

This section contains 2 questions. It contains statements given in two columns, which have to be matched. Statements in column I are labelled as A, B, C and D whereas statements in column II are labelled as p, q, r and s. The answers to these questions have to be appropriately bubbled as illustrated in the following example. If the correct matches are A-p, A-r, B-p, B-s, C-r, C-s and D-q, then the correctly bubbled matrix will look like the following:

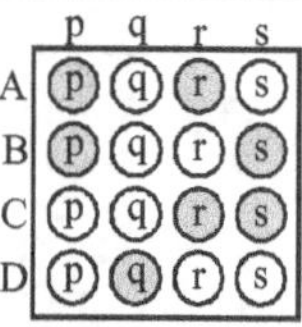

19. Two like point, charges Q_A and Q_B are positioned at points A and B. The electric field strength to the right of charge Q_B on the line that passes through the two charges varies according to a law that is represented shematically in the figure accompanying the problem without employing a definite scale. Assume electric field to be positive if its direction coincides with the positive direction on the x-axis.

Match the two columns.

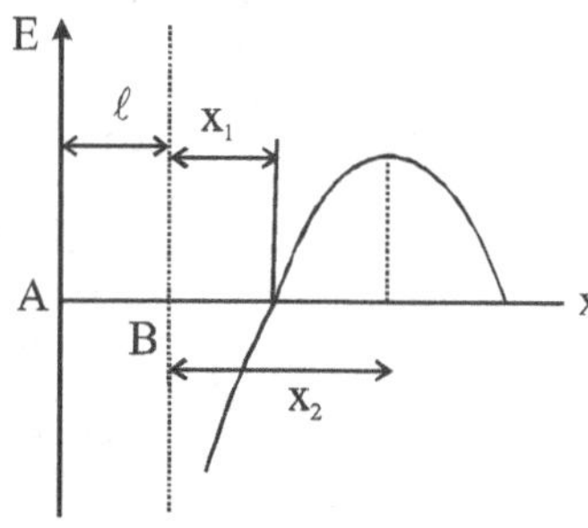

	Column-I		Column-II
(A)	Charge Q_A	(p)	$-ve$
(B)	Charge Q_B	(q)	$+ve$
(C)	$|Q_A/Q_B|$	(r)	$\left(\dfrac{\ell + x_1}{x_1}\right)^2$
(D)	x_2	(s)	$\dfrac{\ell}{(Q_A/Q_B)^{1/3}-1}$

20. For the situation shown in the figure below, match the entries of column I with entries of column II.

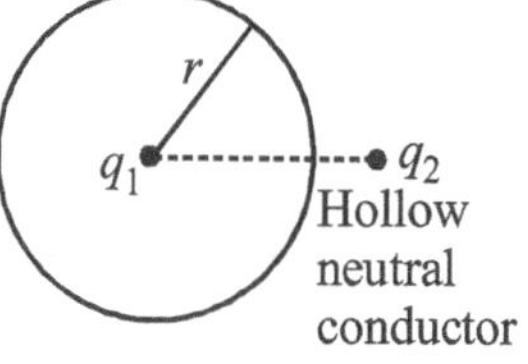

	Column I		Column II
(A)	In the situation shown	(p)	Distribution of charge on inner surface of conductor is uniform
(B)	If outside charge is not present	(q)	Distribution of charge on inner surface of conductor is non-uniform
(C)	If we displace the outside charge while the inside charge remains at centre	(r)	Distribution of charge on outer surface of conductor is uniform
(D)	If the inside charge is displaced by small amount from centre then	(s)	Distribution of charge on outer surface of conductor is non-uniform

<table>
<tr><td rowspan="3">RESPONSE
GRID</td><td>16. ⓐⓑⓒⓓ   17. ⓐⓑⓒⓓ   18. ⓐⓑⓒⓓ</td></tr>
<tr><td>19. A - ⓟⓠⓡⓢ; B - ⓟⓠⓡⓢ; C - ⓟⓠⓡⓢ; D - ⓟⓠⓡⓢ</td></tr>
<tr><td>20. A - ⓟⓠⓡⓢ; B - ⓟⓠⓡⓢ; C - ⓟⓠⓡⓢ; D - ⓟⓠⓡⓢ</td></tr>
</table>

DAILY PRACTICE PROBLEM DPP CP14 - PHYSICS

Total Questions	20	Total Marks	74
Attempted		Correct	
Incorrect		Net Score	
Cut-off Score	24	Qualifying Score	35

$$\text{Net Score} = \sum_{i=\text{I}}^{\text{V}}\left[\left(\text{correct}_i \times MM_i\right) - \left(In_i - NM_i\right)\right]$$

Space for Rough Work

PHYSICS $\boxed{\text{CP15}}$

SYLLABUS : Electrostatic Potential and Capacitance

Max. Marks : 74　　　　　　　　　　　　　　　**Time : 60 min.**

Section I - Straight Objective Type

This section contains 6 multiple choice questions. Each question has 4 choices (a), (b), (c) and (d), out of which **ONLY ONE** is correct.

1. If the electrostatic potential were given by

$\phi = \phi_0(x^2 + y^2 + z^2)$, where ϕ_0 is constant, then the charge density giving rise to the above potential would be

(a)　0　　(b)　$-6\,\phi_0\varepsilon_0$　(c)　$-2\,\phi_0\varepsilon_0$　(d)　$-\dfrac{6\phi_0}{\varepsilon_0}$

2. A dielectric slab is attached to a string of mass per unit length μ, whose other end is fixed to a wall. Capacitor has square plates of side b and separation between the plates is

d. Find the fundamental frequency of vibration of the string. (Dielectric slab remains in equilibrium)

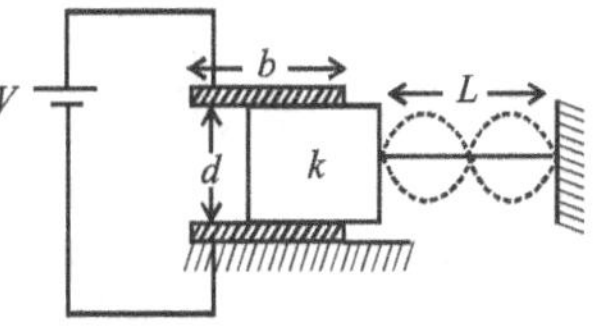

(a)　$\dfrac{1}{2L}\sqrt{\dfrac{\epsilon_0\,bV^2(k-1)\mu}{2d}}$　(b)　$\dfrac{1}{2L}\sqrt{\dfrac{\epsilon_0\,bV^2(k+1)\mu}{2d}}$

(c)　$\dfrac{1}{2L}\sqrt{\dfrac{\epsilon_0\,bV(k-1)}{2d\mu}}$　(d)　$\dfrac{1}{2L}\sqrt{\dfrac{\epsilon_0\,bV^2(k-1)}{2d\mu}}$

RESPONSE GRID	1. ⓐⓑⓒⓓ	2. ⓐⓑⓒⓓ

Space for Rough Work

3. A metal sphere having a radius r_1 charged to a potential V_1 is enveloped by a thin-walled conducting spherical shell of radius r_2 (figure). Determine the potential V_2 acquired by the sphere after it has been connected for a short time to the shell by a conductor.

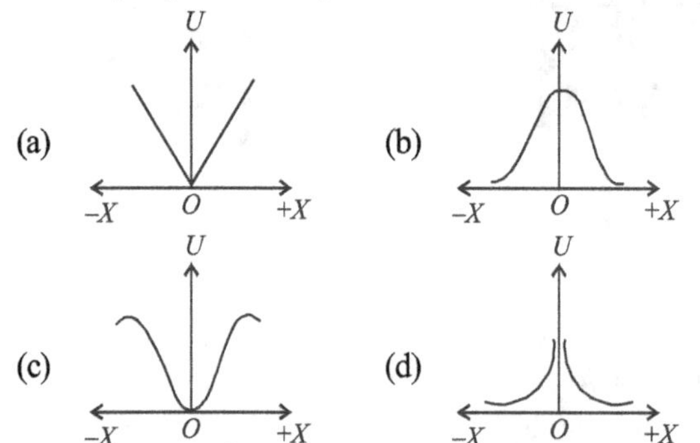

(a) $V_1 \dfrac{2r_1}{r_2}$ (b) $V_1 \dfrac{r_1}{2r_2}$

(c) $V_1 \dfrac{r_1}{r_2}$ (d) $V_1 \dfrac{r_2}{r_1}$

4. Four identical charges are placed at the four vertices of a square lying in YZ plane. A fifth charge is moved along X axis. The variation of potential energy (U) along X axis is correctly represented by

(a)

(b)

(c)

(d)

5. In figure, there is a four way key at the middle. If key is shown from situation BD to AD, then how much charge will flow through point O ?

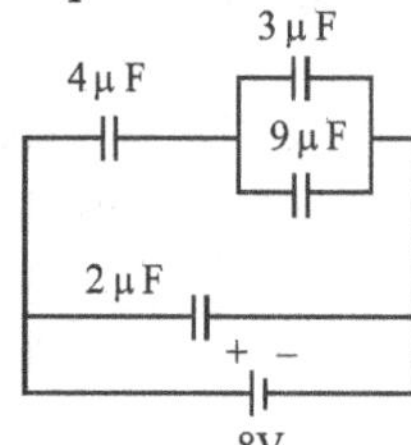

(a) $24\,\mu C$

(b) $36\,\mu C$

(c) $72\,\mu C$

(d) $12\,\mu C$

6. A combination of capacitors is set up as shown in the figure. The magnitude of the electric field, due to a point charge Q (having a charge equal to the sum of the charges on the 4 μ F and 9 μ F capacitors), at a point distance 30 m from it, would equal :

(a) $420\,\text{N/C}$

(b) $480\,\text{N/C}$

(c) $240\,\text{N/C}$

(d) $360\,\text{N/C}$

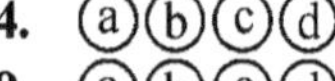
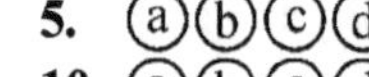

Section II - Multiple Correct Answer Type

This section contains 4 multiple correct answer(s) type questions. Each question has 4 choices (a), (b), (c) and (d), out of which ONE OR MORE is/are correct.

7. A non conducting ring of radius R is charged as shown in figure :

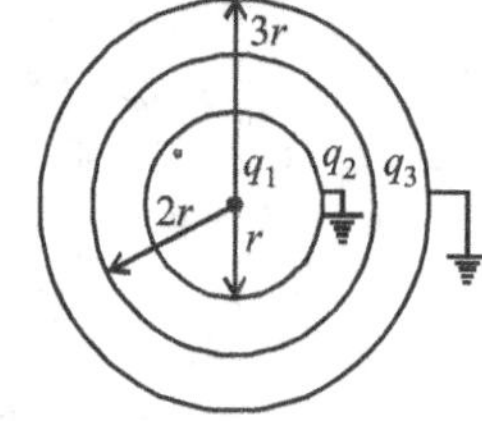

(a) The electric field is zero at the centre of the ring

(b) the electric potential is zero at centre of the ring

(c) the electric potential at the centre is, $V = \dfrac{2q}{4\pi \in_0 R}$

(d) the electric field at the centre is , $E = \dfrac{q}{\pi^2 \in_0 R^2}$

8. Which of the following quantities do not depend on the choice of zero potential or zero potential energy ?
(a) Potential at a point
(b) Potential difference between two points
(c) Potential energy of two-charge system
(d) Change in potential energy of a two-charge system

9. Three concentric conducting spherical shells have radii r, $2r$ and $3r$ and charge q_1, q_2 and q_3 respectively as shown in the figure. Select the correct alternatives

(a) $q_1 + q_3 = -q_2$

(b) $q_1 = -\dfrac{q_2}{4}$

(c) $\dfrac{q_3}{q_1} = 3$

(d) $\dfrac{q_3}{q_2} = -\dfrac{1}{3}$

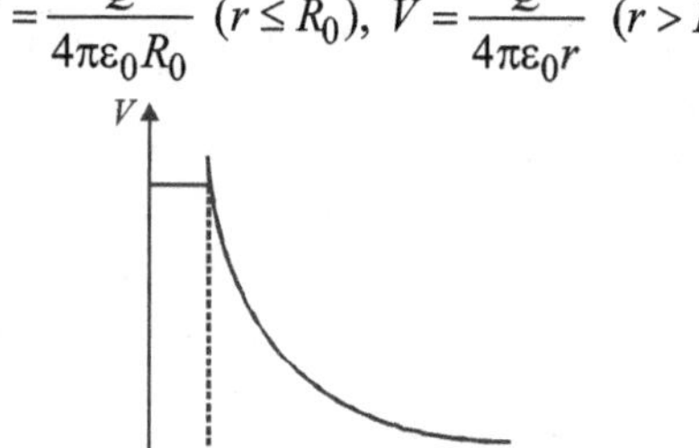

10. A spherical symmetric charge system is centered at origin. Given, Electric potential
$$V = \dfrac{Q}{4\pi\varepsilon_0 R_0} \ (r \le R_0), \quad V = \dfrac{Q}{4\pi\varepsilon_0 r} \ (r > R_0)$$

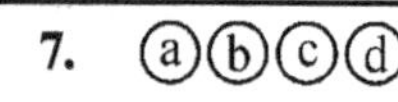

Which of the following statement(s) is/are correct ?
(a) Within $r = 2R_0$ total enclosed net charge is Q
(b) Electric field is discontinued at $r = R_0$
(c) Charge is only present at $r = R_0$
(d) Electrostatic energy is zero for $r < R_0$

Space for Rough Work

Section III - Integer Type

This section contains 4 questions. The answer to each of the questions is a single digit integer ranging from 0 to 9.

11. Two square metal plates of side 1 m are kept 0.01 m apart like a parallel plate capacitor in air in such a way that one of their edges is perpendicular to an oil surface in a tank filled with an insulating oil. The plates are connected to a battery of emf 564 V. The plates are then lowered vertically into the oil at a speed of 0.001 ms^{-1}. Calculate the current (in nano ampere) drawn from the battery during the process. (Dielectric constant of oil = 11, $\varepsilon_0 = 8.85 \times 10^{-12} C^2 N^{-1} m^{-1}$)

12. Two insulated metal spheres of radii 10 cm and 15 cm charged to a potential of 150 V and 100 V respectively, are connected by means of a metallic wire. What is the charge on the first sphere (in e.s.u.) ?

13. Infinite number of identical capacitors (each of capacity 1 µF) are connected as shown in figure. Find the equivalent capacitance (in µF)of system between the terminals shown in figure.

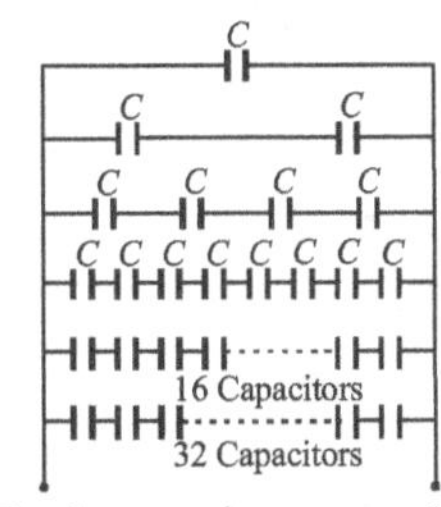

14. A capacitor is charged by a battery. The battery is removed and another identical uncharged capacitor is connected in parallel. The total electrostatic energy of resulting system decreased by a factor of x. Find the value of x.

Section IV - Comprehension Type

Directions (Qs. 15-18) : Based upon the given paragraphs, 4 multiple choice questions have to be answered. Each question has 4 choices (a), (b), (c) and (d), out of which **ONLY ONE** is correct.

PARAGRAPH-1

A non-conducting disc of radius 'a' and uniform surface charge density σ is placed on the ground, with its axis vertical. A particle of mass m and positive charge q is dropped, along the axis of the disc, from a height H with zero initial velocity. The particle has $q/m = 4\pi\varepsilon_0 g/\sigma$.

15. Electrostatic potential at H is

(a) $\dfrac{\sigma}{\varepsilon_0}\left[(a^2+H^2)^{1/2}-H\right]$ (b) $\dfrac{\sigma}{\varepsilon_0}\left[(a^2+H^2)^{1/2}+H\right]$

(c) $\dfrac{\sigma}{2\varepsilon_0}\left[(a^2+H^2)^{1/2}-H\right]$ (d) $\dfrac{\sigma}{2\varepsilon_0}\left[(a^2+H^2)^{1/2}+H\right]$

16. Which of the following is the correct graph of the potential energy of the particle as a function of its height?

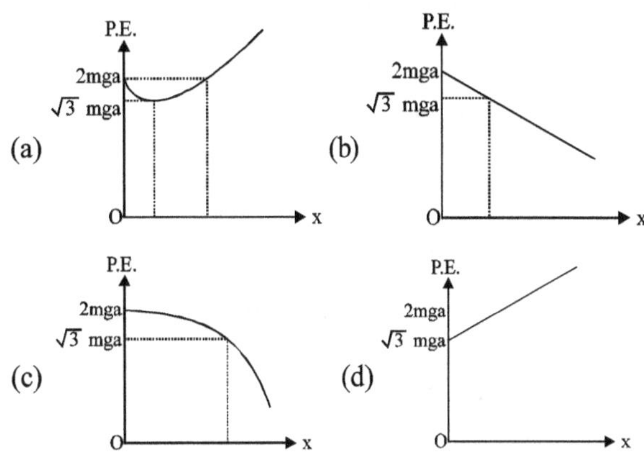

PARAGRAPH-2

A parallel plate condenser consists of two plates of area A and separation d. A slab of thickness t and dielectric constant k is inserted between the plates with its faces parallel to the plates and having the same surface area as shown in the figure. Given $k = 2$.

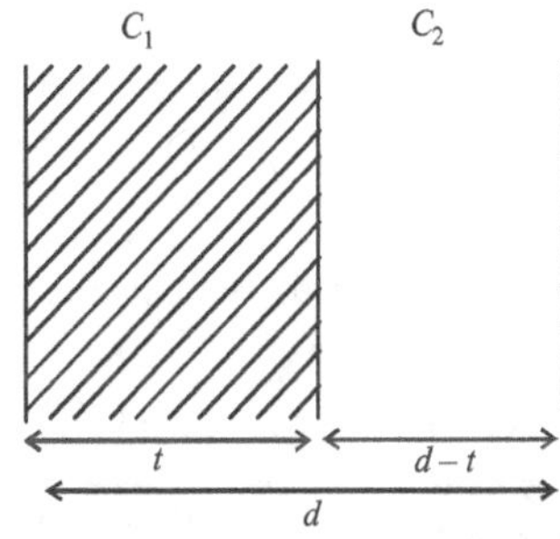

17. The capacitance of the system is

(a) $\dfrac{\varepsilon_0 A}{d-(t/2)}$ (b) $\dfrac{\varepsilon_0 A}{d+(t/2)}$ (c) $\dfrac{\varepsilon_0 A}{d-t}$ (d) $\dfrac{\varepsilon_0 A}{d+t}$

18. For what value of t/d will the capacitance of the system be (3/2) times that of the condenser with air filling the full space
(a) 2/3   (b) 3/2   (c) 1   (d) 1/3

RESPONSE GRID		
11. ⓪①②③④⑤⑥⑦⑧⑨	12. ⓪①②③④⑤⑥⑦⑧⑨	
13. ⓪①②③④⑤⑥⑦⑧⑨	14. ⓪①②③④⑤⑥⑦⑧⑨	15. ⓐⓑⓒⓓ
16. ⓐⓑⓒⓓ 17. ⓐⓑⓒⓓ	18. ⓐⓑⓒⓓ	

Section V - Matrix-Match Type

This section contains 2 questions. It contains statements given in two columns, which have to be matched. Statements in column I are labelled as A, B, C and D whereas statements in column II are labelled as p, q, r and s. The answers to these questions have to be appropriately bubbled as illustrated in the following example. If the correct matches are A-p, A-r, B-p, B-s, C-r, C-s and D-q, then the correctly bubbled matrix will look like the following:

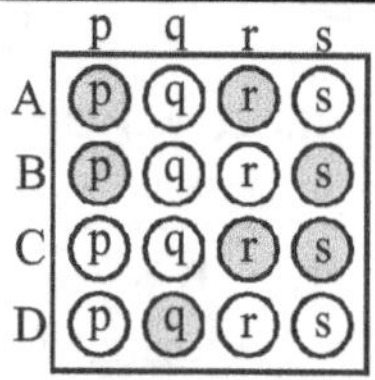

19. A conducting sphere A of radius a, with charge Q is placed concentrically inside a conducting shell B of radius b. B is earthed, C is the common centre of A and B. If P is point between shells A and B at distance r from centre C then for $a = 1$m, $b = 3$m and

$$r = 2\text{m} \left(K = \frac{1}{4\pi \,\epsilon_0} \right)$$

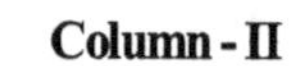

Column - I		**Column - II**	
(A)	Electric field at point P is	(p)	KQ
(B)	Electrical potential at point P is ($v_\infty = 0$)	(q)	zero
(C)	Electric potential difference between A and B is	(r)	$\dfrac{KQ}{4}$
(D)	Electric field outside the shell B at distance 5 m from centre C is	(s)	$\dfrac{KQ}{6}$

20. Match the columns :

Column I

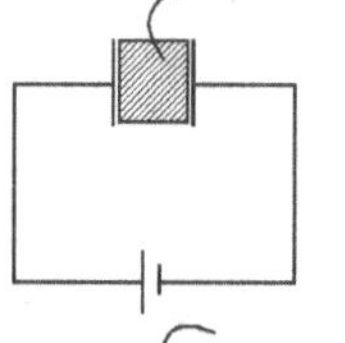

(A) Removal of dielectric when battery is present

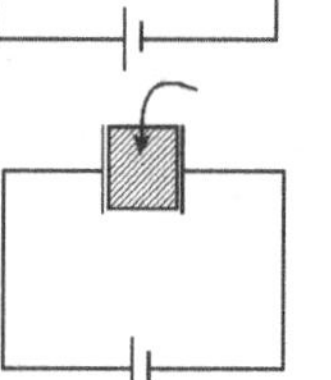

(B) Insertion of dielectric when battery is present

(C) Removal of dielectric when battery is not present

(D) Insertion of dielectric when battery is not present

Column II

(p) Potential difference between plates increases.

(q) Capacitance increases.

(r) Stored energy increases.

(s) Charge present on plates decreases.

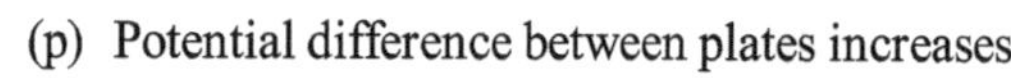

RESPONSE GRID	
19.	A - (p)(q)(r)(s); B - (p)(q)(r)(s); C - (p)(q)(r)(s); D - (p)(q)(r)(s)
20.	A - (p)(q)(r)(s); B - (p)(q)(r)(s); C - (p)(q)(r)(s); D - (p)(q)(r)(s)

DAILY PRACTICE PROBLEM DPP CP15 - PHYSICS

Total Questions	20	Total Marks	74
Attempted		Correct	
Incorrect		Net Score	
Cut-off Score	24	Qualifying Score	35

$$\text{Net Score} = \sum_{i=I}^{V} \left[\left(\text{correct}_i \times MM_i \right) - \left(In_i - NM_i \right) \right]$$

Date : | Start Time : | End Time :

PHYSICS $\boxed{\text{CP16}}$

SYLLABUS : Current Electricity

Max. Marks : 74

Time : 60 min.

GENERAL INSTRUCTIONS

- The Daily Practice Problem Sheet contains 20 Questions divided into 5 sections.
- **Section I** has **5** MCQs with ONLY 1 Correct Option, **3** marks for each correct answer and **−1** for each incorrect answer.
- **Section II** has **4** MCQs with ONE or MORE THAN ONE Correct options.
- For each question, marks will be awarded in one of the following categories:
- Full marks: **+4** If only the bubble(s) corresponding to all the correct option(s) is (are) darkened.
- Partial marks: **+1** For darkening a bubble corresponding to each correct option provided NO INCORRECT option is darkened.
- Zero marks: If none of the bubbles is darkened.
- Negative marks: **−2** In all other cases.
- **Section III** has **4** Single Digit Integer Answer Type Questions, **3** marks for each Correct Answer and 0 marks in all other cases.
- **Section IV** has Comprehension/Matching Cum-Comprehension Type Questions having **5** MCQs with ONLY ONE correct option, **3** marks for each Correct Answer and 0 marks in all other cases.
- **Section V** has **2** Matching Type Questions, **2** mark for the correct matching of each row and 0 marks in all other cases.
- You have to evaluate your Response Grids yourself with the help of Solutions.

Section I - Straight Objective Type

This section contains 5 multiple choice questions. Each question has 4 choices (a), (b), (c) and (d), out of which **ONLY ONE** is correct.

1. Ends of two wires A and B having resistivity $\rho_A = 3 \times 10^{-5}\ \Omega m$ and $\rho_B = 6 \times 10^{-5}\ \Omega m$ of same cross section area are joined together to form a single wire. If the resistance of the joined wire does not change with temperature, then find the ratio of their lengths, given that temperature coefficient of resistivity of wire A and B is $\alpha_A = 4 \times 10^{-5}/°C$ and $\alpha_B = -6 \times 10^{-6}/°C$. Assume that mechanical dimensions do not change with temperature.

(a) $\dfrac{3}{7}$ (b) $\dfrac{10}{3}$ (c) $\dfrac{3}{10}$ (d) $\dfrac{1}{2}$

2. The resistance R_{AB} between points A and B of the frame made of thin homogeneous wire (figure), assuming that the number of successively embedded equilateral triangles (with sides decreasing by half) tends to infinity, if side AB is equal to a, and the resistance of unit length of the wire is

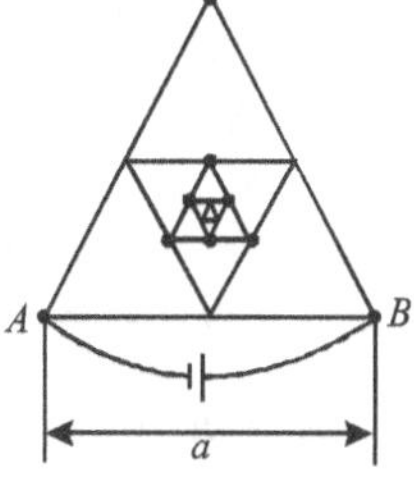

(a) $\dfrac{a\rho\,(\sqrt{7}-1)}{3}$ (b) $\dfrac{a\rho\,(\sqrt{7}+1)}{3}$

(c) $\dfrac{2a\rho\,(\sqrt{7}+1)}{3}$ (d) $a\rho\,(\sqrt{7}+1)$

RESPONSE GRID   1. ⓐⓑⓒⓓ   2. ⓐⓑⓒⓓ

Space for Rough Work

3. A wire of length L and 3 identical cells of negligible internal resistances are connected in series. Due to the current, the temperature of the wire is raised by ΔT in a time t. A number N of similar cells is now connected in series with a wire of the same material and cross-section but of length $2L$. The temperature of the wire is raised by the same amount ΔT in the same time t. The value of N is
   (a) 4   (b) 6   (c) 8   (d) 9

4. A potentiometer is an accurate and versatile device to make electrical measurement of e.m.f. because the method involves
   (a) cells
   (b) potential gradients
   (c) a combination of cells, galvanometer and resistances
   (d) a condition of no current flow through the galvanometer

5. An infinite line charge of uniform electric charge density λ lies along the axis of an electrically conducting infinite cylindrical shell of radius R. At time t = 0, the space inside the cylinder is filled with a material of permittivity ε and electrical conductivity σ. The electrical conduction in the material follows Ohm's law. Which one of the following graphs best describes the subsequent variation of the magnitude of current density j(t) at any point in the material?

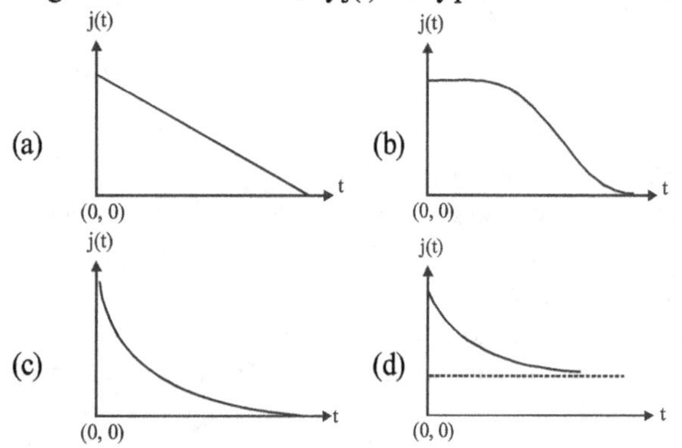

(a) ... (b) ... (c) ... (d)

Section II - Multiple Correct Answer Type

This section contains 4 multiple correct answer(s) type questions. Each question has 4 choices (a), (b), (c) and (d), out of which **ONE OR MORE** is/are correct.

6. A battery of emf $E_0 = 5V$ and internal resistance 5Ω is connected across a long uniform AB of length 1m and resistance per unit length $5\Omega m^{-1}$. Two cells of $E_1 = 1V$ and $E_2 = 2\,V$ are connected as shown in the figure.

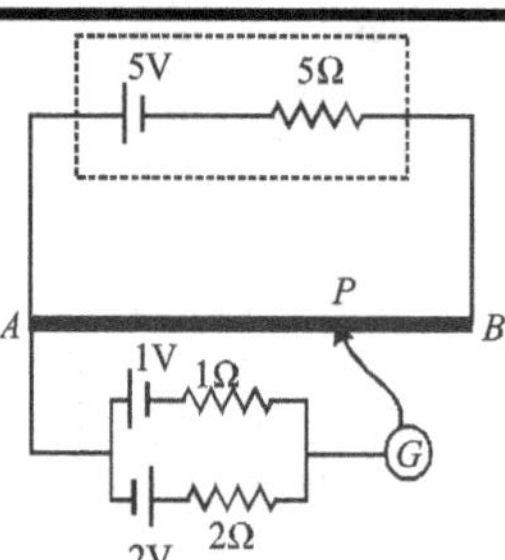

   (a) The null point is at A
   (b) If jockey is touched to point B the current in the galvanometer will be going towards B
   (c) When jockey is connected to point A no current is flowing through $1\,V$ battery
   (d) The null point is at distance of $8/15$m from A

7. An incandescent bulb has a thin filament of tungsten that is heated to high temperature by passing an electric current. The hot filament emits black–body radiation. The filament is observed to break up at random locations after a sufficiently long time of operation due to non–uniform evaporation of tungsten from the filament. If the bulb is powered at constant voltage, which of the following statement(s) is(are) true?
   (a) The temperature distribution over the filament is uniform
   (b) The resistance over small sections of the filament decreases with time
   (c) The filament emits more light at higher band of frequencies before it breaks up
   (d) The filament consumes less electrical power towards the end of the life of the bulb

8. Choose the correct options for the circuit shown.

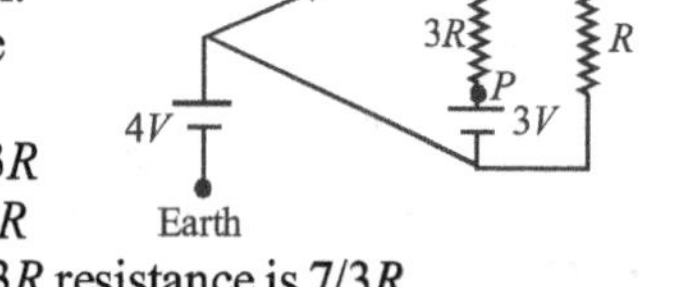

   (a) Potential of the point P is $7V$
   (b) Current in the $3R$ resistance is $7/R$
   (c) Current in the $3R$ resistance is $7/3R$
   (d) Potential of the point P is $3V$

9. Two conducting spheres of radii r and $2r$ are placed at very large separation. Each spheres possesses charge Q. These spheres are connected with a conducting wire of resistance R. Then, which of the following is true ?
   (a) Initial current is $\dfrac{Q}{8\pi\varepsilon_0 rR}$
   (b) Initial current is $\dfrac{Q}{4\pi\varepsilon_0 rR}$
   (c) Current reduces to half the initial current after time $12\pi \in_0 rR \ln 2$
   (d) Current reduces to half the initial current after time $\dfrac{8\pi \in_0 rR \ln 2}{3}$

Section III - Integer Type

This section contains 4 questions. The answer to each of the questions is a single digit integer ranging from 0 to 9.

10. Four resistances carrying a current as shown in the diagram are immersed in a box containing ice at 0°C. If 0.4 x kg ice must be put in the box every 10 minute to keep the average quantity of ice in the box constant, then find the value of x. Latent heat of ice = 80 cal/g

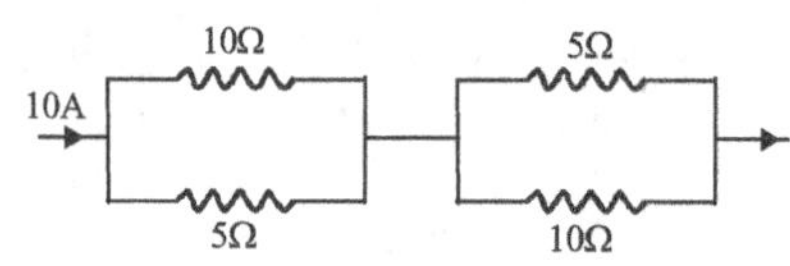

RESPONSE	3. (a)(b)(c)(d)	4. (a)(b)(c)(d)	5. (a)(b)(c)(d)	6. (a)(b)(c)(d)	7. (a)(b)(c)(d)
GRID	8. (a)(b)(c)(d)	9. (a)(b)(c)(d)	10. (0)(1)(2)(3)(4)(5)(6)(7)(8)(9)		

11. A heater is designed to operate with a power of 1000 watts in a 100 volt line. It is connected in a combination with a resistance of 10 ohm and a resistance R to a 100 volt mains as shown in the figure. What should be the value of R (in ohm) so that the heater operates with a power of 62.5 watt ?

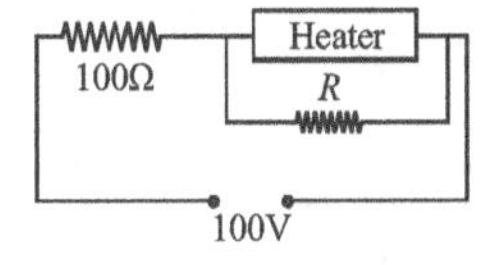

12. The current through a wire depends on time as $i = (20 + 4t)$. If the charge crossed through a section of the wire in 10 second is $x \times 10^2$ C, find the value of x.

13. A part of circuit in a steady state along with the currents flowing in the branches, the values of resistances etc., is shown in the figure. The energy (in mJ) stored in the capacitor $C\,(4\mu F)$ is $\dfrac{x}{10}$. Find the value of x.

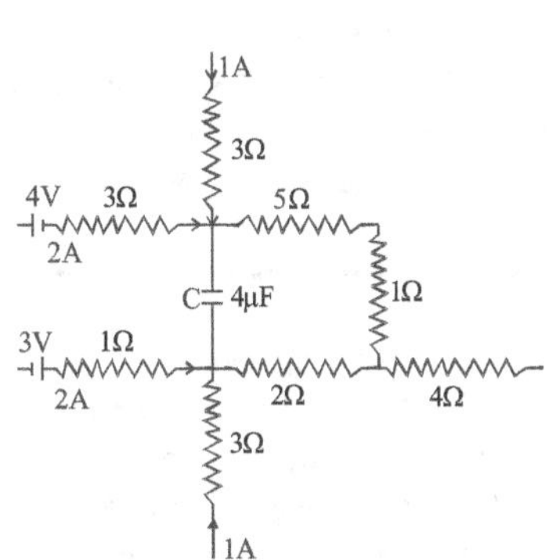

Section IV - Comprehension/Matching Cum-Comprehension Type

Directions (Qs. 14 and 15) : Based upon the given paragraph, 2 multiple choice questions have to be answered. Each question has 4 choices (a), (b), (c) and (d), out of which **ONLY ONE** is correct.

PARAGRAPH

Consider a block of conducting material of resistivity 'ρ' shown in the figure. Current 'I' enters at 'A' and leaves from 'D'. We apply superposition principle to find voltage 'ΔV' developed between 'B' and 'C'. The calculation is done in the following steps:

(i) Take current 'I' entering from 'A' and assume it to spread over a hemispherical surface in the block.

(ii) Calculate field E(r) at distance 'r' from A by using Ohm's law $E = \rho j$, where j is the current per unit area at 'r'.

(iii) From the 'r' dependence of E(r), obtain the potential V(r) at r.

(iv) Repeat (i), (ii) and (iii) for current 'I' leaving 'D' and superpose results for 'A' and 'D'.

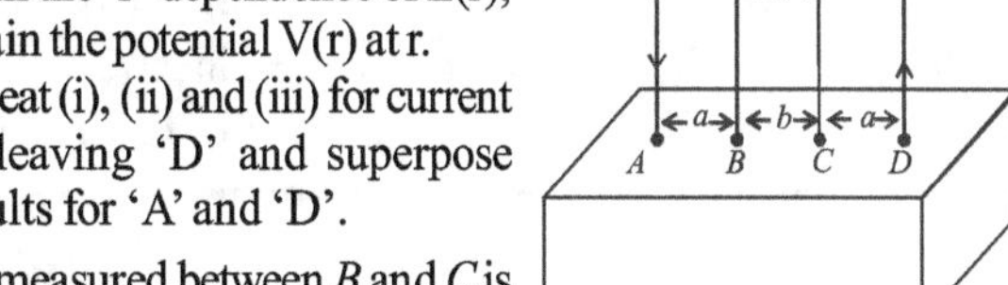
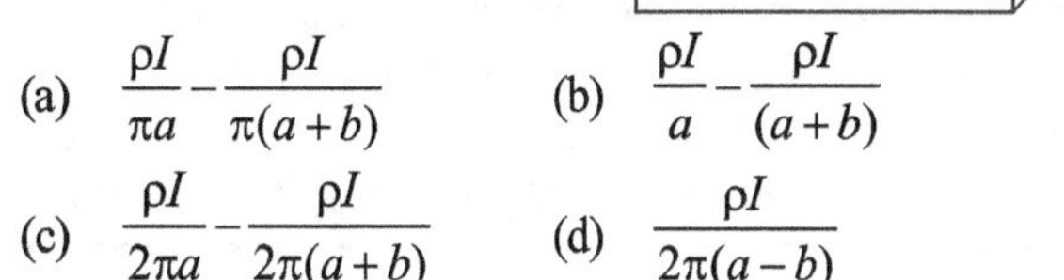

14. ΔV measured between B and C is

(a) $\dfrac{\rho I}{\pi a} - \dfrac{\rho I}{\pi(a+b)}$

(b) $\dfrac{\rho I}{a} - \dfrac{\rho I}{(a+b)}$

(c) $\dfrac{\rho I}{2\pi a} - \dfrac{\rho I}{2\pi(a+b)}$

(d) $\dfrac{\rho I}{2\pi(a-b)}$

15. For current entering at A, the electric field at a distance 'r' from A is

(a) $\dfrac{\rho I}{8\pi r^2}$

(b) $\dfrac{\rho I}{r^2}$

(c) $\dfrac{\rho I}{2\pi r^2}$

(d) $\dfrac{\rho I}{4\pi r^2}$

Directions (Qs. 16-18) : This passage contains a table having 3 columns and 4 rows. Based on the table, there are three questions. Each question has four options (a), (b), (c) and (d) **ONLY ONE** of these four options is correct.

Two or more resistors are said to be connected in parallel if the same potential difference exists across all resistors. Column I shows different combination of resistances. Column II shows the equivalent resistance of the combination. A cell of emf 60 volts and internal resistance 1 Ω is connected across M and N.

Column I	Column II	Column III
I. 7Ω 3Ω 10Ω 5Ω M 10Ω N	(i) 2 Ω	(P) 20 A
II. 3Ω 3Ω 6Ω 3Ω 6Ω 3Ω M 3Ω N	(ii) 5 Ω	(Q) 10 A
III. N r r r M r	(iii) $\dfrac{4r}{3}$	(R) $\dfrac{180}{4r+3}$ A

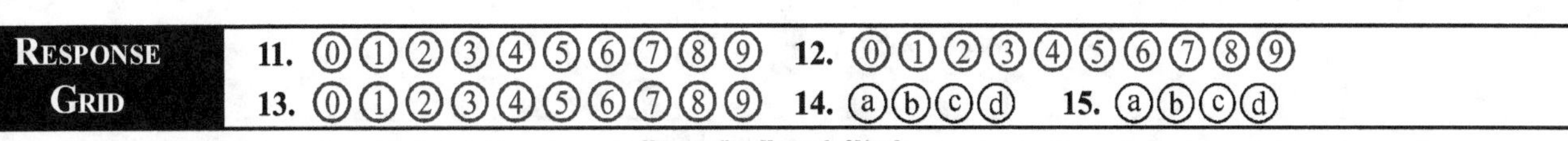
Space for Rough Work

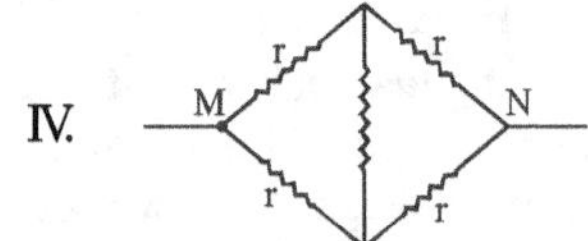

(iv) r

(S) $\dfrac{60}{r+1}$ A

---

16. If resistance r is 3 Ω, in the combination shown in Column I (III), then the equivalent resistance of the combination and current through the cell respectively are (4 Ω, 12 A); Which of the following is correct matching satisfying the condition?

(a) III (iv) S (b) III (iii) R (c) I (iv) P (d) III (ii) Q

17. Which of the following shows the correct matching?

(a) I (ii) Q (b) II (i) P (c) IV (ii) S (d) Both (a) and (b)

18. Which of the following shows the incorrect matching?

(a) III (iv) S (b) IV (iii) R (c) I (ii) Q (d) Both (a) and (b)

Section V - Matrix-Match Type

This section contains 2 questions. It contains statements given in two columns, which have to be matched. Statements in column I are labelled as A, B, C and D whereas statements in column II are labelled as p, q, r and s. The answers to these questions have to be appropriately bubbled as illustrated in the following example. If the correct matches are A-p, A-r, B-p, B-s, C-r, C-s and D-q, then the correctly bubbled matrix will look like the following:

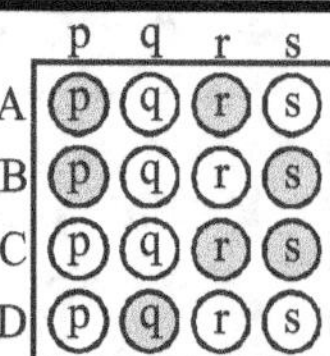

19. Match the columns.

Column-I	Column-II
(A) With increase in temperature	(p) Drift velocity increases
(B) With increase in length	(q) Resistance increases
(C) With increase in area of cross-section	(r) Resistance decreases
(D) With increase in volume	(s) Number of conduction electrons increases

20. Consider a network of resistances each of value of R as shown in figure.

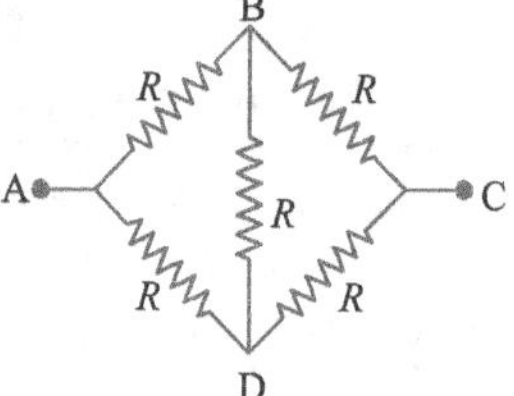

Column-I	Column-II
(A) Equivalent of net work between A and C is	(p) same
(B) Equivalent resistance between A an B	(q) 5/8 R
(C) Potential of B and D when voltage source is applied across A and C is	(r) R
(D) Potential of B and D when voltage source is applied across A and B is	(s) different

---

<table>
<tr><td rowspan="3">RESPONSE GRID</td><td>16. (a)(b)(c)(d) 17. (a)(b)(c)(d) 18. (a)(b)(c)(d)</td></tr>
<tr><td>19. A-(p)(q)(r)(s); B-(p)(q)(r)(s); C-(p)(q)(r)(s); D-(p)(q)(r)(s)</td></tr>
<tr><td>20. A-(p)(q)(r)(s); B-(p)(q)(r)(s); C-(p)(q)(r)(s); D-(p)(q)(r)(s)</td></tr>
</table>

DAILY PRACTICE PROBLEM DPP CP16 - PHYSICS

Total Questions	20	Total Marks	74
Attempted		Correct	
Incorrect		Net Score	
Cut-off Score	24	Qualifying Score	35

$$\text{Net Score} = \sum_{i=I}^{V}\left[\left(\text{correct}_i \times MM_i\right) - \left(In_i - NM_i\right)\right]$$

DPP - Daily Practice Problems

Chapter-wise Sheets

Date : [____] Start Time : [____] End Time : [____]

PHYSICS $\boxed{\text{CP17}}$

SYLLABUS : Moving Charges and Magnetism

Max. Marks : 74 **Time : 60 min.**

GENERAL INSTRUCTIONS

- The Daily Practice Problem Sheet contains 20 Questions divided into 5 sections.
  Section I has **5** MCQs with ONLY 1 Correct Option, **3** marks for each correct answer and **−1** for each incorrect answer.
  Section II has **4** MCQs with ONE or MORE THAN ONE Correct options.
  For each question, marks will be awarded in one of the following categories:
  Full marks: **+4** If only the bubble(s) corresponding to all the correct option(s) is (are) darkened.
  Partial marks: **+1** For darkening a bubble corresponding to each correct option provided NO INCORRECT option is darkened.
  Zero marks: If none of the bubbles is darkened.
  Negative marks: **−2** In all other cases.
  Section III has **4** Single Digit Integer Answer Type Questions, **3** marks for each Correct Answer and 0 marks in all other cases.
  Section IV has Comprehension/Matching Cum-Comprehension Type Questions having **5** MCQs with ONLY ONE correct option, **3** marks for each Correct Answer and 0 marks in all other cases.
  Section V has **2** Matching Type Questions, **2** mark for the correct matching of each row and 0 marks in all other cases.
- You have to evaluate your Response Grids yourself with the help of Solutions.

Section I - Straight Objective Type

This section contains 5 multiple choice questions. Each question has 4 choices (a), (b), (c) and (d), out of which **ONLY ONE** is correct.

1. Two identical wires A and B, each of length 'l', carry the same current I. Wire A is bent into a circle of radius R and wire B is bent to form a square of side 'a'. If B_A and B_B are the values of magnetic field at the centres of the circle and square respectively, then the ratio $\dfrac{B_A}{B_B}$ is:

   (a) $\dfrac{\pi^2}{16}$ (b) $\dfrac{\pi^2}{8\sqrt{2}}$ (c) $\dfrac{\pi^2}{8}$ (d) $\dfrac{\pi^2}{16\sqrt{2}}$

2. A particle of mass m and charge q enters a region of magnetic field (as shown) with speed v. There is a region in which the magnetic field is absent, as shown. The particle after entering the region collides elastically with a rigid wall. Time after which the velocity of particle becomes antiparallel to its initial velocity is

   (a) $\dfrac{m}{2qB}(\pi+4)$

   (b) $\dfrac{m}{qB}(\pi+2)$

   (c) $\dfrac{m}{4qB}(\pi+2)$

   (d) $\dfrac{m}{4qB}(2\pi+3)$

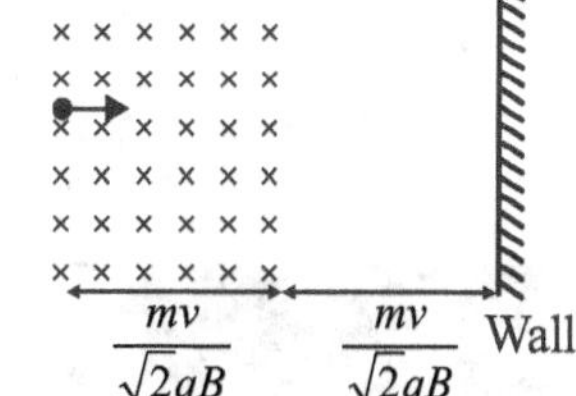

RESPONSE GRID	1. ⓐⓑⓒⓓ	2. ⓐⓑⓒⓓ

Space for Rough Work

3. A charged particle moves in a uniform magnetic field with its velocity vector making an angle of 120° with the direction of the magnetic field. The path of the particle will be (ignore any effects due to radiation)
   (a) a circle
   (b) a helix with uniform pitch
   (c) a helix with non-uniform pitch
   (d) a parabola

4. The figure shows two infinite semi-cylindrical shells: 1 and 2. Shell-1 carries current i_1, in inward direction normal to the plane of paper, while shell-2 carries same current i_1, in opposite direction. A long straight conductor lying along the common axis of the shells is carrying current i_2 in direction same as that of current in shell-1. Force per unit length on the wire is

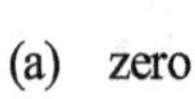

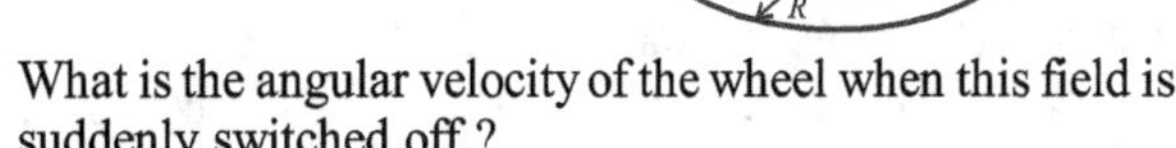

   (a) zero   (b) $\dfrac{\mu_0 i_1 i_2}{2\pi r}$

   (c) $\dfrac{2\mu_0 i_1 i_2}{\pi r}$ (d) $\dfrac{2\mu_0 i_1 i_2}{\pi^2 r}$

5. A line charge λ per unit length is pasted uniformly on to the rim of a wheel of mass m and radius R. The wheel has light non-conducting spokes and is free to rotate about a vertical axis as shown in figure. A uniform magnetic field extends over a radial region given by
$$B = -B_0\,\vec{k}\quad (r \le a;\ a < R)$$
$$= 0\ (\text{otherwise})$$

What is the angular velocity of the wheel when this field is suddenly switched off ?

   (a) $\dfrac{-2B\pi a^2 r}{mR}\vec{k}$ (b) $\dfrac{-B\pi a^2 r}{3mR}\vec{k}$

   (c) $\dfrac{-B\pi a^2 \lambda}{2mR}\vec{k}$ (d) $\dfrac{-B\pi a^2 \lambda}{mR}\vec{k}$

Section II - Multiple Correct Answer Type

This section contains 4 multiple correct answer(s) type questions. Each question has 4 choices (a), (b), (c) and (d), out of which **ONE OR MORE** is/are correct.

6. Two coaxial solenoids 1 and 2 of the same length are set so that one is inside the other. The number of turns per unit length are n_1 and n_2. The current i_1 and i_2 are flowing in opposite directions. The magnetic field inside the inner solenoid is zero. This is possible when

   (a) $i_1 \ne i_2$ and $n_1 = n_2$ (b) $i_1 = i_2$ and $n_1 \ne n_2$

   (c) $i_1 = i_2$ and $n_1 = n_2$ (d) $i_1 n_1 = i_2 n_2$

7. Two long thin, parallel conductors carrying equal currents in the same direction are fixed parallel to the x-axis, one

passing through $y = a$ and the other through $y = -a$. The resultant magnetic field due to the two conductors at any point is B. Which of the following are correct?

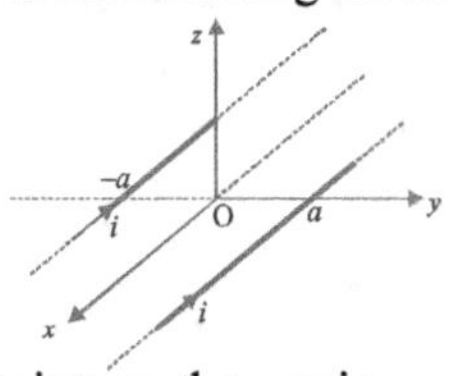

   (a) $B = 0$ for all points on the x-axis
   (b) At all points on the y-axis, excluding the origin, B has only a z-component.
   (c) At all points on the z-axis, excluding the origin, B has only a y-component.
   (d) B cannot have an x-component

8. A large plate with uniform surface charge density σ is moving with constant speed v as shown in the figure. The magnetic field at a small distance from plate is

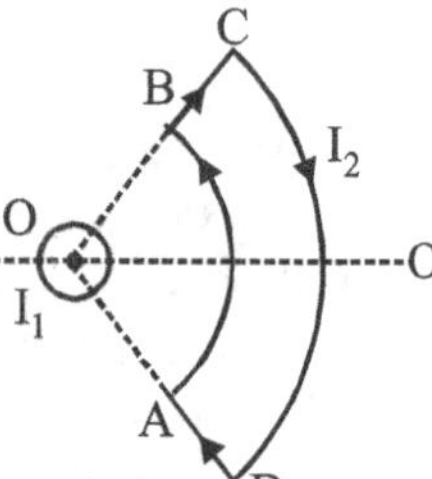

   (a) $\mu_0 \sigma\, v$ in magnitude
   (b) $\dfrac{\mu_0 \sigma v}{2}$ in magnitude
   (c) perpendicular to plate
   (d) parallel to plate

9. A long current carrying wire, carrying current I_1 such that I_1 is flowing out from the plane of paper is placed at O. A steady state current I_2 is flowing in the loop $ABCD$

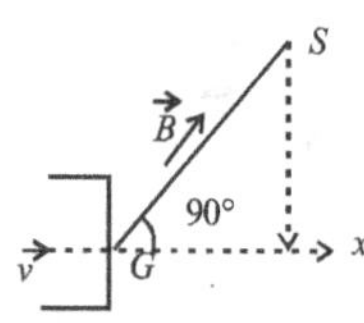

   (a) the net force is zero
   (b) the net torque is zero
   (c) as seen from O, the loop will rotate in clockwise along OO' axis
   (d) as seen from O, the loop will rotate in anticlockwise direction along OO' axis

Section III - Integer Type

This section contains 4 questions. The answer to each of the questions is a single digit integer ranging from 0 to 9.

10. A toroid having a square cross section, 5.00 cm on a side, and an inner radius of 15.0 cm has 500 turns and carries a current of 0.80 A. What is the magnetic field inside the toroid at the outer radius of the toroid in (10^{-4})T?

11. An electron gun G emits electrons of energy 2keV travelling in the positive x-direction. The electrons are required to hit the spot S where $GS = 0.1$m, and the line GS makes an angle of 60° with the x-axis as shown in the fig.

A uniform magnetic field $\vec{B}$ exists parallel to GS in the region outside the electron gun. Find the minimum value of B (in mT) needed to make the electrons hit S.

<table>
<tr><td rowspan="3">RESPONSE
GRID</td><td>3. ⓐⓑⓒⓓ</td><td>4. ⓐⓑⓒⓓ</td><td>5. ⓐⓑⓒⓓ</td><td>6. ⓐⓑⓒⓓ</td><td>7. ⓐⓑⓒⓓ</td></tr>
<tr><td>8. ⓐⓑⓒⓓ</td><td>9. ⓐⓑⓒⓓ</td><td colspan="3">10. ⓪①②③④⑤⑥⑦⑧⑨</td></tr>
<tr><td colspan="5">11. ⓪①②③④⑤⑥⑦⑧⑨</td></tr>
</table>

12. Two parallel wires in the plane of the paper are distance X_0 apart. *A* point charge is moving with speed u between the wires in the same plane at a distance X_1 from one of the wires. When the wires carry current of magnitude I in the same direction, the radius of curvature of the path of the point charge is R_1. In contrast, if the currents I in the two wires have directions opposite to each other, the radius of curvature of the path is R_2. If $\dfrac{X_0}{X_1} = 3$, the value of $\dfrac{R_1}{R_2}$ is

13. A cylindrical cavity of diameter a exists inside a cylinder of diameter $2a$ as shown in the figure. Both the cylinder and the cavity are infinitely long. A uniform current density J flows along the length. If the magnitude of the magnetic field at the point P is given by $\dfrac{N}{12}\mu_0 aJ$, then the value of N is

Section IV - Comprehension/Matching Cum-Comprehension Type

Directions (Qs. 14 and 15) : Based upon the given paragraph, 2 multiple choice questions have to be answered. Each question has 4 choices (a), (b), (c) and (d), out of which **ONLY ONE** is correct.

PARAGRAPH

Curves in the graph shown give, as functions of radial distance r, the magnitude B of the magnetic field inside and outside four long wires a, b, c and d, carrying currents that are uniformly distributed across the cross-sections of the wires. Overlapping portions of the plots are indicated by double labels.

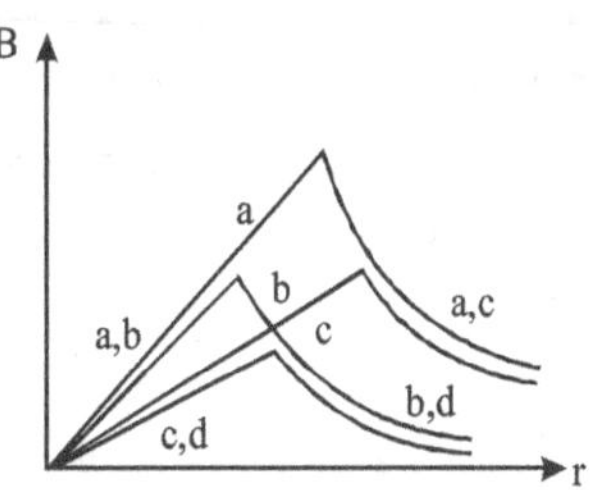

14. Which wire has the greatest radius?
    (a) a   (b) b   (c) c   (d) d

15. The current density in wire a is
    (a) greater than in wire c
    (b) less than in wire c
    (c) equal to that in wire c
    (d) not comparable to that of in wire c due to lack of information

Directions (Qs. 16-18) : This passage contains a table having 3 columns and 4 rows. Based on the table, there are three questions. Each question has four options (a), (b), (c) and (d) **ONLY ONE** of these four options is correct.

A charge particle of mass m moves at a speed of v. It enters a region of uniform magnetic field ($\vec{B}$) at a point S and leaves the region of the field at the point T as shown in column (II). Column (III) shows the corresponding length $\overline{ST}$ or arc length $\widehat{ST}$. Column (I) gives the charge on particle.

Column I		Column II		Column III	
I.	$Q = +q$	(i)		(P)	$\overline{ST} = \sqrt{2}\,\dfrac{mv}{qB}$
II.	$Q = -q$	(ii)		(Q)	$\mathrm{Arc}\ \widehat{ST} = \dfrac{11}{7}\dfrac{mv}{qB}$
III.	$Q = +2q$	(iii)		(R)	$\overline{ST} = \dfrac{mv}{qB}$
IV.	$Q = -2q$	(iv)		(S)	$\mathrm{Arc}\ \widehat{ST} = \dfrac{33}{7}\dfrac{mv}{qB}$

16. If a proton is projected in the uniform magnetic field, which of the following combination best explains the path of the proton ?
    (a) I (i) P   (b) III (iii) Q   (c) I (iii) P   (d) IV (iv) Q

17. If an electron is projected in the uniform magnetic field, which of the following combination best explains the path of the electron?
    (a) III (iii) R   (b) II (iv) S   (c) II (ii) S   (d) IV (i) P

18. Which of the following combination is wrongly matched ?
    (a) III (i) R   (b) IV (ii) Q   (c) III (i) Q   (d) I (iii) R

Section V - Matrix-Match Type

This section contains 2 questions. It contains statements given in two columns, which have to be matched. Statements in column I are labelled as A, B, C and D whereas statements in column II are labelled as p, q, r and s. The answers to these questions have to be appropriately bubbled as illustrated in the following example. If the correct matches are A-p, A-r, B-p, B-s, C-r, C-s and D-q, then the correctly bubbled matrix will look like the following:

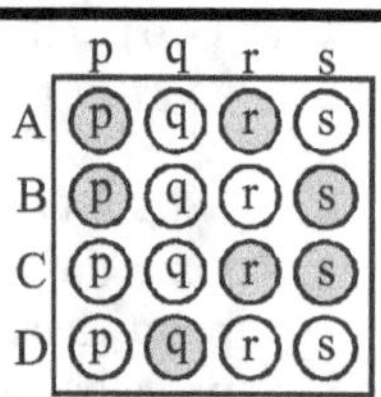

19. A frame ABCD is rotating with angular velcoity ω about an axis which passes through the point O perpendicular to the plane of Paper as shown in the figure. A uniform magnetic field $\vec{B}$ is applied into the plane of the paper in the region as shown. Match the Column I and II.

Column-I		Column -II	
(A)	Potential difference between A and O	(p)	zero
(B)	Potential difference between O and D	(q)	$B\omega L^2/2$
(C)	Potential difference between C and D	(r)	$B\omega L^2$
(D)	Potential difference between A and D	(s)	constant

20. A square loop of uniform conducting wire as shown in figure. A current-I (in amperes) enters the loop from one end and leaves the loop from opposite end as shown in figure. The length of one side of square loop is ℓ metre. The wire has uniform cross section area and uniform linear mass density. In four situations of column-I, the loop is subjected to four different uniform and constant magnetic field. Under the conditions of column I, match the column-I with corresponding results of column-II. (B_0 in column I is a positive non-zero constant).

Column-I		Column-II	
(A)	$\vec{B} = B_0\hat{i}$ in tesla	(p)	magnitude of net force on loop is $\sqrt{2}B_0 I\ell$ newton
(B)	$\vec{B} = B_0\hat{j}$ in tesla	(q)	magnitude of net force on loop is zero
(C)	$\vec{B} = B_0(\hat{i} + \hat{j})$ in tesla	(r)	magnitude of net torque on loop about its centre is zero
(D)	$\vec{B} = B_0\hat{k}$ in tesla	(s)	magnitude of net force on loop is $B_0 I\ell$ newton and it is perpendicular to the plane of loop.

RESPONSE GRID	**19.** A - Ⓟ Ⓠ Ⓡ Ⓢ; B - Ⓟ Ⓠ Ⓡ Ⓢ; C - Ⓟ Ⓠ Ⓡ Ⓢ; D - Ⓟ Ⓠ Ⓡ Ⓢ	
	20. A - Ⓟ Ⓠ Ⓡ Ⓢ; B - Ⓟ Ⓠ Ⓡ Ⓢ; C - Ⓟ Ⓠ Ⓡ Ⓢ; D - Ⓟ Ⓠ Ⓡ Ⓢ	

DAILY PRACTICE PROBLEM DPP CP17 - PHYSICS

Total Questions	20	Total Marks	74
Attempted		Correct	
Incorrect		Net Score	
Cut-off Score	24	Qualifying Score	35

$$\text{Net Score} = \sum_{i=\text{I}}^{\text{V}} \left[\left(\text{correct}_i \times MM_i \right) - \left(In_i - NM_i \right) \right]$$

Date :   **Start Time :**   **End Time :**

PHYSICS $\boxed{\text{CP18}}$

SYLLABUS : Electromagnetic Induction

Max. Marks : 74   **Time : 60 min.**

GENERAL INSTRUCTIONS

- The Daily Practice Problem Sheet contains 20 Questions divided into 5 sections.
  Section I has **6** MCQs with ONLY 1 Correct Option, **3** marks for each correct answer and **−1** for each incorrect answer.
  Section II has **4** MCQs with ONE or MORE THAN ONE Correct options.
  For each question, marks will be awarded in one of the following categories:
  Full marks: **+4** If only the bubble(s) corresponding to all the correct option(s) is (are) darkened.
  Partial marks: **+1** For darkening a bubble corresponding to each correct option provided NO INCORRECT option is darkened.
  Zero marks: If none of the bubbles is darkened.
  Negative marks: **−2** In all other cases.
  Section III has **4** Single Digit Integer Answer Type Questions, **3** marks for each Correct Answer and 0 marks in all other cases.
  Section IV has Comprehension Type Questions having **4** MCQs with ONLY ONE corect option, 3 marks for each Correct Answer and 0 marks in all other cases.
  Section V has **2** Matching Type Questions, **2** mark for the correct matching of each row and 0 marks in all other cases.
- You have to evaluate your Response Grids yourself with the help of Solutions.

Section I - Straight Objective Type

This section contains 6 multiple choice questions. Each question has 4 choices (a), (b), (c) and (d), out of which **ONLY ONE** is correct.

1. A rod PQ of length L moves with a uniform velocity v parallel to a long straight wire carrying a current i. The end P remains at a distance r from the wire. The emf induced across the rod is

(a) $\dfrac{\mu_0 i v^2}{2\pi}\ln\left(\dfrac{r+L}{r}\right)$

(b) $\dfrac{\mu_0 i^2 v^2}{2\pi}\ln\left(\dfrac{r^2+L}{r}\right)$

(c) $\dfrac{\mu_0 i v}{2\pi}\ln\left(\dfrac{r+L}{r}\right)$

(d) $\dfrac{\mu_0 i v}{2\pi}\ln\left(\dfrac{r^2+L^2}{L^2}\right)$

2. A cylindrical region of radius 1 m has instantaneous homogenous magnetic field of 5T and it is increasing at a rate of 2T/s. A regular hexagonal loop ABCDEFA of side 1 m is being drawn in to the region with a constant speed of 1 m/s as shown in the figure. What is the magnitude of emf developed in the loop just after the instant shown when the corner A of the hexagon is coinciding with the centre of the circle ?

(a) $5/\sqrt{3}\,V$

(b) $2\pi/3\ V$

(c) $\left(5\sqrt{3}+2\pi/3\right)V$

(d) $\left(5\sqrt{3}+\pi\right)V$

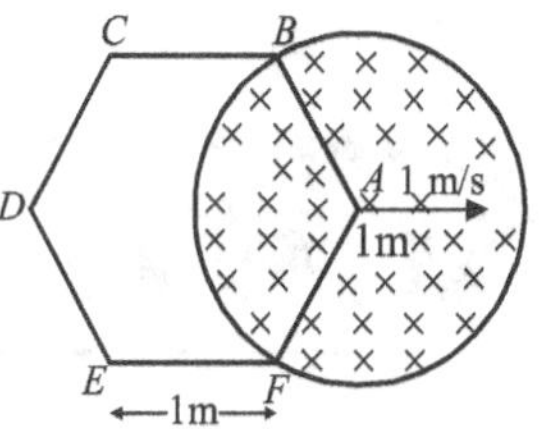

RESPONSE GRID   **1.** ⓐⓑⓒⓓ   **2.** ⓐⓑⓒⓓ

Space for Rough Work

3. A coil of wire having inductance and resistance has a conducting ring placed coaxially within it. The coil is connected to a battery at time $t = 0$, so that a time-dependent current $1_1(t)$ starts flowing through the coil. If $I_2(t)$ is the current induced in the ring, and $B(t)$ is the magnetic field at the axis of the coil due to $I_1(t)$, then as a function of time $(t > 0)$, the product $I_2(t)\,B(t)$
 (a) increases with time
 (b) decreases with time
 (c) does not vary with time
 (d) passes through a maximum

4. A rectangular loop is being pulled at a constant speed v, through a region of certain thickness d, in which a uniform magnetic field B is set up. The graph between position x of the right hand edge of the loop and the induced emf E will be

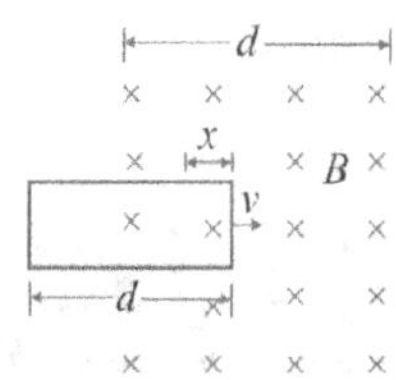

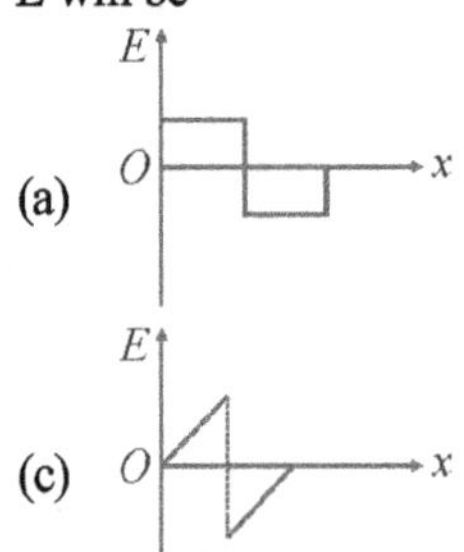
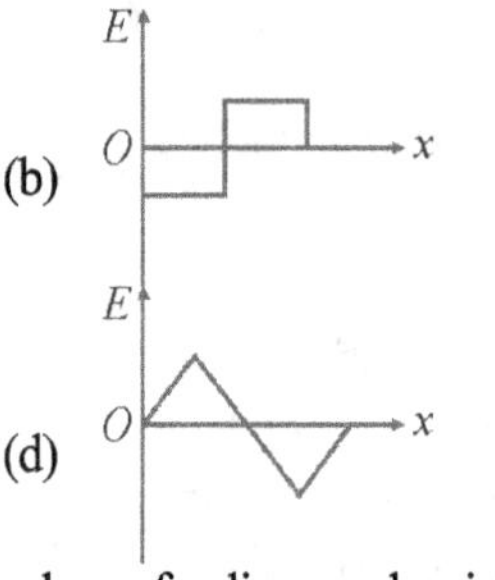

5. Shown in the figure is a circular loop of radius r and resistance R. A variable magnetic field of induction $B = B_0 e^{-t}$ is established inside the coil. If the key (K) is closed, the electrical power developed right after closing the switch is equal to

 (a) $\dfrac{B_0^2 \pi r^2}{R}$ (b) $\dfrac{B_0 10 r^3}{R}$

 (c) $\dfrac{B_0^2 \pi^2 r^4 R}{5}$ (d) $\dfrac{B_0^2 \pi^2 r^4}{R}$

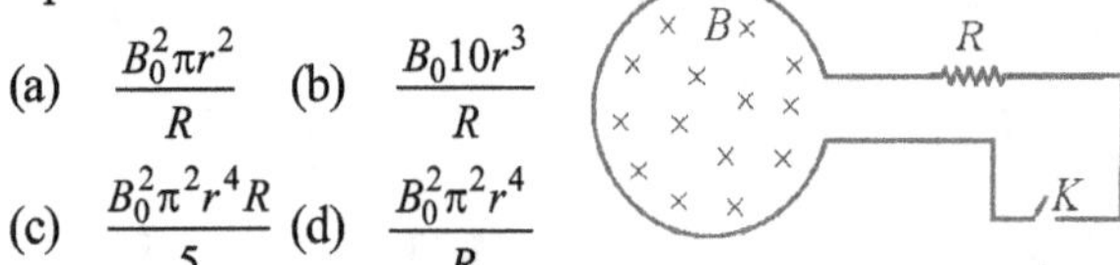

6. PQ is an infinite current carrying conductor. AB and CD are smooth conducting rods on which a conductor EF moves with constant velocity v as shown. The force needed to maintain constant speed of EF is

 (a) $\dfrac{1}{vR}\left[\dfrac{\mu_0 Iv}{2\pi}\ln\left(\dfrac{b}{a}\right)\right]^2$

 (b) $\left[\dfrac{\mu_0 Iv}{2\pi}\ln\left(\dfrac{a}{b}\right)\right]^2 \dfrac{1}{vR}$

 (c) $\left[\dfrac{\mu_0 Iv}{2\pi}\ln\left(\dfrac{b}{a}\right)\right]^2 \dfrac{v}{R}$ (d) $\dfrac{v}{R}\left[\dfrac{\mu_0 Iv}{2\pi}\ln\left(\dfrac{a}{b}\right)\right]^2$

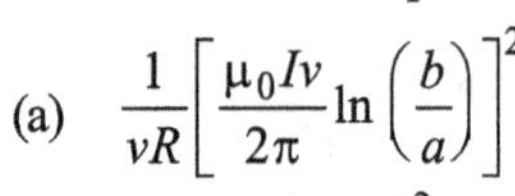
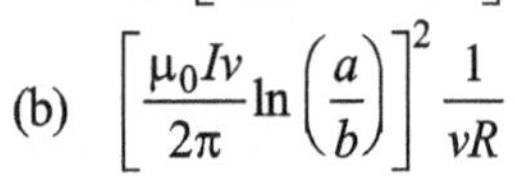
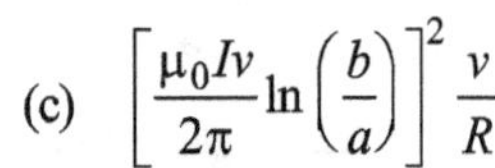
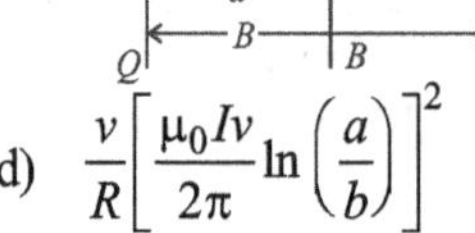

Section II - Multiple Correct Answer Type

This section contains 4 multiple correct answer(s) type questions. Each question has 4 choices (a), (b), (c) and (d), out of which **ONE OR MORE** is/are correct.

7. A non-conducting ring of mass m and radius R has a charge Q uniformly distributed over its circumference. The ring is placed on a rough horizontal surface such that the plane of the ring is parallel to the surface. A vertical magnetic field $B = B_0 t^2$ tesla is switched on. After 2 second from switching on the magnetic field the ring is just about to rotate about vertical axis through its centre. Then
 (a) the induced electric field is quadratic in time t
 (b) the force tangential to the ring is $B_0 Q R t$
 (c) until 2 seconds, the friction force does not come into play
 (d) the friction coefficient between the ring and the surface is $\dfrac{2 B_0 R Q}{mg}$

8. Two circular coils P and Q are fixed coaxially and carry currents I_1 and I_2 respectively

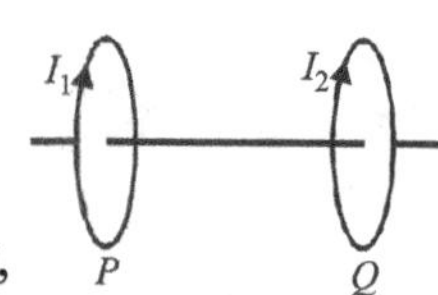

 (a) if $I_2 = 0$ & P moves towards Q, a current in the same direction as I_1 is induced in Q
 (b) if $I_1 = 0$ & Q moves towards P, a current in the opposite direction to that of I_2 is induced in P.
 (c) when $I_1 \neq 0$ and $I_2 \neq 0$ are in the same direction then the two coils tends to move apart.
 (d) when $I_1 \neq 0$ and $I_2 \neq 0$ are in opposite direction then the coils tends to move apart.

9. A rod OA of length l is rotating (about end O) over a conducting ring in crossed magnetic field B with constant angular velocity ω as shown in figure

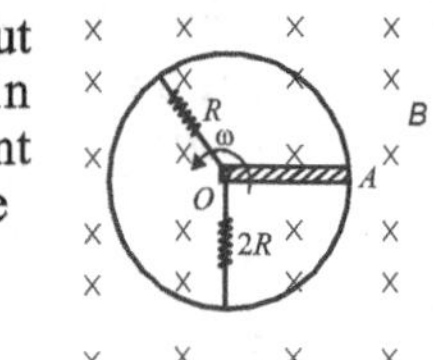

 (a) Current flowing through the rod is $\dfrac{3 B \omega l^2}{4R}$
 (b) Magnetic force acting on the rod is $\dfrac{3 B^2 \omega l^3}{4R}$
 (c) Torque due to magnetic force acting on the rod is $\dfrac{3 B^2 \omega l^4}{8R}$
 (d) Magnitude of external force that acts perpendicularly at the end of the rod to maintain the constant angular speed is $\dfrac{3 B^2 \omega l^3}{8R}$

Response	**3.** ⓐⓑⓒⓓ	**4.** ⓐⓑⓒⓓ	**5.** ⓐⓑⓒⓓ	**6.** ⓐⓑⓒⓓ	**7.** ⓐⓑⓒⓓ
Grid	**8.** ⓐⓑⓒⓓ	**9.** ⓐⓑⓒⓓ				

10. Two metallic square frames P and Q of side ℓ and 2ℓ respectively move in opposite directions with speed $2v$ and v on a conducting surface.

There is a uniform magnetic field $\vec{B}$ 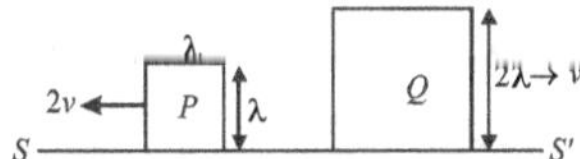

perpendicular to the planes of the frame. Then

(a) the emf induced in each of the vertical sides of frame P will be $2B\ell v$

(b) the upper point of P will be at a higher potential

(c) the emf's of the two coils are additive

(d) the upper point of Q will be at a low potential

Section III - Integer Type

This section contains 4 questions. The answer to each of the questions is a single digit integer ranging from 0 to 9.

11. Two coils are wound on the same iron rod so that the flux generated by one also passes through the other. The primary has 100 loops and secondary has 200 loops. When a current of 2 A flows through the primary, the flux in it is 25×10^{-4} Wb. The value of M (in mH) between the coils is $5x$. Find the value of x.

12. The current in a coil of self-induction 2.0 henry is increasing according to $i = 2 \sin t^2$ ampere. Find the amount of energy spent during the period when the current changes from 0 to 2 ampere.

13. In the figure a 120-turn coil of radius 1.8 cm and resistance 5.3Ω is placed outside a solenoid. The 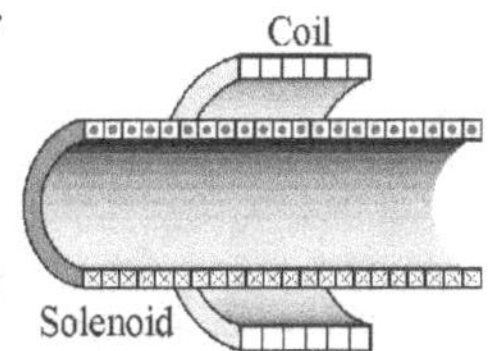

current in the solenoid is 1.5 A and it reduces to zero at a steady rate in 25 ms. $10x$ mA is current appears in the coil. The number of turns per unit length of the solenoid is 220 turns/cm and its diameter $D = 3.2$ cm. Find the value of x.

14. A circular wire loop of radius R is placed in the x-y plane centered at the origin O. A square loop of side $a(a<<R)$ having two turns is placed with its centre at $z = \sqrt{3}R$ along the axis of the circular wire loop, as shown in figure. The plane of the square loop makes an angle of $45°$ 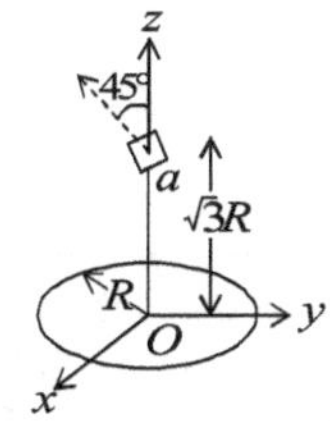

with respect to the z-axis. If the mutual inductance between the loops is given by $\dfrac{\mu_0 a^2}{2^{p/2}R}$, then the value of p is

Section IV - Comprehension Type

Directions (Qs. 15-18) : Based upon the given paragraphs, 4 multiple choice questions have to be answered. Each question has 4 choices (a), (b), (c) and (d), out of which ONLY ONE is correct.

PARAGRAPH-1

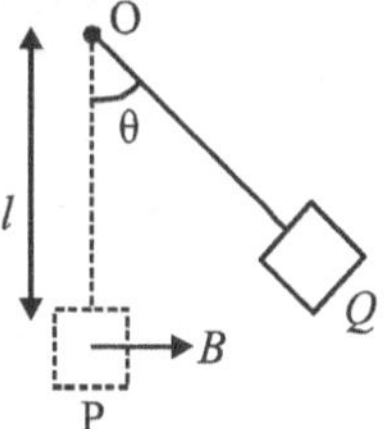

Faraday's Law states that the change of magnetic flux with any closed loop produces induced emf and current in the loop. Magnitude of current produced $\left\{ i = \dfrac{e}{R} = -\left(\dfrac{d\phi}{dt}\right)\dfrac{1}{R}\right\}$.

The cause of induced current is the rate of change of flux. Then using this concept in the situation where a wire frame of area 4×10^{-4} m^2 and resistance 10Ω is suspended from a thread 2 m long in a vertical plane. Now a horizontal magnetic field of 1 tesla is introduced and the arrangement is made to oscillate from its equilibrium position as shown in the figure.

15. The magnetic flux with loop will be maximum in the position

(a) P   (b) Q

(c) between P and Q   (d) $\theta = 45°$

16. For small angle θ, such that maximum displacement of $x_0 = 1$ cm and $\left(\theta_0 = \dfrac{x_0}{\ell}\right)$ find the induced e.m.f as a function of time 't' when $t = 0$ is equilibrium position

(a) $5 \times 10^{-9} \sin(10t)$ (b) $5\sqrt{5} \times 10^{-9} \sin(2\sqrt{5}t)$

(c) $5 \sin(\sqrt{10}t)$ (d) $10^{-6} \sin(5t)$

PARAGRAPH-2

A magnetic field $\vec{B} = \left(\dfrac{B_0 y}{a}\right)\hat{k}$ is into the

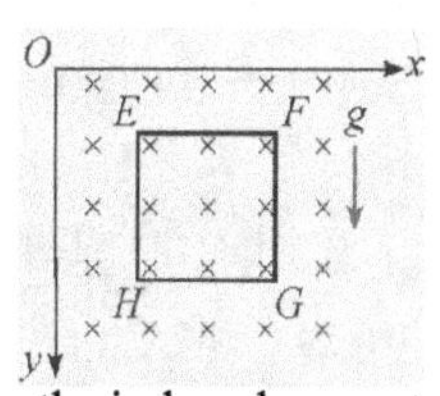

paper in the $+z$ direction. B_0 and a are positive constants. A square loop $EFGH$ of side a and mass m and resistance R, in xy-plane, start falling under the influence of gravity. Note the directions of x and y axes in figure.

17. If v is the speed of the loop at any time, the induced current in the loop is :

(a) $\dfrac{B_0 av}{R}$ anticlockwise   (b) $\dfrac{2B_0 av}{R}$ anticlockwise

(c) $\dfrac{2B_0 av}{R}$ clockwise   (d) $\dfrac{B_0 av}{R}$ anticlockwise

18. The terminal speed of the loop is

(a) $\dfrac{mgR}{B_0^2 a^2}$ (b) $\dfrac{mgR}{B_0 a}$ (c) $\dfrac{2mgR}{B_0^2 a^2}$ (d) $\dfrac{mgR}{2B_0^2 a^2}$

RESPONSE GRID

10. ⓐⓑⓒⓓ   11. ⓪①②③④⑤⑥⑦⑧⑨   12. ⓪①②③④⑤⑥⑦⑧⑨
13. ⓪①②③④⑤⑥⑦⑧⑨   14. ⓪①②③④⑤⑥⑦⑧⑨   15. ⓐⓑⓒⓓ
16. ⓐⓑⓒⓓ   17. ⓐⓑⓒⓓ   18. ⓐⓑⓒⓓ

Section V - Matrix-Match Type

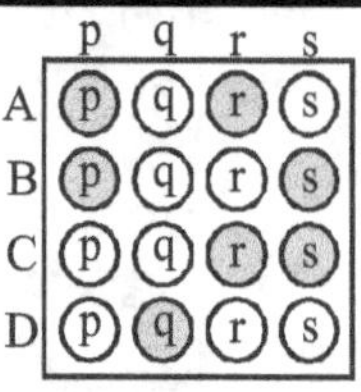

This section contains 2 questions. It contains statements given in two columns, which have to be matched. Statements in column I are labelled as A, B, C and D whereas statements in column II are labelled as p, q, r and s. The answers to these questions have to be appropriately bubbled as illustrated in the following example. If the correct matches are A-p, A-r, B-p, B-s, C-r, C-s and D-q, then the correctly bubbled matrix will look like the following:

19. Time varying magnetic field is present in a circular region of radius R. Then

Column-I

(A) If a rod is placed along the diameter of the magnetic field

(B) Induced electric field at a point within magnetic field (r < R)

(C) Induced electric field at a point out side the magnetic field (r > R)

(D) Induced electric field in a conductor has a component parallel to length of conductor

Column-II

(p) Electric field is perpendicular to the length of the rod.

(q) Constant along the length of conductor.

(r) $-\dfrac{r}{2}\dfrac{dB}{dt}$

(s) $-\dfrac{R^2}{2r}\dfrac{dB}{dt}$

20. **Column-I**

(A) A rod rotates in a uniform transverse magnetic field as shown, about hinge at O. Potential difference between points A and B

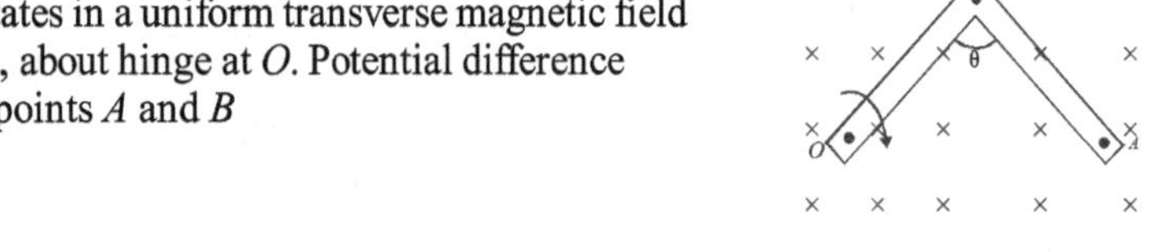

(B) A conducting loop is moved in a region of transverse constant magnetic field (infinite region), downward the plane of paper, as shown. Value of induced current i

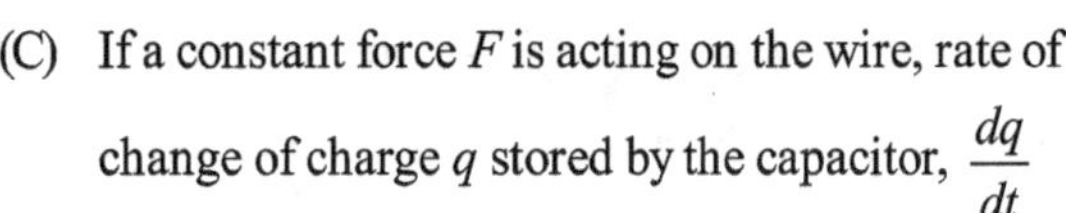

(C) If a constant force F is acting on the wire, rate of change of charge q stored by the capacitor, $\dfrac{dq}{dt}$

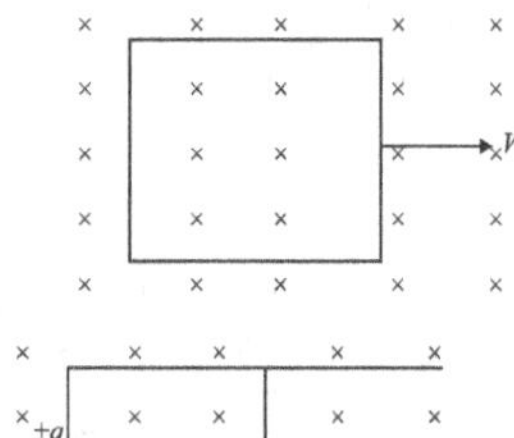

(D) A square loop is rotated about diagonal in a region of uniform magnetic field as shown. Value of i at an instant

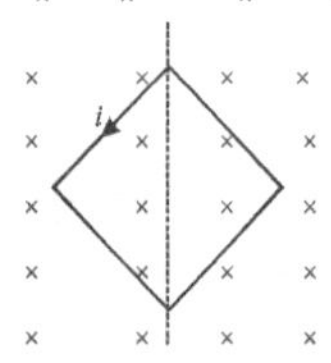

Column-II

(p) may be zero

(q) must be zero

(r) may be negative/positive

(s) must be positive

RESPONSE GRID	
19. A - p q r s ; B - p q r s ; C - p q r s ; D - p q r s	
20. A - p q r s ; B - p q r s ; C - p q r s ; D - p q r s	

DAILY PRACTICE PROBLEM DPP CP18 - PHYSICS

Total Questions	20	Total Marks	74
Attempted		Correct	
Incorrect		Net Score	
Cut-off Score	24	Qualifying Score	35

$$\text{Net Score} = \sum_{i=1}^{V}\left[\left(\text{correct}_i \times MM_i\right) - \left(In_i - NM_i\right)\right]$$

Space for Rough Work

Date : [ ]   Start Time : [ ]   End Time : [ ]

PHYSICS $\boxed{\textbf{CP19}}$

SYLLABUS : Alternating Current

Max. Marks : 74   **Time : 60 min.**

GENERAL INSTRUCTIONS

- The Daily Practice Problem Sheet contains 20 Questions divided into 5 sections.
- **Section I** has **5** MCQs with ONLY 1 Correct Option, **3** marks for each correct answer and **−1** for each incorrect answer.
- **Section II** has **4** MCQs with ONE or MORE THAN ONE Correct options.
- For each question, marks will be awarded in one of the following categories:
- Full marks: **+4** If only the bubble(s) corresponding to all the correct option(s) is (are) darkened.
- Partial marks: **+1** For darkening a bubble corresponding to each correct option provided NO INCORRECT option is darkened.
- Zero marks: If none of the bubbles is darkened.
- Negative marks: **−2** In all other cases.
- **Section III** has **4** Single Digit Integer Answer Type Questions, **3** marks for each Correct Answer and 0 marks in all other cases.
- **Section IV** has Comprehension/Matching Cum-Comprehension Type Questions having **5** MCQs with ONLY ONE correct option, **3** marks for each Correct Answer and 0 marks in all other cases.
- **Section V** has **2** Matching Type Questions, **2** mark for the correct matching of each row and 0 marks in all other cases.
- You have to evaluate your Response Grids yourself with the help of Solutions.

Section I - Straight Objective Type

This section contains 5 multiple choice questions. Each question has 4 choices (a), (b), (c) and (d), out of which **ONLY ONE** is correct.

1. In a series LCR circuit, the difference of the frequencies at which current amplitude falls to $\dfrac{1}{\sqrt{2}}$ of the current amplitude at resonance is

(a) $\dfrac{R}{2\pi L}$ (b) $\dfrac{R}{\pi L}$

(c) $\dfrac{2R}{\pi L}$ (d) $\dfrac{3R}{2\pi L}$

2. In figure given below if $Z_L = Z_c$ and reading of ammeter is 1A then the value of source voltage in volt.

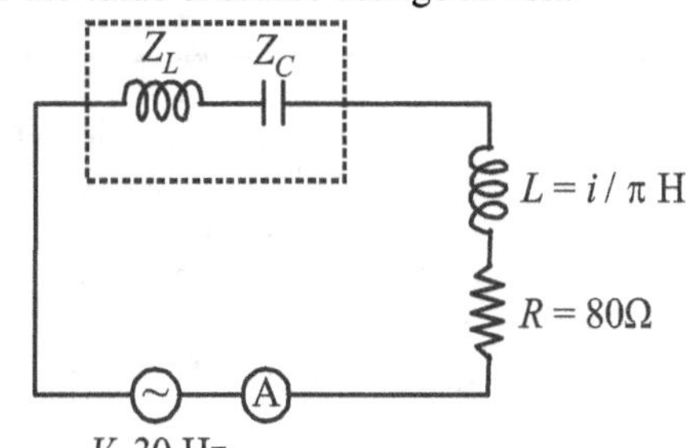

(a) 80   (b) 60
(c) 100   (d) 40

RESPONSE GRID	1. ⓐⓑⓒⓓ	2. ⓐⓑⓒⓓ

Space for Rough Work

3. A resistor of resistance R, capacitor of capacitance C and inductor of inductance L are connected in parallel to AC power source of voltage $\varepsilon_0 \sin \omega t$. The maximum current through the resistance is half of the maximum current through the power source. Then value of R is

(a) $\dfrac{\sqrt{3}}{\left|\omega C - \dfrac{1}{\omega L}\right|}$

(b) $\sqrt{3}\left|\dfrac{1}{\omega C} - \omega L\right|$

(c) $\sqrt{5}\left|\dfrac{1}{\omega C} - \omega L\right|$

(d) $2\left|\dfrac{1}{\omega C} - \omega L\right|$

4. In the circuits (i) and (ii) switches S_1 and S_2 are closed at $t = 0$ and are kept closed for a long time. The variation of current in the two circuits for $t \geq 0$ are roughly shown by figure (figures are schematic and not drawn to scale):

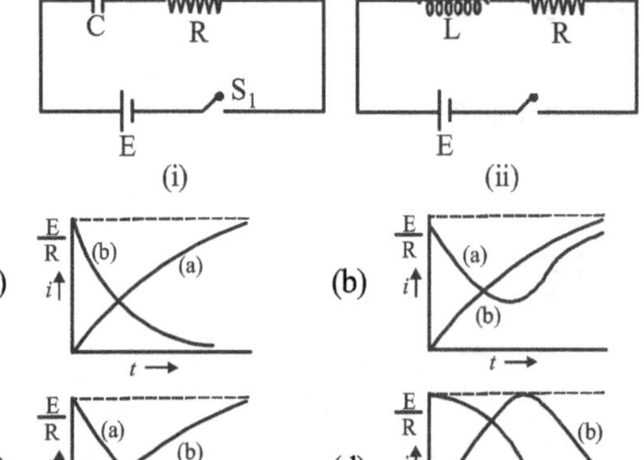

5. When resonance is produced in a series LCR circuit, then which of the following is not correct ?

(a) Current in the circuit is in phase with the applied voltage

(b) Inductive and capacitive reactances are equal

(c) If R is reduced, the voltage across capacitor will increase

(d) Impedance of the circuit is maximum

Section II - Multiple Correct Answer Type

This section contains 4 multiple correct answer(s) type questions. Each question has 4 choices (a), (b), (c) and (d), out of which **ONE OR MORE** is/are correct.

6. A series R– C circuit is connected to AC voltage source. Consider two cases; (A) when C is without a dielectric medium and (B) when C is filled with dielectric of constant 4. The current I_R through the resistor and voltage V_C across the capacitor are compared in the two cases. Which of the following is/are true?

(a) $I_R^A > I_R^B$ (b) $I_R^A < I_R^B$ (c) $V_C^A > V_C^B$ (d) $V_C^A < V_C^B$

7. Graph shows variation of source emf V and current i in a series RLC circuit, with time. Choose the correct option(s) from the following.

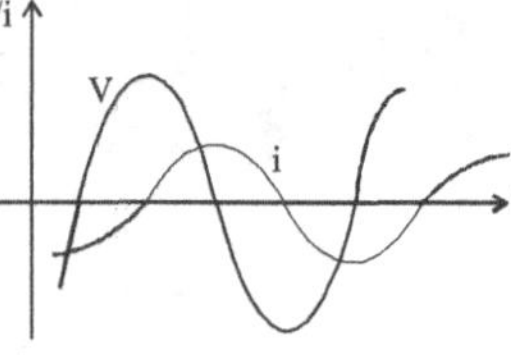

(a) To increase the rate at which energy is transferred to the resistive load, L should be decreased

(b) To increase the rate at which energy is transferred to the resistive load, C should be decreased

(c) The circuit is more inductive than capacitive

(d) The current leads the emf in the circuit

8. Two inductors of self-inductances L_1 and L_2 and of resistances R_1 and R_2 (not shown here) respectively, are connected in the circuit as shown in figure. At the instant $t = 0$, key K is closed. Choose the correct options for which the galvanometer will show zero deflection at all times after the key is closed.

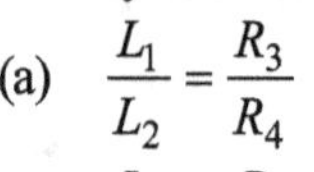

(a) $\dfrac{L_1}{L_2} = \dfrac{R_3}{R_4}$

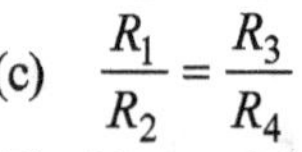

(b) $\dfrac{L_1}{L_2} = \dfrac{R_1}{R_2}$

(c) $\dfrac{R_1}{R_2} = \dfrac{R_3}{R_4}$

(d) None of these

9. Key is in position 2 for time t. Thereafter, it is in position 1. Resistance of the bulb and inductance of inductor are marked in the figure. Choose the correct alternative(s).

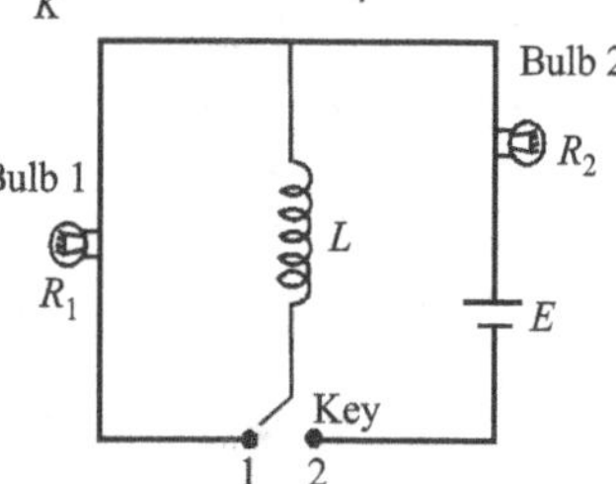

(a) Bulb 2 dies as soon as key is switched into position 1

(b) Time in which brightness of bulb 1 becomes half its maximum brightness does not depend on t

(c) In $t = \infty$, total heat produced in bulb 1 is $\dfrac{LE^2}{2R_2^2}$

(d) Ratio of maximum power consumption of bulbs depends on time

Section III - Integer Type

This section contains 4 questions. The answer to each of the questions is a single digit integer ranging from 0 to 9.

10. An inductor of inductance 100 mH is connected in series with a resistance, a variable capacitance and an AC source of frequency 2.0 kHz. If $(9x)$nF be the value of the capacitance so that maximum current may be drawn into the circuit then find the value of x.

<table>
<tr><td rowspan="2">**RESPONSE GRID**</td><td>**3.** ⓐⓑⓒⓓ</td><td>**4.** ⓐⓑⓒⓓ</td><td>**5.** ⓐⓑⓒⓓ</td><td>**6.** ⓐⓑⓒⓓ</td><td>**7.** ⓐⓑⓒⓓ</td></tr>
<tr><td>**8.** ⓐⓑⓒⓓ</td><td>**9.** ⓐⓑⓒⓓ</td><td colspan="3">**10.** ⓪①②③④⑤⑥⑦⑧⑨</td></tr>
</table>

11. In the given AC circuit, when switch S is at position 1, the source emf leads current by $\dfrac{\pi}{6}$.

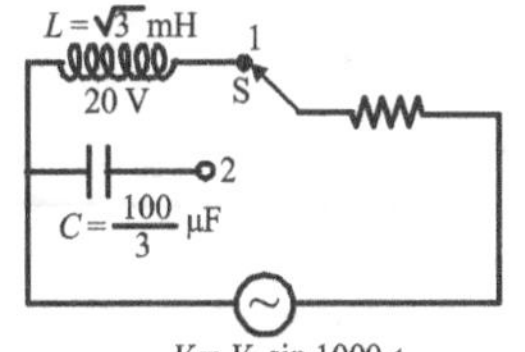

Now, if the switch is at position 2, then source e.m.f. leads current by $\dfrac{\pi}{x}$. Find the value of x.

12. A 100 V AC source of frequency 500 Hz is connected to LCR circuit with $L = 8.1$ mH, $C = 12.5$ μF and $R = 10\,\Omega$, all connected in series. The potential across the resistance is $25\,x$ V. Find the value of x.

13. A 60 Hz AC source of voltage 160 V impressed across an LR-circuit results in a current of 2 A. If the power dissipation is 200 W the maximum value of the back emf arising in the inductance is $25\,x$ V. Find the value of x.

Section IV - Comprehension/Matching Cum-Comprehension Type

Directions (Qs. 14 and 15) : Based upon the given paragraph, 2 multiple choice questions have to be answered. Each question has 4 choices (a), (b), (c) and (d), out of which **ONLY ONE** is correct.

PARAGRAPH

In a series L-R circuit, connected with a sinusoidal A.C. source, the maximum potential difference across L and R are respectively 3 volts and 4 volts.

14. At an instant the potential difference across resistor is 2 volts. The potential difference in volt, across the inductor at the same instant will be
    (a) $3\cos 30°$ (b) $3\cos 60°$
    (c) $3\cos 45°$ (d) $3\cos 15°$

15. At the same instant, the magnitude of the potential difference in volt, across the A.C. source may be
    (a) $4+3\sqrt{3}$ (b) $\dfrac{4+3\sqrt{3}}{2}$ (c) $1+\dfrac{\sqrt{3}}{2}$ (d) $2+\dfrac{\sqrt{3}}{2}$

Directions (Qs. 16-18) : This passage contains a table having 3 columns and 4 rows. Based on the table, there are three questions. Each question has four options (a), (b), (c) and (d) **ONLY ONE** of these four options is correct.

Alternating current in a circuit may be controlled by resistance, inductance and capacitance. Column II and Column III represents the phasor diagram and impedance of an AC-circuit containing different elements respectively. The applied emf (E) and current produced (I) may be represented as $E = E_0 \sin \omega t$ and $I = I_0 \sin(\omega t + \phi)$ with $I_0 = E_0/Z$ (Z = impedance) Here 'X' and 'Y' have different meaning with different units for different circuits shown in the column I.

Column I	Column II	Column III
I. X Resistance — Resistor only ($E = E_0 \sin \omega t$)	(i)	(P) $Z = \dfrac{1}{\omega X}$
II. X Capacitance — Capacitor only ($E = E_0 \sin \omega t$)	(ii)	(Q) $Z = X$
III. X Resistance Y Inductance — L-R series circuit ($E = E_0 \sin \omega t$)	(iii)	(R) $Z = \sqrt{x^2 + \omega^2 Y^2}$
IV. X Resistance Y Capacitance — C-R series circuit ($E = E_0 \sin \omega t$)	(iv)	(S) $Z = \sqrt{x^2 + \dfrac{1}{\omega^2 Y^2}}$

16. If the potential difference across the capacitor of capacitance Y unit shown in the C-R series circuit is $\dfrac{E}{\sqrt{(X\,Y\omega)^2+1}}$ then the correct matching for the circuit is

(a) IV (iii) Q (b) IV (iii) S (c) III (iv) S (d) IV (ii) P

17. Which of the following shows the correct matching for L-R series circuit?

(a) III (iii) R (b) III (iv) R (c) III (i) P (d) III (ii) Q

18. Which of the following is wrongly matched?

(a) I (ii) Q (b) II (i) P (c) IV (iv) R (d) IV (iii) S

Section V - Matrix-Match Type

This section contains 2 questions. It contains statements given in two columns, which have to be matched. Statements in column I are labelled as A, B, C and D whereas statements in column II are labelled as p, q, r and s. The answers to these questions have to be appropriately bubbled as illustrated in the following example. If the correct matches are A-p, A-r, B-p, B-s, C-r, C-s and D-q, then the correctly bubbled matrix will look like the following:

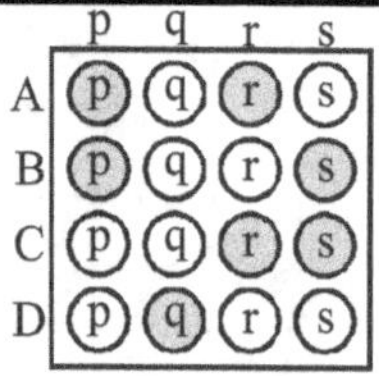

19. Consider the circuit shown in figure given below and match the columns.

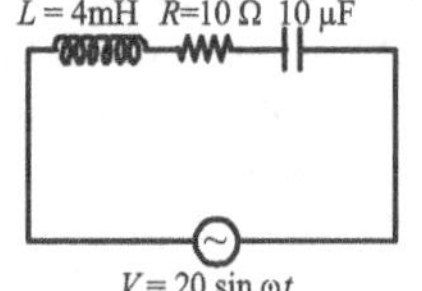

Column-I

(A) For $\omega = 5,000$ rad/sec

(B) For $\omega = 2,500$ rad/sec

(C) For $\omega = 75,00$ rad/sec

(D) For $\omega = 5,000$ rad/sec and $R = 20\Omega$ in place of 10Ω

Column-II

(p) The current in circuit leads the voltage

(q) The current and voltage in circuit are in same phase

(r) The peak current in circuit is less than $2A$

(s) Voltage in circuit leads the current.

20. In an LCR sereis circuit connected to an ac source, the supply voltage is $V = V_0 \sin\left(100\pi t + \dfrac{\pi}{6}\right)$. $V_L = 40\ V$, $V_R = 40V$, $Z = 5\Omega$ and $R = 4\Omega$. Match the two columns.

Column I

(A) Peak current (in A)

(B) V_0 (in volts)

(C) Effective value of applied voltage (in volts)

(D) X_C (in Ω)

Column II

(p) $10\sqrt{2}$

(q) $50\sqrt{2}$

(r) 50

(s) 1

<table>
<tr><td rowspan="3">RESPONSE GRID</td><td colspan="3">16. ⓐⓑⓒⓓ   17. ⓐⓑⓒⓓ   18. ⓐⓑⓒⓓ</td></tr>
<tr><td colspan="3">19. A - ⓟⓠⓡⓢ ; B - ⓟⓠⓡⓢ ; C - ⓟⓠⓡⓢ ; D - ⓟⓠⓡⓢ</td></tr>
<tr><td colspan="3">20. A - ⓟⓠⓡⓢ ; B - ⓟⓠⓡⓢ ; C - ⓟⓠⓡⓢ ; D - ⓟⓠⓡⓢ</td></tr>
</table>

DAILY PRACTICE PROBLEM DPP CP19 - PHYSICS

Total Questions	20	Total Marks	74
Attempted		Correct	
Incorrect		Net Score	
Cut-off Score	24	Qualifying Score	35

$$\text{Net Score} = \sum_{i=1}^{V}\left[\left(\text{correct}_i \times MM_i\right) - \left(In_i - NM_i\right)\right]$$

Space for Rough Work

Date : [ ] Start Time : [ ] End Time : [ ]

PHYSICS $\boxed{\text{CP20}}$

SYLLABUS : Electromagnetic Waves

Max. Marks : 74 **Time : 60 min.**

GENERAL INSTRUCTIONS

- The Daily Practice Problem Sheet contains 20 Questions divided into 5 sections.
  Section I has **6** MCQs with ONLY 1 Correct Option, **3** marks for each correct answer and **−1** for each incorrect answer.
  Section II has **4** MCQs with ONE or MORE THAN ONE Correct options.
  For each question, marks will be awarded in one of the following categories:
  Full marks: **+4** If only the bubble(s) corresponding to all the correct option(s) is (are) darkened.
  Partial marks: **+1** For darkening a bubble corresponding to each correct option provided NO INCORRECT option is darkened.
  Zero marks: If none of the bubbles is darkened.
  Negative marks: **−2** In all other cases.
  Section III has **4** Single Digit Integer Answer Type Questions, **3** marks for each Correct Answer and 0 marks in all other cases.
  Section IV has Comprehension Type Questions having **4** MCQs with ONLY ONE corect option, 3 marks for each Correct Answer and 0 marks in all other cases.
  Section V has **2** Matching Type Questions, **2** mark for the correct matching of each row and 0 marks in all other cases.
- You have to evaluate your Response Grids yourself with the help of Solutions.

Section I - Straight Objective Type

This section contains 6 multiple choice questions. Each question has 4 choices (a), (b), (c) and (d), out of which **ONLY ONE** is correct.

1. The energy of electromagnetic wave in vacuum is given by the relation

(a) $\dfrac{E^2}{2\varepsilon_0}+\dfrac{B^2}{2\mu_0}$ (b) $\dfrac{1}{2}\varepsilon_0 E^2+\dfrac{1}{2}\mu_0 B^2$

(c) $\dfrac{E^2+B^2}{c}$ (d) $\dfrac{1}{2}\varepsilon_0 E^2+\dfrac{B^2}{2\mu_0}$

2. The figure here gives the electric field of an electromagnetic wave at a certain point and a certain instant. The wave is transporting energy in the negative z-direction.

The direction of the magnetic field of the wave at that point and instant is

(a) $+$ ve x-direction
(b) $-$ve x-direction
(c) $+$ve z-direction
(d) $-$ve y-direction

3. A lamp emits monochromatic green light uniformly in all directions. The lamp is 3% efficient in converting electrical power to electromagnetic waves and consumes 100 W of power. The amplitude of the electric field associated with the electromagnetic radiation at a distance of 5 m from the lamp will be nearly:

(a) 1.34 V/m (b) 2.68 V/m (c) 4.02 V/m (d) 5.36 V/m

RESPONSE GRID	1. ⓐⓑⓒⓓ	2. ⓐⓑⓒⓓ	3. ⓐⓑⓒⓓ

———— Space for Rough Work ————

4. An electromagnetic wave going through vacuum is described by $E = E_0 \sin(kx - \omega t)$; $B = B_0 \sin(kx - \omega t)$. Which of the following equations is true?

(a) $E_0 k = B_0 \omega$
(b) $E_0 \omega = B_0 k$
(c) $E_0 B_0 = \omega k$
(d) $E_0 B_0 k = \omega$

5. An electromagnetic wave of frequency 1×10^{14} hertz is propagating along z-axis. The amplitude of electric field is 4 V/m. If $\varepsilon_0 = 8.8 \times 10^{-12}$ $C^2/N\text{-}m^2$, then average energy density of electric field will be:

(a) 35.2×10^{-10} J/m^3
(b) 35.2×10^{-11} J/m^3
(c) 35.2×10^{-12} J/m^3
(d) 35.2×10^{-13} J/m^3

6. An infinitely long thin wire carrying a uniform linear static charge density λ is placed along the z-axis (Fig.). The wire is set into motion along its length with a uniform velocity $\mathbf{v} = v\hat{k}_z$. Calculate the poynting vector $\mathbf{S}$ 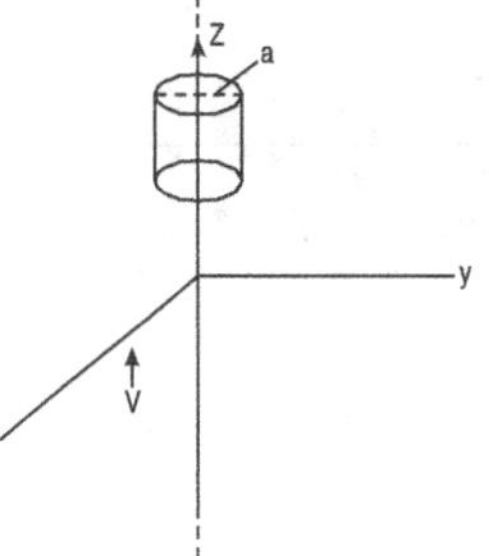

$$= \frac{1}{\mu_o} (\mathbf{E} \times \mathbf{B}).$$

(a) $\dfrac{-\lambda^2 v}{4\pi^2 \varepsilon_0 a^2} \hat{k}$
(b) $\dfrac{-\lambda^2 v}{4\pi^2 \varepsilon_0 a^2} \hat{j}$
(c) $\dfrac{\lambda^2 v}{4\pi^2 \varepsilon_0 a^2} \hat{k}$
(d) $\dfrac{\lambda^2 v}{4\pi^2 \varepsilon_0 a^2} \hat{j}$

Section II - Multiple Correct Answer Type

This section contains 4 multiple correct answer(s) type questions. Each question has 4 choices (a), (b), (c) and (d), out of which **ONE OR MORE** is/are correct.

7. Select the correct statement(s) from the following.
(a) Wavelength of microwaves is greater than that of ultraviolet rays.
(b) The wavelength of infrared rays is lesser than that of ultraviolet rays.
(c) The wavelength of microwaves is lesser than that of infrared rays
(d) Gamma ray has shortest wavelength in the electromagnetic spectrum

8. An electromagnetic wave of intensity I falls on a surface kept in vacuum and exerts radiation pressure P on it. Which of the following statements are true?
(a) Radiation pressure is I/c if the wave is totally absorbed
(b) Radiation pressure is I/c if the wave is totally reflected
(c) Radiation pressure is $2I/c$ if the wave is totally reflected
(d) Radiation preassure is $5I/c$ if the wave is totally absorbed

9. Select the correct statement(s) from the following.
(a) Displacement current comes into play in a region where electric field is changing with time.
(b) Displacement current $I_D = \varepsilon_0 \dfrac{\partial \phi E}{\phi t}$
(c) In case of a steady electric flux linked with a region the displacement current is minimum.
(d) $I_{rms} = \dfrac{2\varepsilon_0 E}{t}$

10. The amplitude of an electromagnetic wave in vacuum is doubled with no other changes made to the wave. As a result of this doubling of the amplitude, which of the following statements are incorrect?
(a) The speed of wave propagation changes only
(b) The frequency of the wave changes only
(c) The wavelength of the wave changes only
(d) The time period of the wave changes only

Section III - Integer Type

This section contains 4 questions. The answer to each of the questions is a single digit integer ranging from 0 to 9.

11. The electric field associated with an e.m. wave in vacuum is given by $\vec{E} = \hat{i}\, 40 \cos (kz - 6 \times 10^8 t)$, where E, z and t are in volt/m, meter and seconds respectively. Find the value of wave vector k in m^{-1}.

RESPONSE	4. (a)(b)(c)(d)	5. (a)(b)(c)(d)	6. (a)(b)(c)(d)	7. (a)(b)(c)(d)	8. (a)(b)(c)(d)
GRID	9. (a)(b)(c)(d)	10. (a)(b)(c)(d)	11. (0)(1)(2)(3)(4)(5)(6)(7)(8)(9) 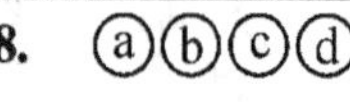		

Space for Rough Work

12. If the velocity of light in free space is 3×10^8 m/sec then the value of wavelength of electromagnetic wave of frequency 2×10^6 Hz is 25 x m. Find the value of x.

13. A light beam travelling in the x-direction is described by the electric field $E_y = 300 \sin \omega \left(t - \dfrac{x}{c} \right)$. An electron is constrained to move along the y-direction with a speed of 2.0×10^7 m/s. If ratio of the maximum electric force and the maximum magnetic force on the electron is $5x \times 10^{10}$. Find the value of x

14. A laser beam has intensity $2.5 \times 10^{14} \dfrac{W}{m^2}$. If the amptitude of magnetic field in the beam is $16\,k \times 10^{-2}$ T. Find the value of k

---

Section IV - Comprehension Type

Directions (Qs. 15-18) : Based upon the given paragraphs, 4 multiple choice questions have to be answered. Each question has 4 choices (a), (b), (c) and (d), out of which **ONLY ONE** is correct.

PARAGRAPH-1

A parallel-plate capacitor has square plate 1.0 m of a side as shown in figure. A current of 2.0 A displacement current charges the capacitor, producing a uniform electric field $\vec{E}$ between the plates, with $\vec{E}$ perpendicular to the plates.

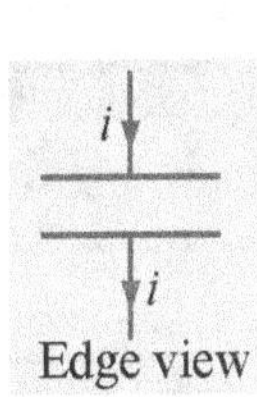

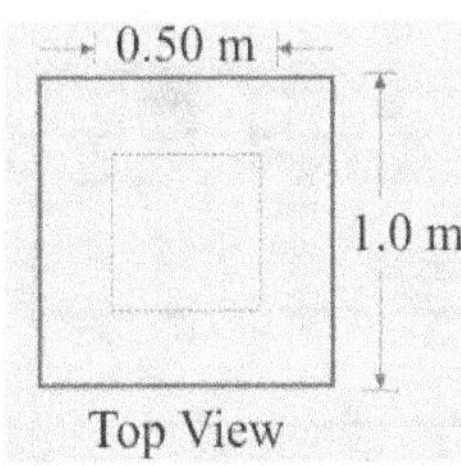

15. The value of dE/dt in the region

   (a) $1.1 \times 10^{11}\ V/m$ (b) $2.1 \times 10^{11}\ V/m$

   (c) $2.3 \times 10^{11}\ V/m$ (d) $3.4 \times 10^{11}\ V/m$

16. The value of $\oint \vec{B}.d\vec{\ell}$ around the square dashed path

   (a) zero   (b) $0.63\ \mu$T-m

   (c) $0.75\ \mu$T-m   (d) $0.83\ \mu$Tm

PARAGRAPH-2

An EM-wave consists of oscillating electric and magnetic fields. An EM-wave travelling along an x-axis has an electric field $\vec{E}$ and a magnetic field $\vec{B}$ with magnitudes which depend on x and t :

$$E = E_0 \sin(kx - \omega t) \quad \text{and} \quad B = B_0 \sin(kx - \omega t).$$

Electric field induces the magnetic field and vice-versa. The speed of EM-waves is c, which can be written as

$$c = \frac{E}{B} = \frac{1}{\sqrt{\mu_0\, \in_0}}$$

17. The magnetic field in a plane electromagnetic wave is given by $B_y = 2 \times 10^{-7} \sin (0.5 \times 10^3 x + 1.5 \times 10^{11} t)$ T. What is the frequency of the wave?

   (a) 23.9 GHz   (b) 29.3 GHz

   (c) 32.9 GHz   (d) 39.2 GHz

18. The correct expression for the electric field is

   (a) $E_x = 60 \sin (0.5 \times 10^3 x + 1.5 \times 10^{11} t)$ V/m

   (b) $E_z = 60 \sin (0.5 \times 10^3 x + 1.5 \times 10^{11} t)$ V/m

   (c) $E_y = 30 \sin (5 \times 10^3 x + 1.5 \times 10^{11} t)$ V/m

   (d) $E_z = 30 \sin (5 \times 10^3 x + 1.5 \times 10^{11} t)$ V/m

---

RESPONSE GRID		
12. ⓪①②③④⑤⑥⑦⑧⑨	**13.** ⓪①②③④⑤⑥⑦⑧⑨	
14. ⓪①②③④⑤⑥⑦⑧⑨	**15.** ⓐⓑⓒⓓ **16.** ⓐⓑⓒⓓ **17.** ⓐⓑⓒⓓ	
18. ⓐⓑⓒⓓ		

Space for Rough Work

Section V - Matrix-Match Type

This section contains 2 questions. It contains statements given in two columns, which have to be matched. Statements in column I are labelled as A, B, C and D whereas statements in column II are labelled as p, q, r and s. The answers to these questions have to be appropriately bubbled as illustrated in the following example. If the correct matches are A-p, A-r, B-p, B-s, C-r, C-s and D-q, then the correctly bubbled matrix will look like the following:

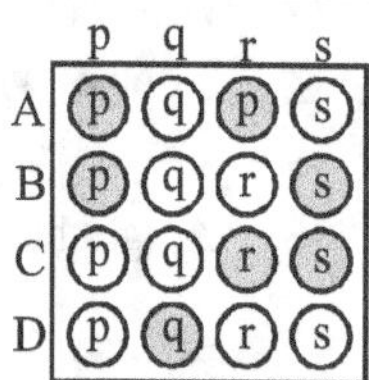

19. Match the Column-I (Phenomenon associated with electromagnetic radiation) with Column-II (Part of electromagnetic spectrum)

Column I
(A) Doublet of sodium
(B) Wavelength corresponding to temperature associated with the isotropic radiation filling all space
(C) Wavelength emitted by atomic hydrogen in interstellar space
(D) Wavelength of radiation arising from two close energy levels in hydrogen

Column II
(p) Visible radiation
(q) Microwave
(r) Short radio wave
(s) X-rays

20. Match the Column-I (Wavelength range of electromagnetic spectrum) with Column-II (Method of production of these waves).

Column I
(A) $700\,nm$ to $1\,mm$
(B) $1\,nm$ to $400\,nm$
(C) $< 10^{-3}\,nm$
(D) $1\,mm$ to $0.1\,m$

Column II
(p) Vibration of atoms and molecules.
(q) Inner shell electrons in atoms moving from higher energy level to a lower level.
(r) Radioactive decay of the nucleus.
(s) Magnetron valve.

RESPONSE GRID	
19. A - p q r s ; B - p q r s ; C - p q r s ; D - p q r s	
20. A - p q r s ; B - p q r s ; C - p q r s ; D - p q r s	

DAILY PRACTICE PROBLEM DPP CP20 - PHYSICS

Total Questions	20	Total Marks	74
Attempted		Correct	
Incorrect		Net Score	
Cut-off Score	24	Qualifying Score	35

$$\text{Net Score} = \sum_{i=1}^{V}\left[\left(\text{correct}_i \times MM_i\right) - \left(In_i - NM_i\right)\right]$$

Space for Rough Work

Date :

Start Time :

End Time :

PHYSICS $\boxed{\text{CP21}}$

SYLLABUS : Ray Optics and Optical Instruments

Max. Marks : 74

Time : 60 min.

GENERAL INSTRUCTIONS

- The Daily Practice Problem Sheet contains 20 Questions divided into 5 sections.
  Section I has **5** MCQs with ONLY 1 Correct Option, **3** marks for each correct answer and **−1** for each incorrect answer.
  Section II has **4** MCQs with ONE or MORE THAN ONE Correct options.
  For each question, marks will be awarded in one of the following categories:
  Full marks: **+4** If only the bubble(s) corresponding to all the correct option(s) is (are) darkened.
  Partial marks: **+1** For darkening a bubble corresponding to each correct option provided NO INCORRECT option is darkened.
  Zero marks: If none of the bubbles is darkened.
  Negative marks: **−2** In all other cases.
  Section III has **4** Single Digit Integer Answer Type Questions, **3** marks for each Correct Answer and 0 marks in all other cases.
  Section IV has Comprehension/Matching Cum-Comprehension Type Questions having **5** MCQs with ONLY ONE correct option, **3** marks for each Correct Answer and 0 marks in all other cases.
  Section V has **2** Matching Type Questions, **2** mark for the correct matching of each row and 0 marks in all other cases.
- You have to evaluate your Response Grids yourself with the help of Solutions.

Section I - Straight Objective Type

This section contains 5 multiple choice questions. Each question has 4 choices (a), (b), (c) and (d), out of which **ONLY ONE** is correct.

1. A thin convex lens made from crown glass $\left(\mu = \dfrac{3}{2}\right)$ has focal length f. When it is measured in two different liquids having refractive indices $\dfrac{4}{3}$ and $\dfrac{5}{3}$, it has the focal lengths f_1 and f_2 respectively. The correct relation between the focal lengths is:

(a) $f_1 = f_2 < f$

(b) $f_1 > f$ and f_2 becomes negative

(c) $f_2 > f$ and f_1 becomes negative

(d) f_1 and f_2 both become negative

2. Light is incident from a medium into air at two possible angles of incidence (A) 20° and (B) 40°. In the medium, light travels 3.0 cm in 0.2 ns. The ray will :

(a) suffer total internal reflection in both cases (A) and (B)

(b) suffer total internal reflection in case (B) only

(c) have partial reflection and partial transmission in case (B)

(d) have 100% transmission in case (A)

RESPONSE GRID   1. ⓐⓑⓒⓓ   2. ⓐⓑⓒⓓ

Space for Rough Work

3. A transparent sphere of radius R has a cavity of radius $R/2$ as shown in figure. Find the refractive index of the sphere if a parallel beam of light falling on left surface focuses at point P.

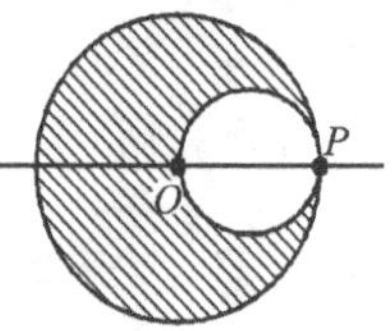

(a) $\mu = \dfrac{3+\sqrt{5}}{2}$ (b) $\mu = \dfrac{3-\sqrt{5}}{2}$

(c) $\mu = 3+\sqrt{5}$ (d) $\mu = \dfrac{1+\sqrt{5}}{2}$

4. A point object is located at a distance 15cm. from the pole of a concave mirror of focal length 10cm on its principal axis is moving with a velocity $(8\hat{i}+11\hat{j})$ cm/s and velocity of mirror is $(4\hat{i}+2\hat{j})$ cm/s as shown. If $\vec{v}$ is the velocity of image, then find the value of $|\vec{v}|$ in (cm/s).

(a) 20

(b) 30

(c) 10

(d) 40

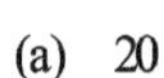
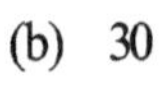

5. If the optical axis of convex and concave lenses are separated by a distance 5 mm as shown in the figure. Find the coordinate of the final image formed by the combination if parallel beam of light is incident on convex lens, origin is at optical centre.

(a) (25 cm, 0.5 cm)

(b) (25 cm, 0.25 cm)

(c) (25 cm, – 0.5 cm)

(d) (25 cm, – 0.25 cm)

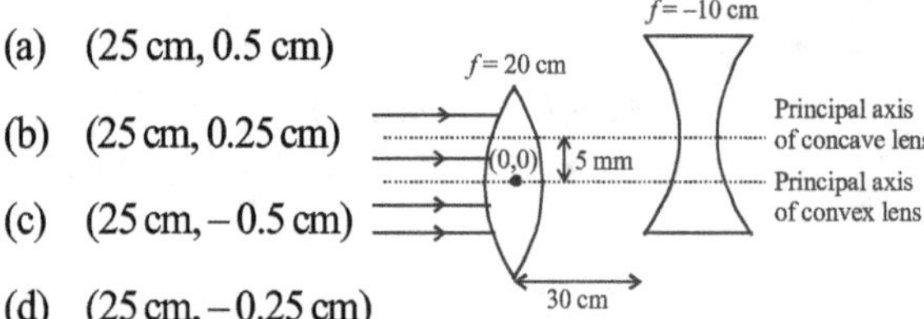

Section II - Multiple Correct Answer Type

This section contains 4 multiple correct answer(s) type questions. Each question has 4 choices (a), (b), (c) and (d), out of which **ONE OR MORE** is/are correct.

6. A plano–convex lens is made of a material of refractive index n. When a small object is placed 30 cm away in front of the curved surface of the lens, an image of double the size of the object is produced. Due to reflection from the convex surface of the lens, another faint image is observed at a distance of 10 cm away from the lens. Which of the following statement(s) is(are) true?

(a) The refractive index of the lens is 2.5

(b) The radius of curvature of the convex surface is 45 cm

(c) The faint image is erect and real

(d) The focal length of the lens is 20 cm

7. An object of length 2 cm is placed perpendicular to the principal axis of a convex lens of focal length 12 cm. If the object is at a distance of 8 cm from lens, then

(a) height of the image is 6 cm

(b) image formed is erect

(c) magnification is 3

(d) image distance is 24 cm

8. Remote objects are viewed through a converging lens with a focal length $F = 9$ cm placed at a distance $a = 36$cm in front of the eye. Assume that the radius r of the pupil is approximately 1.5 mm. Choose the correct options.

(a) The minimum radius of the screen that should be placed behind the lens so that the entire field of view is covered is 0.5mm.

(b) The minimum radius of the screen that should be placed behind the lens so that the entire field of view is covered is 1.0 mm.

(c) The screen must be placed in the plane S with its centre at point B.

(d) The screen must be placed perpendicular to the plane S with its centre at point B.

9. A planet is observed by an astronomical refracting telescope having an objective of focal length 16 m and an eyepiece of focal length 2 cm.

(a) The distance between the objective and the eyepiece is 16.02 m

(b) The angular magnification of the planet is – 800

(c) The image of the planet is inverted

(d) The objective is larger then the eyepiece

Section III - Integer Type

This section contains 4 questions. The answer to each of the questions is a single digit integer ranging from 0 to 9.

10. The convex surface of a thin concavo-convex lens of glass of refractive index 1.5 has a radius of curvature 20 cm. The concave surface has a radius of curvature 60 cm. The convex side is silvered and placed on a horizontal surface.

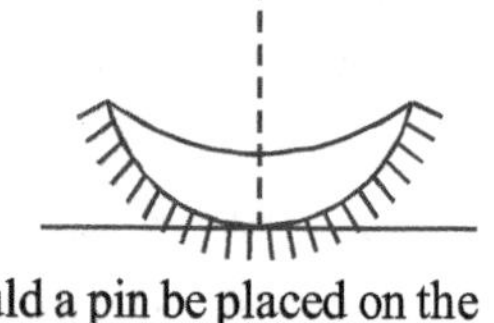

At 3x distance (in centimetre) should a pin be placed on the optical axis such that its image is formed at the same place. Calculate the value of x.

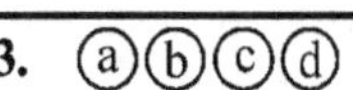

RESPONSE GRID	**3.** ⓐⓑⓒⓓ	**4.** ⓐⓑⓒⓓ	**5.** ⓐⓑⓒⓓ	**6.** ⓐⓑⓒⓓ	
	7. ⓐⓑⓒⓓ	**8.** ⓐⓑⓒⓓ	**9.** ⓐⓑⓒⓓ	**10.** ⓪①②③④⑤⑥⑦⑧⑨	

11. AB and CD are surfaces of two slabs as shown in figure. The medium between the slabs has refractive index 2, refractive index of slab above AB is $\sqrt{2}$ and below CD is $\sqrt{3}$. $(10x)°$ is the minimum angle of incidence, so that the ray is totally reflected by both the slabs. Find the value of x.

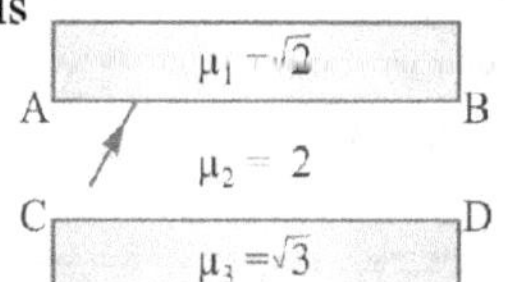

12. A thin plano-convex lens of focal length f is split into two halves and one of the halves is shifted along the optical axis.

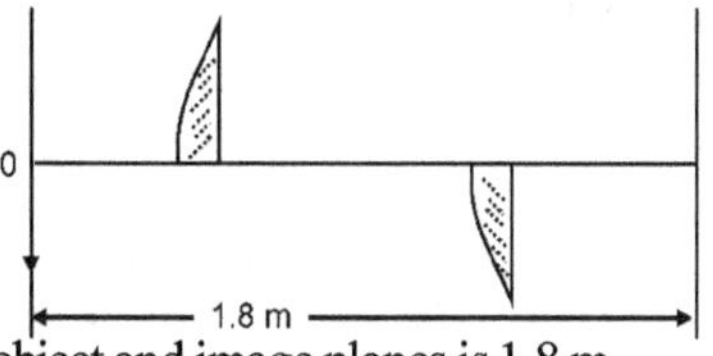

The separation between object and image planes is 1.8 m. The magnification of the image formed by one of the half-lenses is 2. If $\dfrac{x}{5}$ is the focal-length of the lens (in m) then find the value of x.

13. A telescope has an objective of focal length 50 cm and an eye piece of focal length 5 cm. The least distance of distinct vision is 25 cm. The telescope is focussed for distinct vision on a scale 200 cm away from the objective. Calculate x, if $\dfrac{425}{x}$ is the separation (in cm) between the objective and the eye-piece.

Section IV - Comprehension/Matching Cum- Comprehension Type

Directions (Qs. 14 and 15) : Based upon the given paragraph, 2 multiple choice questions have to be answered. Each question has 4 choices (a), (b), (c) and (d), out of which **ONLY ONE** is correct.

PARAGRAPH

A concave mirror of radius of curvature 20cm is shown in the figure. A circular disc of diameter $(1.0 + 0.2t)$ cm is placed on the principal axis of mirror with its plane perpendicular to the principal axis at a distance 15cm from the pole of the mirror.

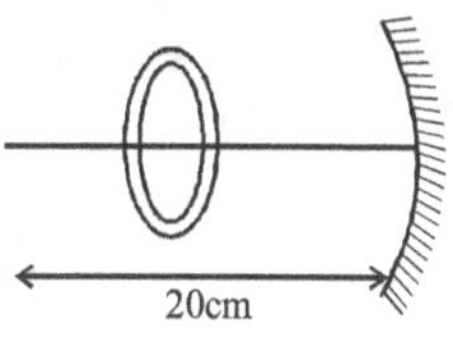

14. The image formed by the mirror will be in the shape of a
    (a) circular disc
    (b) elliptical disc with major axis horizontal
    (c) elliptical disc with major axis vertical
    (d) distorted disc

15. In the above question, the area of the image of the disc at $t = 1$ second is
    (a) $1.2\,\pi\,cm^2$ (b) $1.44\,\pi\,cm^2$
    (c) $1.52\,\pi\,cm^2$ (d) $1.64\,\pi\,cm^2$

Directions (Qs. 16-18) : This passage contains a table having 3 columns and 4 rows. Based on the table, there are three questions. Each question has four options (a), (b), (c) and (d) **ONLY ONE** of these four options is correct.

A lens of focal length f is cut into two equal parts as shown in figure. 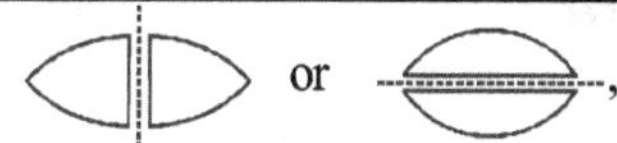 or

Column I shows different combinations of these two parts. Column II gives equivalent focal length of the combination and column III the corresponding power.

Column I		Column II		Column III	
I.		(i)	∞	(P)	1/2f
II.		(ii)	f/2	(Q)	0
III.		(iii)	f	(R)	1/f
IV.		(iv)	2f	(S)	2/f

16. If focal length of complete lens is f, then the correct matching is
    (a) III (iii) R   (b) III (ii) R   (c) III (i) R   (d) III (ii) Q

17. If focal length of the complete lens is f = 10cm, then focal length of the combination shown in figure Column I (IV) is 10cm. Which of the following is the correct matching satisfying the above condition?
    (a) IV (iii) R   (b) IV (i) R   (c) IV (ii) S   (d) III (i) Q

18. Which of the following options shows the correct matching?
    (a) I (ii) S   (b) II (i) Q   (c) III (iv) R   (d) Both (a) and (b)

Space for Rough Work

Section V - Matrix-Match Type

This section contains 2 questions. It contains statements given in two columns, which have to be matched. Statements in column I are labelled as A, B, C and D whereas statements in column II are labelled as p, q, r and s. The answers to these questions have to be appropriately bubbled as illustrated in the following example. If the correct matches are A-p, A-r, B-p, B-s, C-r, C-s and D-q, then the correctly bubbled matrix will look like the following:

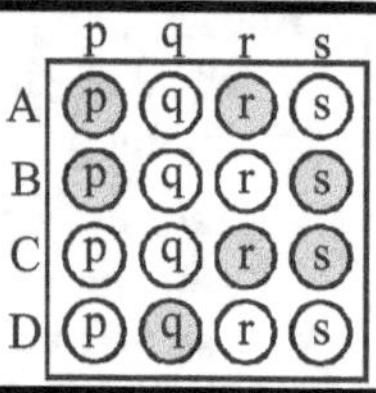

19. A convex lens of refractive index μ_2 is kept in a medium of refractive index μ_1 as shown.

Match the two columns:

Column-I

(A) On increasing value of μ_1 lens will be

(B) If $\mu_1 > \mu_2$

(C) When lens is cut into two parts along yy', then for any one part

(D) μ_1 is increased but $\mu_1 < \mu_2$

Column-II

(p) $|f|$ increases and lens will be converging

(q) $|f|$ may decrease or increase and lens will be diverging

(r) $|f|$ increases and nature of lens remains unchanged

(s) $|f|$ increases then decreases

20. A ray of light strikes at the boundary separating two media at angle θ. μ_1 and μ_2 are refractive indices of media with $(\mu_2 > \mu_1)$.

Column I

(A) When $\theta < \sin^{-1}\left(\dfrac{\mu_1}{\mu_2}\right)$ then deviation in the path of ray is

(B) Maximum deviation in the path of ray for refraction at boundary

(C) Maximum deviation in the path of ray for reflection at the boundary

(D) Deviation in the path at grazing angle of incidence

Column II

(p) $\dfrac{\pi}{2} - \sin^{-1}\left(\dfrac{\mu_1}{\mu_2}\right)$

(q) $\pi - 2\sin^{-1}\left(\dfrac{\mu_1}{\mu_2}\right)$

(r) Zero

(s) $\sin^{-1}\left(\dfrac{\mu_2}{\mu_1}\sin\theta\right) - \theta$

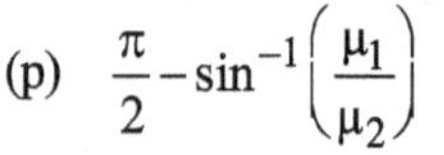

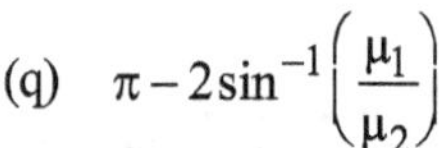

RESPONSE GRID	
19. A - (p)(q)(r)(s); B - (p)(q)(r)(s); C - (p)(q)(r)(s); D - (p)(q)(r)(s)	
20. A - (p)(q)(r)(s); B - (p)(q)(r)(s); C - (p)(q)(r)(s); D - (p)(q)(r)(s)	

DAILY PRACTICE PROBLEM DPP CP21 - PHYSICS

Total Questions	20	Total Marks	74
Attempted		Correct	
Incorrect		Net Score	
Cut-off Score	24	Qualifying Score	35

$$\text{Net Score} = \sum_{i=1}^{V}\left[\left(\text{correct}_i \times MM_i\right) - \left(In_i - NM_i\right)\right]$$

Date :   **Start Time :**   **End Time :**

PHYSICS $\boxed{\text{CP22}}$

SYLLABUS : Wave Optics

Max. Marks : 74   **Time : 60 min.**

GENERAL INSTRUCTIONS

- The Daily Practice Problem Sheet contains 20 Questions divided into 5 sections.

  Section I has **6** MCQs with ONLY 1 Correct Option, **3** marks for each correct answer and **–1** for each incorrect answer.

  Section II has **4** MCQs with ONE or MORE THAN ONE Correct options.

  For each question, marks will be awarded in one of the following categories:

  Full marks: **+4** If only the bubble(s) corresponding to all the correct option(s) is (are) darkened.

  Partial marks: **+1** For darkening a bubble corresponding to each correct option provided NO INCORRECT option is darkened.

  Zero marks: If none of the bubbles is darkened.

  Negative marks: **–2** In all other cases.

  Section III has **4** Single Digit Integer Answer Type Questions, **3** marks for each Correct Answer and 0 marks in all other cases.

  Section IV has Comprehension Type Questions having **4** MCQs with ONLY ONE corect option, 3 marks for each Correct Answer and 0 marks in all other cases.

  Section V has **2** Matching Type Questions, **2** mark for the correct matching of each row and 0 marks in all other cases.

- You have to evaluate your Response Grids yourself with the help of Solutions.

Section I - Straight Objective Type

This section contains 6 multiple choice questions. Each question has 4 choices (a), (b), (c) and (d), out of which **ONLY ONE** is correct.

1. In Young's double slit experiment, the distance between slits and the screen is 1.0 m and monochromatic light of 600 nm is being used. A person standing near the slits is looking at the fringe pattern. When the separation between the slits is varied, the interference pattern disappears for a particular distance d_0 between the slits. If the angular resolution of the eye is $\dfrac{1°}{60}$, the value of d_0 is close to :

   (a) 1 mm   (b) 3 mm   (c) 2 mm   (d) 4 mm

2. Two beams, A and B, of plane polarized light with mutually perpendicular planes of polarization are seen through a polaroid. From the position when the beam A has maximum intensity (and beam B has zero intensity), a rotation of polaroid through 30° makes the two beams appear equally bright. If the initial intensities of the two beams are I_A and I_B respectively, then $\dfrac{I_A}{I_B}$ equals:

   (a) 3   (b) $\dfrac{3}{2}$

   (c) 1   (d) $\dfrac{1}{3}$

RESPONSE GRID	1. ⓐⓑⓒⓓ 2. ⓐⓑⓒⓓ

Space for Rough Work

3. The slits $S_1 - S_2$ is illuminated by a light source S emitting light of wavelength λ. The slits are separated by a distance d. A plane mirror is placed at a distance D in front of the slits and a screen is placed at a distance 2D behind the slits. The screen receives light reflected only by the plane mirror. The fringe-width of the interference pattern on the screen is

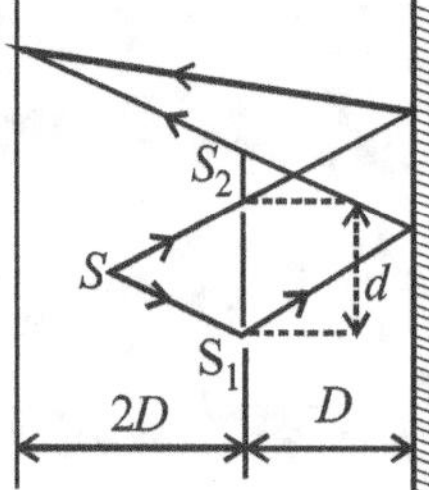

(a) $\dfrac{D\lambda}{d}$ (b) $\dfrac{2D\lambda}{d}$ (c) $\dfrac{3D\lambda}{d}$ (d) $\dfrac{4D\lambda}{d}$

4. In a *YDSE* experiment, if a slab whose refractive index can be varied is placed in front of one of the slits then the variation of resultant intensity at mid-point of screen with 'μ' will be best represented by ($\mu \geq 1$). [Assume slits of equal width and there is no absorption by slab; mid point of screen is the point where waves interfere with zero phase difference in absence of slab]

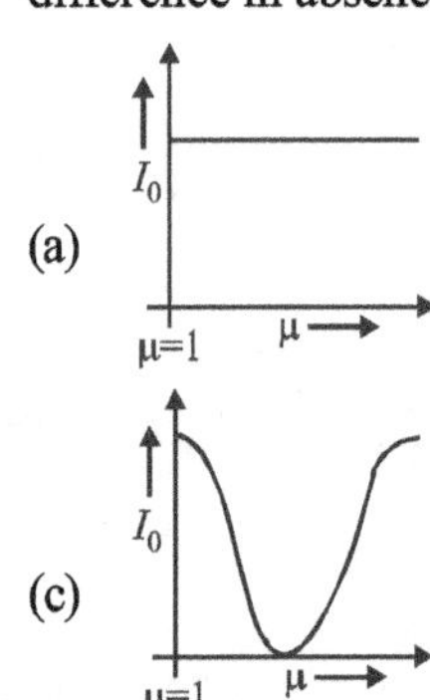
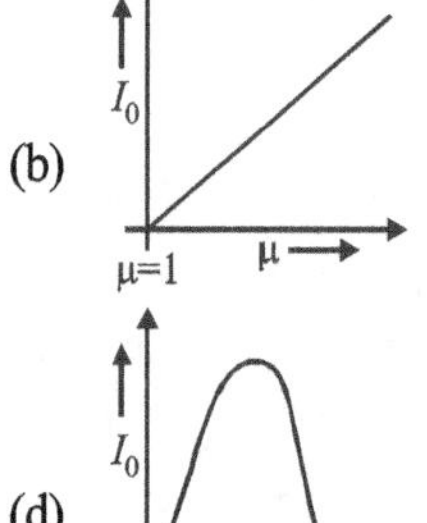

5. A broad source of light ($I = 680$ nm) illuminates normally two glass plates 120 mm long that touch at one end and are separated by a wire 0.034 mm in diameter at the other end.

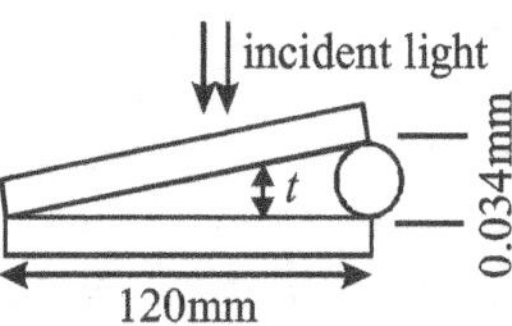

The total number of bright fringes that appear over the 120 mm distance is –

(a) 50   (b) 100   (c) 200   (d) 400

6. The contrast in the fringes in an interference pattern depends on
(a) fringe width
(b) wavelength
(c) intensity ratio of the sources
(d) distance between the slits

Section II - Multiple Correct Answer Type

This section contains 4 multiple correct answer(s) type questions. Each question has 4 choices (a), (b), (c) and (d), out of which **ONE OR MORE** is/are correct.

7. If one of the slits of a standard Young's double slit experiment is covered by a thin parallel sided glass slab so that it transmits only one half the light intensity of the other, then
(a) the fringe pattern will get shifted towards the covered slit
(b) the fringe pattern will get shifted away from the covered slit
(c) the bright fringes will become less bright and the dark ones will become more bright
(d) the fringe width will remain unchanged

8. Two point monochromatic and coherent sources of light of wavelength λ are placed on the dotted line in front of an infinite screen. The source emit waves in phase with each other. The distance between S_1 and S_2 is d while their distance from the screen is much larger. Then

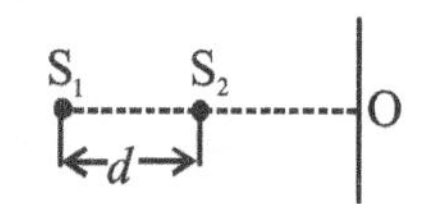

(a) if d is $\dfrac{3\lambda}{2}$, at O minima will be observed
(b) if d is $\dfrac{11\lambda}{6}$, then intensity at O will be $\dfrac{3}{4}$ of maximum intensity
(c) If d is 3λ, O will be a maxima
(d) if d is $\dfrac{7\lambda}{6}$, the intensity at O will be $\dfrac{3}{4}$ of maximum intensity

9. In the Young's double slit experiment, the interference pattern is found to have an intensity ratio between the bright and dark fringes as 9. This implies that
(a) the intensities at the screen due to the two slits are 5 units and 4 units respectively
(b) the intensities at the screen due to the two slits are 4 units and 1 units respectively
(c) the amplitude ratio is 3
(d) the amplitude ratio is 2

Space for Rough Work

10. If screen is shifted in x direction away from source, then which of the following is incorrect?

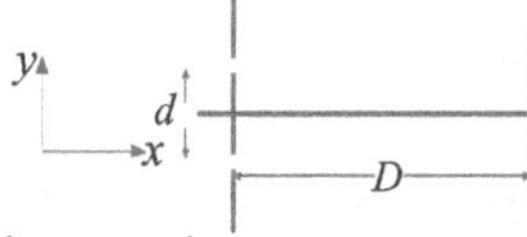

(a) Central maxima is shifted along y-axis
(b) Position of all maximas except the central maxima change
(c) Fringe width remains constant
(d) Angular width changes due to shifting

Section III - Integer Type

This section contains 4 questions. The answer to each of the questions is a single digit integer ranging from 0 to 9.

11. In Young's experiment, the source is red light of wavelength 7×10^{-7} m. When a thin glass plate of refractive index 1.5 at this wavelength is put in the path of one of the interfering beams, the central bright fringe shifts by 10^{-3} m to the position previously occupied by the 5th bright fringe. Find the thickness (in μm) of the plate.

12. Screen S is illuminated by two point sources A and B. Another source C sends a parallel beam of light towards point P on the screen (see figure). Line AP is normal to the screen and the lines AP, BP and CP are in one plane. The distance AP, BP and CP are 3 m, 1.5 m and 1.5 m respectively. The radiant powers of sources A and B are 90 watts and 180 watts respectively. The beam from C is of intensity 20 watt/m^2. Calculate x if $7x$ is the intensity (in W/m^2) at P on the screen.

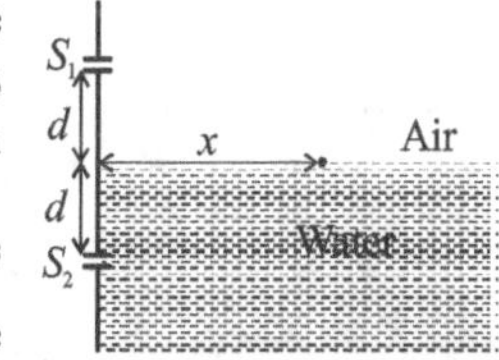

13. In *YDSE* a light containing two wavelengths 500 nm and 700 nm are used. $\dfrac{7}{x}$ is the minimum distance (in mm) where maxima of two wavelengths coincide. Given $D/d = 10^3$, where D is the distance between the slits and the screen and d is the distance between the slits. Find the value of x.

14. A Young's double slit interference arrangement with slits S_1 and S_2 is immersed in water (refractive index $= \dfrac{4}{3}$) as shown in the figure. The positions of maximum on the surface of water are given by $x^2 = p^2m^2\lambda^2 - d^2$, where λ is the wavelength of light in air (refractive index=1), $2d$ is the separation between the slits and m is an integer. The value of p is

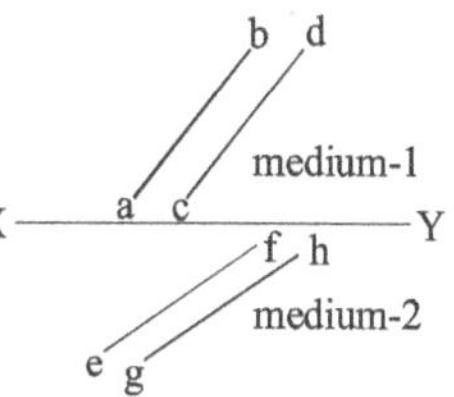

Section IV - Comprehension Type

Directions (Qs. 15-18) : Based upon the given paragraphs, 4 multiple choice questions have to be answered. Each question has 4 choices (a), (b), (c) and (d), out of which **ONLY ONE** is correct.

PARAGRAPH-1

For the Young's double slit experiment a monochromatic light source is used whose wavelength is λ strikes on the slits, separated by distance d as shown in the figure.

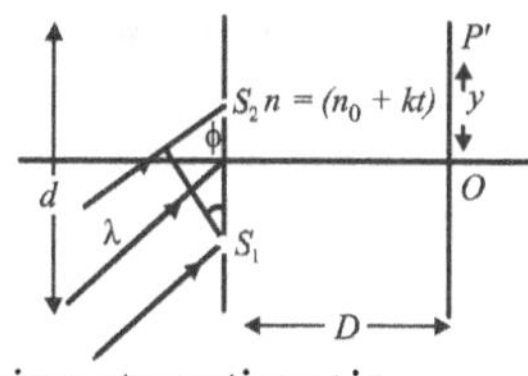

15. The y co-ordinate of central maxima at any time t is

(a) $\dfrac{D\sin\phi}{n_0 + kt}$ (b) $\dfrac{D\cos\phi}{n_0 + kt}$ (c) $\dfrac{D\sin\phi}{\left(n_0 + kt\right)^2}$ (d) $\dfrac{D\cos\phi}{\left(n_0 + kt\right)^2}$

16. The velocity of central maxima at any time t as a function of time t is

(a) $\dfrac{-2kD\sin\phi}{(n_0 + kt)^2}$

(b) $\dfrac{-kD\sin\phi}{(n_0 + kt)^2}$

(c) $\dfrac{-2kD\sin\phi}{(n_0 + kt)}$

(d) $\dfrac{-kD\sin\phi}{(n_0 + kt)}$

PARAGRAPH-2

The figure shows a surface XY separating two transparent media, medium-1 and medium-2. The line ab and cd represent waveforms of a light wave travelling in medium-1 and incident on *XY*. The lines ef and gh represent wavefronts of the light wave in medium-2 after refraction.

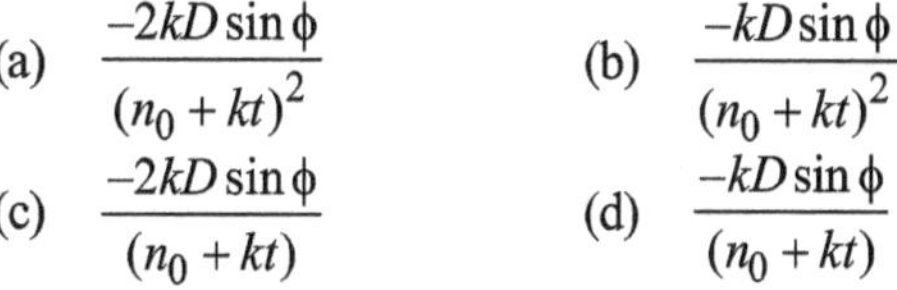

17. Light travels as a
(a) parallel beam in each medium
(b) convergent beam in each medium
(c) divergent beam in each medium
(d) divergent beam in one medium and convergent beam in the other medium.

18. The phases of the light wave at c, d, e and f are ϕ_c, ϕ_d, ϕ_e and ϕ_f respectively. It is given that $\phi_c \neq \phi_f$
(a) ϕ_c cannot be equal to ϕ_d
(b) ϕ_d can be equal to ϕ_e
(c) $(\phi_d - \phi_f)$ is equal to $(\phi_c - \phi_e)$
(d) $(\phi_d - \phi_c)$ is not equal to $(\phi_f - \phi_e)$

RESPONSE GRID	**10.** ⓐⓑⓒⓓ **11.** ⓪①②③④⑤⑥⑦⑧⑨ **12.** ⓪①②③④⑤⑥⑦⑧⑨ **13.** ⓪①②③④⑤⑥⑦⑧⑨ **14.** ⓪①②③④⑤⑥⑦⑧⑨ **15.** ⓐⓑⓒⓓ **16.** ⓐⓑⓒⓓ **17.** ⓐⓑⓒⓓ **18.** ⓐⓑⓒⓓ

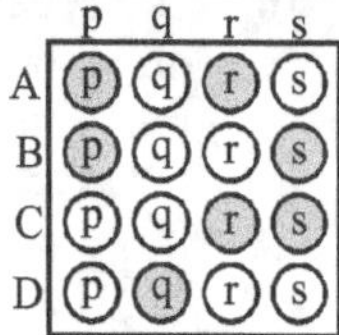

Section V - Matrix-Match Type

This section contains 2 questions. It contains statements given in two columns, which have to be matched. Statements in column I are labelled as A, B, C and D whereas statements in column II are labelled as p, q, r and s. The answers to these questions have to be appropriately bubbled as illustrated in the following example. If the correct matches are A-p, A-r, B-p, B-s, C-r, C-s and D-q, then the correctly bubbled matrix will look like the following:

19.

	Column-I		Column-II
(A)	If Young's double slit experiment is performed in water instead of air then the fringe pattern will	(p)	equal
(B)	A plane wave front is incident normally on a circular operature and diffraction pattern is obtained on the screen on another side of aperture. On displacing the screen towards operture, the number of HPZ exposed through the aperture is	(q)	more
(C)	If the wavelength of a wave is large than the degree of diffraction observed	(r)	increase
(D)	For best contrast between maxima and minima in the interference pattern of Young's double slit experiment the intensity of light emerging out of the two slits should	(s)	shrink

20. In column I S_1 and S_2 represent coherent point sources, S represents a point source. λ = wavelength of light emitted by the sources. Match the two columns.

Column-I   **Column-II**

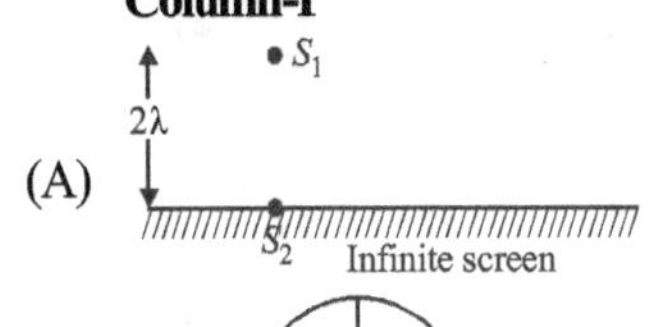

(A)		(p)	Number of maxima = 2
(B)		(q)	Number of minima = 2
(C)		(r)	Number of maxima = 4
(D)		(s)	Number of maxima = 7

RESPONSE GRID	19. A - (p)(q)(r)(s); B - (p)(q)(r)(s); C - (p)(q)(r)(s); D - (p)(q)(r)(s)	
	20. A - (p)(q)(r)(s); B - (p)(q)(r)(s); C - (p)(q)(r)(s); D - (p)(q)(r)(s)	

DAILY PRACTICE PROBLEM DPP CP22 - PHYSICS

Total Questions	20	Total Marks	74
Attempted		Correct	
Incorrect		Net Score	
Cut-off Score	24	Qualifying Score	35

$$\text{Net Score} = \sum_{i=1}^{V} \left[\left(correct_i \times MM_i \right) - \left(In_i - NM_i \right) \right]$$

Space for Rough Work

Date : [   ]   Start Time : [   ]   End Time : [   ]

PHYSICS $\boxed{\text{CP23}}$

SYLLABUS : Dual Nature of Radiation and Matter

Max. Marks : 74   **Time : 60 min.**

GENERAL INSTRUCTIONS

- The Daily Practice Problem Sheet contains 20 Questions divided into 5 sections.
  Section I has **6** MCQs with ONLY 1 Correct Option, **3** marks for each correct answer and **−1** for each incorrect answer.
  Section II has **4** MCQs with ONE or MORE THAN ONE Correct options.
  For each question, marks will be awarded in one of the following categories:
  Full marks: **+4** If only the bubble(s) corresponding to all the correct option(s) is (are) darkened.
  Partial marks: **+1** For darkening a bubble corresponding to each correct option provided NO INCORRECT option is darkened.
  Zero marks: If none of the bubbles is darkened.
  Negative marks: **−2** In all other cases.
  Section III has **4** Single Digit Integer Answer Type Questions, **3** marks for each Correct Answer and 0 marks in all other cases.
  Section IV has Comprehension Type Questions having **4** MCQs with ONLY ONE corect option, 3 marks for each Correct Answer and 0 marks in all other cases.
  Section V has **2** Matching Type Questions, **2** mark for the correct matching of each row and 0 marks in all other cases.
- You have to evaluate your Response Grids yourself with the help of Solutions.

Section I - Straight Objective Type

This section contains 6 multiple choice questions. Each question has 4 choices (a), (b), (c) and (d), out of which **ONLY ONE** is correct.

1. Radiation of wavelength λ, is incident on a photocell. The fastest emitted electron has speed v. If the wavelength is changed to $\dfrac{3\lambda}{4}$, the speed of the fastest emitted electron will be:

(a) $= v\left(\dfrac{4}{3}\right)^{\frac{1}{2}}$

(b) $= v\left(\dfrac{3}{4}\right)^{\frac{1}{2}}$

(c) $> v\left(\dfrac{4}{3}\right)^{\frac{1}{2}}$

(d) $< v\left(\dfrac{4}{3}\right)^{\frac{1}{2}}$

RESPONSE GRID   1. ⓐⓑⓒⓓ

Space for Rough Work

2. An α-particle having a de-Broglie wavelength λ_i collides with a stationary carbon nucleus. The α-particle moves off in a different direction as shown below.

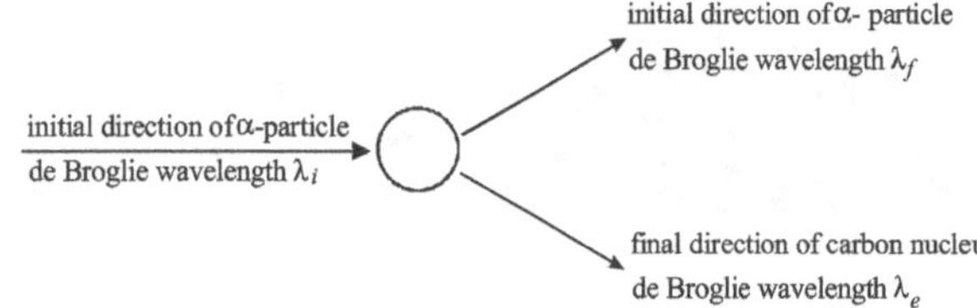

After the collision, the de Broglie wavelengths of the α-particle and the carbon nucleus are λ_f and λ_e respectively. Which of the following relations about de–Broglie wavelengths is correct

(a) $\lambda_i < \lambda_f$ (b) $\lambda_i > \lambda_f$ (c) $\lambda_f = \lambda_e$ (d) $\lambda_i = \lambda_e$

3. To decrease the cut-off wavelength of continuous X-rays by 25%, the potential difference across X-ray tube must be

(a) increased by $\dfrac{100}{3}\%$ (b) decreased by $\dfrac{100}{3}\%$

(c) increased by 25%   (d) decreased by 25%

4. In the photoelectric experiment, if we use a monochromatic light, the I-V curve is as shown. If work function of the metal is 2eV, estimate the power of light used. (Assume efficiency of photoemission = $10^{-3}\%$, i.e., number of photoelectrons emitted are $10^{-3}\%$ of number of photons incident on metal)

(a) 2W

(b) 5W

(c) 7W

(d) 10W

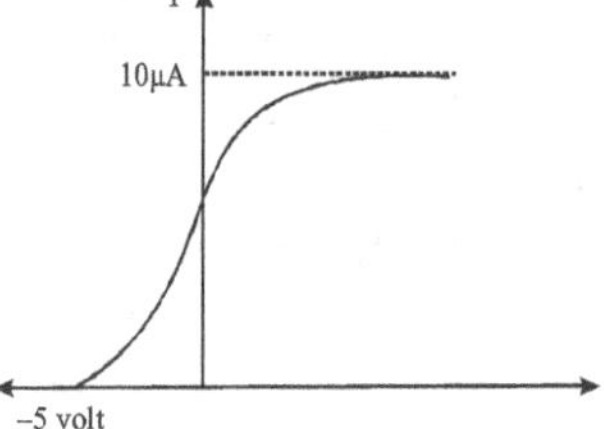

5. The ratio of the λ_{min} in a Coolidge tube to $\lambda_{deBroglie}$ of the electrons striking the target depends on accelerating potential V as

(a) $\dfrac{\lambda_{min}}{\lambda_{de\,Broglie}} \propto \sqrt{V}$ (b) $\dfrac{\lambda_{min}}{\lambda_{de\,Broglie}} \propto V$

(c) $\dfrac{\lambda_{min}}{\lambda_{de\,Broglie}} \propto \dfrac{1}{\sqrt{V}}$ (d) $\dfrac{\lambda_{min}}{\lambda_{de\,Broglie}} \propto \dfrac{1}{V}$.

6. The electric field of a light wave at a point is $E = (100\,\text{N/c})$ $\sin[(3 \times 10^{15}\,\text{s}^{-1})t]\sin[(6 \times 10^{15}\,\text{s}^{-1})t]$ where t is time in seconds. This light falls on a metal surface having work function of $2\,eV$, then maximum possible kinetic energy of photoelectrons is about

(a) 16 eV   (b) 7 eV   (c) 6 eV   (d) 4 eV

Section II - Multiple Correct Answer Type

This section contains 4 multiple correct answer(s) type questions. Each question has 4 choices (a), (b), (c) and (d), out of which **ONE OR MORE** is/are correct.

7. Two photocathodes are illuminated by the light emitted by a single source. The dependence of photocurrent versus voltages between cathode and anode is shown by curves 1 and 2 as shown in the figure. (I/I_{max} represents ratio of photocurrent to saturaion current)

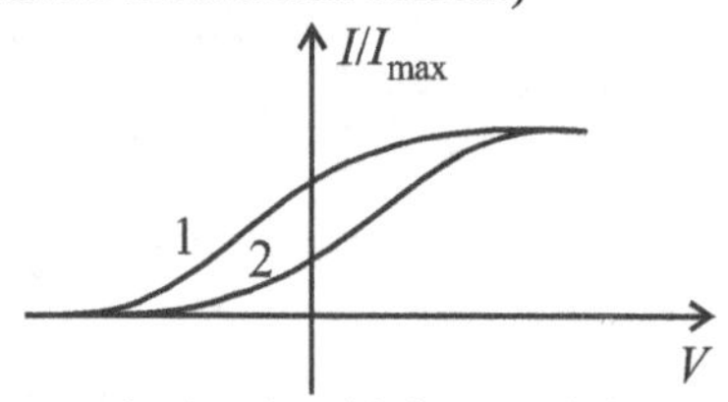

(a) Photocathode 1 has higher work function than 2

(b) Photocathode 2 has higher work function than 1

(c) Saturation current may be different for 1 and 2

(d) Saturation current must be same for 1 and 2

8. The collector plate in an experiment on photoelectric effect is kept vertically above the emitter plate. Light source is put on and a saturation photocurrent is recorded. An electric field is switched on which has a vertically downward direction. Which of the following is/are incorrect?

(a) the photocurrent will increase

(b) the kinetic energy of the electrons will increase

(c) the stopping potential will decrease

(d) the threshold wavelength will increase

9. The graph between the stopping potential (V_0) and $\left(\dfrac{1}{\lambda}\right)$ is shown in the figure. ϕ_1, ϕ_2 and ϕ_3 are work functions. Which of the following is/are correct?

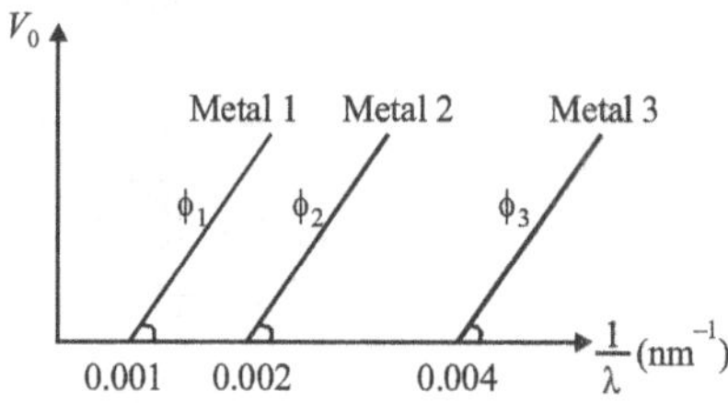

(a) $\phi_1 : \phi_2 : \phi_3 = 1 : 2 : 4$

(b) $\phi_1 : \phi_2 : \phi_3 = 4 : 2 : 1$

(c) $\tan\theta \propto \dfrac{hc}{e}$

(d) ultravioletlight can be used to emit photoelectrons from metal 2 and metal 3 only

Space for Rough Work

10. Photoelectric effect supports quantum nature of light because
    (a) there is a minimum frequency of light below which no photoelectrons are emitted
    (b) the maximum kinetic energy of photo electrons depends only on the frequency of light and not on its intensity
    (c) even when the metal surface is faintly illuminated, the photoelectrons leave the surface immediately
    (d) electric charge of the photoelectrons is quantized

Section III - Integer Type

This section contains 4 questions. The answer to each of the questions is a single digit integer ranging from 0 to 9.

11. A silver sphere of radius 1 cm and work function 4.7 eV is suspended from an insulating thread in free space. It is under continuous illumination of 200 nm wavelength of light. As photoelectrons are emitted, the sphere gets charged and acquires a potential. The maximum number of photoelectrons emitted from the sphere is $A \times 10^z$ (where $1 < A < 10$). The value of 'z' is

12. The work functions of Silver and Sodium are 4.6 and 2.3 eV, respectively. Determine the ratio of the slope of the stopping potential versus frequency plot for Silver to that of Sodium.

13. A photon of energy 8.6 eV is incident on a metal surface of threshold freequency 1.6×10^{15} Hz, then the maximum kinetic energy (in ev) of photoelectrons emitted is ($h = 6.6 \times 10^{-34}$ Js)

14. A monochromatic source of light operating at 200W emits 4×10^{20} photons per second. The wavelength of the light is 100x nm. Find the value of x.

Section IV - Comprehension Type

Directions (Qs. 15-18) : Based upon the given paragraphs, 4 multiple choice questions have to be answered. Each question has 4 choices (a), (b), (c) and (d), out of which **ONLY ONE** is correct.

PARAGRAPH-1

The diagram shows the basic setup for the production of X-rays. A_1 and A_2 are two ammeters, which have readings 2.55 A and 2.566A respectively. F is a filament which is also the cathode. The potential difference applied between P and Q is 50000V. Assume that all X-ray photons have the maximum possible energy and that one X-ray photons is emitted for every 100

electrons incident on the target. You may assume that the kinetic energy of the other electrons reappear as heat in the tube.

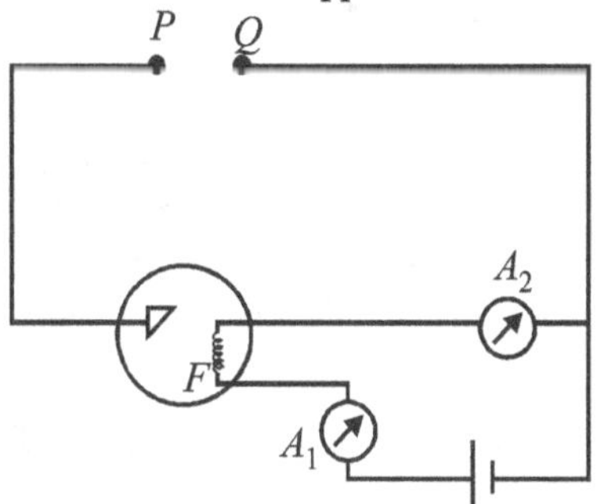

15. The number of X-ray photons produced per second is approximately
    (a) 10^{12} (b) 10^{15} (c) 10^{18} (d) 10^{21}

16. The rate at which heat is produced in the X-ray tube is approximately
    (a) 79.2 W   (b) 204W   (c) 2040 W   (d) 792 W

PARAGRAPH-2

A physicist wishes to eject electrons by shining light on a metal surface. The light source emits light of wavelength of 450 nm. The table lists the only available metals and their work functions.

Metal	W_0 (eV)
Barium	2.5
Lithium	2.3
Tantalum	4.2
Tungsten	4.5

17. Which option correctly identifies the metal that will produce the most energetic electrons and their energies ?
    (a) Lithium, 0.45 eV   (b) Tungston, 1.75 eV
    (c) Lithium, 2.30 eV   (d) Tungston, 2.75 eV

18. Suppose photoelectric experiment is done separately with these metals with light of wavelength 450 nm. The maximum magnitude of stopping potential amongst all the metals is-
    (a) 2.75 volt   (b) 4.5 volt
    (c) 0.45 volt   (d) 0.25 volt

Section V - Matrix-Match Type

This section contains 2 questions. It contains statements given in two columns, which have to be matched. Statements in column I are labelled as A, B, C and D whereas statements in column II are labelled as p, q, r and s. The answers to these questions have to be appropriately bubbled as illustrated in the following example. If the correct matches are A-p, A-r, B-p, B-s, C-r, C-s and D-q, then the correctly bubbled matrix will look like the following:

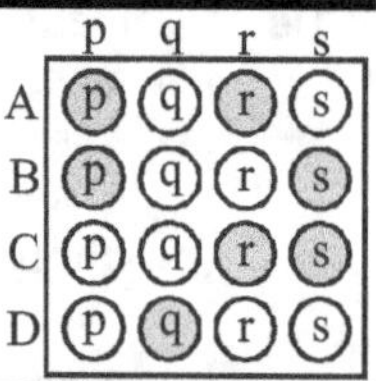

19. In the photoelectric effect experiment, if v is frequency of radiation and I is intensity in terms of number of photons incident per second per unit area, then match the following

Column-I		Column-II
(A) If v is increased keeping I and work function constant	(p)	stopping potential increases
(B) If I is increased keeping v and work function constant.	(q)	saturation current increases
(C) If distance between cathode and anode is increased.	(r)	maximum kinetic energy of photoelectron increases
(D) Work function is decreased keeping v and I constant	(s)	stopping potential remains same

20. **Match the following**

Column-I		Column-II
(A) Radiation pressure	(p)	particle nature of radiation
(B) Threshold wavelength	(q)	Stopping potential
(C) Maximum kinetic energy of photoelectron	(r)	Maximum wavelength of incident photons for photoelectric effect
(D) Quantisation of angular momentum of electron	(s)	de Broglie hypothesis

<table>
<tr><td rowspan="2">Response Grid</td><td>19. A - p q r s ; B - p q r s ; C - p q r s ; D - p q r s</td></tr>
<tr><td>20. A - p q r s ; B - p q r s ; C - p q r s ; D - p q r s</td></tr>
</table>

DAILY PRACTICE PROBLEM DPP CP23 - PHYSICS

Total Questions	20	Total Marks	74
Attempted		Correct	
Incorrect		Net Score	
Cut-off Score	24	Qualifying Score	35

$$\text{Net Score} = \sum_{i=I}^{V} \left[\left(\text{correct}_i \times MM_i \right) - \left(In_i - NM_i \right) \right]$$

Space for Rough Work

DPP - Daily Practice Problems

Chapter-wise Sheets

Date : | Start Time : | End Time :

PHYSICS $\boxed{\text{CP24}}$

SYLLABUS : Atoms

Max. Marks : 74 **Time : 60 min.**

GENERAL INSTRUCTIONS

- The Daily Practice Problem Sheet contains 20 Questions divided into 5 sections.
  Section I has **5** MCQs with ONLY 1 Correct Option, **3** marks for each correct answer and **–1** for each incorrect answer.
  Section II has **4** MCQs with ONE or MORE THAN ONE Correct options.
  For each question, marks will be awarded in one of the following categories:
  Full marks: **+4** If only the bubble(s) corresponding to all the correct option(s) is (are) darkened.
  Partial marks: **+1** For darkening a bubble corresponding to each correct option provided NO INCORRECT option is darkened.
  Zero marks: If none of the bubbles is darkened.
  Negative marks: **–2** In all other cases.
  Section III has **4** Single Digit Integer Answer Type Questions, **3** marks for each Correct Answer and 0 marks in all other cases.
  Section IV has Comprehension/Matching-cum-Comprehension Type Questions having **5** MCQs with ONLY ONE correct option, **3** marks for each Correct Answer and 0 marks in all other cases.
  Section V has **2** Matching Type Questions, **2** mark for the correct matching of each row and 0 marks in all other cases.
- You have to evaluate your Response Grids yourself with the help of Solutions.

Section I - Straight Objective Type

This section contains 5 multiple choice questions. Each question has 4 choices (a), (b), (c) and (d), out of which **ONLY ONE** is correct.

1. Suppose potential energy between electron and proton at separation r is given by $U = K \ln (r)$, where K is a constant. For such a hypothetical hydrogen atom, the ratio of energy difference between energy levels ($n = 1$ and $n = 2$) and ($n = 2$ and $n = 4$) is

(a) 1 (b) 2 (c) 3 (d) 4

2. If in hydrogen atom, radius of nth Bohr orbit is r_n, frequency of revolution of electron in n^{th} orbit is f_n, choose the correct option.

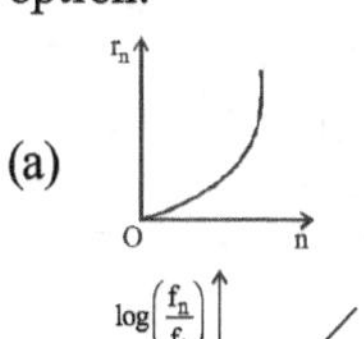
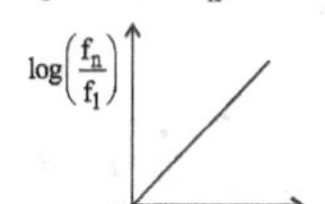

(a) (b)

(c) (d) Both (a) and (b)

Space for Rough Work

3. A sample of hydrogen gas is excited by means of a monochromatic radiation. In the subsequent emission spectrum, 10 different wavelengths are obtained, all of which have energies greater than or equal to the energy of the absorbed radiation. It follows that the initial quantum number of the state (before absorbing radiation) was

(a) 5   (b) 4

(c) 3   (d) 2

4. A diatomic molecule is made of two masses m_1 and m_2 which are separated by a distance r. If we calculate its rotational energy by applying Bohr's rule of angular momentum quantization, its energy will be given by : (n is an integer)

(a) $\dfrac{(m_1+m_2)^2 n^2 h^2}{2m_1^2 m_2^2 r^2}$ (b) $\dfrac{n^2 h^2}{2(m_1+m_2)r^2}$

(c) $\dfrac{2n^2 \hbar^2}{(m_1+m_2)r^2}$ (d) $\dfrac{(m_1+m_2)n^2 \hbar^2}{2m_1 m_2 r^2}$

5. An electron in a hydrogen atom makes a transition from $n = n_1$ to $n = n_2$. The time period of electron in the initial state is eight times that in the final state. Then which of the following statement is true ?

(a) $n_1 = 3n_2$ (b) $n_1 = 4n_2$

(c) $n_1 = 2n_2$ (d) $n_1 = 5n_2$

Section II - Multiple Correct Answer Type

This section contains 4 multiple correct answer(s) type questions. Each question has 4 choices (a), (b), (c) and (d), out of which **ONE OR MORE** is/are correct.

6. Suppose the potential energy between electron and proton at a distance r is given by $-\dfrac{Ke^2}{3r^3}$. Application of Bohr's theory to hydrogen atom in this case shows that –

(a) energy in the nth orbit is proportional to n^6

(b) energy is proportional to m^{-3} (m : mass of electron)

(c) energy the nth orbit is proportional to n^{-2}

(d) energy is proportional to m^3 (m = mass of electron)

7. Let A_n be the area enclosed by the nth orbit in a hydrogen atom. The graph of $\ln(A_n/A_1)$ against $\ln(n)$ –

(a) will pass through origin

(b) will a straight line with slope-4

(c) will be a monotonically increasing nonlinear curve

(d) will be a circle

8. Highly excited states for hydrogen–like atoms (also called Rydberg states) with nuclear charge Ze are defined by their principal quantum number n, where n>>1. Which of the following statement(s) is(are) true?

(a) Relative change in the radii of two consecutive orbitals does not depend on Z

(b) Relative change in the radii of two consecutive orbitals varies as 1/n

(c) Relative change in the energy of two consecutive orbitals varies as $1/n^3$

(d) Relative change in the angular momenta of two consecutive orbitals varies as 1/n

9. The radius of the orbit of an electron in a Hydrogen-like atom is $4.5\,a_0$, where a_0 is the Bohr radius. Its orbital angular momentum is $\dfrac{3h}{2\pi}$. It is given that h is Planck constant and R is Rydberg constant. The possible wavelength(s), when the atom de-excites, is (are)

(a) $\dfrac{9}{32R}$ (b) $\dfrac{9}{16R}$ (c) $\dfrac{9}{5R}$ (d) $\dfrac{4}{3R}$

Section III - Integer Type

This section contains 4 questions. The answer to each of the questions is a single digit integer ranging from 0 to 9.

10. A hydrogen like atom (atomic number Z) is in a higher excited state of quantum number n. The excited atom can make a transition to the first excited state by successively emitting two photons of energy 10.2 and 17.0 eV respectively. Alternately, the atom from the same excited state can make a transition to the second excited state by successively emitting two photons of energies 4.25 eV and 5.95 eV respectively. Determine the value of n. (Ionization energy of H-atom = 13.6 eV)

11. Let neutron be a point mass and hydrogen atom a solid sphere. A neutron makes a head on collision with a hydrogen atom in ground state kept at rest. The coefficient of restitution for collision is $e = 1/2$. The minimum kinetic energy of colliding neutron (in eV) so that hydrogen atom is excited to higher energy level such that magnitude of electrostatic potential energy in the excited state is one-eighth of K.E. of electron in ground state is 4x. Find the value of x. (mass of neutron = mass of hydrogen).

12. A hydrogen-like atom (described by the Bohr model) is observed to emit six wavelengths, originating from all possible transitions between a group of levels. These levels have energies between -0.85 eV and -0.544 eV (including both these values). Find the atomic number of the atom. (Take hc = 1240 eV-nm, ground state energy of hydrogen atom =−13.6 eV)

<table>
<tr><td rowspan="3">Response Grid</td><td>3. ⓐⓑⓒⓓ</td><td>4. ⓐⓑⓒⓓ</td><td>5. ⓐⓑⓒⓓ</td><td>6. ⓐⓑⓒⓓ</td><td>7. ⓐⓑⓒⓓ</td></tr>
<tr><td>8. ⓐⓑⓒⓓ</td><td>9. ⓐⓑⓒⓓ</td><td colspan="3">10. ⓪①②③④⑤⑥⑦⑧⑨</td></tr>
<tr><td colspan="2">11. ⓪①②③④⑤⑥⑦⑧⑨</td><td colspan="3">12. ⓪①②③④⑤⑥⑦⑧⑨</td></tr>
</table>

13. Electrons in hydrogen like atom $(Z = 3)$ make transitions from the fifth to the fourth orbit and from the fourth to the third orbit. The resulting radiations are incident normally on a metal plate and eject photoelectrons. The stopping potential for the photoelectrons ejected by the shorter wavelength is 3.95 volts. Calculate the work function of the metal (ine V).

(Rydberg constant $= 1.094 \times 10^7 \, \text{m}^{-1}$)

Section IV - Comprehension/Matching Cum-Comprehension Type

Directions (Qs. 14 and 15) : Based upon the given paragraph, 2 multiple choice questions have to be answered. Each question has 4 choices (a), (b), (c) and (d), out of which **ONLY ONE** is correct.

PARAGRAPH

A small particle of mass m moves in such a way that the potential energy of particle is given as $U = -\dfrac{1}{2} m\alpha^2 r^2$ where α is constant and r is the distance of particle from centre. If Bohr's model of quantization of angular momentum and circular orbit is valid for the particle, answer the following questions ($h =$ Planck's constant)

14. Kinetic energy of particle in n^{th} orbit is

(a) $\dfrac{nh\alpha}{4\pi}$ (b) $\dfrac{n^2 h\alpha}{4\pi^2}$

(c) $\dfrac{nh\alpha}{2\pi}$ (d) $\sqrt{\dfrac{n^2 h^2 \alpha}{\pi}}$.

15. Total energy of particle in its orbits is

(a) $-\dfrac{nh\alpha}{4\pi}$ (b) $\dfrac{nh\alpha}{2\pi}$ (c) zero (d) $-\dfrac{nh\alpha}{2\pi}$

Directions (Qs. 16-18) : This passage contains a table having 3 columns and 4 rows. Based on the table, there are three questions. Each question has four options (a), (b), (c) and (d) **ONLY ONE** of these four options is correct.

According to Bohr's model, electron revolves in circular orbits around the nucleus under the influence of coulombic force of attraction in defined stationary orbits, for which angular momentum, $\text{mvr} = \dfrac{nh}{2\pi}$. Column I, II & III give different relation between Z = atomic number, n = orbit number, and different physical quantities like angluar velocity, energy, current, ionization energy. (Here A_0, B_0, C_0 and D_0 are constants)

	Column I		Column II		Column III
I.	Ionisation energy of an electron in n^{th} Bohr's orbit	(i)	Inversely proportional to n	(P)	$A_0 \dfrac{Z^2}{n^3} \, (\text{Sec}^{-1})$
II.	Current developed due to motion of an electron in n^{th} orbit	(ii)	Inversely proportional to n^3	(Q)	$B_0 \dfrac{Z}{n}$
III.	Velocity of an electron in n^{th} Bohr's orbit	(iii)	Directly proportional to Z^2	(R)	$C_0 \dfrac{Z^2}{n^3}$
IV.	Angular speed of an electron in n^{th} Bohr's orbit	(iv)	Directly proportional to Z	(S)	$D_0 \dfrac{Z^2}{n^2}$

16. If the value of current developed due to motion of an electron in 3rd Bohr's orbit (for $Z = 3$) is $\dfrac{1}{3} \times$ constant then correct match satisfying the above condition will be:

  (a) II (iii) R   (b) IV (iii) P   (c) II (ii) P   (d) I (iv) S

17. Which of the following shows the correct matching?

  (a) II (ii) Q   (b) III (i) Q   (c) IV (ii) Q   (d) I (i) R

18. Which of the following does not show the correct matching?

  (a) IV (ii) P   (b) II (iii) R   (c) II (ii) R   (d) I (iv) Q

Section V - Matrix-Match Type

This section contains 2 questions. It contains statements given in two columns, which have to be matched. Statements in column I are labelled as A, B, C and D whereas statements in column II are labelled as p, q, r and s. The answers to these questions have to be appropriately bubbled as illustrated in the following example. If the correct matches are A-p, A-r, B-p, B-s, C-r, C-s and D-q, then the correctly bubbled matrix will look like the following:

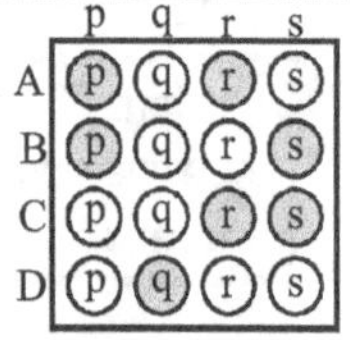

19. Match the different kinds of radiations emitted by a hydrogen atom given in Column I with the corresponding electron transitions given in Column II.

Column-I	Column-II
(A) Ultraviolet light	(p) $n = 6 \rightarrow n = 3$
(B) Visible light	(q) $n = 3 \rightarrow n = 1$
(C) Infrared radiation	(r) $n = 4 \rightarrow n = 2$
(D) Microwaves	(s) $n = 7 \rightarrow n = 6$

20. Using Bohr's model, match the following (where the letters n and Z have usual meaning).

Column I	Column II
(A) Due to revolving electron, the magnetic field produced at its centre is proportional to	(p) n^{-5}
(B) Magnetic moment of revolving electron is proportional to	(q) n
(C) De-Broglie wavelength of revolving electron is proportional to	(r) Z^3
(D) Areal velocity of revolving electron about nucleus is proportional to	(s) independent of Z

<table>
<tr><td rowspan="3">RESPONSE GRID</td><td colspan="3">16. ⓐⓑⓒⓓ   17. ⓐⓑⓒⓓ   18. ⓐⓑⓒⓓ</td></tr>
<tr><td colspan="3">19. A - ⓟⓠⓡⓢ; B - ⓟⓠⓡⓢ; C - ⓟⓠⓡⓢ; D - ⓟⓠⓡⓢ</td></tr>
<tr><td colspan="3">20. A - ⓟⓠⓡⓢ; B - ⓟⓠⓡⓢ; C - ⓟⓠⓡⓢ; D - ⓟⓠⓡⓢ</td></tr>
</table>

DAILY PRACTICE PROBLEM DPP CP24 - PHYSICS

Total Questions	20	Total Marks	74
Attempted		Correct	
Incorrect		Net Score	
Cut-off Score	24	Qualifying Score	35

$$\text{Net Score} = \sum_{i=1}^{V} \left[\left(correct_i \times MM_i \right) - \left(In_i - NM_i \right) \right]$$

Space for Rough Work

Date :   Start Time :   End Time :

PHYSICS   

SYLLABUS : Nuclei

Max. Marks : 74   **Time : 60 min.**

GENERAL INSTRUCTIONS

- The Daily Practice Problem Sheet contains 20 Questions divided into 5 sections.
- **Section I** has **6** MCQs with ONLY 1 Correct Option, **3** marks for each correct answer and **–1** for each incorrect answer.
- **Section II** has **4** MCQs with ONE or MORE THAN ONE Correct options.
- For each question, marks will be awarded in one of the following categories:
- Full marks: **+4** If only the bubble(s) corresponding to all the correct option(s) is (are) darkened.
- Partial marks: **+1** For darkening a bubble corresponding to each correct option provided NO INCORRECT option is darkened.
- Zero marks: If none of the bubbles is darkened.
- Negative marks: **–2** In all other cases.
- **Section III** has **4** Single Digit Integer Answer Type Questions, **3** marks for each Correct Answer and 0 marks in all other cases.
- **Section IV** has Comprehension Type Questions having **4** MCQs with ONLY ONE corect option, 3 marks for each Correct Answer and 0 marks in all other cases.
- **Section V** has **2** Matching Type Questions, **2** mark for the correct matching of each row and 0 marks in all other cases.
- You have to evaluate your Response Grids yourself with the help of Solutions.

Section I - Straight Objective Type

This section contains 6 multiple choice questions. Each question has 4 choices (a), (b), (c) and (d), out of which **ONLY ONE** is correct.

1. A radioactive sample S_1 having an activity $5\mu Ci$ has twice the number of nuclei as another sample S_2 which has an activity of $10\ \mu Ci$. The half lives of S_1 and S_2 can be

(a) 20 years and 5 years, respectively

(b) 20 years and 10 years, respectively

(c) 10 years each

(d) 5 years each

RESPONSE GRID	1. ⓐⓑⓒⓓ

Space for Rough Work

2. Binding energy per nucleon vs mass number curve for nuclei is shown in the Figure. W, X, Y and Z are four nuclei indicated on the curve. The process that would release energy is

(a) $Y \to 2Z$

(b) $W \to X + Z$

(c) $W \to 2Y$

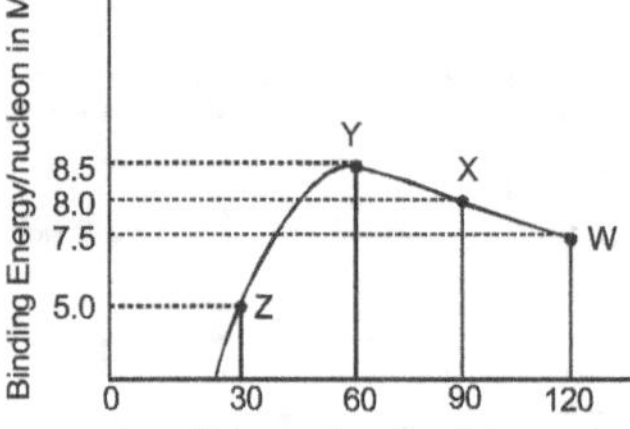

(d) $X \to Y + Z$

3. A sample of radioactive substance has 10^6 nuclei. If half life is 20 seconds, the number of nuclei left in the sample after 10 seconds is

(a) 10^4

(b) 2×10^5

(c) 7×10^5

(d) 11×10^5

4. The nuclear binding energies of the elements P and Q are E_P and E_Q respectively. Three nuclei of elements Q fuse to form one nucleus of element P. In this process the energy released is 'e'. The correct relation between E_P, E_Q and e will be

(a) $E_Q = 3E_P + e$

(b) $E_Q = 3E_P - e$

(c) $E_P = 3E_Q + e$

(d) $E_P = 3E_Q - e$

5. A radioactive source in the form of metal sphere of diameter 10^{-3} m emits beta particle at a constant rate of 6.25×10^{10} particles per second. If the source is electrically insulated, how long will it take for its potential to rise by 1.0 volt, assuming that 80% of the emitted beta particles escape from the source?

(a) $6.95\ \mu$ sec

(b) $0.95\ \mu$ sec

(c) $1.95\ \mu$ sec

(d) $2.15\ \mu$ sec

6. Half life of a radioactive substance is 20 minute. Difference between points of time when it is 33% disintegrated and 67% disintegrated is approximately

(a) 40 minute

(b) 10 minute

(c) 15 minute

(d) 20 minute

Section II - Multiple Correct Answer Type

This section contains 4 multiple correct answer(s) type questions. Each question has 4 choices (a), (b), (c) and (d), out of which **ONE OR MORE** is/are correct.

7. A fission reaction is given by $^{236}_{92}U \to {}^{140}_{54}Xe + {}^{94}_{38}Sr + x + y$,

where x and y are two particles. Considering $^{236}_{92}U$ to be at rest, the kinetic energies of the products are denoted by K_{Xe}, K_{Sr}, K_x(2 MeV) and K_y(2 MeV), respectively. Let the binding energies per nucleon of $^{236}_{92}U$, $^{140}_{54}Xe$ and $^{94}_{38}Sr$ be 7.5 MeV, 8.5 MeV and 8.5 MeV, respectively. Considering different conservation laws, the incorrect option(s) is(are)

(a) $x = n, y = n, K_{Sr} = 129$ MeV, $K_{Xe} = 86$ MeV

(b) $x = p, y = e^-, K_{Sr} = 129$ MeV, $K_{Xe} = 86$ MeV

(c) $x = p, y = n, K_{Sr} = 129$ MeV, $K_{Xe} = 86$ MeV

(d) $x = n, y = n, K_{Sr} = 86$ MeV, $K_{Xe} = 129$ MeV

8. The mass number of a nucleus is

(a) always less than its atomic number

(b) always more than its atomic number

(c) sometimes equal to its atomic number

(d) sometimes more than and sometimes equal to its atomic number

9. The initial nucleus of uranium series is $_{92}U^{238}$ and the final nucleus is $_{82}Pb^{206}$. When uranium decays to lead by emitting α and β particles then number of

(a) α-particles produced is 8

(b) β-particles produced is 6

(c) α-particles produced is 6

(d) β-particles produced is 8

10. A radioactive battery, consists of N_0 atoms of a radioelement emitting α-rays with a disintegration constant λ, of which a fraction f is captured at the anode A and converted into a current. A charged capacitor C initially charged as shown in the figure and a resistance R are connected across the battery. Choose the correct options

(The battery contained N_0 atoms at $t = 0$.)

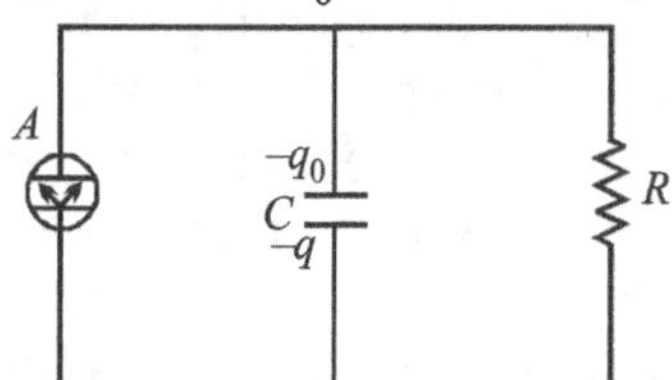

(a) The charge across the capacitor as a function of time t, is $\left(-q_1 e^{-\frac{t}{RC}} + q_2 e^{-\lambda t}\right)$

(b) Time when the charge on the capacitor become zero is $\dfrac{1}{\dfrac{1}{RC} - \lambda} \ln\left(\dfrac{q_1}{q_2}\right)$

(c) Time when the charge on the capacitor becomes zero is $\dfrac{1}{\dfrac{1}{RC} + \lambda} \ln\left(\dfrac{q_1}{q_2}\right)$

(d) The charge across the capacitor as a function of time t is $\left(-q_1 e^{-\frac{t}{RC}} - q_2 e^{-\lambda t}\right)$

RESPONSE	2. ⓐⓑⓒⓓ	3. ⓐⓑⓒⓓ	4. ⓐⓑⓒⓓ	5. ⓐⓑⓒⓓ	6. ⓐⓑⓒⓓ
GRID	7. ⓐⓑⓒⓓ	8. ⓐⓑⓒⓓ	9. ⓐⓑⓒⓓ	10. ⓐⓑⓒⓓ	

Section III - Integer Type

This section contains 4 questions. The answer to each of the questions is a single digit integer ranging from 0 to 9.

11. To determine the half life of a radioactive element, a student plots a graph of $ln\left|\dfrac{dN(t)}{dt}\right|$ versus t. Here $\left|\dfrac{dN(t)}{dt}\right|$ is the rate of radioactive decay at time t. If the number of radioactive nuclei of this element decreases by a factor of p after 4.16 years, the value of p is

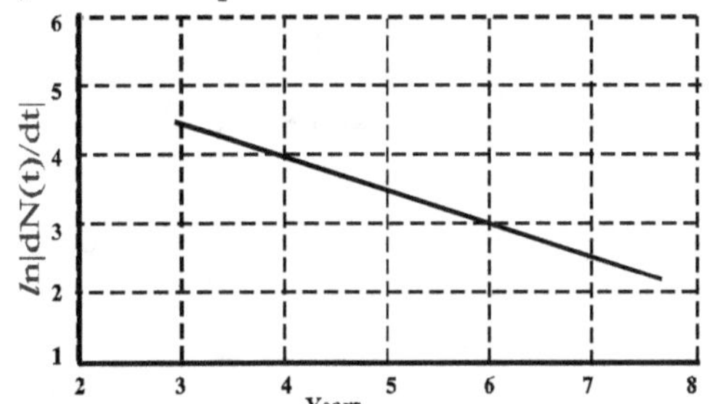

12. In an α-decay the kinetic energy of α-particle is 48 MeV and Q-value of the reaction is 50 MeV. The mass number of the mother nucleus is X. Find the value of X/25.

(Assume that daughter nucleus is in ground state)

13. There are two radioactive substances A and B. Decay constant of B is two times that of A. Initially, both have equal number of nuclei. After n half lives of A, rate of disintegration of both are equal. The value of n is

14. In a nuclear reaction ^{235}U undergoes fission liberating 200 MeV of energy. The reactor has a 10% efficiency and produces 1000 MW power. If the reactor is to function of 10 years, the total mass (in mega gram) of uranium required is $8x$. Find the value of x.

Section IV - Comprehension Type

Directions (Qs. 15-18) : Based upon the given paragraphs, 4 multiple choice questions have to be answered. Each question has 4 choices (a), (b), (c) and (d), out of which **ONLY ONE** is correct.

PARAGRAPH-1

A sample contains two radioactive nuclei X and Y with half lives 2 hr and 1 hr respectively. The nucleus X-decays into the nucleus Y and Y decays into a stable nucleus Z. At time t = 0 the activities of the components in the sample were equal and were each equal to A_0.

$$X \xrightarrow{\ t_{1/2}=2\,hr\ } Y \xrightarrow{\ t_{1/2}=1\,hr\ } Z$$

Suppose that N_X, N_Y are the number of nuclei of X and Y, respectively, at time t. It is given that

$$\lambda_Y N_Y = \lambda_X(N_X + N_Y) + C_1\, e^{-\lambda_Y . t} \ \ldots\ldots\ldots (i)$$

where λ_X, λ_Y are the decay constants of X and Y; C_1 is an arbitrary constant.

15. The value of C_1 is

(a) $-\dfrac{A_0}{2}$ (b) $-A_0$

(c) $-2A_0$ (d) 0

16. Number of nuclei of Y at time t is equal to (t is in hour)

(a) $\dfrac{A_0}{\ln 2}[2^{1-t/2} - 2^{-t}]$ (b) $\dfrac{A_0}{\ln 2}[2^{-t/2} - 2^{-t}]$

(c) $\dfrac{A_0}{\ln 2}[2^{t} - 2^{-t}]$ (d) $\left(\dfrac{A_0}{\ln 2}\right)e^{-2t}$

PARAGRAPH-2

Gold nucleus ($_{79}Au^{198}$) can decay into mercury nucleus ($_{80}Hg^{198}$) by two decay schemes shown in figure. (i) it can emit a β particle (β_1) and come to ground state by either emitting one γ ray (γ_1) or emitting two γ rays (γ_3 & γ_4) (ii) it can emit one β particle (β_2) and come to ground state by emitting γ_2 ray.

Atomic masses : $^{198}Au = 197.9682$ amu,

$^{198}Hg = 197.9662$ amu , 1 amu $= 930$ MeV/c^2. The energy levels of the nucleus are shown in figure.

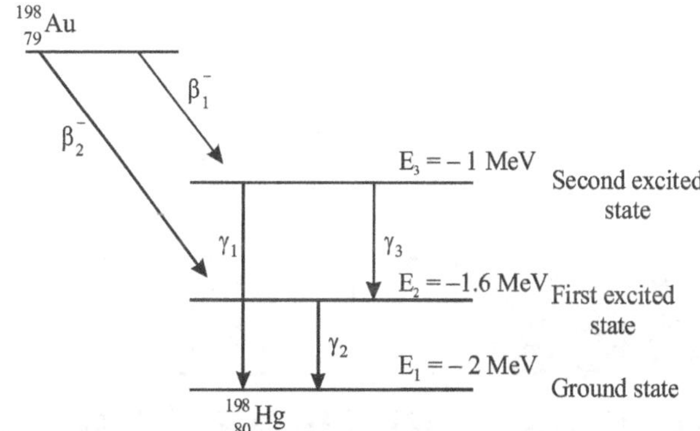

17. What is the maximum kinetic energy of emitted β_2 particles?

(a) 1.44 MeV   (b) 0.59 MeV

(c) 1.86 MeV   (d) 1.46 MeV

18. The wavelength of emitted γ rays are in the order of

(a) $\lambda_{\gamma 2} > \lambda_{\gamma 3} > \lambda_{\gamma 1}$ (b) $\lambda_{\gamma 3} > \lambda_{\gamma 2} > \lambda_{\gamma 1}$

(c) $\lambda_{\gamma 1} > \lambda_{\gamma 2} > \lambda_{\gamma 3}$ (d) $\lambda_{\gamma 3} = \lambda_{\gamma 2} = \lambda_{\gamma 1}$

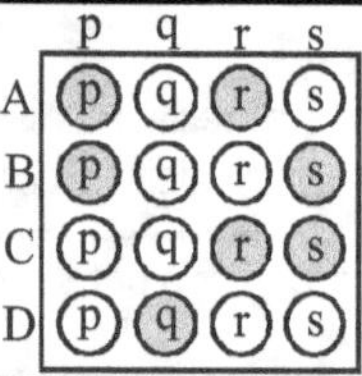

Section V - Matrix-Match Type

This section contains 2 questions. It contains statements given in two columns, which have to be matched. Statements in column I are labelled as A, B, C and D whereas statements in column II are labelled as p, q, r and s. The answers to these questions have to be appropriately bubbled as illustrated in the following example. If the correct matches are A-p, A-r, B-p, B-s, C-r, C-s and D-q, then the correctly bubbled matrix will look like the following:

19. Match the processes given in Column I with the nuclear reactions given in Column II. Symbol Q stands for energy released.

Column-I		**Column-II**
(A) Alpha decay	(p)	$^{235}_{92}U + {}^{1}_{0}n \rightarrow {}^{141}_{56}Ba + {}^{92}_{36}Kr + \left({}^{1}_{0}n\right) + Q$
(B) Beta decay	(q)	$^{3}_{1}H + {}^{2}_{1}H \rightarrow {}^{4}_{2}He + Q$
(C) Nuclear fission	(r)	$^{230}_{90}Th \rightarrow {}^{226}_{90}Ra + {}^{4}_{2}He + Q$
(D) Nuclear fusion	(s)	$^{137}_{55}Cs \rightarrow {}^{137}_{56}Ba + e^{-} + \overline{v} + Q$

20. Column-II gives certain systems undergoing a process. Column-I suggests changes in some of the parameters related to the system. Match the statements in Column-I to the approapriate process(es) from Column-II.

Column-I		**Column-II**
(A) The energy of the system is increased	(p)	*System :* A capacitor, initially uncharged *Process :* It is connected to a battery
(B) Mechanical energy is provided to the system, which is converted into energy of random motion of its parts	(q)	*System :* A gas in an adiabatic container fitted with an adiabatic piston *Process:* The gas is compressed by pushing the piston
(C) Internal energy of the system is converted into its mechanical energy	(r)	*System:* A heavy nucleus, initially at rest *Process:* The nucleus fissions into two fragments of nearly equal masses and some neutrons are emitted
(D) Mass of the system is decreased	(s)	*System:* A resistive wire loop *Process:* The loop is placed in a time varying magnetic field perpendicular to its plane

RESPONSE GRID	
19. A - (p)(q)(r)(s); B - (p)(q)(r)(s); C - (p)(q)(r)(s); D - (p)(q)(r)(s)	
20. A - (p)(q)(r)(s); B - (p)(q)(r)(s); C - (p)(q)(r)(s); D - (p)(q)(r)(s)	

DAILY PRACTICE PROBLEM DPP CP25 - PHYSICS

Total Questions	20	Total Marks	74
Attempted		Correct	
Incorrect		Net Score	
Cut-off Score	24	Qualifying Score	35

$$\text{Net Score} = \sum_{i=1}^{V}\left[\left(correct_i \times MM_i\right) - \left(In_i - NM_i\right)\right]$$

Space for Rough Work

1. **(b)** Measured length of rod = 3.50 cm
For vernier scale with 1 Main Scale Division = 1 mm
9 Main Scale Division = 10 Vernier Scale Division,
Least count = 1 MSD – 1 VSD
$$= 0.1\,mm$$

2. **(a)** The dimensions of radius of gyration
$$= \text{dimensions of } L$$
$$= G^{½}\,h^{½}\,c^{-3/2}.$$

3. **(a)** $I = I_0 \sin^2\theta \Rightarrow \theta = \sin^{-1}\sqrt{\dfrac{I}{I_0}}$

$$d\theta = \frac{1}{2}\frac{\sqrt{I_0}}{\sqrt{I_0 - I}}\frac{dI}{\sqrt{I_0}\sqrt{I}}$$

$$\frac{d\theta}{\theta} = \frac{1}{2}\frac{dI}{\sqrt{I\,(I_0 - I)}\sin^{-1}\sqrt{I/I_0}}$$

$$= \frac{0.0020}{2\times\sqrt{5\times15}\times\dfrac{\pi}{6}} = \frac{2\times10^{-3}}{10\sqrt{3}\times\dfrac{\pi}{6}}$$

$$= \frac{12}{\pi\sqrt{3}}\times10^{-4} = \frac{4}{\pi}\sqrt{3}\times10^{-4}$$

$$\therefore\ \% \text{ error} = \frac{4}{\pi}\sqrt{3}\times10^{-2}\%$$

4. **(a)** Fractional error $-\dfrac{\Delta M}{M}$ as $\Delta M_A = \Delta M_B$

as $M_B > M_A \Rightarrow \dfrac{\Delta M_A}{M_A} > \dfrac{\Delta M_B}{M_B}$

5. **(b)** The time period of a simple pendulum is given by

$$T = 2\pi\sqrt{\frac{\ell}{g}}\ \therefore\ T^2 = 4\pi^2\frac{\ell}{g} \Rightarrow g = 4\pi^2\frac{\ell}{T^2}$$

$$\Rightarrow\ \frac{\Delta g}{g}\times100 = \frac{\Delta \ell}{\ell}\times100 + 2\frac{\Delta T}{T}\times100$$

Case (i)
$\Delta\ell = 0.1$ cm, $\ell = 64$cm, $\Delta T = 0.1$s, $T = 128$s

$$\therefore\ \frac{\Delta g}{g}\times100 = 0.3125$$

Case (ii)
$\Delta\ell = 0.1$ cm, $\ell = 64$cm, $\Delta T = 0.1$s, $T = 64$s

$$\therefore\ \frac{\Delta g}{g}\times100 = 0.46875$$

Case (iii)
$\Delta\ell = 0.1$ cm, $\ell = 20$cm, $\Delta T = 0.1$s, $T = 36$s

$$\therefore\ \frac{\Delta g}{g}\times100 = 1.055$$

Clearly, the value of $\dfrac{\Delta g}{g}\times100$ will be least in case (i).

6. **(a, b)** The quantities specific heat and latent heat both contain a term 'energy per unit mass'. However energy itself contains mass and hence the dimensions of both these quantities do not contain mass.

7. **(a, c)** As the length of the string of simple pendulum is exactly 1 m (given), therefore the error in length $\Delta l = 0$. Further the possibility of error in measuring time is 1s in 40s.

$$\therefore\ \frac{\Delta t}{t} = \frac{\Delta T}{T} = \frac{1}{40}$$

The time period $T = \dfrac{40}{20} = 2$ seconds

$$\therefore\ \frac{\Delta T}{T} = \frac{1}{40} \Rightarrow \frac{\Delta T}{2} = \frac{1}{40} \Rightarrow \Delta T = 0.05\,sec$$

We know that $T = 2\pi\sqrt{\dfrac{\ell}{g}} \Rightarrow T^2 = 4\pi^2\dfrac{l}{g}$

$$\therefore\ g = 4\pi^2\frac{\ell}{T^2}$$

$$\therefore\ \frac{\Delta g}{g}\times100 = \frac{\Delta l}{l}\times100 + 2\frac{\Delta T}{T}\times100$$

$$\therefore\ \frac{\Delta g}{g}\times100 = 0 + 2\left(\frac{1}{40}\right)\times100 = 5$$

8. **(a, b, c)** Let the dependence of mass (M) on velocity (v), acc. due to gravity (g) and density (ρ) be as

$$M = v^x g^y \rho^z$$

Substituting the dimensions of v, g and ρ in R.H.S.

$$ML^0T^0 = [LT^{-1}]^x[LT^{-2}]^y[ML^{-3}]^z$$

or $ML^0T^0 = M^z L^{x+y-3z}T^{-x-2y}$
Comparing the dimensions on both sides (i.e. the equating the powers of M, L and T), we get
$z = 1, x + y - 3z = 0$ and $-x - 2y = 0$
Solving, we get, $x = 6, y = -3$ and $z = 1$

$$\therefore\ \text{Mass }[M] = v^6 g^{-3}\rho$$

$\therefore$ Unit of mass

$$= \frac{3\times(10^8)^6}{(9.81)^3}\times13600 = 1.05\times10^{52}\,kg$$

Similarly, it can be shown that, the length (L) will be given by $L = v^2/g$.

$$\therefore\ \text{Unit of length} = \frac{(3\times10^8)^2}{9.81} = 9.17\times10^{15}\,m$$

and time T is given by $T = v/g$.

$$\therefore\ \text{Unit of time} = \frac{(3\times10^8)}{9.81} = 3.06\times10^7\,s$$

9. **(a, b)** $\left[\dfrac{L}{R}\right] = [CR] = [\text{Time}]$

$$\left[\dfrac{1}{\sqrt{\varepsilon_0 \mu_0}}\right] = \left[\dfrac{E}{B}\right] = [\text{velocity}]$$

10. **3** Given $t = d^{a/2}, r^{b/2}, s^{c/2}$. Substituting dimensions, we have

$$(T) = (ML^{-3})^{a/2} (L)^{b/2} (MT^{-2})^{c/2}$$

$$= M^{(a+c)/2}. L^{(-3a/2 + b/2)} T^{-c}$$

Equating powers of L, we have,

$$-\dfrac{3}{2}a + \dfrac{b}{2} = 0 \qquad \text{Given} \quad a = 1.$$

$$\therefore \ -\dfrac{3}{2} + \dfrac{b}{2} = 0 \text{ or } b = 3.$$

11. **3** $d \propto \rho^x S^y f^z$

$$M^0 L^1 T^0 = M^x L^{-3x} M^y T^{-y} T^{-z}$$
$$M^0 L^1 T^0 = M^{x+y} L^{-3x} T^{-y-z}$$
$$\therefore x + y = 0, \ -3x = 1$$

$$\therefore \ x = -\dfrac{1}{3} \text{ and } y = \dfrac{1}{3}$$

$$\therefore n = 3$$

12. **2** % error in $M = \dfrac{\Delta M}{M} \times 100 = \dfrac{0.2}{20} \times 100 = 1\%$

% error in $V = \dfrac{\Delta V}{V} \times 100 = \dfrac{0.1}{10} \times 100 = 1\%$

% error in r = % error in M + % error in V = 1% + 1% = 2%

13. **1**

Maximum percentage error in Y is given by

$$Y = \dfrac{W}{\dfrac{\pi D^2}{4}} \times \dfrac{L}{X}$$

$$\left(\dfrac{\Delta Y}{Y}\right)_{max} = 2\left(\dfrac{\Delta D}{D}\right) + \dfrac{\Delta X}{X} + \dfrac{\Delta L}{L}$$

$$= 2\left(\dfrac{0.001}{0.05}\right) + \left(\dfrac{0.001}{0.125}\right) + \left(\dfrac{0.1}{110}\right) = 0.0489$$

So, maximum percentage error = 4.89%
It is given that

$$W = 50 \text{ N}; D = 0.05 \text{ cm}; = 0.05 \times 10^{-2} \text{m};$$
$$X = 0.125 \text{ cm} = 0.125 \times 10^{-2} \text{m};$$
$$L = 110 \text{ cm} = 110 \times 10^{-2} \text{m}$$

$$Y = \dfrac{50 \times 4 \times 110 \times 10^{-2}}{3.14 (0.05 \times 10^{-2}) \times (0.125 \times 10^{-2})}$$

$$= 2.24 \times 10^{11} \text{N/m}^2$$

$$\therefore \ \Delta Y = 0.0489 \times 2.24 \times 10^{11} = 1.09 \times 10^{10} \text{ N/m}^2$$

$$\simeq 1 \times 10^{10} \text{ N/m}^2$$

14. **(b)** **15.** **(c)**

16. **(c)** x in e^x is a dimensionless quantity
So, $[x] = [M^0 L^0 T^0] = [\pi] = [\text{Plane angle}]$

17. **(d)** [Angular Frequency] = [Angular velocity]
$= [M^0 L^0 T^{-1}]$
[Plane angle] = $[\pi]$ = $[M^0 L^0 T^0]$
which are independent of mass and length so will remain unaffected.

18. **(c)** $\dfrac{1}{[\text{Angular frequency}]} = \dfrac{[X]}{[\text{Angular velocity}]}$

$\Rightarrow [X] = [\text{Angular velocity}] / [\text{Angular Frequency}]$

$$= \dfrac{\left[M^0 L^0 T^{-1}\right]}{\left[M^0 L^0 T^{-1}\right]} = [M^0 L^0 T^0]$$

19. **A-s; B-p, r; C-q; D-q**

20. **A-q, r; B-p; C-s; D-s**

Capacitance   coulomb-volt^{-1}, coulomb^2-joule^{-1}
Inductance   ohm-sec
Magnetic Induction   newton (ampere-metre)$^{-1}$

$\because$ (A) $q = CV; U = \dfrac{1}{2} CV^2$

(B) $L = \dfrac{\phi_m}{I}$

(C) $F = I\ell B$

(D) Magnetic flux density $= \dfrac{\phi}{\text{Area}}$

1. **(d)** Since $0 = (v\sin\theta)t + \frac{1}{2}(-a)t^2 \Rightarrow t = \frac{2v\sin\theta}{a}$

Also, $h = (v\cos\theta)t + \frac{1}{2}gt^2$

$$\Rightarrow h = \frac{2v^2}{a}\sin\theta\left(\cos\theta + \frac{g}{a}\sin\theta\right)$$

2. **(b)**

$$\tan\beta = \frac{v_{girl} + v_{rain}\sin\alpha}{v_{rain}\cos\alpha}$$

$$\Rightarrow \tan\beta = \frac{8 + 10\sin\alpha}{10\cos\alpha}$$

3. **(a)** Arc length = radius × angle

So, $|\vec{B} - \vec{A}| = |\vec{A}|\,\Delta\theta$

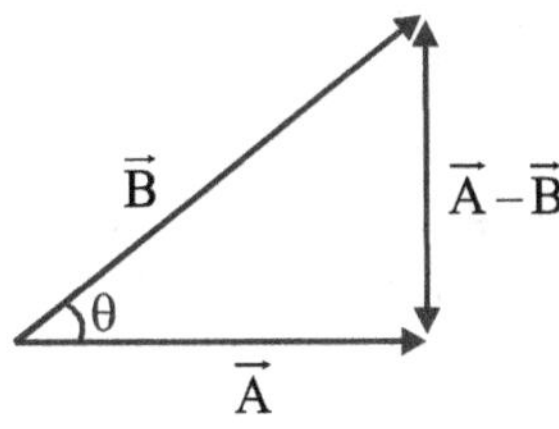

4. **(b)** $10 - v\cos 60° = 0$

$v = 20\,\text{m/s}$

$$H = \frac{v^2\sin^2 60°}{2g} = 15\,\text{m}$$

5. **(b)** As when they collide $vt + \frac{1}{2}\left(\frac{72v^2}{25\pi R}\right)t^2 - \pi R = vt$

$$\therefore t = \frac{5\pi R}{6v}$$

Now, angle covered by $A = \pi + \frac{vt}{R}$

Put t, $\therefore$ angle covered by $A = \frac{11\pi}{6}$

6. **(a, b)**

(a) $v_{hel/water} = v_{sub/water} + v_{hel/sub}$

$$= 17\hat{j} + (-5)\hat{k} = (17\hat{j} - 5\hat{k})\,\text{m/s}$$

(b) $v_{hel/air} = v_{hel/water} + v_{water/air} = v_{hel/water} - v_{air/water}$

$$= (17\hat{j} - 5\hat{k}) - 12\hat{i} = (-12\hat{i} + 17\hat{j} - 5\hat{k})\,\text{m/s}$$

7. **(a, c)** $t = \dfrac{d}{v\cos\theta}$

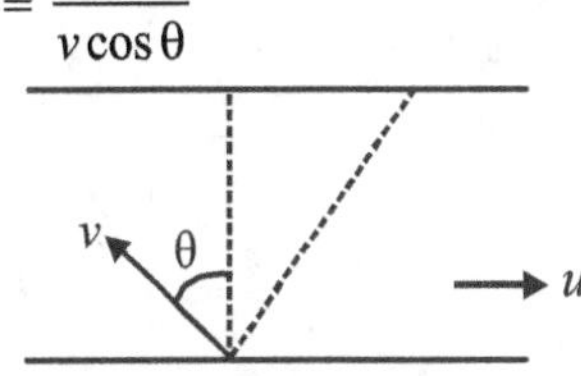

8. **(b, c)** Initial velocity of particle in vector form can be written as

$$x = (u - v\sin\theta)t$$

$$= \frac{ud}{v}\sec\theta - d\tan\theta$$

For x to minimum

$$\frac{dx}{d\theta} = 0 \Rightarrow \sin\theta = \frac{v}{u}$$

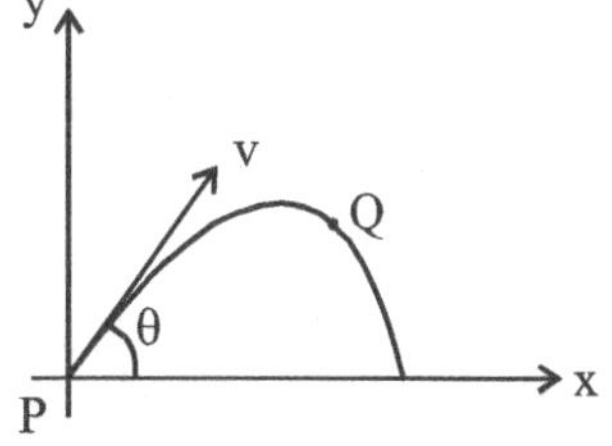

$$\overrightarrow{v_P} = v\cos\theta\,\hat{i} + v\sin\theta\,\hat{j} \qquad \text{...(1)}$$

Velocity of particle at any time t will be:

$$\overrightarrow{v_Q} = v\cos\theta\,\hat{i} + (v\sin\theta - gt)\hat{j} \qquad \text{...(2)}$$

Given that $\overrightarrow{v_P} \perp \overrightarrow{v_Q}$

$\therefore \quad \overrightarrow{v_P}\cdot\overrightarrow{v_Q} = 0$

or $\quad v^2\cos^2\theta + v^2\sin^2\theta - v\sin\theta\,gt = 0$

or $\quad v^2 = v\sin\theta\,gt$ or $t = \dfrac{v}{g}\text{cosec}\,\theta$

Substituting this value of t in Eq. (2), we get

$$\overrightarrow{v_Q} = v\cos\theta\,\hat{i} + \left(v\sin\theta - \frac{v}{\sin\theta}\right)\hat{j}$$

or $\quad |\overrightarrow{v_Q}| = \sqrt{v^2\cos^2\theta + v^2\sin^2\theta + \dfrac{v^2}{\sin^2\theta} - 2v^2}$

$$= v\cot\theta$$

9. **(a, c)** Time taken to reach x-y plane is given by

$$\frac{1}{2}gt^2 = 5 \Rightarrow t = 1\,\text{sec}$$

Initial horizontal velocity of bob is $3\hat{j}$

$y = 3 \times 1 = 3\,\text{m}$

$\therefore x = 2\,\text{m}, y = 3\,\text{m}$

10. **5** From the perspective of observer A, considering vertical motion of the ball from the point of throw till it reaches back at the initial height.

$U_y = +5\sqrt{3}\,\text{m/s}, \ S_y = 0, \ a_y = -10\text{m/s}^2, \ t = ?$

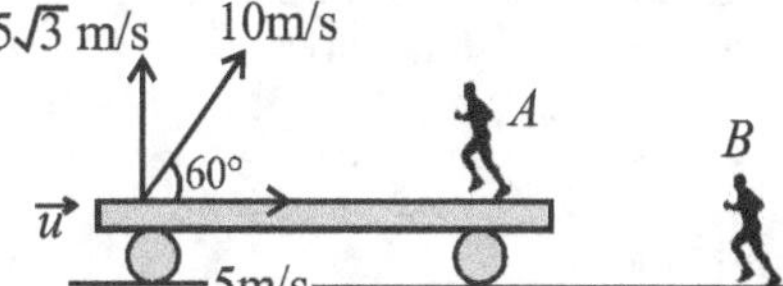

Applying $S = ut + \dfrac{1}{2} at^2 \Rightarrow 0 = 5\sqrt{3}t - 5t^2$

$\therefore \quad t = \sqrt{3}$ sec

Considering horizontal motion from the perspective of observer B. Let u be the speed of train at the time of throw.

The horizontal distance travelled by the ball $= (u + 5)\sqrt{3}$.

The horizonal distance travelled by the boy

$$= \left[u\sqrt{3} + \dfrac{1}{2} a(\sqrt{3})^2 \right] + 1.15$$

As the boy catches the ball therefore

$$(u+5)\sqrt{3} = u\sqrt{3} + \dfrac{3}{2} a + 1.15$$

$\therefore \ 5\sqrt{3} = 1.5a + 1.15 \quad \therefore \ 7.51 = 1.5a$

$\therefore a \approx 5 \ \text{m/s}^2$

11. 1   Let t = time taken by shot fired from the gun horizontally

t + x = time taken by shot fired at an angle 60° with horizontal.

u = $5\sqrt{3}$ m/s, g = 10 m/s²

$u \cos 60°(t + x) = ut \qquad \qquad$ ...(1)   horizontally

$u \sin 60°(t + x) - \dfrac{1}{2} g(t + x)^2 = 0 - \dfrac{1}{2} gt^2 \quad$ ...(2)

                        vertically

Solving (1) & (2) we get x = 1 sec = required time internal

12. 3   Let us take velocity of swimmer with respect to water is v and that of river current is v_r. The swimmer which crosses the river along the straight line AB, has to swim in upstream direction such that its resultant velocity becomes toward AB as shown in figure. If the width of river is assumed to be d, then

Resultant velocity of first swimmer is $v_1 = \sqrt{v^2 - v_r^2}$

Time taken by her to cross the river is

$$t = \dfrac{d}{\sqrt{v^2 - v_r^2}} = \dfrac{d}{\sqrt{2.5^2 - 2^2}} = \dfrac{d}{1.5} \ \text{hr}.$$

Second swimmer if swims along AB, she is drifted towards point C, due to river flow as shown in figure and then she has to walk down to reach point B with velocity u.

Here crossing velocity of second swimmer is v, as its is swimming along normal direction.

Time taken to cross the river by her is,

$$t_1 = \dfrac{d}{v} = \dfrac{d}{1.5} \ \text{hr}$$

Her drift due to river flow is,

$$x = v_r \times \dfrac{d}{v}$$

Time taken to reach point B by walking is,

$$t_2 = \dfrac{x}{u} = \dfrac{v_r d}{uv} = \dfrac{2 \times d}{u \times 2.5} = \dfrac{d}{1.25u} \ \text{hr}$$

Given that both the swimmers reach the destination simultaneously, so we have

$$t = t_1 + t_2 \ \text{or} \ \dfrac{d}{1.5} = \dfrac{d}{2.5} + \dfrac{d}{1.25u}$$

or   **u = 3.0 km/hr.**

13. 5

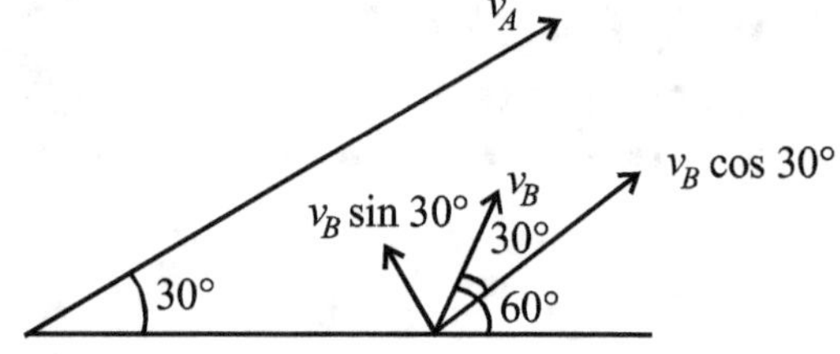

Here

$$v_A = v_B \cos 30°$$

$$\therefore \ 100\sqrt{3} = v_B \times \dfrac{\sqrt{3}}{2}$$

$$\therefore \ v_B = 200 \ \text{ms}^{-1}$$

$$\text{Time} = \dfrac{\text{displacement}}{\text{velocity}}$$

$$\therefore \ t_0 = \dfrac{500}{v_B \sin 30°} = \dfrac{500}{200 \times \sin 30°} = 5 \ \text{sec}$$

14. (b) $v_x = a$ and $v_y = bx$

At any time t, $x = v_x t = at \qquad$ ...(i)

For y, we have $\dfrac{dy}{dt} = bx$

$$= b\,(at)$$

$\therefore \qquad dy = (abt)\,dt$

or $\qquad y = \displaystyle\int_0^t abt \ dt = \dfrac{abt^2}{2} \qquad$ ...(ii)

From equation (i), $t = \dfrac{x}{a}$

Hence $\qquad y = \dfrac{ab}{2} t^2 = \dfrac{ab}{2} \left(\dfrac{x}{a} \right)^2$

or $\qquad y = \dfrac{bx^2}{2a} \qquad$ ...(iii)

15. (c)   The curvature radius can be calculated by

$$\dfrac{1}{R} = \dfrac{\left| \dfrac{d^2 y}{dx^2} \right|}{\left[1 + \left(\dfrac{dy}{dx} \right)^2 \right]^{3/2}}$$

From equation (iii) $\dfrac{dy}{dx} = \dfrac{d(bx^2 / 2a)}{dx} = \dfrac{bx}{a}$

and $\qquad \dfrac{d^2 y}{dx^2} = \dfrac{b}{a}$

Thus, $R = \dfrac{\left[1 + \left(\dfrac{dy}{dx} \right)^2 \right]^{3/2}}{\left| \dfrac{d^2 y}{dx^2} \right|} = \dfrac{\left[1 + \left(\dfrac{bx}{a} \right)^2 \right]^{3/2}}{\left(\dfrac{b}{a} \right)}$

$$= \dfrac{a}{b} \left[1 + \left(\dfrac{bx}{a} \right)^2 \right]^{3/2}$$

16. **(c)** during the upward journey of projectile velocity of the body decreases and finally becomes zero at the top but then after the direction of velocity changes and goes on increasing while acceleration remains constant throughout the journey $a = -g$.

17. **(d)** When velocity-time graph is straight line the corresponding acceleration-time graph will be straight line parallel to time-axis i.e., constant acceleration.

18. **(a)** For case IV displacement time graph shows that body is in rest.

19. **(A) – p, (B) – p, (C) q, s ; (D) r, s**

If angle between constant acceleration vector $\vec{a}$ and velocity $\vec{v}$ is zero or $180°$ then path is straight line otherwise path must be parabolic.

20. **(A) $\rightarrow$ q; (B) $\rightarrow$ p, r; (C) $\rightarrow$ p, r; (D) $\rightarrow$ q, r**

(A) For same range, angles of projection are θ and $(90° - \theta)$

$R_1 = R_2, T_1 \neq T_2, h_1 \neq h_2, v_{y_1} \neq v_{y_2}$, same speed

(B) For same height, $v_{y_1} = v_{y_2}, T_1 = T_2$

(C) $t = \sqrt{\dfrac{2h}{g}}, \; v_y^2 = 2gh$

(D) $v^2 = u^2 + 2gh$

$v_y^2 = u_y^2 + 2gh$

θ above horizontal

$\quad -h = u \sin \theta t - (1/2) g t^2 \qquad \text{.... (1)}$

θ below horizontal

$\quad -h = -u \sin \theta \, t - (1/2) g t^2 \quad \text{.... (2)}$

From (1) and (2), t will be different.

1. **(a)** For the impending motion, block A must slip up and block C down the inclined plane. Since the normal force between A and B is less than that between block B and C, the maximum frictional force (limiting friction) will be reached first between A and B while B and C will stay together.

From FBD of block A:

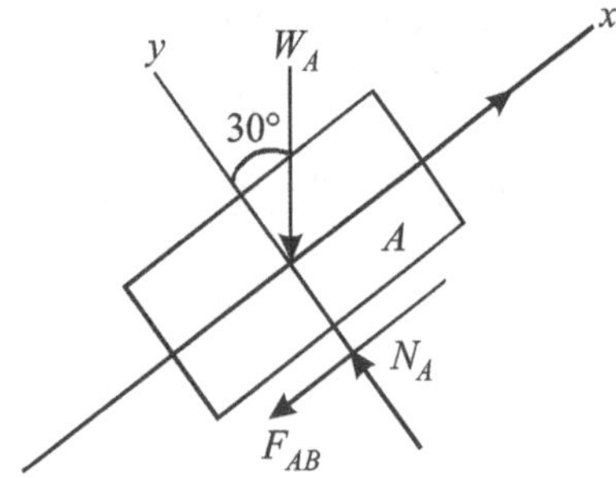

Writing equilibrium equations :

$$\Sigma F_y = 0 \ ;$$
$$N_A - W_A \cos 30° = 0$$
$$N_A = W_A \cos 30°$$
$$N_A = 20\sqrt{3}\,\text{N}$$

Also for impending motion if F_{AB} is frictional force between blocks A and B, then

$$F_{AB} = \mu_s.N_A = 20\sqrt{3}\ \mu_s N \qquad \text{.........(1)}$$

$$\Sigma F_x = 0 :$$
$$T - W_A \sin 30° - F_{AB} = 0$$
$$T - 40.\frac{1}{2} - 20\sqrt{3}\mu_s = 0$$
$$T = 20\,(1 + \sqrt{3}\mu_s) \qquad \text{.........(2)}$$

From FBD of block B and C combined

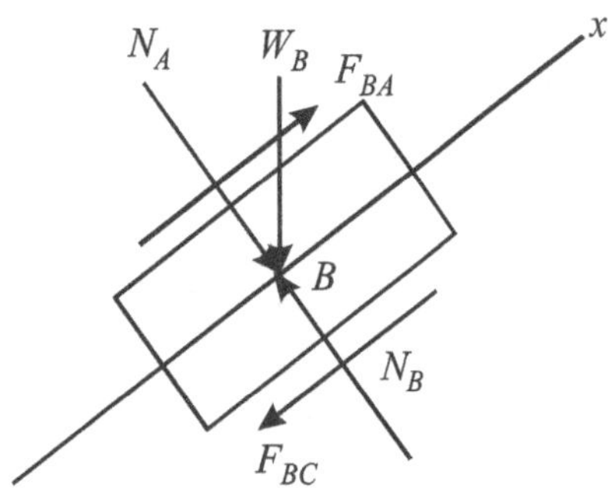

Writing equilibrium equation

$$\Sigma F_y = 0 \ ;$$
$$N_C - N_A - (W_B + W_C)\cos 30° = 0$$
$$N_C - 20\sqrt{3} - 110.\frac{\sqrt{3}}{2} = 0$$
$$N_C = 75\sqrt{3}\ \text{N}$$

Also for impending motion :

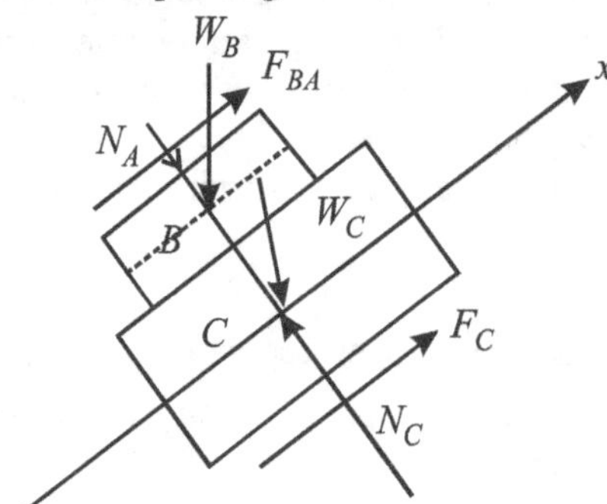

$$F_C = \mu_s.N_C = 75\sqrt{3}\ \mu_s \qquad \text{.........(3)}$$

For $\Sigma F_x = 0$, we have
$$T_A + (F_{BA} + F_C) - (W_B + W_C)\sin 30° = 0$$
$$T + [20\sqrt{3} + 75\sqrt{3}\mu_s] - \frac{110}{2} = 0$$
$$T = (55 - 95\sqrt{3}\mu_s)$$

Since tension is same, so from (2) and (4), we get

$$20\,(1 + \sqrt{3}\mu_s) = (55 - 95\sqrt{3}\ \mu_s)$$

Solving for μ_s we get, $115\sqrt{3}.\mu_s = 35$

or $\mu_s = \dfrac{35}{115\sqrt{3}} = 0.1757$

$\therefore$ Minimum $\mu_s = 0.1757$

2. **(c)**

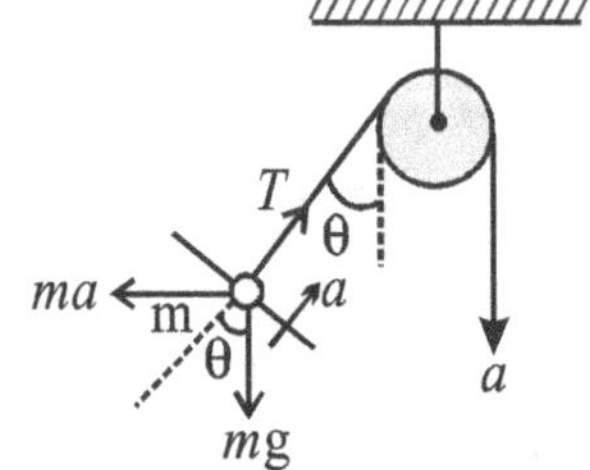

(Force diagram in the frame of the car)
Applying Newton's law perpendicular to string
$$mg \sin\theta = ma \cos\theta$$

$$\Rightarrow \ \tan\theta = \frac{a}{g}$$

Applying Newton's law along string

$$\Rightarrow T - m\sqrt{g^2 + a^2} = ma$$

or $T = m\sqrt{g^2 + a^2} + ma$

3. **(c)**

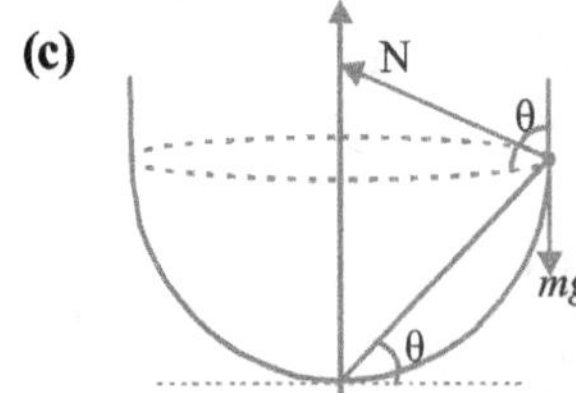

$N \cos \theta = mg$ and $N \sin \theta = m\omega^2 r$

$$\therefore \quad \tan\theta = \frac{\omega^2 r}{g} \quad \ldots(i)$$

Given $\quad y = x^2$

$$\therefore \quad \frac{dy}{dx} = 2x$$

or $\quad \tan\theta = 2 \times 1 = 2 \quad \ldots(ii)$

From above equations, we get

$$\omega = \sqrt{2g} \quad (r = 1\,m)$$

4. **(a)** At limiting equilibrium, $\mu = \tan\theta$

$$\tan\theta = \mu = \frac{dy}{dx} = \frac{x^2}{2} \text{ (from question)}$$

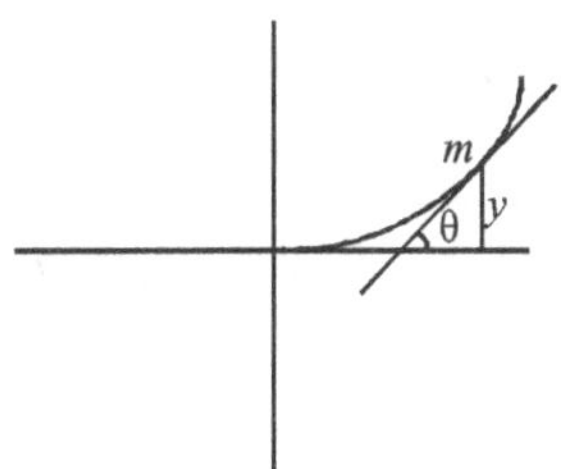

$\because$ Coefficient of friction $\mu = 0.5$

$$\therefore \quad 0.5 = \frac{x^2}{2}$$

$$\Rightarrow \quad x = \pm 1$$

Now, $y = \dfrac{x^3}{6} = \dfrac{1}{6}\,m$

5. **(c)** FBD in reference frame of the lift

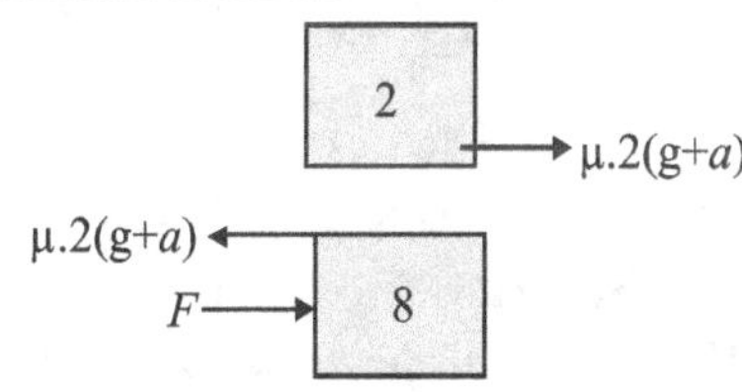

$$a_2 = \frac{1}{5}\left(g + \frac{g}{4}\right) = \frac{g}{4} = 2.5 \, m/s^2$$

$$a_8 = \frac{30 - \left[\mu.2\left(g + \dfrac{g}{4}\right)\right]}{8}$$

$$= \frac{30 - \left[\dfrac{1}{5} \times 2 \times \dfrac{50}{4}\right]}{8} = \frac{25}{8}\, m/s^2$$

6. **(c, d)** Here we choose the x-axis along the incline with positive upward. All the forces on the block are shown in figure.

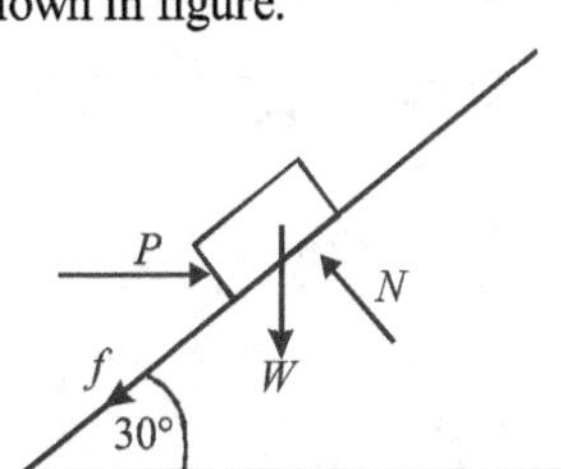

From $\Sigma F_x = ma_x$ we have $P \cos 30° - W \sin 30° - f = ma_x$, where $m = 20$ kg, $W = mg = 196$ N, and $f = 80$ N

For $a_x = 0$, $P = 206$ N.

For $a_x = 0.75 \, m/s^2$, $P = 223$ N

7. **(c, d)** From figure, $\Sigma F_{ver} = R_1 \cos 30° - W = ma_{ver} = 0$ and $\Sigma F_{hor} = R_2 - R_1 \sin 30° = ma$.

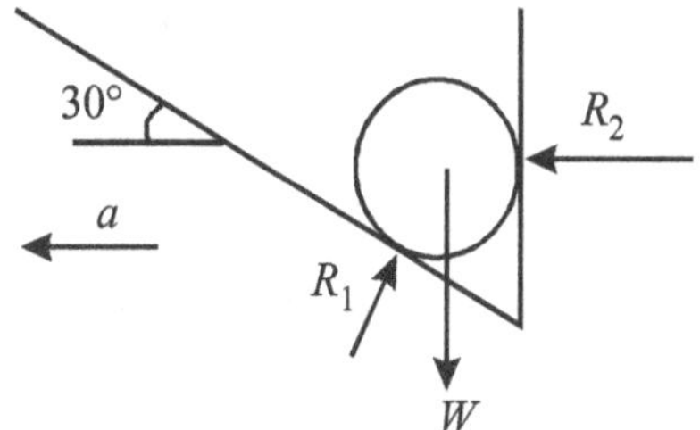

Thus, the acting forces are

$$R_1 = \frac{W}{\cos 30°} = 1.15W$$

$$R_2 = R_1 \sin 30° + \frac{W}{g}a$$

$$= (1.15\,W)(0.5) + \frac{W}{g}a$$

$$= W\left(0.58 + \frac{a}{g}\right)$$

8. **(a, b, c, d)** Let T = tension in the string, F = force of friction between C and P.

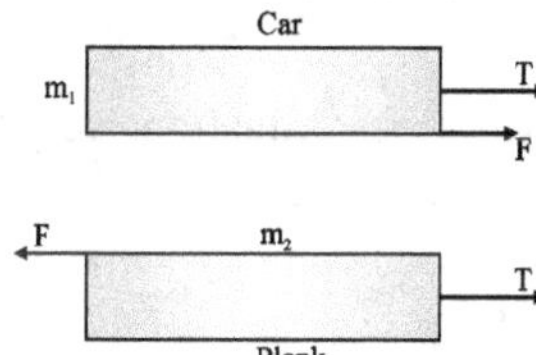

If the string is under tension, the acceleration of C to the right = acceleration of P to the left = a.

$$T + F = m_1 a \qquad F - T = m_2 a$$

$$\therefore \quad T = \frac{1}{2}(m_1 - m_2)a \quad \text{or } T > 0 \text{ if } m_1 > m_2.$$

If $m_1 < m_2$, T becomes < 0, i.e., it becomes slack.

If $m_1 = m_2$, $T = 0$

9. **(b, c, d)**

Let N be the normal reaction (Reading of the weighing machine)

at $A \Rightarrow \quad N_A - mg = \dfrac{mv^2}{r}$

put $v \therefore \ N_A - mg = mg \Rightarrow N_A = 2mg = 2W$

Also, at E, $\ N_E + mg = \dfrac{mv^2}{r} = mg \quad \therefore \ N_E = 0$

hence $\ N_A > N_E$ by 2W

Now at G, $N_G = \dfrac{mv^2}{r} = mg = W = N_c$

Also $\quad \dfrac{N_E}{N_A} = 0$ and $\dfrac{N_A}{N_C} = 2$

10. 6

If θ is the angle which the inclined plane makes with the vertical direction, then the acceleration of the block sliding down the plane of length ℓ will be $g\cos\theta$.

Using the formula, $s = ut + \dfrac{1}{2}at^2$, we have $s = \ell$, $u = 0$,

$t = t$ and $a = g\cos\theta$.

So $\ell = 0 \times t + \dfrac{1}{2}g\cos\theta\, t^2 = \dfrac{1}{2}(g\cos\theta)t^2$ ...(i)

Taking vertical downward motion of the block, we get

$\therefore\ h = 0 + \dfrac{1}{2}g(t/2)^2 = \dfrac{1}{2}gt^2/4$ ...(ii)

Dividing (ii) by (i), we get $\dfrac{h}{\ell} = \dfrac{1}{4\cos\theta}$ $\quad [\because \cos\theta = h/\ell]$

or $\cos\theta = \dfrac{1}{4\cos\theta}$; or $\cos^2\theta = \dfrac{1}{4}$; or $\cos\theta = \dfrac{1}{2}$

or $\theta = \mathbf{60°}$

11. 2 For m not to slide over M, acceleration of the triangular block should be $g\tan\theta$.

If m_0 is the required mass, then

$mg - T = m_0\,(g\tan\theta)$ $\qquad$ ...(i)

and $T = (M+m)g\tan\theta$

or $\qquad T = 2g\tan\theta$ $\qquad$ ...(ii)

$\qquad\qquad \cot\theta = 2$ $\qquad$ ...(iii)

After simplifying above equation, we get $m_0 = 2$ kg.

12. 1 Before cutting string

$N_1 = T = Mg/2$

After cutting string

$Mg - N_2 = Ma$ $\qquad$ ...(i)

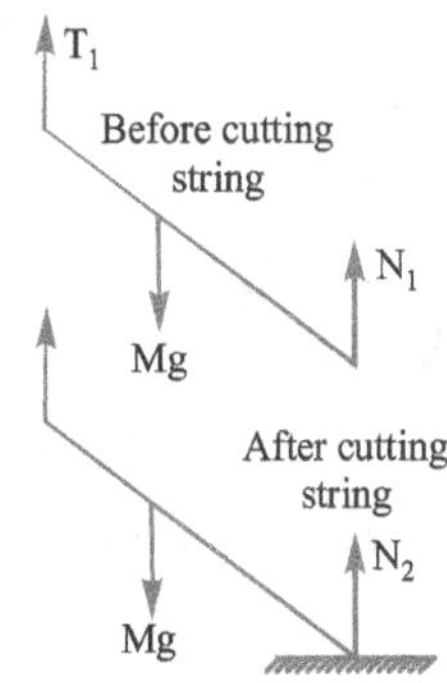

$N_2\ell\sin\theta = M\alpha(2\ell)^2/12$ $\qquad$ ...(ii)

By constraint that lower end will have acceleration only in horizontal direction.

$\ell\alpha\sin\theta = a$ $\qquad$ ...(iii)

From (i), (ii) and (iii)

$\Rightarrow \qquad\qquad N_2 = Mg/(3\sin^2\theta + 1)$

$\Rightarrow \qquad\qquad N_1/N_2 = (3\sin^2\theta + 1)/2 = 1$

13. 1

$10\,t = 2T$

$\Rightarrow T = 5t$

Block A will lose contact when

$T = m_A g$

$5t = m_A g$

$\Rightarrow t_1 = \dfrac{m_A g}{5}\sec = \mathbf{2sec}$

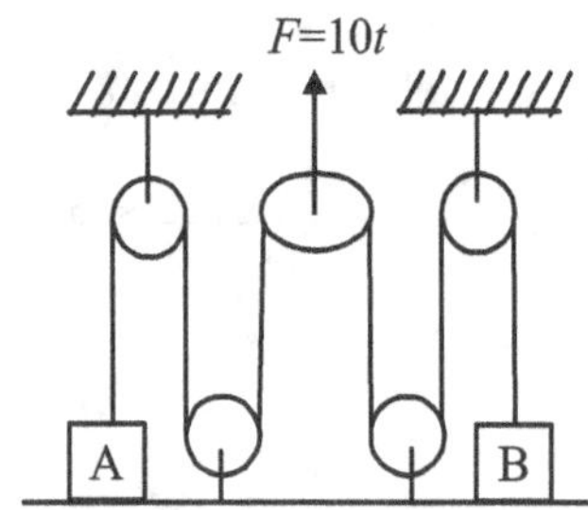

While block B will lose contact, when

$T' = m_B g$

$\Rightarrow 5t = 2m_B g$

or $\quad t_2 = \dfrac{2g}{5}\sec = 4$ sec

At $t_1 \le t$ for block A

$T - mg = ma$

$5t - mg = \dfrac{mdv}{dt}$

$\Rightarrow m\displaystyle\int_0^v dv = \int_{t_1}^{t_2} (5t - mg)dt$

$v = \mathbf{10\ m/s}$

14. (a) If F = 50N, force on 5 kg block = 10N

So friction force = 10N

15. (b) Until the 10 kg block is sticked with ground (F = 40N), No force will be felt by 5 kg block.

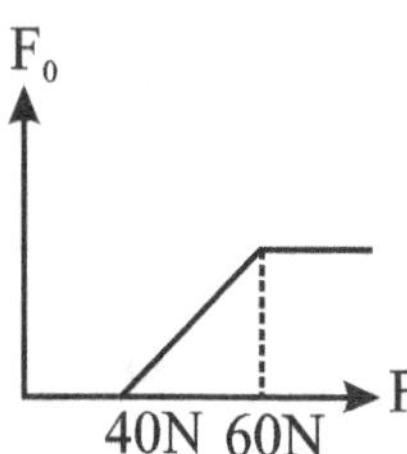

After F = 40 N, the friction force on 5 kg increases, till F = 60 N and after that, the kinetic friction start acting on 5 kg block, which will be constant (20N).

16. (a)

All the body of mass m_1, m_2 and m_3 will move with the same acceleration $= \dfrac{F}{m_1 + m_2 + m_3}$

$= \dfrac{12}{1+2+3} = 2\,\text{ms}^{-2}$

17. (b)

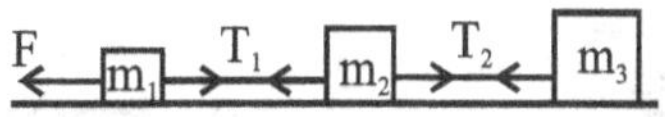

$$F - T_1 = m_1 a \quad \text{...(i)}$$

F.B.D. of m_1: $F - T_1 = m_1 a$ ...(i)

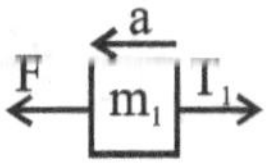

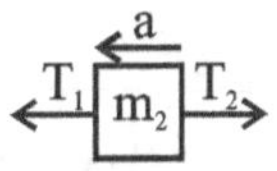

$$T_1 - T_2 = m_2 a \quad \text{.... (ii)}$$

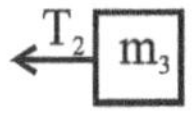

$$T_2 = m_3 a \quad \text{....(iii)}$$

(i) + (ii) + (iii)

$$a = F/(m_1 + m_2 + m_3)$$

$$T_2 = m_3 F \Big/ m_1 + m_2 + m_3 = \frac{3 + 12}{1 + 2 + 3} = 6N$$

$$T_1 = m_2 a + T_2 = (m_2 + m_3)\, F/(m_1 + m_2 + m_3)$$

$$= \frac{(2 + 3)12}{1 + 2 + 3} = 10N$$

18. (d) For situation (I),

$$f_1 = \frac{(m_2 + m_3)\,F}{m_1 + m_2 + m_3}, \quad f_2 = \frac{m_3 f}{m_1 + m_2 + m_3}$$

Situation (II), $f_1 = \dfrac{m_1 F}{m_1 + m_2 + m_3}$,

$$f_2 = \frac{(m_1 + m_2)\,F}{m_1 + m_2 + m_3}$$

Situation (III), $T_1 = \dfrac{m_1 F}{m_1 + m_2 + m_3}$,

$$T_2 = \frac{(m_1 + m_2)\,F}{m_1 + m_2 + m_3}$$

Situation (IV), $T_1 = \dfrac{(m_2 + m_3)\,F}{m_1 + m_2 + m_3}$,

$$T_2 = \frac{m_3 F}{m_1 + m_2 + m_3}$$

19. **(A) → r; (B) → p; (C) → q; (D) → q**

Gravity force (mg) will remain constant and always directed towards the centre of the earth. Normal force depends on cos θ, whereas centrifugal force and friction force depends on sin θ. As θ first decreases then increases. Normal force first increases then decreases whereas centrifugal force and friction force first decreases then increases.

20. **(A) → p, q; (B) → s; (C) → s; (D) → p, s**

(A) $20 - 0.5 \times 2 \times 10 = ma$; $a = 5 \text{ m/s}^2$, $f = 10N$

Tension at mid point,

$$T - 0.5 \times 1 \times 10 = 1 \times 5 \Rightarrow T = 10\,N$$

(B) Speed constant $\Rightarrow a = 0$

Pulling force = mg sin θ + f

(C) $F_{net} = 7.5 - 0.75 \times g \times \sin 30° - \dfrac{1}{\sqrt{3}} \times 0.75 g \cos 30°$

$$= 7.5 - 0.75 g \times \frac{1}{2} - \frac{1}{\sqrt{3}} 0.75 g \frac{\sqrt{3}}{2} = 0$$

(D) $F_{net} = 20 - 2g = 0$; $T - 1g = 1 \times 0 \Rightarrow T = 10\,N$

1. **(d)** $\qquad W = mgh + \dfrac{1}{2}kx^2$

$\qquad\qquad = mg(a\sin\theta) + \dfrac{1}{2}k(a\theta)^2$

$\qquad\qquad = Wa\sin\theta + \dfrac{1}{2}ka^2\theta^2 \,.$

2. **(d)** The velocity of particle after falling through height h

$\qquad u = \sqrt{2gh} \qquad\qquad ...(i)$

After first rebounding, the velocity of ball is eu and after attaining maximum height it will come to the ground with same velocity eu. So, after second rebounding its velocity will be e^2u.

Similarly, after third fourth ... etc reboundings its velocities will be e^2u, e^4u, ... etc.

Since, it first rebounds with velocity eu so if it attains height h then from

$\qquad v^2 = u^2 - 2gh$

$\qquad \therefore \quad 0 = e^2u^2 - 2gh_1$

or $\quad h_1 = \dfrac{e^2u^2}{2g} = \dfrac{e^2\,2gh}{2g} = e^2h$ [from Eq. (i)]

The same height the ball travels while approaching ground. Now, it rebounds with velocity e^2u so if it attains a height h_2 then

$\qquad 0 = e^4u^2 - 2gh_2$

or $\quad h_2 = e^4h$

The similar process will follow for further reboundings Hence, the total distance travelled by the practice before it stops rebounding.

$\qquad = h + 2h_1 + 2h_2 + ...\infty$

$\qquad = h + 2e^2h + 2e^4h + ...\infty$

$\qquad = h + 2e^2h\left(1 + e^2 + e^4 + ...\infty\right)$

$\qquad = h + 2e^2h\left(\dfrac{1}{1-e^2}\right)$

$\qquad = h\left(1 + \dfrac{2e^2}{1-e^2}\right) = \left(\dfrac{1+e^2}{1-e^2}\right)h$

3. **(b)** $\quad$ K.E. $= \dfrac{1}{2}mv^2 = \dfrac{1}{2}m\left[u + at\right]^2 = \dfrac{1}{2}m\left[0 + gt\right]^2$

$\qquad \therefore \; K.E = \dfrac{1}{2}mgt^2 \qquad \therefore \; K.E \propto t^2 \qquad ...(1)$

First the kinetic energy will increase as per eq (1). As the balls touches the ground it starts deforming and loses its K.E. (K.E. converting into elastic potential energy). When the deformation is maximum, K.E. = 0.

The ball then again regain its shape when its elastic potential energy changes into K.E. As the ball moves up it loses K.E. and gain gravitational potential energy. These characteristics are according to graph (b).

4. **(b)** Because momentum of the two-ball system is conserved, $\vec{p}_{Pi} + 0 = \vec{p}_{Pf} + \vec{p}_B$.

Because the Ping-Pong $\vec{p}_{Pf} = -\vec{p}_{Pi}$.

As a consequence, $\vec{p}_B = 2\vec{p}_{Pi}$. Kinetic energy can be expressed as $K = p^2/2m$. Because of the much larger mass of the bowling ball, its kinetic energy is much smaller than that of the Ping-Pong ball.

5. **(b)** Speed just before collision $= \sqrt{2g\ell\,(1-\cos\theta_0)}$

Speed just after collision $= e\sqrt{2g\ell\,(1-\cos\theta_0)}$

From conservation of energy,

$\qquad \dfrac{1}{2}me^2[2g\ell\,(1-\cos\theta_0)] = mg\ell\,(1-\cos\theta)$

$\qquad \therefore \; \theta = \cos^{-1}\{1 - e^2(1-\cos\theta_0)\}$

6. **(a, b, c)** Work by centripetal force $= 0$

because $F_C \perp$ to displacement

Area under F-x curve $= \int F.dx = W.$

By definition, for conservative force work is independent of path length.

[Pressure $\times$ volume] = [work]

7. **(b, c, d)** If $\vec{F}$ is conservative, then

$\qquad F_x = -\dfrac{\partial U}{\partial x}, F_y = -\dfrac{\partial U}{\partial y}$

and so $\dfrac{\partial F_x}{\partial y} = -\dfrac{\partial^2 U}{\partial y\partial x} = -\dfrac{\partial^2 U}{\partial x\partial y} = \dfrac{\partial F_y}{\partial x}$

But, for the given force,

$\qquad \dfrac{\partial F_x}{\partial y} = 2x^2y$ and $\dfrac{\partial F_y}{\partial x} = 2xy^2$

Hence, the given force is not conservative.

The work done by $\vec{F}$ is given by

$\qquad W = \int \vec{F}.d\vec{s} = (x^2y^2\hat{i} + x^2y^2\hat{j}).(dx\,\hat{i} + dy\,\hat{j})$

$\qquad\quad = \int x^2y^2\,dx + \int x^2y^2\,dy$

Along AB, $y = 0$ and so $W_{AB} = 0$.

Along BC, $dx = 0$ and

$\qquad W_{BC} = \int_0^a a^2y^2 dy = \dfrac{a^5}{3}$

Thus, $W_{ABC} = W_{AB} + W_{BC} = \dfrac{a^5}{3}$(J)

Along AD, $x = 0$ and so $W_{AD} = 0$.
Along DC, $dy = 0$ and

$$W_{DC} = \int_0^a x^2 a^2 dx = \frac{a^5}{3}$$

Thus, $W_{ADC} = W_{AD} + W_{DC} = \frac{a^5}{3}$ (J)

Along AC, $x = y$ and $dx = dy$. Thus,

$$W_{AC} = 2\int_0^a x^4 dx = \frac{2a^5}{3}$$ (J)

8. (a, b) We denote the spring constant, the relaxed length, and the collar mass by k, ℓ_0, and m, respectively. We let v_i and ℓ_i represent the initial collar speed and spring length, v and ℓ represent the instantaneous speed and spring length at some other time. The conservation of mechanical energy implies that

$$\frac{1}{2}mv^2 + \frac{1}{2}k\,(\ell - \ell_0)^2 = \frac{1}{2}mv_i^2 + \frac{1}{2}k\,(\ell_i - \ell_0)^2$$

Since $v_i = 0$, we have

$$v = \sqrt{\frac{k}{m}}\,[(\ell_i - \ell_0)^2 - (\ell - \ell_0)^2]^{1/2}$$

Referring to figure,

$$\ell_i = \sqrt{(0.20)^2 + (0.15)^2} = 0.25\,\text{m}$$

As the collar passes point A, $\ell = \ell_A = 0.20\,\text{m}$. With $\ell_0 = 0.10$ m, $k = 500$ N/m, and $m = 10$ kg, we obtain

$$v_A = \sqrt{\frac{500}{10}}[(0.25 - 0.10)^2 - (0.20 - 0.10)^2]^{1/2}$$

$$= \sqrt{50}\,\sqrt{0.0225 - 0.0100} = 0.791\,\text{m/s}$$

As the collar passes point B, $\ell = \ell_B$

$$= \sqrt{(0.20)^2 + (0.10)^2} = 0.2236\,\text{m}.$$

Then we have,

$$v_B = \sqrt{50}\,[(0.15)^2 - (0.1236)^2]^{1/2} = 0.601\,\text{m/s}$$

9. (a, b, d) Maximum extension will be at the moment when both masses stop momentarily after going down. Applying W-E theorem from starting to that instant

$$k_f - k_t = W_{gr} + W_{sp} + W_{ten.}$$

$$0 - 0 = 2Mgx + \left(-\frac{1}{2}Kx^2\right) + 0$$

$$\Rightarrow \quad x = \frac{4Mg}{K}$$

System will have maximum KE when net force on the system becomes zero. Therefore,

$$2Mg = T \quad \text{and} \quad T = kx \Rightarrow x = \frac{2Mg}{K}$$

Hence KE will be maximum when 2M mass has gone down by $\dfrac{2Mg}{K}$

Applying W/E theorem

$$k_f - 0 = 2Mg.\frac{2Mg}{K} - \frac{1}{2}K\frac{4M^2g^2}{K} \Rightarrow k_f = \frac{2M^2g^2}{K^2}$$

Maximum energy of spring $= \dfrac{1}{2}K\left(\dfrac{4Mg}{K}\right)^2 = \dfrac{8M^2g^2}{K}$

Therefore maximum spring energy $= 4 \times$ maximum K.E.

10. 3 (K.E.)' $= 50\%$ of K.E. after hit i.e.,

$$\frac{1}{2}mv'^2 = \frac{50}{100} \times \frac{1}{2}mv^2 \Rightarrow v' = \frac{v}{\sqrt{2}}$$

Coefficient of restitution $= \dfrac{1}{\sqrt{2}}$

Now, total distance travelled by object is

$$H = h\left(\frac{1+e^2}{1-e^2}\right) = h\left(\frac{1+\frac{1}{2}}{1-\frac{1}{2}}\right) = 3h$$

11. 5 Here Δ K.E. $= W = P \times t$

$$\therefore \frac{1}{2}mv^2 = P \times t$$

$$\therefore v = \sqrt{\frac{2Pt}{m}} = \sqrt{\frac{2 \times 0.5 \times 5}{0.2}} = 5\,\text{ms}^{-1}$$

12. 6 $F = f + mg \sin\theta$

$\qquad = \mu N + mg \sin\theta$

$\qquad = \mu\, mg \cos\theta + mg \sin\theta$

$$W = \int_{a/2}^0 F ds$$

$$= \int_{a/2}^0 (\mu mg \cos\theta + mg \sin\theta)\,(Rd\theta)$$

$$= mg R \int_{r/2}^0 (\mu \cos\theta + \sin\theta)d\theta$$

$$= mg R\,|\mu\sin\theta - \cos\theta\,|_{r/2}^0 = -mg R\,(1+\mu)$$

$$= 2 \times 10 \times \frac{1}{5}\,(1 + 0.5) = 6\,\text{J}.$$

13. 3 For maxmum K.E, $F = 0$, or $1 - x^2 = 0$, $\therefore x = \pm 1$.

$$W = \Delta K$$

or $\displaystyle\int_0^1 F dx = k_f - k_i$

or $\displaystyle\int_0^1 (1-x^2)\,dx = k_f - 0$

or $\left| x - \dfrac{x^3}{3}\right|_0^1 = k_f$

$\therefore \quad k_f = \dfrac{2}{3}$

Given $\quad \dfrac{2}{3} = \dfrac{2}{n}$

$\therefore \quad n = 3$

14. **(c)** By conservation of mechanical energy, we have

$$\Delta U = U_f - U_i = \left(Mg\dfrac{\ell}{2} + mg\ell \right) - 0$$

$$= \left(\dfrac{M}{2} + m \right) g\ell$$

15. **(a)** $\quad \dfrac{1}{2} mv^2 = Mg\dfrac{\ell}{2} + mg\ell$

$\therefore \quad v = \sqrt{\dfrac{Mg\ell + 2mg\ell}{m}}.$

16. **(a)** Kinetic energy of the projectile decreases during the upward journey, becomes zero at the maximum height & then kinetic energy goes on increasing during the return journey.

17. **(c)** When spring is compressed or elangated by a length x from its natural length, the potential energy of the spring increases by $\dfrac{1}{2}k\,x^2$.

18. **(a)**

19. **A-r; B-p; C-q; D-s**

Initial position, $KE = 0$,

Equilibrium, KE is maximum

Work done on block by gravity $= mgx$

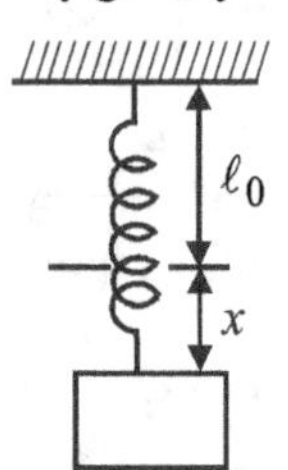

Magnitude of work done on block by spring $= \dfrac{1}{2}k\,x^2$

By conservation of energy, total mechanical energy will be conserved.

20. $\text{(A)} \rightarrow p\,;\text{(B)} \rightarrow p;\,\text{(C)} \rightarrow r\,;\text{(D)} \rightarrow q$

1. **(b)** Centre of mass of the rod is given by:

$$x_{cm} = \frac{\int_0^L (ax + \frac{bx^2}{L})\,dx}{\int_0^L (a + \frac{bx}{L})\,dx}$$

$$= \frac{\frac{aL^2}{2} + \frac{bL^2}{3}}{aL + \frac{bL}{2}} = \frac{L\left(\frac{a}{2} + \frac{b}{3}\right)}{a + \frac{b}{2}}$$

Now $\dfrac{7L}{12} = \dfrac{\frac{a}{2} + \frac{b}{3}}{a + \frac{b}{2}}$

On solving we get, $b = 2a$

2. **(b)** Since v is changing (decreasing), L is not conserved in magnitude. Since it is given that a particle is confined to rotate in a circular path, it cannot have spiral path. Since the particle has two accelerations a_c and a_t therefore the net acceleration is not towards the centre.

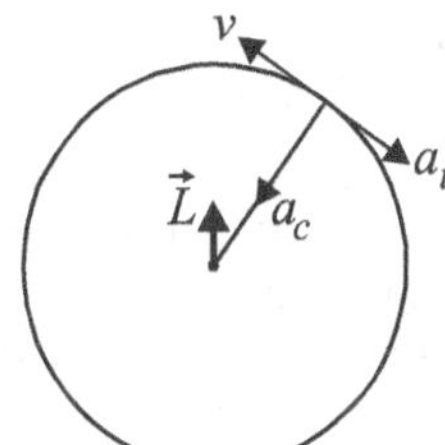

The direction of $\vec{L}$ remains same even when the speed decreases.

3. **(b)** We know that $|\vec{\tau}| = \left|\dfrac{d\vec{L}}{dt}\right|$ where $L = I\omega$

$\therefore \quad \tau = \dfrac{d}{dt}(I\omega) = \omega\dfrac{dI}{dt}$ ...(i)

From the situation it is clear that the moment of inertia for (rod + insect) system is increasing.

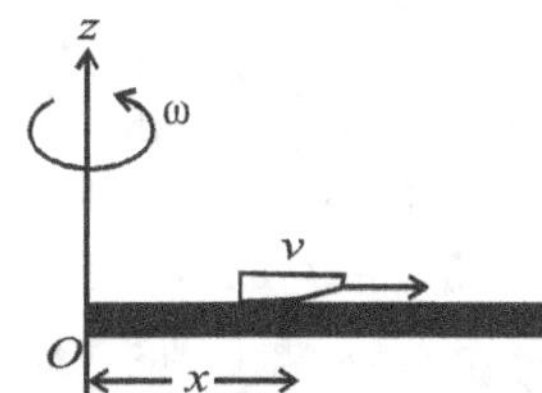

Let at any instant of time 't', the insect is at a distance x from O. At this instant, the moment of inertia of the system is

$I = \dfrac{1}{3}ML^2 + mx^2$ ...(ii)

From (i) & (ii)

$$\tau = \omega\frac{d}{dt}\left[\frac{1}{3}ML^2 + mx^2\right] = \omega\,m\frac{d}{dt}(x^2)$$

$$= 2\omega mx\frac{dx}{dt} = 2\omega mxv$$

$$= 2\omega mv^2t \qquad [\because x = vt]$$

$$\therefore \qquad \tau \propto t \qquad (\text{till } t = T)$$

When the insect stops moving, $\vec{L}$ does not change and therefore τ becomes constant.

4. **(d)** By the concept of energy conservation

$$\frac{1}{2}mv^2 + \frac{1}{2}I\omega^2 = mg\left(\frac{3v^2}{4g}\right)$$

For rolling motion $v = R\omega$

$$\therefore \quad \frac{1}{2}mv^2 + \frac{1}{2}I\frac{v^2}{R^2} = \frac{3}{4}mv^2$$

$$\therefore \quad \frac{1}{2}I\frac{v^2}{R^2} = \frac{3}{4}mv^2 - \frac{1}{2}mv^2 = \frac{1}{4}mv^2$$

$$\frac{1}{2}I\frac{v^2}{R^2} = \frac{1}{4}mv^2$$

$$\Rightarrow \quad I = \frac{1}{2}mR^2$$

This is the formula of the moment of inertia of the disc.

5. **(a)** The given body can be considered as a right circular cone ABC from which a cone ADE and a cylindrical $PQRS$ have been cut out as shown.

Let the x-axis be along the base and y-axis as the axis of symmetry. For the cone ABC of height h is :

$$\frac{h_2}{r_1} = \frac{h}{r}$$

or $\dfrac{h - 20}{5} = \dfrac{h}{10}$

$\Rightarrow 2h - 40 = h \Rightarrow h = 40\,\text{cm}.$

Volume $V_1 = \dfrac{1}{3}\pi r^2 h$

$$= \frac{1}{3}\pi(10)^2 \times 40 = \frac{4000}{3}\pi\,\text{cm}^3$$

Position of CG on y-axis,

$$y_1 = \frac{1}{4} \times 40 = 10\,\text{cm}.$$

For cone ADE, Volume

$$V_2 = \frac{1}{3}\pi r_1^2 h_2 = \frac{1}{3}\pi(5)^2 \times 20 = \frac{500}{3}\pi\,\text{cm}^3$$

Position of CG on y-axis,

$$y_2 = 20 + \frac{1}{4} \times 20 = 25 \, \text{cm}.$$

For cylindrical hole

Volume, $V_3 = \pi r_3^2 h_1 = \pi \left(\frac{5}{2}\right)^2 \times 20 = 125\,\pi \, \text{cm}^3$

Position of CG on y-axis, $y_3 = \frac{h_1}{2} = \frac{20}{2} = 10 \, \text{cm}.$

The given body has a volume $= V_1 - V_2 - V_3$

$\therefore$ Position of CG of given body on y-axis

$$\bar{y} = \frac{\Sigma V_y}{\Sigma V} = \frac{V_1 y_1 - V_2 y_2 - V_3 y_3}{V_1 - V_2 - V_3}$$

$$= \frac{\dfrac{4000}{3}\pi \times 10 - \dfrac{500}{3}\pi \times 25 - 125\pi \times 10}{\dfrac{4000}{3}\pi - \dfrac{500}{3}\pi - 125\pi}$$

$$\bar{y} = \frac{40000 - 12500 - 3750}{4000 - 500 - 375} = \frac{23750}{3125} = 7.6 \, \text{cm}$$

6. **(a, b, d)** Let $\omega_1 =$ the initial angular velocity of the disc.
$\omega_2 =$ the final common angular velocity of the disc and the ring.

For the disc, $I_1 = \frac{1}{2}mr^2$

For the ring, $I_2 = mr^2$
By conservation of angular momentum,

$$L = I_1\omega_1 - (I_1 + I_2)\omega_2$$

or $\omega_2 = \dfrac{I_1\omega_1}{I_1 + I_2} = \omega_1/3$

Initial kinetic energy $= E_1 = \frac{1}{2}I_1\omega_1^2$

Final kinetic energy $= E_2 = \frac{1}{2}(I_1 + I_2)\omega_2^2$

Heat produced $=$ loss in kinetic energy $= E_1 - E_2$.
Ratio of heat produced to initial kinetic energy

$$= \frac{E_1 - E_2}{E_1} = \frac{2}{3}.$$

7. **(a, b, c, d)** $I_z = \dfrac{m(\ell\sin\theta)^2}{12} + m\left(\dfrac{\ell}{2}\cos\theta\right)^2 + m\dfrac{(\ell\cos\theta^2)}{12}$

$$+ m\left(\frac{\ell}{2}\sin\theta\right)^2 + \frac{m\ell^2}{12} + \frac{m\ell^2}{12}$$

$$= \frac{m\ell^2}{12} + \frac{m\ell^2}{4} + \frac{m\ell^2}{12} + \frac{m\ell^2}{12}$$

$$= \frac{m\ell^2}{2} \quad \text{(constant independent of } \theta\text{)}$$

$[I_z$ will be maximum for any value of θ (Obviously)]

8. **(a, b, c)** $\vec{\tau} = \dfrac{d\vec{L}}{dt}$

Given that

$$\vec{\tau} = \vec{A} \times \vec{L} \Rightarrow \frac{d\vec{L}}{dt} = \vec{A} \times \vec{L}$$

From cross-product rule, $\dfrac{d\vec{L}}{dt}$ is always perpendicular to the

plane containing $\vec{A}$ and $\vec{L}$.
By the dot product definition

$$\vec{L}.\vec{L} = L^2$$

Differentiating with respect to time

$$\vec{L}\cdot\frac{d\vec{L}}{dt} + \vec{L}\cdot\frac{d\vec{L}}{dt} = 2L\frac{dL}{dt} \Rightarrow 2\vec{L}\cdot\frac{d\vec{L}}{dt} = 2L\frac{dL}{dt}$$

Since, $\dfrac{d\vec{L}}{dt}$ i.e. $\vec{\tau}$ is perpendicular to $\vec{L}$

$$\therefore \ \vec{L}\cdot\frac{d\vec{L}}{dt} = 0 \ \Rightarrow \ \frac{dL}{dt} = 0$$

$\Rightarrow \ L = $ constant
Thus, the magnitude of L always remains constant.

As $\vec{A}$ is a constant vector and it is always perpendicular to $\vec{\tau}$,

Also, $\vec{L}$ is perpendicular to $\vec{A}$

$\because \ \vec{L} \perp \vec{A} \quad \therefore \ \vec{L}.\vec{A} = 0$

Thus, it can be concluded that component of $\vec{L}$ along $\vec{A}$ is zero i.e., always constant.

9. **(a, b, c)** The possible forces are shown in figure.

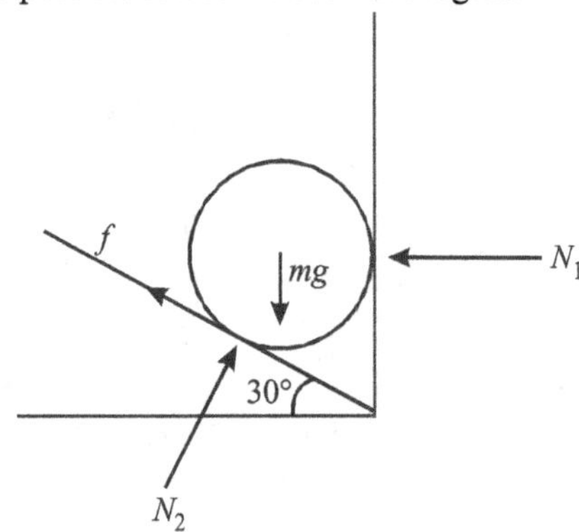

If we take moments about an axis through the center of the sphere, only f can have a torque and $\Sigma \tau = 0$ implies $f = 0$.
Then $\Sigma F_y = 0$ yields
$N_2 \cos 30° = mg = (10 \, \text{kg}) \, (9.8 \, \text{m/s}^2)$
$\Sigma F_x = 0$ yields $N_2 \sin 30° - N_1 = 0$,
or $N_1 = 56.5 \, \text{N}, \ N_2 = 113 \, \text{N}$

10. **1** By Newton's second law

$$F_2 - F_1 = ma$$

$\therefore \qquad F_1 = F_2 - ma$

$$= 5 - 1 \times 2 = 3 \, \text{N}.$$

For rotational equilibrium, taking moment of forces about centre of mass, we get

$$F_1 \times \frac{l}{2} - F_2\left(\frac{l}{2} - y\right) = 0$$

$$3 \times \frac{l}{2} - 5\left(\frac{l}{2} - 0.2\right) = 0$$

$$\therefore \qquad l = 1\,\text{m}.$$

11. **9**

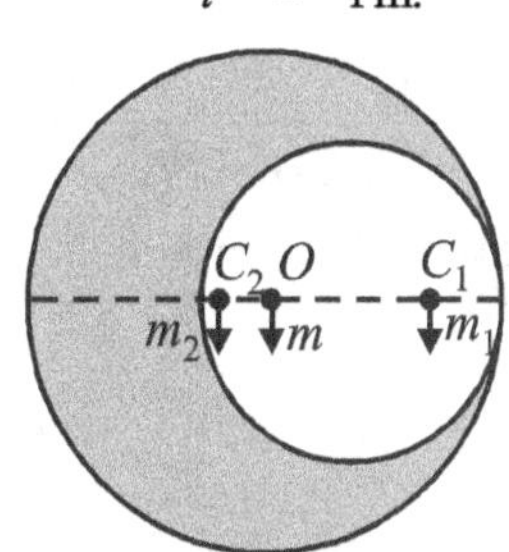

Area of whole plate $= \pi\,(56/2)^2 = 784\,\pi$ sq. cm.

Area of cutout portion $= \pi\,(42/2)^2 = 441\,\pi$ sq. cm. ;

Area of remaining portion $= 784\pi - 441\pi = 343\,\pi\,\text{cm}^2$;

As mass $\propto$ area.

$$\therefore \quad \frac{\text{mass of cutout portion}}{\text{mass of remaining portion}} = \frac{m_1}{m_2} = \frac{441\pi}{343\pi} = \frac{9}{7}$$

Let C_2 be centre of mass of remaining portion and C_1 be centre of mass of cutout portion.

O is centre of mass of the whole disc.;

$OC_1 = r_1 = 28 - 21 = 7$ cm.

$OC_2 = r_2 = ?$;

Equating moments of masses about O,

we get $m_2 \times r_2 = m_1 \times r_1 \Rightarrow r_2 = \dfrac{m_1}{m_2} \times r_1 = \dfrac{9}{7} \times 7 = 9$

$\therefore$ Centre of mass of remaining portion is at 9 cm to the left of centre of disc.

12. **3**

$$FR = I\alpha$$

where R is the radius of the disc.

$$F = \frac{1}{2} MR\alpha$$

$$= \frac{1}{2} MR\left(\frac{d\omega}{dt}\right) = \frac{1}{2} MR(6)$$

$$= \frac{1}{2} \times 5 \times 0.2 \times 6 = 3.0\,\text{N}$$

13. **6** $\quad I = \displaystyle\int_0^R (dm) r^2$

$$\therefore \quad I = \int_0^R \rho \times 4\pi r^2 \, dr \times r^2$$

$$\therefore \quad I = 4\pi \int_0^R \rho\, r^4 \, dr$$

$$\therefore \quad I_A = 4\pi \int_0^R k\,\frac{r}{R} \times r^4 \, dr = \frac{4\pi K}{R}\int_0^R r^5 \, dr$$

$$= \frac{4\pi K}{R}\left(\frac{R^6}{6}\right) = 4\pi K\,\frac{R^5}{6}$$

$$I_B = 4\pi \int_0^R K\left(\frac{r}{R}\right)^5 r^4 \, dr = \frac{4\pi K}{R^5} \times \frac{R^{10}}{10} = 4\pi K\,\frac{R^5}{10}$$

$$\therefore \quad \frac{I_B}{I_A} = \frac{6}{10} \Rightarrow n = 6$$

14. **(c)** As shown in the figure that all of the angular velocities are in the same direction, so we can regard ω_A, ω_B, and ω as the components of angular velocity along the rotation axis. Conservation of angular momentum then gives

$$I_A\omega_A + I_B\omega_B = (I_A + I_B)\omega$$

$$\omega = \frac{I_A\omega_A + I_B\omega_B}{I_A + I_B}$$

15. **(a)** The initial kinetic energy is

$$K_1 = \frac{1}{2} I_A\omega_A^2 + \frac{1}{2} I_B\omega_B^2$$

$$= \frac{1}{2}\,(0.040\,\text{kg.m}^2)\,(50\,\text{rad/s})^2 +$$

$$\frac{1}{2}\,(0.020\,\text{kg.m}^2)\,(200\,\text{rad/s})^2$$

The final kinetic energy is

$$K_2 = \frac{1}{2}(I_A + I_B)\omega_2 = \frac{1}{2}\,(0.040\,\text{kg.m}^2$$

$$+ 0.020\,\text{kg.m}^2)\,(100\,\text{rad/s})^2 = 300\,\text{J}$$

16. **(b)** As we know that moment of inertia of solid sphere along its diameter is $\dfrac{2}{5}\text{MR}^2$.

Using parallel axes theorem $I_{\text{tangent}} = I_{\text{cm}} + MR^2$

$$= \frac{2}{5}\text{MR}^2 + \text{MR}^2 = \frac{7}{5}\text{MR}^2$$

So the radius of gyration $= \sqrt{\dfrac{7}{5}}\,R$

17. **(b)** MOI along tangent in the plane is

$$\frac{5}{4}\text{MR}^2$$

$$I_{\text{along tangent}} = I_{\text{diameter (c.m.)}} + MR^2$$

$$\Rightarrow \quad \frac{5}{4}\text{MR}^2 = I_{\text{diameter}} + MR^2$$

$$\Rightarrow \quad I_{\text{diameter}} = \frac{5}{4}\text{MR}^2 - MR^2 = \frac{MR^2}{4}$$

18. **(a)** Moment of inertia of thin spherical shell along the tangent is $\dfrac{5}{3}\text{MR}^2$ and radius of gyration is $\sqrt{\dfrac{5}{3}}R$

so, $I = \dfrac{5}{3} \times 2 \times \left(\sqrt{15}\right)^2 = 50\,\text{kg m}^2$,

radius of gyration $= \sqrt{\dfrac{5}{3}} \times \sqrt{15} = 5\,\text{m}$

19. $A \to p, q, r; B \to p, q, r; C \to p, q; D \to p, q, r;$

(A) Since all forces on disc pass through point of contact with horizontal surface, the angular momentum of disc about point on ground in contact with disc is conserved. Also the angular momentum of disc in all cases is conserved about any point on the line passing through point of contact and parallel to velocity of centre of mass. The K.E. of disc is decreased in all cases due to work done by friction.

From calculation of velocity of lowest point on disc, the direction of friction in case A, B and D is towards left and in case C is towards right.

The direction of frictional force cannot change in any given case.

20. **A-p; B-r, s; C-q; D-r**

$$\vec{v} = 3\hat{i} \, , \, a_t = 0, \, L = mvr_\perp = (mr^2)\omega \;;$$

$$\omega = \frac{12}{\sqrt{9t^2 + 16}}$$

$$\text{distance} = |\vec{r}| = \sqrt{(3t)^2 + (4)^2} \;;$$

$$\frac{d}{dt}(\text{distance}) = \left(\frac{3t}{\sqrt{(3t)^2 + (4)^2}} \right)$$

this is increasing function with time (t).

1. **(c)** $-\dfrac{GM_e m}{10R_e} + \dfrac{1}{2}mv_i^2 = -\dfrac{GM_e m}{R_e} + \dfrac{1}{2}mv_f^2$

   $\therefore\quad v_f^2 = v_i^2 + \dfrac{2GM_e}{R_e}\left(1 - \dfrac{1}{10}\right).$

2. **(c)** $W = m(V_2 - V_1)$

   when, $V_1 = -\left[\dfrac{GM_1}{a} + \dfrac{GM_2}{\sqrt{2}a}\right],$

   $V_2 = -\left[\dfrac{GM_2}{a} + \dfrac{GM_1}{\sqrt{2}a}\right]$

   $\therefore\quad W = \dfrac{Gm(M_2 - M_1)}{a\sqrt{2}}(\sqrt{2} - 1).$

3. **(b)** $\dfrac{1}{2}mv^2 = 2\left[\dfrac{GMm}{L}\right] \Rightarrow v = 2\sqrt{\dfrac{GM}{L}}$

   The potential energy is a combined property of the three mass system. The kinetic energy of mass m is only its energy which decreases as it moves.
   (b) is the correct option.

   $$\text{M} \bullet\!\!-\!-\!-\!-\!-\!-\!-\!-\!\overset{\uparrow v}{\underset{m}{\bullet}}\!-\!-\!-\!-\!-\!-\!-\!-\!\bullet \text{M}$$

   $$\mid\!\!\longleftarrow\!\!-\!\!-\!\!-\ 2L\ -\!\!-\!\!\longrightarrow\!\!\mid$$

4. **(c)** **For $r \geq R$**
   Force on the test mass m is $F = m \times |E_g|$
   Where E_g is the gravitational field intensity at the point of observation

   $\therefore\quad \dfrac{mv^2}{r} = m \times \left[\dfrac{GM}{r^2}\right]$ where M is the total mass of the spherical system.

   $\therefore\quad v \propto \dfrac{1}{\sqrt{r}}$

   For r < R Again $F' = m\left|E_g'\right|$

   $\therefore\quad \dfrac{mv^2}{r} = m\left[\dfrac{GM}{R^3} \times r\right]$

   $\Rightarrow v \propto r$

5. **(a)** Let v_1 and v_2 be the velocity required for the satellite in order to maintain its motion along the circular orbits C_1 and C_2 respectively.

   Then $\quad v_1 = \sqrt{\dfrac{GM}{3R}}$ and $v_2 = \sqrt{\dfrac{GM}{6R}}$

   Now, let v'_1 and v'_2 be the velocities of the satellite at A and B while the transfer is pursued from orbit C_1 to C_2. Evidently, the points A and B will be the positions of perigee and apogee for the satellite along its elliptical path.
   Conserving angular momentum
   $v'_1(3R) = v'_2(6R)$

   $\Rightarrow v'_2 = \dfrac{v'_1}{2}$

   Conserving energy between A and B, we have

   $\dfrac{1}{2}m\,(v'_1)^2 - \dfrac{GMm}{3R} = \dfrac{1}{2}m(v'_2)^2 - \dfrac{GMm}{6R}$

   $\Rightarrow v'^2_1 - v'^2_2 = 2GM\left(\dfrac{1}{6R}\right)$

   $\Rightarrow v'^2_1 - \dfrac{v'^2_1}{4} = \dfrac{GM}{3R}$

   $\Rightarrow \dfrac{3v'^2_1}{4} = \dfrac{GM}{3R} \Rightarrow v'_1 = \dfrac{2}{3}\sqrt{\dfrac{GM}{R}}$

   So, $\quad v'_2 = \dfrac{1}{3}\sqrt{\dfrac{GM}{R}}$

   Now, change in energy required at point A

   $\Delta E_1 = \dfrac{1}{2}mv'^2_1 - \dfrac{1}{2}mv_1^2$

   $\Rightarrow \dfrac{m}{2}\left[\dfrac{4}{9}(gR) - \dfrac{gR}{3}\right] \Rightarrow \dfrac{m}{2}\left(\dfrac{gR}{9}\right) = \dfrac{mgR}{18}$

   Similarly change in energy required at point B

   $\Delta E_2 = \dfrac{1}{2}mv_2^2 - \dfrac{1}{2}mv'^2_2 = \dfrac{m}{2}\left[\dfrac{gR}{6} - \dfrac{gR}{9}\right]$

   $\qquad = \dfrac{m}{2}\left(\dfrac{gR}{18}\right) = \dfrac{mgR}{36}$

6. **(a, b, c, d)** Given that the velocity of the satellite is

   $v = 30400 \times \dfrac{5}{18}$ m/s $= 8444.44$ m/s

   Let us calculate the orbital velocity v_0 for the satellite to move along a circular orbit of height 320 km.

   $\because\quad v_0 = \sqrt{\dfrac{GM}{r}} = \sqrt{\dfrac{gR^2}{r}}$

   $\qquad = \sqrt{\dfrac{9.8 \times (6.4 \times 10^6)^2}{672 \times 10^4}} = 7728.73$ m/s

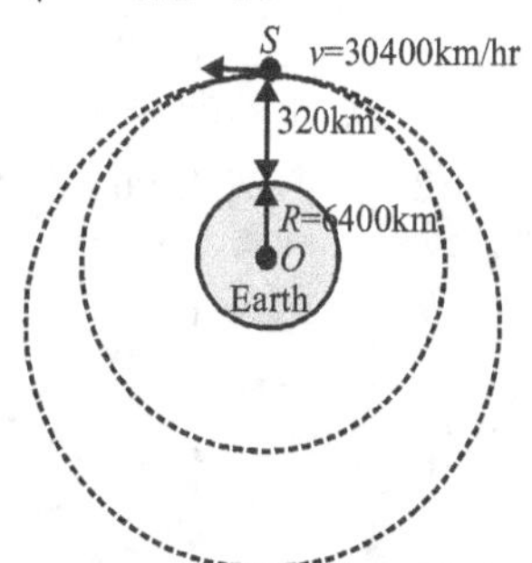

   Also, the escape velocity for the satellite in this position is given by $v_e = \sqrt{2}\,v_0 = 10930.08$ m/s

Evidently, $7728.73 < 8444.44 < 10930.08$
i.e., $v_0 < v < v_e$
So, the satellite moves along an elliptical orbit, with the position of launch as the perigee. (figure).

(b) Let r_{max} be the maximum distance of the satellite from the earth's centre, and v' the corresponding velocity.
From, conservation law of angular momentum and energy between perigee and apogee, we have
$$8444.44\,(672 \times 10^4) = v'(r_{max})$$
and $\dfrac{1}{2}(8444.44)^2 - \dfrac{gR^2}{672 \times 10^4} = \dfrac{1}{2}v'^2 - \dfrac{gR^2}{r_{max}}$

Eliminating v' from the above two equations, we have
$$3565.43 \times 10^4 \left[1 - \left(\frac{672}{r'}\right)^2\right]$$
$$= \frac{9.8 \times (640 \times 10^4)^2}{10^4}\left[\frac{1}{672} - \frac{1}{r'}\right]$$
where $r' = \dfrac{r_{max}}{10^4}\,m$

$$\Rightarrow 3565.43 \times 10^4 \left(\frac{r'^2 - (672)^2}{r'^2}\right)$$
$$= 4014.08 \times 10^7 \left[\frac{r' - 672}{672r'}\right]$$

$$\Rightarrow r' + 672 = 1.675\,r' \Rightarrow r' = \frac{672}{0.675} = 995\,m$$
$$\therefore r_{max} = 995 \times 10^4 m$$
$\Rightarrow$ The maximum height of the satellite
$$= r_{max} - R = 9950 - 6400 = 3550\,\text{km}.$$

(c) The semi-major axis of the elliptical path will be
$$a = \frac{r_{max} + r_{min}}{2} = \left(\frac{995 + 672}{2}\right) \times 10^4\,m$$
$$= 833.5 \times 10^4\,m$$
From Kepler's IIIrd law, of planetary motion,
$$T = 2\pi\sqrt{\frac{a^3}{GM}} \Rightarrow T = 2\pi\sqrt{\frac{a^3}{gR^2}}$$
$$\Rightarrow T = 2\pi\sqrt{\frac{(833.5 \times 10^4)^3}{9.8 \times (64 \times 10^5)^2}}$$
$$= 2 \times 3.14 \times 1201.06 = 7546.5\,\text{sec.} = 2.09\,\text{hrs.}$$

(d) The escape velocity is given by
$$v_e = \sqrt{2}v_0 = 10930.08\,\text{m/s}$$

7. **(a, b, d)** $F(r) = -\dfrac{k}{r^n}$
$$\Rightarrow U(r) = -\int F(r)\,dr = -\frac{k}{(n-1)}\cdot\frac{1}{r^{n-1}}$$
If L is the angular momentum of the particle of mass m in an orbit of radius r, then

Kinetic energy $= \dfrac{L^2}{2I} = \dfrac{L^2}{2mr^2} = K(r)$

Since total energy $E(r) = U(r) + K(r)$
$$\Rightarrow E(r) = -\frac{k}{(n-1)}\cdot\frac{1}{r^{n-1}} + \frac{L^2}{2mr^2}$$
The criterion that a circular orbit of radius r_0 be stable is that $E(r)$ is minimum.
For $E(r)$ to be minimum, 2 conditions must be fulfilled.
$$\Rightarrow \left.\frac{\partial E}{\partial r}\right|_{r=r_0} = 0 \text{ and } \left.\frac{\partial^2 E}{\partial r^2}\right|_{r=r_0} > 0,$$

using both conditions $(3-n)\dfrac{L^2}{m} > 0$
This is possible only when $n < 3$.
We also note that inverse square law belongs to this category $n = -1$ also gives stable circular orbits [Law of direct distance]. But $n = 3$ gives circular orbits which are unstable [Inverse cube law]

8. **(a, c)** From fig.

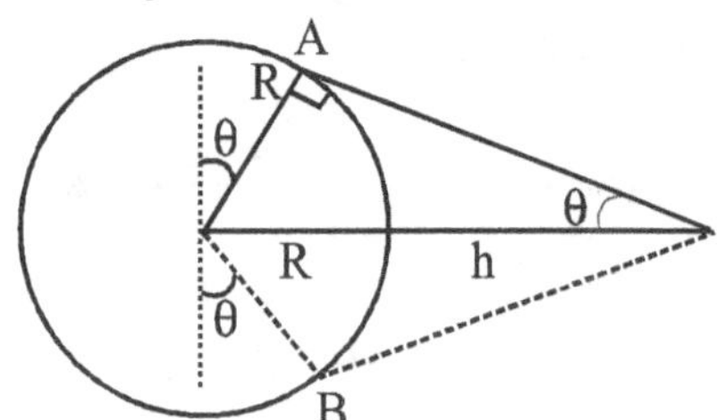

Min. colatitude, $\sin\theta = \dfrac{R}{R+h}$

Curved area AB on earth $= 2\pi R^2(1 - \sin\theta)$
Area on earth escaped from satellite
$$= 4\pi R^2 - 2\pi R^2(1 - \sin\theta) = 2\pi R^2(1 + \sin\theta)$$

9. **(a, c)** Kinetic energy on the surface of earth $= \dfrac{1}{2}mv_0^2$

Potential energy on the surface of earth $= \dfrac{-GMm}{R}$

Total energy $= \dfrac{1}{2}mv_0^2 - \dfrac{GMm}{R}$

Kinetic energy at a height $h = \dfrac{1}{2}mv^2$

Potential energy at this height $= \dfrac{-GMm}{(R+h)}$

Total energy $= \dfrac{1}{2}mv^2 - \dfrac{GMm}{R+h}$
By the principle of conservation of energy,
$$\frac{1}{2}mv^2 - \frac{GMm}{R+h} = \frac{1}{2}mv_0^2 - \frac{GMm}{R}$$

$$\frac{1}{2}(v_0^2 - v^2) = \frac{GM}{R} - \frac{GM}{R+h}$$

But $GM = gR^2$

$$\therefore \frac{1}{2}(v_0^2 - v^2) = \frac{gR^2 h}{R(R+h)}$$

$$v_0^2 - v^2 = \frac{2gRh}{R+h} = \frac{2gh}{1+\dfrac{h}{R}}$$

At maximum height $v = 0$.

The initial velocity $v_0 = (90\%)v_{escape} = 0.9\sqrt{2gR}$
then

$$(0.9\sqrt{2gR})^2 - 0 = \frac{2gh_{max}}{1+\dfrac{h_{max}}{R}} ;$$

$$0.81\,R = \frac{h_{max}}{1+\dfrac{h_{max}}{R}}$$

$0.81\,R + 0.81\,h_{max} = h_{max}$
$0.19\,h_{max} = 0.81\,R$
Maximum height reached by the rocket

$$h_{max} = \frac{0.81R}{0.19} = 4.26\,R$$

10. 4

$g = \dfrac{GM}{R^2}$; If R decreases then g increases. Taking logarithm

of both the sides;
$\log g = \log G + \log M - 2\log R$

Differentiating it we get $\dfrac{dg}{g} = 0 + 0 - \dfrac{2\,dR}{R}$;

$$\therefore \frac{dg}{g} = -2\left(\frac{-2}{100}\right) = \frac{4}{100}$$

$\therefore$ % increase in $g = \dfrac{dg}{g} \times 100 = \dfrac{4}{100} \times 100 = \mathbf{4\%}$

11. 4

$$\left(\frac{T_A}{T_B}\right)^2 = \left(\frac{R_A}{R_B}\right)^3 \qquad \text{(Kepler law)};$$

$$\therefore \left(\frac{8\,T_B}{T_B}\right)^2 = \left(\frac{R_A}{R_B}\right)^3$$

or $\quad 64 = \left(\dfrac{R_A}{R_B}\right)^3$

or $\quad (4)^3 = \left(\dfrac{R_A}{R_B}\right)^3$

or $\quad 4 = \dfrac{R_A}{R_B}$

$\therefore \quad \mathbf{R_A = 4\,R_B}$

12. 8

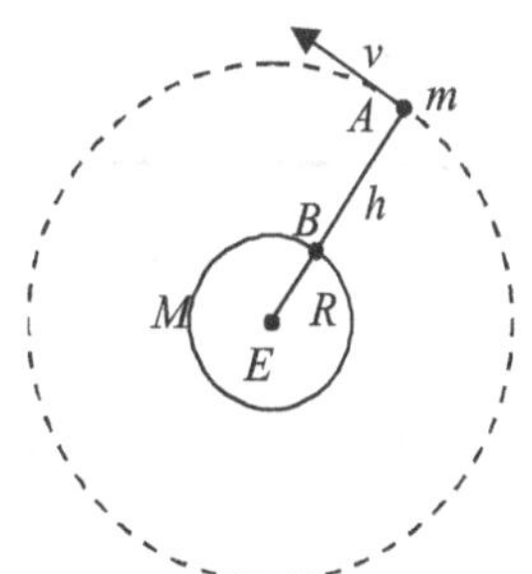

For the satellite in the circular orbit, we have

$$\frac{mv_s^2}{(R+h)} = \frac{GMm}{(R+h)^2}$$

$$\Rightarrow \quad v_s^2 = \frac{GM}{R+h}$$

$$\Rightarrow \quad \left(\frac{1}{2}\sqrt{\frac{2GM}{R}}\right)^2 = \frac{GM}{R+h} \quad \left(\because v_s = \frac{1}{2}v_e\right)$$

$$\Rightarrow \quad \frac{GM}{2R} = \frac{GM}{R+h}$$

$\Rightarrow \quad R + h = 2R$
$\Rightarrow \quad h = R$

When the satellite is stopped, its kinetic energy is zero. When it falls freely on to the Earth, its potential energy decreases and converts into kinetic energy.

$\therefore \quad (P.E.)_A - (P.E.)_B = K.E.$

$$\Rightarrow \quad \frac{-GMm}{2R} - \left(\frac{-GMm}{R}\right) = \frac{1}{2}mv^2$$

$$\Rightarrow \quad v = \sqrt{\frac{GM}{R}} = \sqrt{gR} = \sqrt{10 \times 6.4 \times 10^6} = \mathbf{8000\ m/s}$$

13. 2 Let h be the height to which the bullet rises

then, $\quad g^1 = g\left(1+\dfrac{h}{R}\right)^{-2}$

$$\Rightarrow \quad \frac{g}{4} = g\left(1+\frac{h}{R}\right)^{-2}$$

$\Rightarrow \quad h = R$

We know that $v_e = \sqrt{\dfrac{2GM}{R}} = v\sqrt{N}$ (given) ...(i)

Now applying conservation of energy for the throw
Loss of kinetic energy = Gain in gravitaional potential energy

$$\therefore \quad \frac{1}{2}mv^2 = -\frac{GMm}{2R} - \left(-\frac{GMm}{R}\right)$$

$$\therefore \quad v = \sqrt{\frac{GM}{R}} \qquad \qquad \text{...(ii)}$$

Comparing (i) & (ii) $\qquad N = 2$

14. (c) Given, mass of sphere of radius 1 m $= M$.

$\therefore$ Mass of the whole sphere of radius 4 m,

$$M_0 = \frac{M \times \dfrac{4}{3}\pi(4)^3}{\dfrac{4}{3}\pi(1)^3} = 64\,M.$$

The gravitation field at B
= field due to whole sphere – field due to sphere A

$$= \frac{GM_0 r}{R^3} - \frac{GM}{AB^2}$$

or $\quad E_B = \frac{G(64\,M) \times 2}{4^3} - \frac{GM}{4^2}$

$$= \frac{31}{16} GM.$$

15. (b) The radius of the given circle is 6 m. Obviously the point will lie outside the sphere in yz – plane.

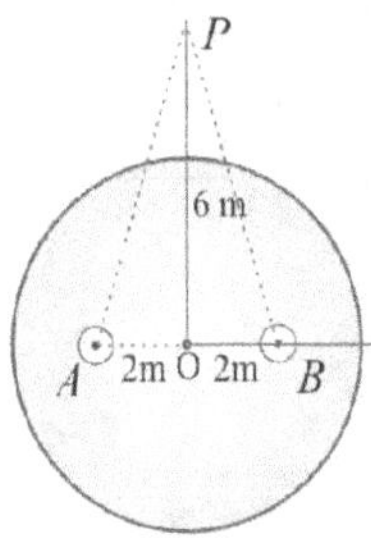

The distance $AP = BP = \sqrt{6^2 + 2^2}$

$$= \sqrt{40}\ \text{m}.$$

The potential at P = Potential due to whole sphere
$\qquad\qquad\qquad - 2$ (potential due to cavity)

$$= \frac{-GM_0}{OP} + 2\left[\frac{GM}{AP}\right]$$

$$= \frac{-G(64\,M)}{6} + \frac{2\,GM}{\sqrt{40}}$$

$$= -10.98\ GM$$

16. (b) $T \propto r^{3/2}$

$$\frac{T_2}{T_1} = \left(\frac{2r}{r}\right)^{3/2} = 2\sqrt{2}$$

$$\Rightarrow T_2 = 2\sqrt{2}\,T_1$$

17. (a) When a satellite revolves around a planet in its orbit, it posses both potential energy (due to its position) and kinetic energy (due to orbital motion)

$$U = \frac{-G\,M\,m}{r} \qquad \left(\begin{array}{l} M = \text{mass of earth} \\ m = \text{mass of stellite} \\ r = \text{radius of orbit} \end{array}\right)$$

$$K.E = \frac{G\,M\,m}{2r}$$

So total energy

$$= U + K.E. = \frac{-G\,M\,m}{r} + \frac{G\,M\,m}{2r} = \frac{-G\,M\,m}{2r}$$

18. (d) $V_{(orbital)} \propto \dfrac{1}{\sqrt{r}}$

Time period $\propto r^{3/2}$

Angular momentum $\propto \sqrt{r}$

Kinetic energy $\propto \dfrac{1}{r}$

19. $(A) \rightarrow q, r; (B) \rightarrow s; (C) \rightarrow q; (D) \rightarrow p$

(A) Kinetic energy of a body projected from the surface of earth at large distance may be zero (body momentarily comes to rest) or positive.

(B) Gravitational potential energy of a bound system must be negative.

(C) Change in potential energy of a point mass if left free to itself, with time may be zero (point mass on horizontal surface) or negative (point mass falling freely vertically).

(D) Change in areal velocity of earth as earth moves from apogee towards perigee is zero as areal velocity remains constant according to Kepler's second law.

20. $(A) \rightarrow p, s; (B) \rightarrow r, s; (C) \rightarrow p, q, s; (D) \rightarrow r, s$

Due to rotation

$g_{eff} = g_0 - \omega^2 R \cos^2 \lambda$

$\therefore$ g changes with λ (altitude angle)

g_0 depends on earth mass

τ on earth $= 0 \Rightarrow$ Angular momentum constant

Escape velocity is independent on direction of projection but depends on earth mass and distance from earth centre.

Gravitational potential, $V = -\dfrac{GM}{r}$.

1. **(b)** Using Hooke's law, $F = kx$ we can write

$$7 = k(a - \ell_0) \qquad \ldots(i)$$

and $\qquad 9 = k(b - \ell_0) \qquad \ldots(ii)$

If ℓ be the length under tension 11 N, then

$$11 = k(\ell - \ell_0) \qquad \ldots(iii)$$

After solving above equations, we get

$$\ell = 2b - a$$

2. **(b)** If T be the tension in the rope, then

$2T = 10 \text{kN}$

$T = 5 \text{kN}.$

$\therefore$ Longitudinal stress in the rope

$$\sigma = \frac{T}{A} = \frac{5 \text{kN}}{10^3 \text{mm}^2} = 5 \text{ Nmm}^{-2}$$

$\therefore$ Extension in the rope

$$= \frac{\text{Stress}}{Y} \times L = \frac{5 \text{ Nmm}^{-2}}{10^3 \text{ Nmm}^{-2}} \times 1500 \text{mm} = 7.5 \text{mm}$$

$\therefore$ Deflection of the load $\delta = \dfrac{7.5}{2} = 3.75 \text{mm}$

3. **(b)** $\Delta L = \dfrac{LF}{AY}$, where $L = 3 \text{m}$,

$A = \pi (1.0 \times 10^{-3} \text{ m})^2 = 3.14 \times 10^{-6} \text{ m}^2$,

and since each wire supports one-quarter of the load,

$$F = \frac{(50 \text{ kg}) (9.8 \text{ m}/\text{s}^2)}{4} = 123 \text{ N}$$

$$\Delta L = \frac{(3\text{m}) (123 \text{N})}{(3.14 \times 10^{-6} \text{m}^2) (1.8 \times 10^{11} \text{N}/\text{m}^2)}$$

$$= 65 \times 10^{-5} \text{ m or } 0.65 \text{ mm}$$

4. **(a)** As stress $\propto$ strain^2 hence graph (a) correctly dipicts.

5. **(b)** Stress $= 1 \text{ kg wt/mm}^2 = 9.8 \text{ N/mm}^2$

$$= 9.8 \times 10^6 \text{ N/m}^2.$$

$$Y = 1 \times 10^{11} \text{N}/\text{m}^2, \qquad \frac{\Delta \ell}{\ell} \times 100 = ?$$

$$Y = \frac{\text{Stress}}{\text{Strain}} = \frac{\text{Stress}}{\Delta \ell / \ell}$$

$$\therefore \frac{\Delta \ell}{\ell} = \frac{\text{Stress}}{Y} = \frac{9.8 \times 10^6}{1 \times 10^{11}}$$

$$\frac{\Delta \ell}{\ell} \times 100 = 9.8 \times 10^{-11} \times 100 \times 10^6$$

$$= 9.8 \times 10^{-3} = 0.0098 \%$$

6. **(d)** For stress to be equal,

$$\frac{T_1}{A_1} = \frac{T_2}{A_2}$$

$$\therefore \frac{T_1}{T_2} = \frac{A_1}{A_2} = \frac{1}{2}.$$

7. **(b, c)** $W = U = \dfrac{e^2 Y}{2} \times \text{Vol.}$

$$= \frac{1}{2} \left(\frac{\ell}{L}\right)^2 Y \times AL = \frac{YA\ell^2}{2L}$$

8. **(b, c, d)** The force at the middle of rod AB will be F. So stress right of middle will be greater than F/A. The force at each section of rod CD is F. So stress at each section is F/A.

9. **(a, b)** The maximum stress that P can withstand before breaking is greater than Q. Therefore (A) is a correct option.

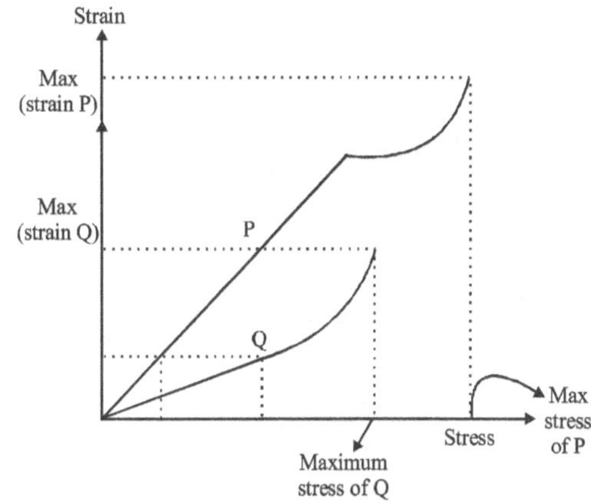

The strain of P is more than Q therefore P is more ductile. Therefore (B) is a correct option.

$$Y = \frac{\text{stress}}{\text{strain}}$$

For a given strain, stress is more for Q. Therefore $Y_Q > Y_P$.

10. **(a, b, c)** $T_B = \dfrac{mg}{3}$ and $T_A = mg + \dfrac{mg}{3} = \dfrac{4mg}{3}$

$$\therefore T_A = 4T_B$$

Stress, $S = \dfrac{T}{\pi r^2}$

(a) For $r_A = r_B$, $S_A = 4S_B$

$\therefore$ A breaks

(b) For $r_A < 2r_B$, $S_A > S_B$

$\therefore$ A breaks

(c) For $r_A = 2r_B$, $S_A = S_B$

$\therefore$ either may break

11. **5** $W = \dfrac{1}{2} \times F \times l = \dfrac{1}{2} mgl$

$$= \frac{1}{2} \times 10 \times 10 \times 1 \times 10^{-3} = 0.05 J$$

12. **1**

If ℓ is the length of wire and A is the area of the cross – section, then mass of the wire

$$m = \rho \ell A$$

Stress $\quad f = \dfrac{mg}{A} = \dfrac{\rho \ell A g}{A} = \rho \ell g$

Thus $\quad 7.8 \times 10^9 = 7.8 \times 10^3 \times \ell \times 10$

$\therefore \quad \ell = 10^5\,\text{m} = 100\,\text{km}$

13. **4** Given that $F/A = 4.8 \times 10^7\ \text{Nm}^{-2}$

$\therefore \quad F = 4.8 \times 10^7 \times A$ or

$$\frac{mv^2}{r} = 4.8 \times 10^7 \times 10^{-6} = 48$$

or $\dfrac{mr^2\omega^2}{r} = 48$ or $\omega^2 = \dfrac{48}{mr}$

$$\omega = \sqrt{\left(\frac{48}{10 \times 0.3}\right)} = \sqrt{16} = 4\ \text{rad/sec}$$

14. **9**

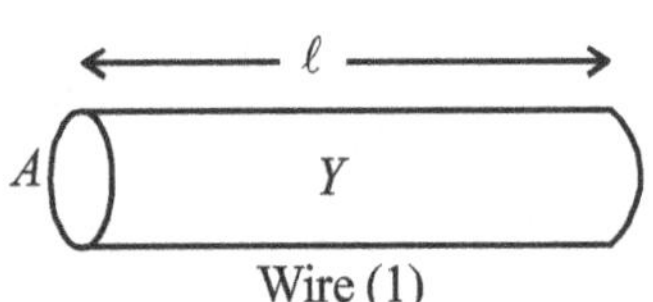

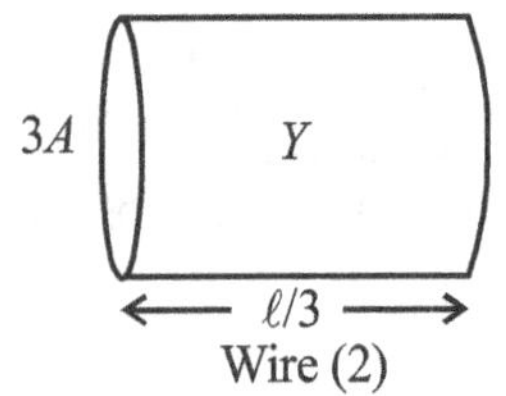

As shown in the figure, the wires will have the same Young's modulus (same material) and the length of the wire of area of cross-section $3A$ will be $\ell/3$ (same volume as wire 1).

For wire 1, $\quad Y = \dfrac{F/A}{\Delta x/\ell}$ ...(i)

For wire 2, $\quad Y = \dfrac{F'/3A}{\Delta x/(\ell/3)}$ ...(ii)

From (i) and (ii), $\dfrac{F}{A} \times \dfrac{\ell}{\Delta x} = \dfrac{F'}{3A} \times \dfrac{\ell}{3\Delta x} \Rightarrow F' = 9F$

15. **(b)**

16. **(b)**

17. **(a)** $\qquad \Delta\ell_{copper} = \Delta\ell_{steel}$

or $\dfrac{F \times 2}{(1.1 \times 10^{11}) \times 2 \times 10^{-4}} = $

$\dfrac{F \times L}{2.0 \times 10^{11} \times 1 \times 10^{-4}}$

or $\qquad L = 1.8\,\text{m}$

18. **(a)** $\quad e_{steel} = f_{steel}/Y_{steel} = \left(\dfrac{3 \times 10^4}{1 \times 10^{-4}}\right)\Big/2 \times 10^{11}$

$= 1.5 \times 10^{-3}$.

19. **(A) → q; (B) → p; (C) → s; (D) → r**

Hooke's law states that for small deformation, the stress in a body is proportional to the corresponding strain.

Young's modulus $Y = \dfrac{\text{Tensile stress}}{\text{Tensile strain}}$

20. **(A) → (r); B → (p, s) ; (C) → (q) ; (D) → (q)**

1. (b) Let us consider an elemental mass dm shown in the shaded portion.

Here

$$P\,4\pi r^2 - (P+dP)\,4\pi r^2$$

$$= \frac{GMr}{R^3}\,\rho\,(4\pi r^2)\,dr$$

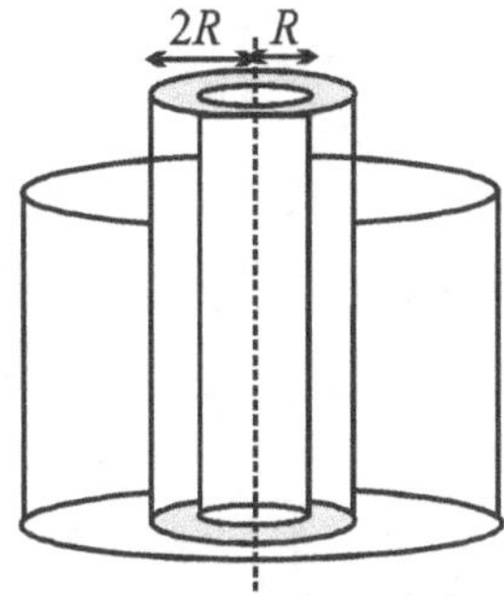

$$\therefore \quad -\int_0^P dp = \frac{GM\rho}{R^3}\int_R^r r\,dr$$

$$\therefore \quad P = \frac{GM\rho}{2R^3}\left[R^2 - r^2\right]$$

$$\therefore \quad \frac{P\,(r=3R/4)}{P\,(r=2R/3)} = \frac{\left[R^2 - \dfrac{9R^2}{16}\right]}{\left[R^2 - \dfrac{4R^2}{9}\right]} = \frac{\dfrac{7R^2}{16}}{\dfrac{5R^2}{9}} = \frac{63}{80}$$

$$\text{and}\quad \frac{P\,(r=3R/5)}{P\,(r=2R/5)} = \frac{\left[R^2 - \dfrac{9R^2}{25}\right]}{\left[R^2 - \dfrac{4R^2}{25}\right]} = \frac{16}{21}$$

B and *C* are correct options.

2. (b) Upward force by capillary tube on top surface of liquid is $f_{up} = 4\sigma a \cos\theta$.

If liquid is raised to a height h then we use

$$4\sigma a \cos = ha^2 \rho g \quad \text{or} \quad h = \frac{4\sigma\cos\theta}{a\rho g}$$

3. (b)

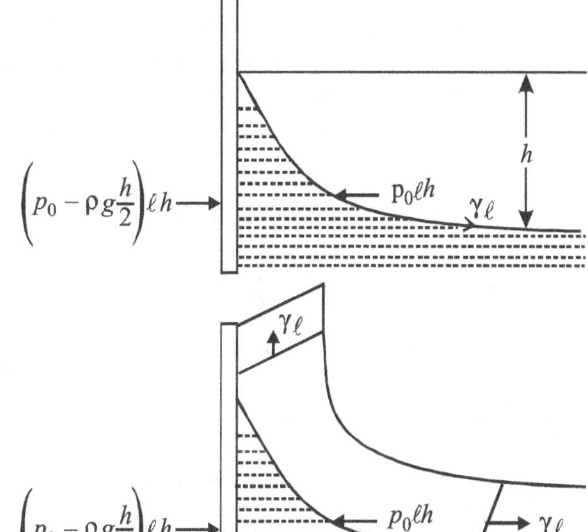

$$mg = v\rho_{wood}\,g = (3\pi R^2 h)\,\rho_{wood}\,g$$

$$(3\pi R^2 h)\,\rho_{wood}\,g = (3\pi R^2 H)\,\rho_w g$$

$$\frac{h\rho_{wood}}{\rho_{water}} = H$$

4. (d) $\dfrac{4}{3}\pi\left(r_1^3 + r_2^3\right)(\sigma - \rho\ g) = 6\pi\eta(r_1 + r_2)v$

and $\dfrac{4}{3}\pi r_2^3(\sigma - \rho)g = T + 6\pi\eta r_1 v$

$$\Rightarrow T = \frac{4}{3}\pi\frac{(r_2^4 - r_1^4)(\sigma - \rho)g}{(r_1 + r_2)}$$

5. (a) No sliding $\Rightarrow$ pure rolling

Therefore, acceleration of the tube = 2a (since COM of cylinders are moving at 'a')

$P_A = P_{atm} + \rho(2a)L$ (From horizontal limb)

Also, $P_A = P_{atm} + \rho g h$ (From vertical lmb)

$$\Rightarrow \quad a = \frac{gH}{2L}$$

6. (a)

Balancing forces in horizontal direction

$$\left(p_0 - \rho g\frac{h}{2}\right)\ell h + \gamma\ell = p_0\ell h \Rightarrow h = \sqrt{\frac{2\gamma}{\rho g}}$$

7. (b,c) As $v_t \propto r^2$

$$\therefore \quad \frac{v_1}{v_2} = \frac{(r)^2}{(r/2)^2} \Rightarrow v_2 = \frac{v_1}{4}.$$

8. (b,d) $F = \rho v Q = \rho A v^2$,

Clearly when velocity becomes two times, the thrust becomes four times.

Energy lost per second, $P = Fv = \rho A v^3$, so it becomes eight times.

9. (b,d) Assume the discharge to be equally divided between the two nozzles.

$$Q_A = Q_B = \frac{3\times 10^{-3}}{60} = 50\times 10^{-6}\ \text{m}^3/\text{s}$$

$$v_A = v_B = \frac{50 \times 10^{-6}}{\pi/4 \times 0.005^2} = 2.54 \, m/s$$

$$v_{\theta A} = 2.54 \cos 30° = 2.2 \, m/s$$

$$v_{\theta B} = 2.54 \cos 45° = 1.8 \, m/s$$

Assume that the water entering the sprinkler through a tap does not involve any angular momentum.

When stationary, the torque due to nozzles action,

for nozzle A, $\tau_A = 1000 \times 50 \times 10^{-6} \times 2.2 \times 0.20$
$$= 0.0220 \, Nm$$

for nozzle B, $\tau_B = 1000 \times 50 \times 10^{-6} \times 1.8 \times 1.5$
$$= 0.0135 \, Nm$$

Total torque due to nozzles A and B,
$$\tau = 0.0355 \, Nm$$

When rotating free, let the angular velocity be ω. Now the absolute velocities of the nozzle-discharge in the circumferential direction are

for nozzle A, $v_{\theta A} = (2.2 - 0.2 \, \omega) \, m/s$

for nozzle B, $v_{\theta B} = (1.8 - 0.15 \, \omega) \, m/s$

There being no external moment, the angular momentum should be conserved,

$$\rho \, Q_A (2.2 - 0.2\omega) \times -0.2 + \rho \, Q_B (1.8 - 0.15\omega)$$
$$\times 0.15 = 0$$

Cancelling ρ and using $Q_A = Q_B$, $\omega = 9.72$ rad/s.

10. **(b, c)** $P_{top}V \qquad = \quad P_{bottom}V'$

$$P_{bottom} \quad = \quad (P_{top} + \rho g h)$$

As $\quad P_{bottom} > P_{top} \, ; \, \therefore \, V > V'.$

11. **3**

For equilibrium
$$F_{net} = 0$$
$$\tau_{net} = 0$$

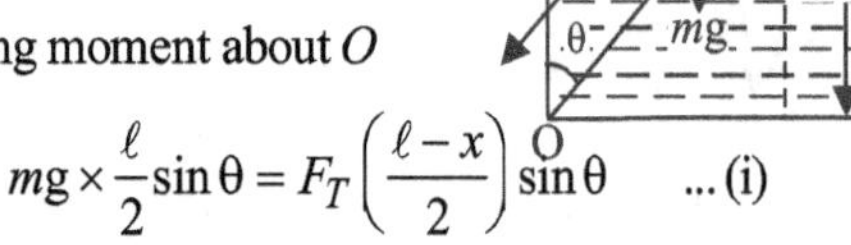

Taking moment about O

$$mg \times \frac{\ell}{2} \sin \theta = F_T \left(\frac{\ell - x}{2} \right) \sin \theta \qquad ...(i)$$

Also F_T = weight of fluid displaced.
$$F_T = [(\ell - x)A] \times \rho g \qquad ...(ii)$$
and $m = (\ell A)0.5 \rho_w \qquad ...(iii)$
where A is the area of cross section of the rod.
From (i), (ii) and (iii)

$$(\ell A)0.5 \rho_w g \times \frac{\ell}{2} \sin \theta = [(u - x)A]\rho_w g \times \left(\frac{\ell - x}{2} \right) \sin \theta$$

Here, $\ell = 1$
$$\therefore \quad (1 - x)^2 = 0.5$$
$$\therefore \quad 1 - x = 0.707$$
$$\Rightarrow \quad x = 0.293 \, m$$
From the diagram
$$\cos \theta = \frac{0.5}{1 - x} = \frac{0.5}{0.707}$$
$$\Rightarrow \quad \theta = \mathbf{45°}$$

12. **4** **For bubble A :**
If P_A is the pressure inside the bubble then

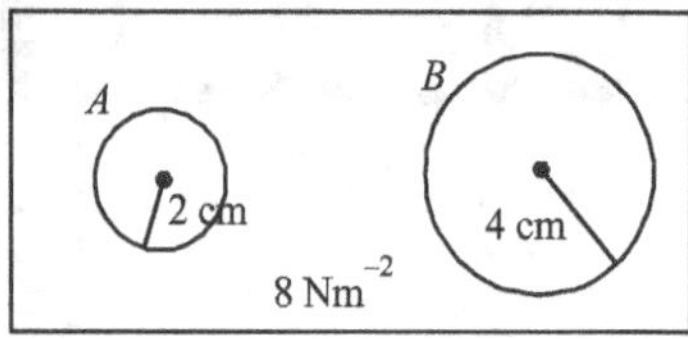

$$P_A - 8 = \frac{4T}{R_A} = \frac{4 \times 0.04}{0.02} = 8 \Rightarrow P_A = 16 N/m^2$$

For bubble B :
If P_B is the pressure inside the bubble then

$$P_B - 8 = \frac{4T}{R_B} = \frac{4 \times 0.04}{0.04} = 4 \Rightarrow P_B = 12 N/m^2$$

$$\therefore \quad \frac{P_B}{P_A} = \frac{4}{3}$$

13. **3** Range, $R = vt = \sqrt{2gh} \times t \qquad ...(i)$

Also $2R = \sqrt{2gh'} \times t \qquad ...(ii)$

From above equations, we get $h' = 4h = 40m$

$\therefore$ Extra height of water = 30 m = 3 atm.

14. **5**

Let the edge of cube be ℓ. When mass is on the cube of wood

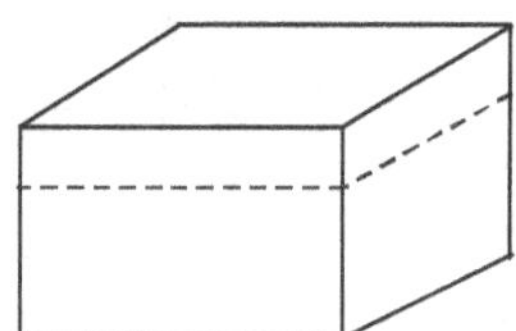

$$200g + \ell^3 d_{wood} g = \ell^3 d_{H_2O} g$$

$$\Rightarrow \quad 200 + \ell^3 d_{wood} = \ell^3 d_{H_2O}$$

$$\Rightarrow \quad \ell^3 d_{wood} = \ell^3 d_{H_2O} - 200 \qquad ...(i)$$

when the mass is removed

$$\ell^3 d_{wood} = (\ell - 2) \ell^2 d_{H_2O} \qquad ...(ii)$$

From (i) and (ii)

$$\ell^3 d_{H_2O} - 200 = (\ell - 2) \ell^2 d_{H_2O}$$

But $d_{H_2O} = 1$

$$\therefore \quad \ell^3 - 200 = \ell^2 (\ell - 2)$$

$$\therefore \quad \ell^3 - 200 = \ell^3 - 2\ell^2 \Rightarrow \ell = \mathbf{10 \, cm}$$

15. **(b)**

16. **(d)**

17. **(b)** Volume of fluid crossing the section of the tube of length ℓ and radius R in unit time

$$V = \int 2\pi r v dr = \int_0^R 2\pi v_0 r \left(\frac{R^2 - r^2}{R^2} \right) dr$$

$$= 2\pi v_0 \left[\frac{R^2}{2} - \frac{R^2}{4} \right] = \pi \frac{v_0 R^2}{2}$$

18. **(c)** Kinetic energy of the fluid within the volume of the tube

$$= \int \frac{1}{2}(dm)\,v^2 = \int \frac{1}{2}(2\pi r\,dr\,\ell\rho)\,v^2$$

$$= \int_0^R \pi r\ell\rho v_0^2 \left(\frac{R^2 - r^2}{R^2}\right)^2 dr$$

$$= \pi\rho v_0^2 \ell \int_0^R \left(r + \frac{r^5}{R^4} - \frac{2r^3}{R^2}\right) dr$$

$$= \pi\rho v_0^2 \ell \left(\frac{R^2}{2} + \frac{R^2}{6} - \frac{R^2}{2}\right) = \frac{\pi\ell\rho v_0^2 R^2}{6}$$

19. **(A) → r; (B) → q; (C) → q; (D) → q**

In A : Same water level implies

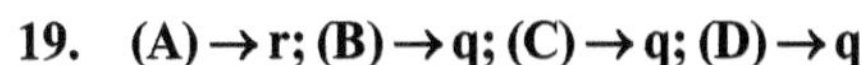

Wt. of fluid displaced is the same as that of object hence both buckets have equal weight.

In B, C : Mass of water in both buckets is equal and B has additional mass of solid object hence B is heavier.

In D : Same water level and object sinks $\rho_0 > \rho_\omega$ i.e. some volume of ρ_ω is replaced by same volume of ρ_0 mass increases.

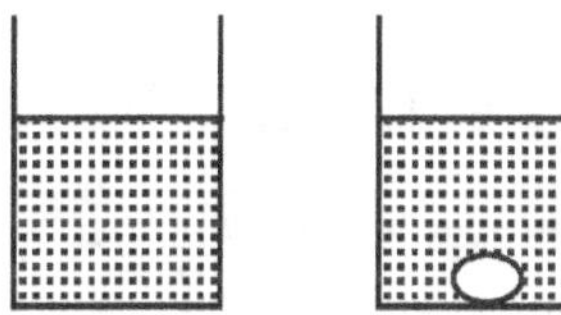

∴ B is heavier.

20. **(A) → p; (B) → q,r,s; (C) → p; (D) → s**

For pipe of uniform cross-section $v_3 = v_4 = v_5 = v$

Applying Bernoulli's equation between (1) and (5), we have

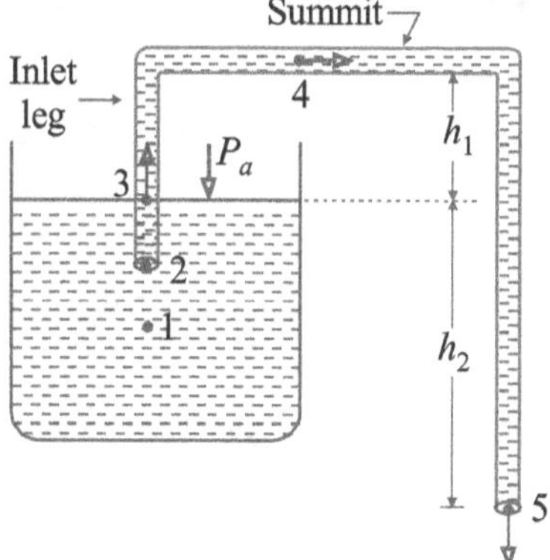

$$P_a = P_a + \frac{1}{2}\rho v_2^2 - \rho g h_2$$

$$\Rightarrow \quad v_2 = \sqrt{2gh_2}$$

Thus for $v_2 > 0$, $h_2 > 0$

Also $\quad P_a = P_3 + \frac{1}{2}\rho v^2 = P_4 + \frac{1}{2}\rho v^2 + \rho g h_1$

$$= P_a + \frac{1}{2}\rho v^2 - \rho g h_2$$

From the above equation following conclusion can be made

(i) $\quad P_4 < P_3 < P_a$

(ii) $\quad \rho g(h_1 + h_2) = P_a - P_4$

$$\Rightarrow (h_1 + h_2) \neq \frac{P_a - P_4}{\rho g}$$

or $\quad h_1 + h_2 < \dfrac{P_a}{\rho g}$

1. **(a)**
$$M_1 g = Mg - V_1 \rho_{\ell_1} g$$
or
$$M_1 g = Mg - V_1 \rho_1 g \qquad \ldots (i)$$
and
$$M_2 g = Mg - V_1[1 + \gamma_g(t_2 - t_1)]\frac{\rho_1}{[1 + \gamma_\ell(t_2 - t_1)]} g \qquad \ldots (ii)$$

After simplifying, we get
$$\gamma_\ell = \gamma_g + \left(\frac{M_2 - M_1}{M - M_2}\right)\frac{1}{(t_2 - t_1)}$$

2. **(c)** The graph shows that for the same temperature difference $(T_2 - T_1)$, less time is taken for x. This means the emissivity is more for x. According to Kirchoff's law, a good emitter is a good absorber as well.

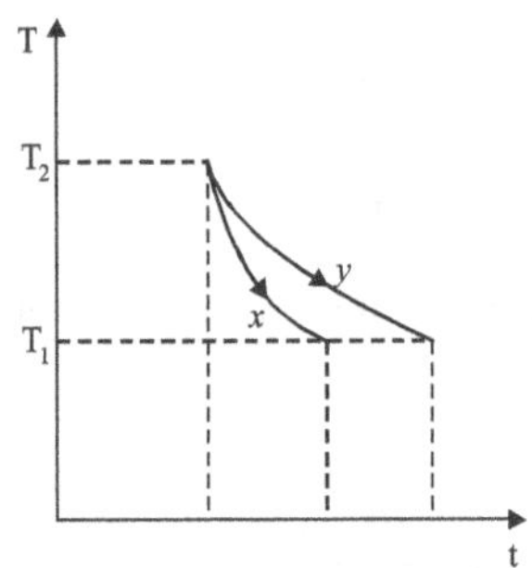

3. **(d)**
$$\left[\frac{-dT}{dr}\right] = \frac{A}{mc}\left[T - T_0\right]$$
$$= \frac{4\pi r^2}{\rho \times \frac{4}{3}\pi r^3 c}\left[T - T_0\right]$$
$$\therefore \quad \left[\frac{-dT}{dr}\right] \propto \frac{1}{\rho r c}$$

4. **(d)** Since tension is the two rods will be same, hence
$$A_1 Y_1 \alpha_1 \Delta\theta = A_2 Y_2 \alpha_2 \Delta\theta$$
$$\Rightarrow A_1 Y_1 \alpha_1 = A_2 Y_2 \alpha_2$$

5. **(c)** Rate of cooling $\dfrac{\Delta\theta}{t} = \dfrac{A\varepsilon\sigma(T^4 - T_0^4)}{mc}$
$$\Rightarrow t \propto \frac{m}{A} \ [\Delta\theta, t, \sigma, (T^4 - T_0^4) \text{ are constant}]$$
$$\Rightarrow t \propto \frac{m}{A} \propto \frac{\text{Volume}}{\text{Area}} \propto \frac{a^3}{a^2} \Rightarrow t \propto a \Rightarrow \frac{t_1}{t_2} = \frac{a_1}{a_2}$$
$$\Rightarrow \frac{100}{t_2} = \frac{1}{2} \Rightarrow t_2 = 200 \sec$$

6. **(d)** The thermal resistance is given by
$$\frac{x}{KA} + \frac{4x}{2KA} = \frac{x}{KA} + \frac{2x}{KA} = \frac{3x}{KA}$$
$$\therefore \frac{dQ}{dt} = \frac{\Delta T}{\frac{3x}{KA}} = \frac{(T_2 - T_1)KA}{3x} = \frac{1}{3}\left\{\frac{A(T_2 - T_1)K}{x}\right\}$$
$$\therefore f = \frac{1}{3}$$

7. **(a, b, c, d)** With the incident radiation, the temperature of black body try to increase, so body emits more energy per unit time. To keep the temperature constant it must absorbs incident radiations with increased rate. The reflection depends on the nature of surface not on the temperature.

8. **(a, d)** Kinetic energy of the sphere,
$$K = \frac{1}{2}I\omega^2$$
$$= \frac{1}{2} \times \frac{2}{5}MR^2(2\pi n)^2$$
$$= \frac{4}{5}\pi^2 n^2 MR^2 .$$

Kinetic energy used to raise, the temperature
$$= 0.5\left(\frac{4}{5}\pi^2 n^2 MR^2\right)$$
$$= \frac{2}{5}\pi^2 n^2 mR^2$$

If ΔT be the raise in temperature of the sphere, then
$$MC\Delta T = \frac{2}{5}\pi^2 n^2 MR^2$$
$$\therefore \quad \Delta T = \frac{2\pi^2 n^2 R^2}{5C} .$$

9. **(a, b, c)**

10. **(b, c)** Material expands outward and so x, r increases. Due to linear expansion diameter of rod will increase.

11. **2**
The rate of flow of heat is given by
$$H = K\frac{2\pi\ell(T_1 - T_2)}{\ln\left(\frac{r_2}{r_1}\right)}$$
$$= \frac{0.15 \times (2\pi \times 0.19)[120 - 30]}{\ln\left(\frac{1.2}{1}\right)}$$
$$\simeq 200 \text{ J/s.}$$

12. 9

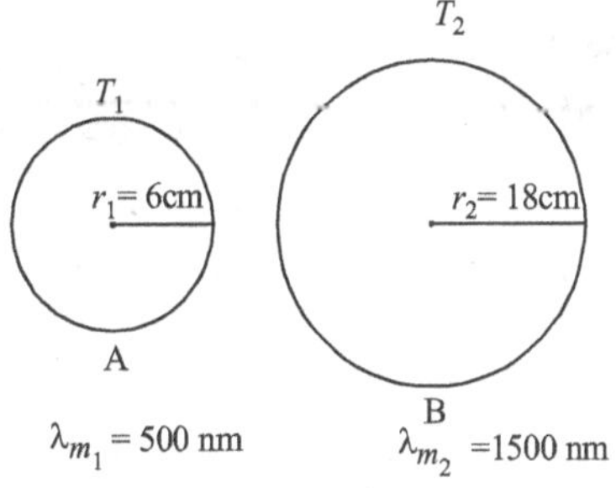

$$\frac{\text{Rate of total energy radiated by A}}{\text{Rate of total energy radiated by B}}$$

$$= \frac{\sigma T_1^4 (4\pi r_1^2)}{\sigma T_2^4 (4\pi r_2^2)} = \left(\frac{T_1}{T_2}\right)^4 \times \left(\frac{r_1}{r_2}\right)^2$$

$$= \left(\frac{\lambda_{m_2}}{\lambda_{m_1}}\right)^4 \left(\frac{r_1}{r_2}\right)^2 \left[\because \frac{T_1}{T_2} = \frac{\lambda_{m_2}}{\lambda_{m_1}} \text{ by Wein 's law}\right]$$

$$= \left(\frac{1500}{500}\right)^4 \left(\frac{6}{18}\right)^2 = 9$$

13. 2

At steady state

Heat conduct through the rod = heat absorbed at the end

or
$$KA\frac{\Delta T}{\Delta x} = \sigma A(T^4 - T_0^4)$$

or
$$K(10^{-4})\left[\frac{15.5 - 0}{0.50}\right] = 6 \times 10^{-8}(10^{-4})(300^4 - 290^4)$$

$$\therefore \quad K = 2\,\text{W/m-}^\circ\text{C.}$$

14. 2
$$\frac{P_A}{P_B} = \frac{A_A T_A^4}{A_B T_B^4} = \frac{A_A}{A_B} \times \frac{\lambda_B^4}{\lambda_A^4}$$

$$\therefore \frac{\lambda_A}{\lambda_B} = \left[\frac{A_A}{A_B} \times \frac{P_B}{P_A}\right]^{\frac{1}{4}} = \left[\frac{R_A^2}{R_B^2} \times \frac{P_B}{P_A}\right]^{\frac{1}{4}} = \left[\frac{400 \times 400}{10^4}\right]^{\frac{1}{4}}$$

$$\therefore \frac{\lambda_A}{\lambda_B} = 2$$

15. (c)

16. (a)

For (Qs. 15 -16)

When the temperature of rods is increased, there will be increase in their lengths and thereby the springs are compressed. Let x_1, x_2 and x_3 be the compresion in the three springs respectively. Then

$$L\alpha\,\Delta T + (L/2)\alpha\,\Delta T = x_1 + x_2 + x_3$$

or
$$\frac{3}{2}L\alpha\,\Delta T = x_1 + x_2 + x_3 \qquad ...(i)$$

The free body diagrams of the rods are shown in figure.

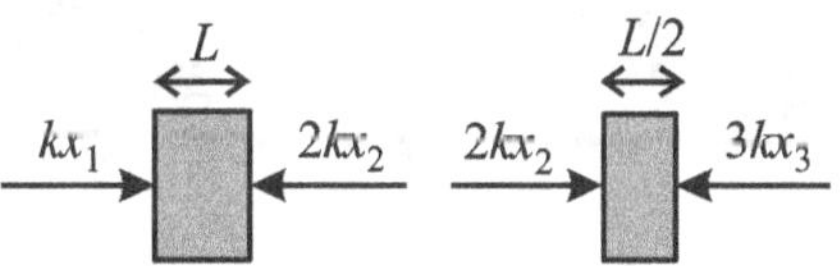

Considering the equilibriums of rods, we have

$$x_1 = 2x_2 = 3x_3 \qquad ...(ii)$$

From eqs. (i) and (ii), we get

$$x_1 + \frac{x_1}{2} + \frac{x_1}{3} = \frac{3}{2}L\alpha\,\Delta T$$

or
$$\frac{11}{4}x_1 = \frac{3}{2}L\alpha\,\Delta T$$

or
$$x_1 = \frac{9}{11}L\alpha\,\Delta T$$

Energy stored in spring of spring constant (k).

$$E_1 = \frac{1}{2}k\,x_1^2 = \frac{1}{2}k\left[\frac{9}{11}L\alpha\,\Delta T\right]^2$$

$$= \frac{81}{242}k\,L^2\alpha^2\Delta T^2$$

Similarly, $E_2 = \dfrac{81}{484}k\,L^2\alpha^2\Delta T^2$

and $E_3 = \dfrac{27}{242}k\,L^2\alpha^2\Delta T^2$

17. (c)

18. (c)

19. (A)→p; (B)→q; (C) →s; (D) →r

Energy emitted per unit time $= \dfrac{d\theta}{dt} = \sigma\varepsilon AT^4 = E$

Energy absorbed per unit time $= E_0 = \sigma\varepsilon AT_0^4$

Net loss of thermal eneregy $= \Delta E = E - E_0 = \sigma\varepsilon A(T^4 - T_0^4)$

20. (A)→q; (B)→p; (C)→ s; (D)→r

For a small temperature difference between a body and its surrounding the rate of cooling of the body is directly propertional to the temperature difference.

$$\frac{dT}{dt} = -k(T - T_0)$$

$$\frac{dT}{(T - T_0)} = -kdt$$

Now integrate both side within proper limit and draw graph

accordingly $\left[\text{use} \int \dfrac{1}{x}dx = \log x\right]$

Here, T = temperature of the body
T_0 = temperature of the surrounding

1. (b)

$$Q = Q_1 + Q_2 + Q_3 + Q_4$$
$$= 6000 - 5500 - 3000 + 3500$$
$$= +1000 \, J$$
$$W = W_1 + W_2 + W_3 + W_4$$
$$= 2500 - 1000 - 1200 + x$$
$$= +300 + x$$

In cyclic process,
$$\Delta U = 0$$

Now, $\quad Q = \Delta U + W$

or $\quad 1000 = 0 + (300 + x)$

$\therefore \quad x = 700 \, J$

$$\eta = \frac{W}{Q_1 + Q_4}$$

$$= \frac{1000}{6000 + 3500} = 10.5\%$$

2. (a) Let l_1 and l_2 be the final lengths of the two parts, then from gas equation :

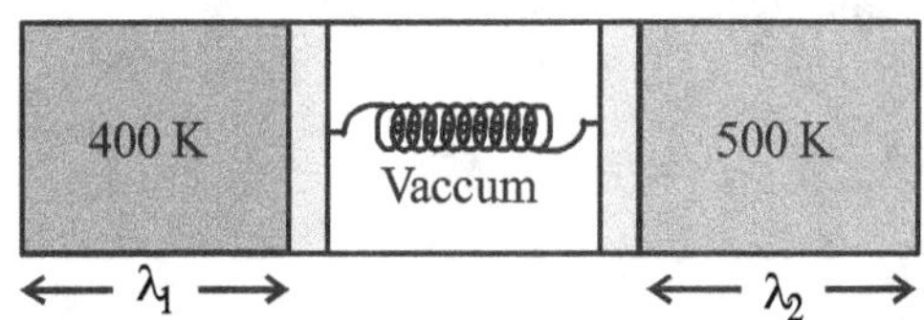

$$\frac{P_0 A l_0}{T_0} = \frac{P A l_1}{T_1} = \frac{P A l_2}{T_2} \qquad ...(i)$$

Considering the equilibrium of piston in initial and final states, we have

$$P_0 A = k x_0 \text{ and } PA = kx$$

or $\quad \dfrac{P}{P_0} = \dfrac{x}{x_0} \qquad ...(ii)$

Decrease in length of spring = total increase in the lengths of the two chambers.

$\therefore \quad x - x_0 = l_1 + l_2 - 2l_0 \qquad ...(iii)$

From eq. (i),

$$l_1 = \frac{P_0 l_0 T_1}{P T_0} \text{ and } l_2 = \frac{P_0 l_0 T_2}{P T_0}$$

Using eq. (ii),

$$l_1 = \frac{x_0 l_0 T_1}{x T_0} \text{ and } l_2 = \frac{x_0 l_0 T_2}{x T_0}$$

Putting these in eq. (iii)

$$x - x_0 = \frac{x_0 l_0}{x T_0} [T_1 + T_2] - 2l_0$$

Substituting the values and solving for x, we get

$$x \approx 1.3 \, m.$$

3. (d) The heat capacity of the solid is

$$\frac{dQ}{d\theta} = 2a\theta + 4b\theta^3.$$

4. (b) Given : $\quad Q_1 = 1000 \, J$
$$Q_2 = 600 \, J$$
$$T_1 = 127°C = 400 \, K$$
$$T_2 = ?$$
$$\eta = ?$$

Efficiency of carnot engine,

$$\eta = \frac{W}{Q_1} \times 100\%$$

or, $\quad \eta = \dfrac{Q_2 - Q_1}{Q_1} \times 100\%$

or, $\quad \eta = \dfrac{1000 - 600}{1000} \times 100\%$

$$\eta = 40\%$$

Now, for carnot cycle $\dfrac{Q_2}{Q_1} = \dfrac{T_2}{T_1}$

$$\frac{600}{1000} = \frac{T_2}{400}$$

$$T_2 = \frac{600 \times 400}{1000}$$
$$= 240 \, K$$
$$= 240 - 273$$

$\therefore \quad T_2 = -33°C$

5. (a) Process AB is isobasic and BC is isothermal, CD isochoric and DA isothermic compression.

6. (b, c) $\dfrac{P^2}{\rho} = k \Rightarrow \dfrac{P^2 RT}{PM} = k \Rightarrow PT = \left(\dfrac{kM}{R}\right) \quad ...(1)$

$$\frac{P^2}{\rho} = \frac{P'^2}{\rho/2} \Rightarrow P' = \frac{P}{\sqrt{2}}$$

Hence from (1), $T' = T\sqrt{2}$.

$PT = $ constant hence P-T curve is a parabola.

7. (a, d) $\quad \eta_1 = 1 - \dfrac{300}{400} = \dfrac{1}{4}$; $\eta_2 = 1 - \dfrac{400}{500} = \dfrac{1}{5}$

$$\eta_3 = 1 - \frac{500}{600} = \frac{1}{6} \; ; \; \eta_4 = 1 - \frac{600}{800} = \frac{1}{4}$$

8. (b, d) Process is not isothermal {for option (a)}.

(b) Volume decreases and temperature decreases
ΔU = negative,
So, ΔQ = negative
(c) Work done in process A $\to$ B $\to$ C is positve
(d) Cycle is clockwise, so work done by the gas is positive

9. **(b, c)** There is a decrease in volume during melting of an ice slab at 273 K. Therefore, negative work is done by ice-water system on the atmosphere or positive work is done on the ice-water system by the atmosphere. Hence, option (b) is correct.

Secondly heat is absorbed during melting (i.e. dQ is positive) and as we have seen, work done by ice-water system is negative (dW is negative.) Therefore, from first law of thermodynamics
$dU = dQ - dW$
change in internal energy of ice-water system, dU will be positive or internal energy will increase.

10. **9**

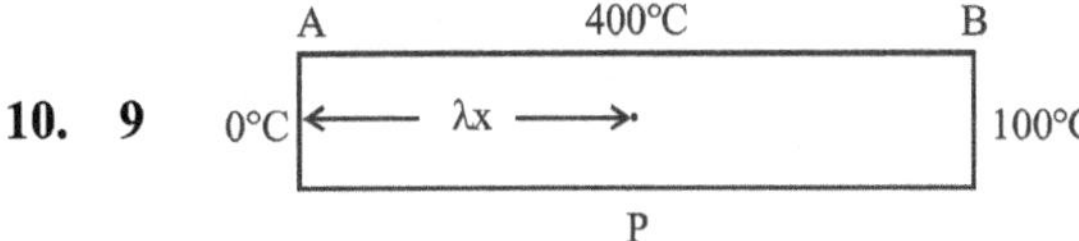

For heat flow from P to 0

$$L_f \frac{dm_1}{dt} = \frac{KA\,400}{\lambda x} \quad ..... \text{(i)}$$

For heat flow from P to B

$$L_{vap} \frac{dm_2}{dt} = \frac{KA\,300}{10x - \lambda x} \quad ..... \text{(ii)} \left[\text{Given } \frac{dm_1}{dt} = \frac{dm_2}{dt} \right]$$

On solving (i) and (ii), we get $\lambda = 9$

11. **2** Applying first law of thermodynamics to path iaf
$Q_{iaf} = \Delta U_{iaf} + W_{iaf}$
$500 = \Delta U_{iaf} + 200 \qquad \therefore \Delta U_{iaf} = 300\,J$
Now,
$Q_{ibf} = \Delta U_{ibf} + W_{ib} + W_{bf}$
$\qquad = 300 + 50 + 100$
$Q_{ib} + Q_{bf} = 450\,J \qquad\qquad ...(1)$
Also $Q_{ib} = \Delta U_{ib} + W_{ib}$
$\therefore Q_{ib} = 100 + 50 = 150\,J \qquad\qquad ...(2)$

From (1) & (2) $\dfrac{Q_{bf}}{Q_{ib}} = \dfrac{300}{150} = 2$

12. **4** Given, $\qquad V = kT^{2/3}$

$$\therefore \qquad dV = k \times \frac{2}{3} T^{-1/3} dT = \frac{2}{3} k T^{-1/3} dT$$

Work done $\qquad dW = PdV$

$$= \frac{RT}{V} dV$$

$$= \frac{RT}{kT^{2/3}} \times \frac{2}{3} kT^{-1/3} dT = \frac{2}{3} R(dT)$$

Total work done $\qquad W = \dfrac{2}{3} R \displaystyle\int_{T_1}^{T_2} dT$

$$= \frac{2}{3} R[T_2 - T_1]$$
$$= 2/3 \times 2 \times 30 = 40\,cal$$

13. **4**
If P_1 be the pressure after expansion, then
$$PV = P_1(3V + V)$$
$$\therefore \qquad P_1 = \frac{P}{4}.$$
For the adiabatic compression, let P_2 be the final pressure, then
$$P_1(4V)^{\gamma} = P_2 V$$
$$\therefore \qquad P_2 = P_1(4)^{1.5}$$
$$= 8\,P_1$$
The change in internal energy,
$$\Delta U = nC_V \Delta T$$
$$= n\frac{R}{\gamma - 1}[T_2 - T_1]$$
$$= \frac{P_2 V_2 - P_1 V_1}{\gamma - 1} = 400\,J.$$

For (Q.14-15):
$m_A = 100\,gm$; $V_A = V_B = 10^{-2}\,m^3$
$P_A = 10^5\,N/m^2.$

In cylinder A, the process is adiabatic, so
$$P_1 V_1^{\gamma} = P_2 V_2^{\gamma}$$
$$10^5(10^{-2})^{1.5} = P_2(25 \times 10^{-4})^{1.5}$$
$$\therefore \qquad P_2 = 8 \times 10^5$$

14. **(d)** For cylinder B,
$$P_f = \frac{F}{A_2} = \frac{8000}{200 \times 10^{-4}}$$
$$= 4 \times 10^5\,N/m^2$$
$$W_B = fx = W_A$$
or $\qquad 8000x = 2000 \Rightarrow x = 0.25m$
$$\Delta V_B = Ax = 200 \times 10^{-4} \times 0.25$$
$$= 50 \times 10^{-4}\,m^3$$
$$\therefore \qquad V_f = 10^{-2} + 50 \times 10^{-4} = 250 \times 10^{-4}\,m^3$$
For cylinder A,
$$10^5 \times 10^{-2} = \frac{100}{M} RT_0 \qquad\qquad ...\text{(i)}$$
For cylinder B,
$$\left(4 \times 10^5\right) \times \left(250 \times 10^{-4}\right) = \frac{m_B}{M} RT_0 \qquad ...\text{(ii)}$$
After solving above equations, we get
$$m_B = 1000\,gm.$$

15. **(c)** So at equilibrium, the force on the connecting rod
$$F = P_2 A_2 = 8 \times 10^5 \times 1000 \times 10^{-4}$$
$$= 8000N$$

16. **(a)** For an Isochoric process, volume remains constant and hence, $dW = PdV = 0$, $dU = dQ = nC_v dT$

17. **(a)** For an Isobaric process, pressure remains constant and hence, $dW = P(V_2 - V_1)$, $dQ = nC_p dT$

18. **(b)** For an Isothermal process, temperature remians constant. As internal energy depends only on temperature $dU = 0 \Rightarrow dQ = dW = \displaystyle\int_{V_1}^{V_2} Pdv$

$$\Rightarrow dQ = nRT \log_e \frac{V_2}{V_1} = 2.303\,nRT \log_{10} \frac{V_2}{V_1}$$

19. (A)$\to$p, s; (B)$\to$q; (C)$\to$q, r; (D)$\to$p,s

(A) $PV = nRT$

$$P = (nRT)\frac{1}{V} = (\text{constant})\frac{1}{V}$$

T = constant i.e. isothermal process

$\because$ V increases, ΔW is positive.

$\Delta Q = \Delta U + \Delta W > 0$

(B) $\Delta Q = 0$

$pdV = \Delta W$ = negative

(C) $PV = nRT$

As volume decreases. T also decreases i.e., $\Delta U > 0$

$PdV = \Delta W < 0$ so $\Delta Q < 0$

(D) For cyclic process $\Delta U = 0$

$\Delta W > 0$ (clockwise), $\Delta Q > 0$

20. (A)$\to$ r; (B)$\to$ p; (C)$\to$ q; (D)$\to$ s

(A)$\to$ r $\qquad \Delta S = \dfrac{\Delta Q}{T} = \dfrac{-mL}{T}$

$$= \frac{-0.5 \times 4200 \times 80}{373}$$

$$\simeq -446 \text{ J/K}$$

(B)$\to$ p $\qquad \Delta S = \dfrac{\Delta Q}{T} = \dfrac{-mL}{T}$

$$= \frac{-0.5 \times 4200 \times 80}{273} \simeq 610 \text{ J/K}$$

(C)$\to$ q $\quad$ As the sides of the rod are insulated, so

$$\Delta S = \frac{\Delta Q}{T} = 0.$$

(D)$\to$ s $\quad$ The total change in entropy

$$\Delta S = 610 - 446 = 164 \text{ J/K}$$

1. **(a)** We have from the gas law

$$(P_0 - \alpha V^2)V = nRT$$

$$T = \frac{(P_0 - \alpha V^2)V}{nR} = f(V)$$

From the maximum temperature

$$\frac{dT}{dV} = 0$$

or $\quad P_0 - 3\alpha V^2 = 0$

$$V = \left(\frac{P_0}{3\alpha}\right)^{1/2}$$

Therefore, corresponding pressure

$$P = P_0 - \alpha \frac{P_0}{3\alpha} = \frac{2P_0}{3}$$

Hence, the sought maximum temperature from the gas law becomes

$$T = \frac{PV}{nR} = \frac{2\dfrac{P_0}{3}\left(\dfrac{P_0}{3\alpha}\right)^{1/2}}{nR} = \frac{2P_0}{3nR}\left(\frac{P_0}{3\alpha}\right)^{1/2}$$

2. **(d)** Avg.K.E. $= \dfrac{5}{2}KT = \dfrac{5}{6}mv^2 \left[\because \dfrac{1}{2}mv^2 = \dfrac{3}{2}KT\right]$

3. **(a)** $PV = \dfrac{m}{M}RT$; $\therefore \dfrac{P}{T} = Cm$

or $\quad \dfrac{\text{slope of } B}{\text{slope of } A} = \dfrac{m_B}{m_A} = \dfrac{3m}{m} = 3$

4. **(d)** $\gamma_{He} = 5/3,\qquad \gamma_{O_2} = 7/5$

$$P_{He}(LA)^{5/3} = P'_{He}\left(\frac{LA}{2}\right)^{5/3} \Rightarrow P'_{He} = P_{He}(2)^{5/3}$$

Similarly, $\quad P'_{O_2} = P_{O_2}\left(\dfrac{L}{L_2}\right)^{7/5}$

$$P_{O_2} = P_{He}, \; P'_{O_2} = P'_{He}$$

taking ratio $\Rightarrow L_2 = \dfrac{L}{2^{25/21}}$

volume of $O_2 = L_2A = \dfrac{LA}{2^{25/21}}$

5. **(b)** From the relation

$$\frac{n_1 + n_2}{\gamma - 1} = \frac{n_1}{\gamma_1 - 1} + \frac{n_2}{\gamma_2 - 1}$$

For monoatomic gas, $\gamma_1 = \dfrac{5}{3}$

For diatomic gas, $\gamma_2 = \dfrac{7}{5}$

$$\therefore \quad \frac{n_1 + n_2}{\gamma - 1} = \frac{n_1}{\left(\dfrac{5}{3} - 1\right)} + \frac{n_2}{\left(\dfrac{7}{5} - 1\right)}$$

or $\quad \dfrac{n_1 + n_2}{\gamma - 1} = \dfrac{3}{2}n_1 + \dfrac{5}{2}n_2$

or $\quad \dfrac{n_1 + n_2}{\gamma - 1} = \dfrac{3n_1 + 5n_2}{2}$

$$\therefore \quad \gamma - 1 = \frac{2n_1 + 2n_2}{3n_1 + 5n_2}$$

or $\quad \gamma = \dfrac{2n_1 + 2n_2}{3n_1 + 5n_2} + 1 = \dfrac{5n_1 + 7n_2}{3n_1 + 5n_2}$

6. **(a, c, d)**
At NTP same volume means same molecules
$\because f_1 = f_2$, so same temperature means same internal energy
$\left(U = \dfrac{f}{2}nRT\right)$. Average velocity is zero.

7. **(c, d)**

$$v_{rms} = \sqrt{\frac{3PV}{M}}$$

$$\therefore \quad K = \frac{1}{2}Mv_{rms}^2 = \frac{3}{2}PV$$

$$K' = \frac{3}{2}(2P \times 2V) = 4K = 4 \times 3000 = 12000 \text{ J}.$$

8. **(b, c)**
For adiabatic process, $PV^\gamma = \text{constant (k)}$
Also $\quad \ell nP + \gamma \ell nV = \ell nk$
$\therefore \qquad \ell nP = -\gamma \ell nV = \ell nk$
As slope of x is greater than y, so
$\gamma_x \gamma_x > \gamma_y$
As $C_v = \dfrac{R}{\gamma - 1}$; so $C_{v_1} < C_{v_2}$

Also $\gamma = 1 + \dfrac{2}{f}$

or $f = \left(\dfrac{2}{\gamma - 1}\right)$; $\therefore \; f_1 < f_2$.

9. **(a, c, d)**

$$\gamma_v = \gamma_p = \frac{1}{273}/K$$

$E = \dfrac{3}{2}RT$ is same for all ideal gases at same temperature.

The mean free path, $\lambda = \dfrac{kT}{\sqrt{2}\pi d^2 P}$; so it increases with decrease in pressure.

10. **2** $V_1 = 200$ m/s, $T_1 = 300$ k, $T_2 = 400$ k, $V_2 = ?$
R.M.S. velocity, $V \propto \sqrt{T}$

$$\frac{V_2}{V_1} = \sqrt{\frac{T_2}{T_1}} \Rightarrow V_2 = V_1\sqrt{\frac{T_2}{T_1}} = 200\sqrt{\frac{400}{300}} = 2 \times \frac{200}{\sqrt{3}} \text{ ms}^{-1}$$

11. 8   The initial pressure of gas

$$P_1 = 830\,mm - 30\,mm$$
$$= 800\,mm$$

and $\qquad T_1 = T$

If P is now pressure in the jar, then final pressure of the gas

$$P_2 = (P - 25)$$

and $\qquad T_2 = \left(T - \dfrac{3T}{100}\right)$

We know that $\qquad \dfrac{P_1}{T_1} = \dfrac{P_2}{T_2}$

or $\qquad \dfrac{800}{T} = \dfrac{P - 25}{\left(T - \dfrac{3T}{100}\right)}$

$\therefore \qquad P \approx 800\,mm\ of\ Hg$

12. 2   The pressure exerted by the weight of the piston

$$= \dfrac{mg}{A}$$
$$= \dfrac{1 \times 10}{10 \times 10^{-4}}$$
$$= 1 \times 10^4\,N/m^2$$

Thus initial pressure of the gas

$$P_1 = 100 \times 10^{-3} + 10^4$$
$$= 110 \times 10^3\,N/m^2$$
$$V_1 = A\ell_1$$
$$= A \times 0.20$$
$$P_2 = 10^4\,N/m^2$$

Using $\qquad P_1 V_1 = P_2 V_2$

or $\qquad P_1(A\ell_1) = P_2(A\ell_2)$

$\therefore \qquad \ell_2 = \dfrac{P_1 \ell_1}{P_2}$

$$= \dfrac{110 \times 10^3}{1 \times 10^4} \times 0.20$$
$$= 2.2\,m$$
$$= 220\,cm$$

13. 9

We have $\qquad \dfrac{v_2}{v_1} = \sqrt{\dfrac{T_1}{T_2}}$

$\therefore \qquad \dfrac{1}{2} = \sqrt{\dfrac{T_1}{T_2}}$

or $\qquad T_2 = 4\,T_1$

$\therefore \qquad \Delta T = T_2 - T_1$

or $\qquad 3T_1 = 3 \times (273 + 16)$
$$= 867\,K$$

The heat required $\qquad Q = \mu C_v \Delta T$

$$= \left[\dfrac{14}{28}\right] \times \dfrac{5}{2} \times 8.31 \times 867$$
$$\approx 9000\,J$$

14. (a)   The time between successive collisions,

$$t = \dfrac{1}{500}\,s$$

The root mean square speed

$$v_{rms} = \dfrac{2\ell}{t}$$

$$= \dfrac{2 \times 1}{1/500}$$
$$= 1000\ m/s.$$

By the definition of rms speed,

$$v_{rms} = \sqrt{\dfrac{3RT}{M}}$$

or $\qquad 100 = \sqrt{\dfrac{3RT}{M}}$

or $\qquad 100 = \sqrt{\dfrac{3 \times 25/3 \times T}{4 \times 10^{-3}}}$

$\therefore \qquad T = 160\,K$

15. (b)   Mean kinetic energy per atom

$$= \dfrac{3}{2}kT$$
$$= \dfrac{3}{2} \times 1.38 \times 10^{-23} \times 160$$
$$= 3.312 \times 10^{-21}\,J.$$

16. (c)   For a diatomic gas, average energy of a molecule

is $\dfrac{5}{2}kT$ if the molecules translate and rotate but

do not vibrate and is $\dfrac{7}{2}kT$ if they vibrate also i.e.,

$$f = 7,\ C_v = \dfrac{7}{2}R\ ,\ C_p = R + C_v = \dfrac{9}{2}R$$

17. (b)   As given for polyatomic gas degree of freedom $f = 6$,

then $C_v = \dfrac{6}{2}R = 3R,$

$$C_p = 4R,\ \gamma = \dfrac{C_p}{C_v} = \dfrac{4}{3} = 1.33$$

18. (c)   For diatomic gas

Case I. (molecule translate & rotate only)

$$C_v = \dfrac{5}{2}R \qquad C_p = \dfrac{7}{2}R \qquad \gamma = 1.40$$

Case II. (molecule translate, rotate & vibrate also)

$$C_v = \dfrac{7}{2}R \qquad C_p = \dfrac{9}{2}R \qquad \gamma = 1.29$$

19. **(A) → r; (B) → s; (C) → p ; (D) → q**

$$V_{rms} = \sqrt{\dfrac{V_1^2 + V_2^2 + \dots + V_n^2}{n}} = \sqrt{\dfrac{3kT}{m}}$$

$$V_{mpv} = \sqrt{\dfrac{2kT}{m}}$$

For an ideal gas molecule

$$U = \dfrac{1}{2}\,fkT\ \text{[energy for 1 mole of gas]}$$

for $f = 1$, $U = \dfrac{1}{2}kT$ (for each degree of freedom)

20. **(A) → (q) ; (B) → (r) ; (C) → (p) ; (D) → (s)**

A real gas behaves as an ideal gas at low pressure and high temperature

1. **(a)** $U(x) = k|x|^3$

$\therefore \quad [k] = \dfrac{[U]}{[x^3]} = \dfrac{ML^2T^{-2}}{L^3} = ML^{-1}T^{-2}$

Now time period may depend on $T \propto (\text{mass})^x$ $(\text{amplitude})^y (k)^z$

$\therefore \quad [M^0 L^0 T] = [M]^x [L]^y [ML^{-1} T^{-2}]^z$

$\qquad = [M^{x+z} L^{y-z} T^{-2z}]$

Equating the powers, we get

$-2z = 1$ or $z = -1/2$

$y - z = 0$ or $y = z = -1/2$

Hence $T \propto (\text{amplitude})^{-1/2} \propto a^{-1/2}$

2. **(b)** The equivalent system is shown in figure.

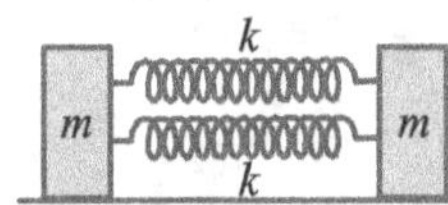

The reduced mass, $\mu = \dfrac{mm}{m+m} = \dfrac{m}{2}$

and $\qquad k_e = 2k.$

$\therefore \qquad \omega = \sqrt{\dfrac{k}{m}} = \sqrt{\dfrac{2k}{m/2}} = 2\sqrt{\dfrac{k}{m}}$

$\qquad\qquad = 2\sqrt{\dfrac{0.1}{0.1}} = 2 \text{ rad/s}$

or $\qquad f = \dfrac{\omega}{2\pi} = \dfrac{2}{2\pi} = \dfrac{1}{\pi} Hz$

3. **(d)** Let us plot the graph of the mathematical equation

$U(x) = K\left[1 - e^{-x^2}\right], \quad F = -\dfrac{dU}{dx} = 2kxe^{-x^2}$

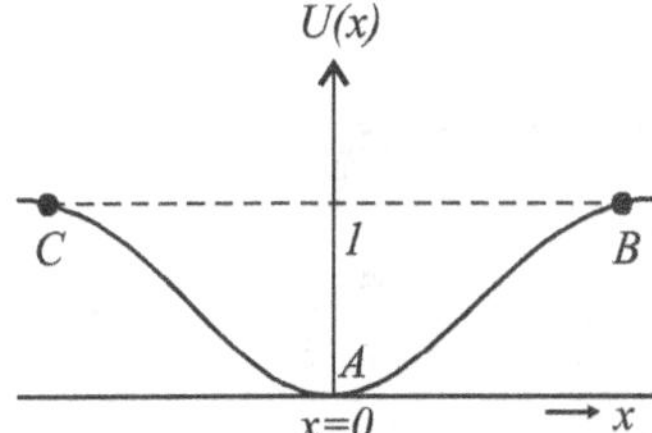

From the graph it is clear that the potential energy is minimum at $x = 0$. Therefore, $x = 0$ is the state of stable equilibrium. Now if we displace the particle from $x = 0$ then for displacements the particle tends to regain the position $x = 0$ with a force $F = \dfrac{2kx}{e^{x^2}}$. Therefore for small values of x we have $F \propto x$.

4. **(b)** From graph it is clear that when $L = 1m, T^2 = 4s^2$

As we know,

$T = 2\pi\sqrt{\dfrac{L}{g}}$

$\Rightarrow \quad g = \dfrac{4\pi^2 L}{T^2}$

$\qquad = 4 \times \left(\dfrac{22}{7}\right)^2 \times \dfrac{1}{4} = \left(\dfrac{22}{7}\right)^2$

$\therefore \quad g = \dfrac{484}{49} = 9.87 \text{m/s}^2$

5. **(a)** $T = \dfrac{2V\sin\theta}{g} \quad \therefore \quad 1 = \dfrac{2V\sin 45°}{g} \quad \therefore v = \sqrt{50} \text{ ms}^{-1}$

6. **(a, c)**

The particle is doing SHM because of the frictional force only. The contact force on the block is

$F = \sqrt{(mg)^2 + f^2} = m\sqrt{g^2 + a^2} = m\sqrt{g^2 + (\omega^2 x)^2}$

This is not proportional to x but proportional to m. The contact force on the platform is F only and this is independent of m.

7. **(a, d)** $\quad U + KE = -2 + 1 = -1 \text{ J (const)}$

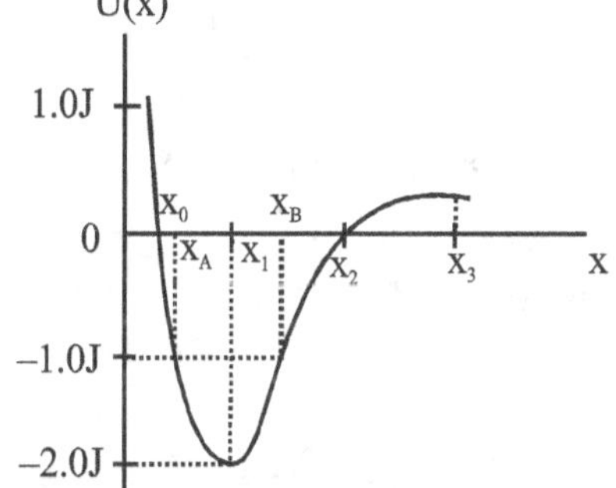

$\therefore \ U_{max} = -1 \text{ J}$ at $x_A \& x_B$ [when $KE = 0$]

$\therefore$ The particle oscillates between x_A and x_B.

8. **(a, b, c, d)**

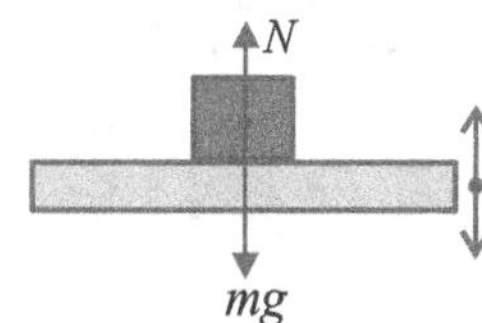

$mg - N = ma$

or $\qquad mg - 0 = m\omega^2 A$

$\therefore \qquad \omega = \sqrt{\dfrac{g}{A}} = \sqrt{\dfrac{10}{0.40}} = 5 \text{s}$

$\qquad T = \dfrac{2\pi}{\omega} = \dfrac{2\pi}{5} \text{ s}.$

$\qquad a_{max} = \omega^2 A = 25 \times 0.4 = 10 \text{ m/s}^2 = g$

When plank moves in upward direction,

$\qquad N = m(g+a) = m(g+g) = 2mg.$

9. **(a, c)** At time t_1, velocity of the particle is negative i.e. going towards $-X_m$. From the graph, at time t_1, its speed is decreases Therefore particle lies in between $-X_m$ and 0.

At time t_2, velocity is positive and its magnitude is less than maximum i.e. it has yet not crossed O.

It lies in between $-X_m$ and 0.

Phase of particle at time t_1 is $(180 + \theta_1)$

Phase of particle at time t_2 is $(270 + \theta_2)$

Phase difference is $90 + (\theta_2 - \theta_1)$

$\theta_2 - \theta_1$ can be negative making $\Delta\phi < 90°$ but cannot be more than $90°$.

10. **4.**

The displacement of a particle in S.H.M. is given by :

$$y = a \sin(\omega t + f)$$

$$\text{velocity} = \frac{dy}{dt} = \omega a \cos(\omega t + f)$$

The velocity is maximum when the particle passes through the mean position i.e.

$$\left(\frac{dy}{dt}\right)_{max} = \omega a$$

The kinetic energy at this instant is given by

$$\frac{1}{2} m \left(\frac{dy}{dt}\right)^2_{max} = \frac{1}{2} m\omega^2 a^2 = 8 \times 10^{-3} \text{ joule}$$

or $\quad \dfrac{1}{2} \times (0.1) \, \omega^2 \times (0.1)^2 = 8 \times 10^{-3}$

Solving we get $\quad \omega = \pm 4$

$\therefore$ Positive vaolue of $\omega = \textbf{4 rad/s.}$

11. **5**

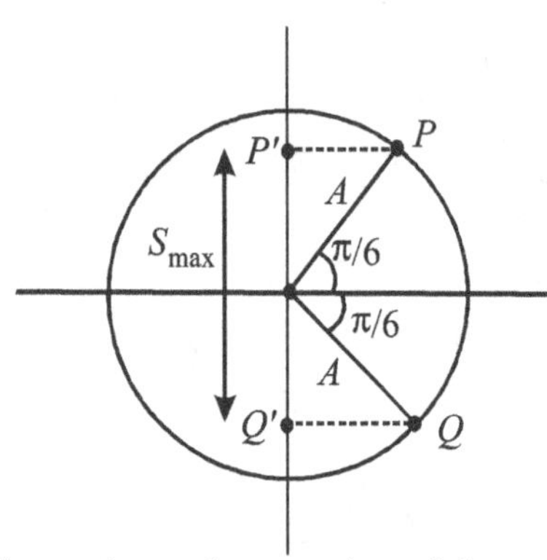

Figure shows the mapping of the two SHMs with circular motions having phase difference

$$\phi = \omega t = \frac{2\pi}{6} \times 1 = \frac{\pi}{3} \text{ rad}$$

The maximum separation between the two particles is

$$S_{max} = 2A \sin\frac{\pi}{6}$$

or $\quad S_{max} = 2 \times 5 \times \dfrac{1}{2} = 5\text{cm}.$

12. **1**

When the rod is slightly displaced from its means position, then restoring force,

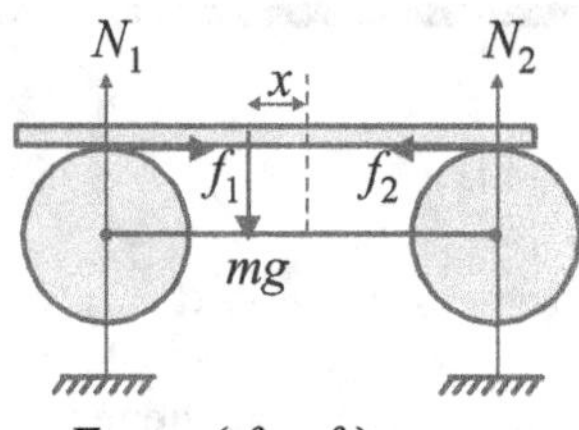

$$\begin{aligned} F &= -(f_1 - f_2) \\ &= -(\mu N_1 - \mu N_2) \\ &= -\mu(N_1 - N_2) \end{aligned}$$

For the vertical equilibrium of the rod, we have

$$N_1 + N_2 = mg \qquad \qquad \text{...(i)}$$

and for rotational equilibrium, we have

$$mg(\ell/2 - x) - N_2\,\ell = 0 \qquad \text{...(ii)}$$

$$\therefore \qquad N_2 = \frac{mg}{\ell}(\ell/2 - x)$$

and $\qquad N_1 = mg - N_2$

$$= mg - \frac{mg}{\ell}\left(\frac{\ell}{2} - x\right)$$

$$= \frac{mg}{\ell}\left[\frac{\ell}{2} + x\right]$$

Thus $\qquad F = \mu\left[\frac{mg}{\ell}\left(\frac{\ell}{2} + x\right) - \frac{mg}{\ell}\left(\frac{\ell}{2} - x\right)\right]$

$$= -\mu\frac{mg}{\ell}(2x)$$

Acceleration of the rod

$$a = \frac{F}{m}$$

$$= \frac{2\mu g}{\ell}(-x)$$

Thus $\qquad T = 2\pi\sqrt{\dfrac{\ell}{2\mu g}}$

$$= \pi\sqrt{\frac{2\ell}{\mu g}} = 10 \text{ sec}$$

13. **3**

We know that $T = 2\pi\sqrt{\left(\dfrac{M}{k}\right)}$,

where k = spring constant.

In first case, $\quad 2 = 2\pi\sqrt{\left(\dfrac{M}{k}\right)} \qquad \text{...(1)}$

In second case, $3 = 2\pi\sqrt{\left(\dfrac{M+4}{k}\right)} \qquad \text{... (2)}$

Squaring of eq. (1) and (2) and then dividing (2) by (1), we have

$$\frac{9}{4} = \frac{M+4}{M} = 1 + \frac{4}{M}$$

Solving we get $M = 3.2 \text{ kg} \approx 3$

14. **(b)** Speed of Q just before collision is

$$V_Q = \omega A = \sqrt{\frac{k}{m}} \, A$$

15. **(a)** The block shall meet after time $t = \dfrac{T}{4}$, where T is time period of either isolated spring block system.

$$t = \frac{T}{4} = \frac{1}{4} 2\pi \sqrt{\frac{m}{k}} = \frac{\pi}{2} \sqrt{\frac{m}{k}}$$

16. **(b)**

$$K = K_1 + 2K_2 = K^1 + 2K^1 = 3K^1$$
$$\Rightarrow T = 2\pi \sqrt{M/3K^1}$$

17. **(a)**

$$K = \frac{K_1 K_2}{K_1 + K_2} \quad \text{but condition given as } K_1 \text{ and } K_2$$
becomes twice

so $\quad K = \dfrac{2K_1 \times 2K_2}{2K_1 + 2K_2} = \dfrac{2K_1 K_2}{K_1 + K_2}$

18. **(c)** In case III, K_1 and $2K_2$ are parallel so $K = K_1 + 2K_2$,
$T = 2\pi \sqrt{M/K_1 + 2K_2}$

19. $A \rightarrow (s); B \rightarrow (q, r); C \rightarrow (p); D \rightarrow (s)$

$\because \quad v = A\omega \cos(\omega t + \phi),$

$\therefore \quad$ The velocity-time graph is (sinusoidal)

Relation between acceleration velocity is

$\dfrac{v^2}{\omega^2} + \dfrac{a^2}{\omega^4} = A^2$ which may be circle if $\omega = 1$ and ellipse if $\omega \neq 1$.

Acceleration-displacement graph is a straight line and acceleration time graph is sinusoidal.

20. $A \rightarrow (r); B \rightarrow (s); C \rightarrow (p); D \rightarrow (q)$

(A) In frame of lift effective acceleration due to gravity is

$$g + \frac{g}{2} = \frac{3g}{2} \text{ downwards.}$$

$$\therefore \quad T = 2\pi \sqrt{\frac{2(3\ell)}{3g}}$$

(B) $\quad T = 2\pi \sqrt{\dfrac{m}{k_{eff}}} = 2\pi \sqrt{\dfrac{m}{k + 2k}} = 2\pi \sqrt{\dfrac{m}{3k}}.$

(C) $\quad T = 2\pi \sqrt{\dfrac{I}{mgd}} = 2\pi \sqrt{\dfrac{\dfrac{m\ell^2}{3}}{mg\dfrac{\ell}{2}}} = 2\pi \sqrt{\dfrac{2\ell}{3g}}$

(D) $\quad T = 2\pi \sqrt{\dfrac{m}{\rho Ag}} = 2\pi \sqrt{\dfrac{(\rho/2) A (2\ell)}{\rho Ag}} = 2\pi \sqrt{\dfrac{\ell}{g}}$

1. (a) At $t=0$, $y=\dfrac{1}{1+x^2}$ or $x=\sqrt{\dfrac{1-y}{y}}=x_1$

At $t=2s$, $y=\dfrac{1}{2+x^2-2x}=\dfrac{1}{1+\left(x-1^2\right)}$

or $\left(x-1^2\right)=\dfrac{1-y}{y}$ or $x=1+\sqrt{\dfrac{1-y}{y}}=x_2$

$\therefore$ Speed of the wave

$$v=\dfrac{\Delta x}{\Delta t}=\dfrac{x_2-x_1}{t_2-t_1}=\dfrac{1}{2-0}=0.5\,\text{m/s}$$

2. (a) $f=\dfrac{1}{2\ell}\sqrt{\dfrac{T}{m}};$

In air : $T=mg=\rho Vg$

$\therefore\; f=\dfrac{1}{2\ell}\sqrt{\dfrac{\rho Vg}{m}}$ ... (i)

In water : $T=mg-$ upthrust

$$=V\rho g-\dfrac{V}{2}\rho_\omega g=\dfrac{Vg}{2}(2\rho-\rho_\omega)$$

$$\therefore\; f'=\dfrac{1}{2\ell}\sqrt{\dfrac{\dfrac{Vg}{2}(2\rho-\rho_\omega)}{m}}$$

$$=\dfrac{1}{2\ell}\sqrt{\dfrac{Vg\rho}{m}}\sqrt{\dfrac{(2\rho-\rho_\omega)}{2\rho}}$$

$$\dfrac{f'}{f}=\sqrt{\dfrac{2\rho-\rho_\omega}{2\rho}}$$

$$f'=f\left(\dfrac{2\rho-\rho_\omega}{2\rho}\right)^{1/2}$$

$$=300\left[\dfrac{2\rho-1}{2\rho}\right]^{1/2}\text{Hz}$$

3. (a) $C=\sqrt{\dfrac{\gamma RT}{M_0}}=\sqrt{\dfrac{5RT}{3M_0}}$

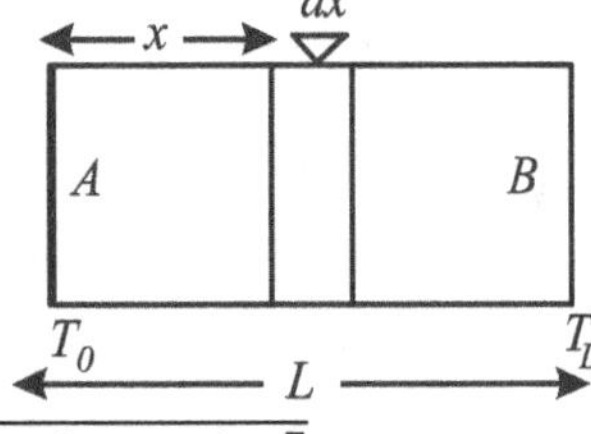

$$dx=C.dt=\sqrt{\dfrac{5R}{3M_0}}\left[T_0+\left(\dfrac{T_L-T_0}{L}\right)\times\right]dt$$

$$t=\dfrac{2L}{\left(\sqrt{T_L}+\sqrt{T_0}\right)}\sqrt{\dfrac{3M}{5R}}$$

4. (d) and $\begin{aligned}A_A&=2,\;f_A=f\\A_B&=1,\;f_B=2f\end{aligned}$

$$\therefore\quad \dfrac{I_A}{I_B}=\dfrac{f_A^2\,A_A^2}{f_B^2\,A_B^2}=1$$

5. (c) The velocity profile of each elementary section of the pulse is shown in figure 1 and figure 2.

When both the pulses completely overlap, the velocity profiles of both the pulses in overlap region are identical. By superposition, velocity of each elementary section doubles. Therefore, KE of each section becomes four times. Hence the $K.E.$ in the complete width of overlap becomes four times.

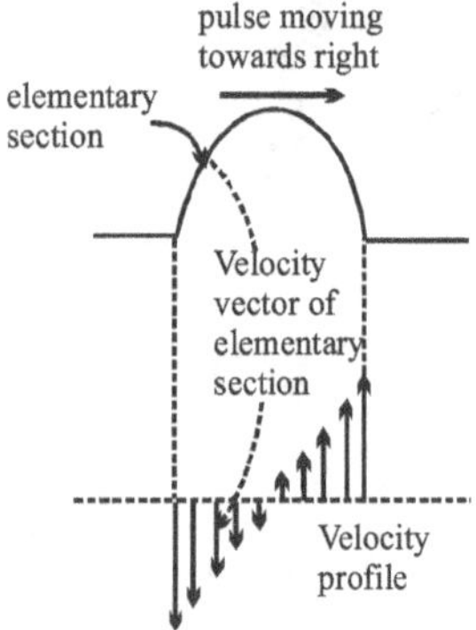
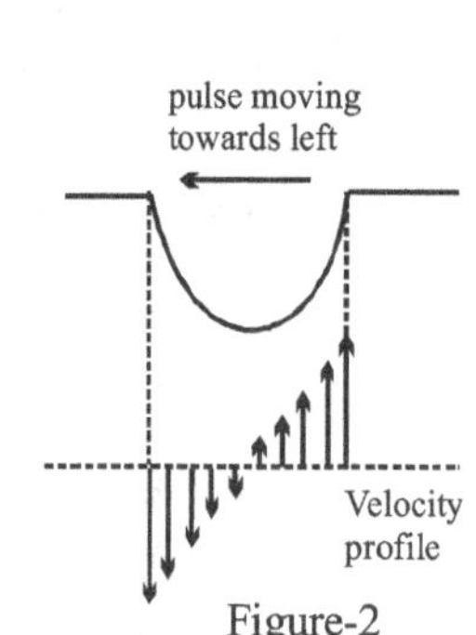

6. (b, c)
The maximum pulse height is 2.0 cm. when
$x-3.0\,t=0$. It is constant.
Speed of the pulse

$$=\dfrac{\text{coefficient of }t}{\text{coefficient of }x}=3.0\,\text{cm/s}$$

7. (b, d)
When sound pulse is reflected through a rigid boundary (closed end of a pipe), no phase change occurs between the incident and reflected pulse i.e., a high pressure pulse is reflected as a high pressure pulse.

When a sound pulse is reflected from open end of a pipe, a phase change of a radian occurs between the incident and the reflected pulse. A high pressure pulse is reflected as a low pressure pulse.

8. (a, b)
The displacement of air column to the right of B is negative (i.e. towards B) while displacement of air column to the left of B is positive (i.e., towards B) so density is maximum at B, similarly density is minimum at D.

9. (a,b,c) Standing waves are produced by two similar waves superposing while travelling in opposite direction.
This can happen in case (a), (b) and (c).

10. 1 $n_1 = \dfrac{1}{2\ell}\sqrt{\left(\dfrac{T}{4\pi r^2 \rho}\right)}$ and $n_2 = \dfrac{1}{4\ell}\sqrt{\left(\dfrac{T}{\pi r^2 \rho}\right)}$

$n = \dfrac{v}{\lambda} = \dfrac{1}{\lambda}\sqrt{\dfrac{T}{m}}$ [where $\dfrac{\lambda}{2}$ = length of string]

$\therefore \dfrac{n_1}{n_2} = 2 \times \dfrac{1}{2} = 1 \left[\because m = \dfrac{\text{mass}}{\text{length}} = \dfrac{\rho \times A \times \text{length}}{\text{length}} = \rho A\right]$

11. 5 $R = \sqrt{3^2 + 4^2} = 5\,\text{mm}$

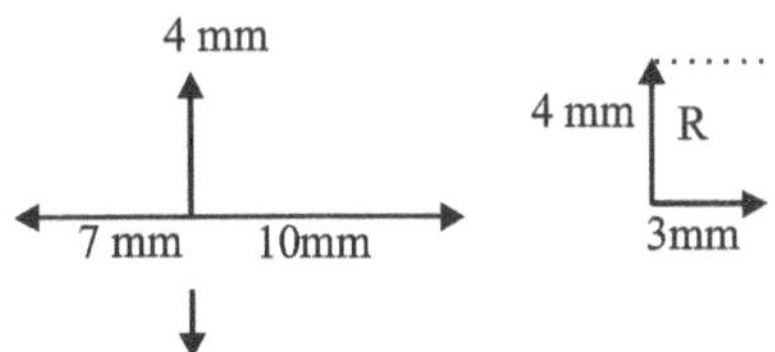

12. 3 Let v be the actual frequency of the whistle. By Doppler's effect

$$v' = v\,\dfrac{v_S}{v_S - v_t}$$

where v_s = Speed of sound = 300 m/s (given)
$v' = 2.2\,\text{kHz} = 220\,\text{Hz}$ (given)

$\therefore \quad 2200 = v\,\dfrac{300}{300 - v_t} \qquad \ldots\text{(i)}$

WHILE THE TRAIN IS RECEDING

$$v'' = v\,\dfrac{v_s}{v_s + v_t}$$

Here, $v' = 1.8\,\text{kHz} = 1800\,\text{Hz}$ (given)

$\therefore \quad 1800 = v\,\dfrac{300}{300 + v_t} \qquad \ldots\text{(ii)}$

Dividing (i) and (ii)

$$\dfrac{2200}{1800} = \dfrac{300}{300 - v_t} \times \dfrac{300 + v_t}{300}$$

$\Rightarrow \dfrac{11}{9} = \dfrac{300 + v_t}{300 - v_t}$

$\Rightarrow 3300 - 11v_t = 2700 = 9v_t$
$\Rightarrow 600 = 20\,v_t$
$\Rightarrow v_t = \textbf{30 m/s}$

13. 8 The frequency of tuning fork, $f = 392\,\text{Hz}$.

Also $\qquad 392 = \dfrac{1}{2 \times 50}\sqrt{F/\mu} \qquad \ldots\ldots\text{(i)}$

After decreasing the length by 2%, we have

$$f' = \dfrac{1}{2(49)}\sqrt{F/\mu} \qquad \ldots\ldots\text{(ii)}$$

From above equations,

$$f' = 400\,\text{Hz}.$$

$\therefore$ Beats frequency = 8 Hz.

14. (a), 15. (b)

When a string oscillates, nodes are produced at its ends. In case of fundamental tone, it vibrates in single loop. Hence, **wavelength of fundamental tone**, $\lambda_0 = 2\ell$ and in case of first overtone it vibrates in two loops as shown in figure. Hence wavelength of first overtone is $\lambda_1 = \ell$.

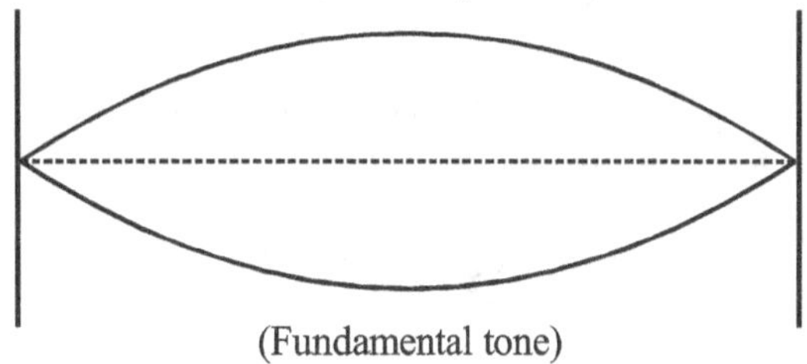

(Fundamental tone)

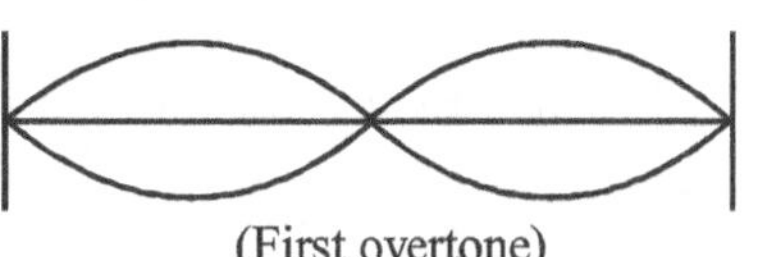

(First overtone)

When stationary performs SHM and displacement amplitude at a point distant x from one end is given by

$$a = a_0 \sin\left(\dfrac{2\pi x}{\lambda}\right) \qquad \ldots\ldots\text{(1)}$$

where a_0 is maximum displacement amplitude which occurs at antinode. Since, tension in string is T, therefore, velocity of transverse wave is given by $v = \sqrt{\dfrac{T}{m}}$ where m is mass per unit length of string.

Fundamental tone : Since, frequency is $n = \dfrac{v}{\lambda}$, therefore, frequency of fundamental tone of the string,

$$n_0 = \dfrac{1}{2\ell}\sqrt{\dfrac{T}{m}}$$

Considering an elemental length dx of string at a distance x from left end, its mass = $m\,dx$.

Its oscillation energy = $\dfrac{1}{2}(m\,dx)\,a^2\,(2\pi n_0)^2$

$$= \dfrac{a_0^2 \pi^2 T}{2\ell^2}\sin^2\left(\dfrac{2\pi x}{2\ell}\right)dx$$

$\therefore$ Total oscillation energy of the string

$$= \dfrac{a_0^2 \pi^2 T}{2\ell^2}\int_0^\ell \sin^2\left(\dfrac{\pi x}{\ell}\right)dx = \dfrac{a_0^2 \pi^2 T}{4\ell}$$

Since, maximum kinetic energy of a particle performing SHM is equal to its oscillation energy, therefore, maximum kinetic

energy of the string in its fundamental tone $= \dfrac{a_0^2 \pi^2 T}{4\ell}$

First overtone : Frequency, $n_1 = \dfrac{v}{\lambda_1} = \dfrac{1}{\ell}\sqrt{\dfrac{T}{m}}$

Considering an elemental length dx of string at a distance from left end, its mass $= m\,dx$.

Its oscillation energy $= \dfrac{1}{2}(m dx)a_0^2 . \sin^2\left(\dfrac{2\pi x}{\ell}\right)(2\pi n_1)^2$

$= \dfrac{2\pi^2 a_0^2 T}{\ell^2}\sin^2\left(\dfrac{2\pi x}{\ell}\right)dx$

$\therefore$ Total oscillation energy of the string

$= \dfrac{2\pi^2 a_0^2 T}{\ell^2}\int_0^\ell \sin^2\left(\dfrac{2\pi x}{\ell}\right)dx$

or maximum kinetic energy of string in its overtone

$= \dfrac{a_0^2 \pi^2 T}{\ell}$

16. (a) For an open organ pipe wavelength and frequency for the first harmonic or fundamental tone
$\lambda = 2l = 2 \times .3 = .6$ m

while $\upsilon = \dfrac{v}{2l} = \dfrac{330}{2 \times .3} = 550$ Hz

17. (b) For first overtone or third harmonic of a closed

organ pipe $\upsilon = \dfrac{3v}{4l}$ and $\lambda = \dfrac{4l}{3}$

18. (c) For first harmonic of open organ pipe

$\upsilon = \dfrac{v}{2l},\ \lambda = 2l.$

Third harmonic of open organ pipe

$\upsilon = \dfrac{3v}{2l},\ \lambda = \dfrac{2}{3}l$

First harmonic of closed organ pipe

$\upsilon = \dfrac{v}{4l},\ \lambda = 4l$

Third harmonic of closed organ pipe

$\upsilon = \dfrac{3v}{4l},\ \lambda = \dfrac{4l}{3}$

19. A→q; B→q; C→q; D→s
(A) and (B) B is displacement node
$\Rightarrow a = 0, v = 0$ and $E = 0$ and deformation maximum $\Rightarrow$ PE max.
(D) B is displacement antinode
$\Rightarrow a = $ max, $KE = 0, PE = 0, V = 0$

20. A→(q); B→(p); C→(s); D→(r)
(A) Intensity due to a source emitting sound uniformly in all directions is given by

$$I = \dfrac{P}{4\pi r^2}$$

So $\quad I_1 = \dfrac{1 \times 10^{-3}}{4\pi(2)^2} = 19.90 \times 10^{-6}$ W/m^2

$\quad I_2 = \dfrac{1 \times 10^{-3}}{4\pi(3)^2} = 8.85 \times 10^{-6}$ W/m^2

(B) The resultant intensity is given by
$$I = I_1 + I_2 + 2\sqrt{I_1 I_2}\cos\phi$$
where $\quad \phi = \dfrac{2\pi}{\lambda}\Delta x.$

Here $\lambda = \dfrac{v}{f} = \dfrac{330}{660} = \dfrac{1}{2}$ and $\Delta x = 3 - 2 = 1$ m

$\therefore \quad \phi = \dfrac{2\pi}{(1/2)} \times 1 = 4\pi$

$I = I_1 + I_2 + 2\sqrt{I_1 I_2}\cos 4\pi$

$\quad = I_1 + I_2 + 2\sqrt{I_1 I_2}$

or $\quad I = (\sqrt{I_1} + \sqrt{I_2})^2$

$\quad = (\sqrt{19.9} + \sqrt{8.85})^2 \times 10^{-6}$
$\quad = 55.3 \times 10^{-6}$ W/m^2

(C) In the case $\quad \phi_0 = \pm\pi$ rad

$\therefore \quad I = [\sqrt{I_1} + \sqrt{I_2} + 2\sqrt{I_1 I_2}\cos(4\pi \pm \pi)]$

$\quad = (\sqrt{I_1} - \sqrt{I_2})^2$

$\quad = (\sqrt{19.9} - \sqrt{8.85})^2 \times 10^{-6}$
$\quad = 2.2 \times 10^{-6}$ W/m^2

(D) For incoherent sources

$I = I_1 + I_2$

$\quad = (19.9 + 8.85) \times 10^{-6}$
$\quad = 28.7 \times 10^{-6}$ W/m^2

1. (c) Given $\vec{E} = E_o\,\hat{x}$

This shows that the electric field acts along $+x$ direction and is a constant. The area vector makes an angle of $45°$ with the electric field. Therefore the electric flux through the shaded portion whose area is

$a \times \sqrt{2}\,a = \sqrt{2}\,a^2$ is $\phi = \vec{E}.\vec{A} = EA\cos\theta = E_0(\sqrt{2}\,a^2)\cos$

$45° = E_0(\sqrt{2}\,a^2) \times \dfrac{1}{\sqrt{2}} = E_0 a^2$

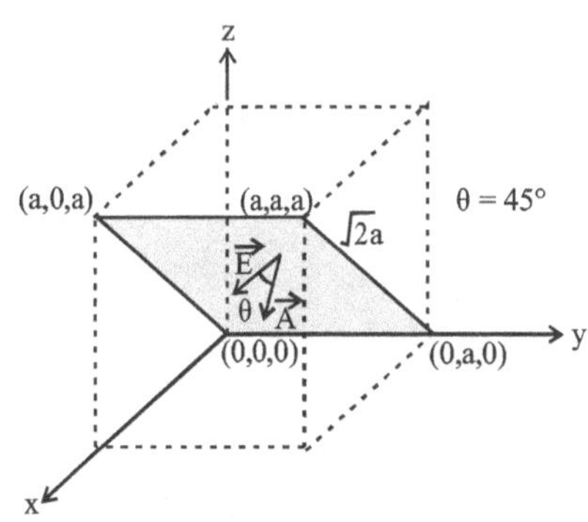

2. (c)

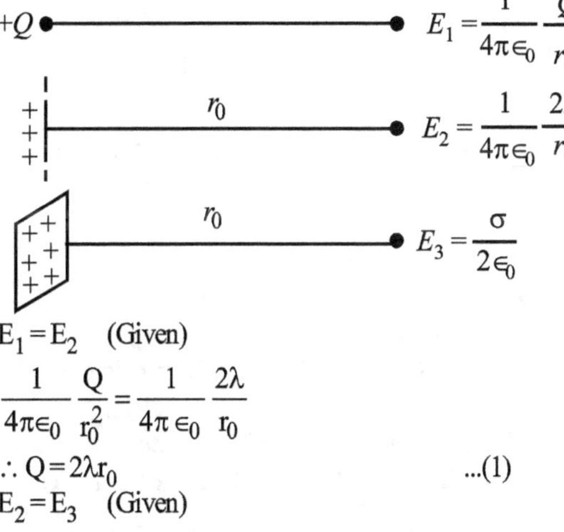

$E_1 = E_2$ (Given)

$\dfrac{1}{4\pi\epsilon_0}\dfrac{Q}{r_0^2} = \dfrac{1}{4\pi\epsilon_0}\dfrac{2\lambda}{r_0}$

$\therefore Q = 2\lambda r_0$ ...(1)

$E_2 = E_3$ (Given)

$\dfrac{1}{4\pi\epsilon_0}\dfrac{2\lambda}{r_0} = \dfrac{\sigma}{2\epsilon_0} \Rightarrow r_0 = \dfrac{\lambda}{\sigma\pi}$

$\therefore$ (b) is incorrect

$E_1 = E_3$ (Given)

$\therefore \dfrac{1}{4\pi\epsilon_0}\dfrac{Q}{r_0^2} = \dfrac{\sigma}{2\epsilon_0} \Rightarrow Q = 2\pi\sigma r_0^2$

$\therefore$ (a) is incorrect

Now $E_1\,(r_0/2) = \dfrac{1}{4\pi\epsilon_0}\dfrac{4Q}{r_0^2}$

$= \dfrac{1}{4\pi\epsilon_0} \times \dfrac{4 \times 2\lambda r_0}{r_0^2} = \dfrac{1}{4\pi\epsilon_0}\dfrac{8\lambda}{r_0}$

and $2E_2\,(r_0/2) = 2\left[\dfrac{1}{4\pi\epsilon_0}\dfrac{4\lambda}{r_0}\right] = \dfrac{1}{4\pi\epsilon_0}\dfrac{8\lambda}{r_0}$

$\therefore$ (c) is correct

$E_2\,(r_0/2) = \dfrac{1}{4\pi\epsilon_0}\dfrac{2\lambda}{r_0/2} = \dfrac{1}{4\pi\epsilon_0}\dfrac{4\lambda}{r_0} = \dfrac{\lambda}{\pi\epsilon_0 r_0}$

$4E_3\,(r_0/2) = \dfrac{4\sigma}{2\epsilon_0} = \dfrac{2\sigma}{\epsilon_0} = \dfrac{2}{\epsilon_0} \times \dfrac{\lambda}{\pi r_0}$

$\therefore$ (d) is incorrect.

3. (a) We have centripetal force equation

$q\left(\dfrac{2k\lambda}{r}\right) = \dfrac{mv^2}{r}$

so $v = \sqrt{\dfrac{2kq\lambda}{m}}$

Now, $T = \dfrac{2\pi r}{v} = 2\pi r\sqrt{\dfrac{m}{2kq\lambda}}$

where $k = \dfrac{1}{4\pi\varepsilon_0}$

4. (b) $\tau = pE\sin\theta$, this is given by the second curve.

5. (b) $F_3 = \dfrac{k(q_b + q_c)q_d}{r^2}$

$F_1 = F_2 = $ zero

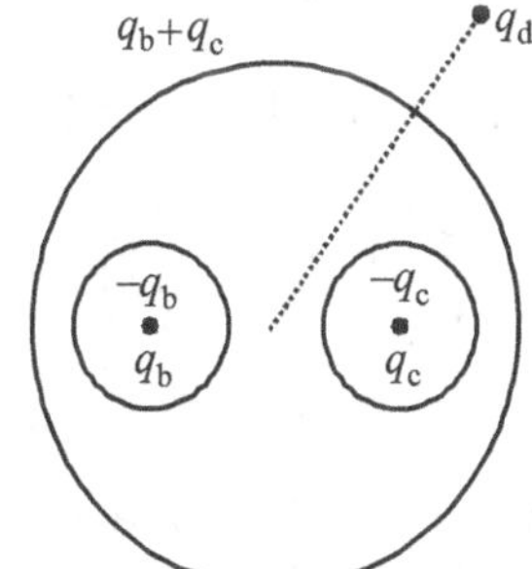

6. (a, c)

The net charge of the dipole is $q_{in} = q - q = 0$, and so

$\phi = \dfrac{q_{in}}{\epsilon_0} = 0.$

The electric field of dipole is not zero anywhere of its vicinity.

7. (b, d)

The electric field at any point inside the shell,

$E = \dfrac{1}{4\pi\epsilon_0}\dfrac{q}{R^2}.$

The electric field at the outer surface

$E = \dfrac{1}{4\pi\epsilon_0}\dfrac{q}{(2R)^2}.$

8. **(a, b)**

Let v_1 and v_2 be the velocities of the first and second balls after the removal of the uniform electric field. By hypothesis, the angle between the velocity v_1 and the initial velocity v is 60°. Therefore, the change in the momentum of the first ball is

$$\Delta p_1 = q_1 E \Delta t = m_1 v \sin 60°.$$

Here we use the condition that $v_1 = v/2$, which implies that the change in the momentum Δp_1 of the first ball occurs in a direction perpendicular to the direction of its velocity v_1. Since $E \parallel \Delta p_1$ and the direction of variation of the second ball momentum is parallel to the direction of Δp_1, we obtain for the velocity of the second ball (it can easily be seen that the charges on the balls have the same sign)

$$v_2 = v \tan 30° = \frac{v}{\sqrt{3}}$$

The corresponding change in the momentum of the second ball is

$$\Delta p_2 = q_2 E \Delta t = \frac{m_2 v}{\cos 30°}$$

Hence we obtain, $\dfrac{q_1}{q_2} = \dfrac{m_1 \sin 60°}{m_2 / \cos 30°}$,

$$\frac{q_2}{m_2} = \frac{4}{3}\frac{q_1}{m_1} = \frac{4}{3}k_1$$

9. **(c, d)**

Let us consider a point P on the overlapping region. The electric field intensity at P due to positively charged sphere

$$= \frac{\overrightarrow{\rho r_1}}{3 \in_0}$$

The electric field intensity at P due to negatively charged sphere $= \dfrac{\overrightarrow{\rho r_2}}{3 \in_0}$. The total electric field,

$$\overrightarrow{E} = \frac{\overrightarrow{\rho r_1}}{3 \in_0} + \frac{\overrightarrow{\rho r_2}}{3 \in_0} = \frac{\rho}{3 \in_0}\left[\overrightarrow{r_1} + \overrightarrow{r_2}\right]$$

$$\overrightarrow{E} = \frac{\rho}{3 \in_0}\overrightarrow{r}$$

Therefore the electric field is same in magnitude and direction option (c) and (d) are correct.

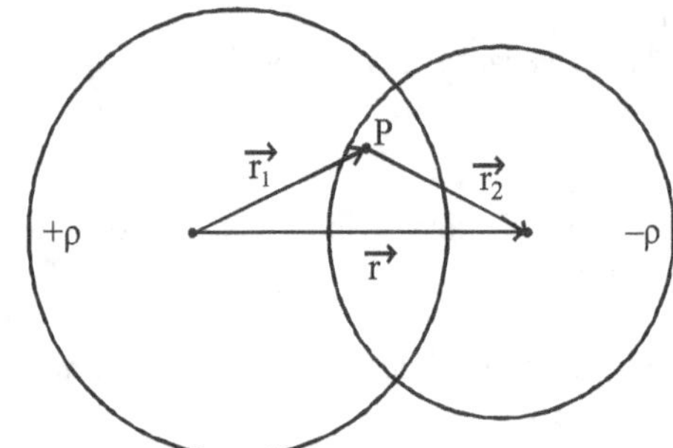

10. **7**

The *FBD* of the device shown in figure. At lowest position of the ball,

$$(T_A + F_e) - mg = \frac{mv_A^2}{\ell} \quad ...(i)$$

At highest position of the ball

$$(T_B + mg) + F_e = \frac{mv_B^2}{\ell}$$

To just complete the circle, $T_B = 0$

$$\therefore \quad mg - F_e = \frac{mv_B^2}{\ell} \quad ...(ii)$$

where $\quad F_e = \dfrac{1}{4\pi \in_0}\dfrac{q^2}{l^2}$

Also $\quad \dfrac{1}{2}mv_A^2 = \dfrac{1}{2}mv_B^2 + mg\,(2\ell) \quad ...(iii)$

After solving above equations and substituting the values, we get

$$v_A = 7\,\text{m/s}$$

11. **3**

The electric force on the dust particle

$$F_e = qE,$$

and viscous force, $F_v = 6\pi\eta rv$.

For constant velocity,

$$F_e - F_v = 0$$

or $\qquad qE = 6\pi\eta rv$

$$\therefore \quad q = \frac{6\pi\eta rv}{E}$$

$$= \frac{6\pi \times 1.6\times 10^{-5} \times 5\times 10^{-17} \times 0.02}{6.28\times 10^5}$$

$$= 0.48\times 10^{-17}\,\text{C}$$

$$= 48\times 10^{-19}\,\text{C}$$

If n be the number of electrons on the dust particle, then

$$n = \frac{q}{e} = \frac{48\times 10^{-19}}{1.6\times 10^{-19}} = 30$$

12. **6**

$r = 1\text{m}$

$Q = 10^{-5}\,\text{C}$

$m = 0.9 \times 10^{-3}\,\text{kg} = \text{mass of particle}$

$q = -10^{-6}\,\text{C} = \text{charge on particle.}$

We know that the electric field due a uniformly. Charged ring of radius r at a point distant x from its center on its axis is given by

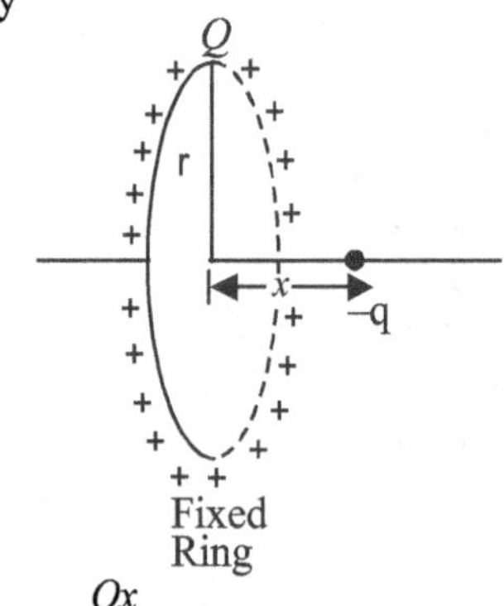

$$E = k\frac{Qx}{(r^2 + x^2)^{3/2}}$$

$\therefore$ Force on the negative charge q will be $F = qE$

$$\therefore \quad F = \frac{-kQq}{(r^2+x^2)^{3/2}} \times x$$

$$\Rightarrow \quad mA = \frac{-kQq}{(r^2+x^2)^{3/2}} \times x$$

$$\Rightarrow \quad A = -k\frac{Qq}{m(r^2+x^2)^{3/2}} \times x$$

$\Rightarrow$ The motion is simple harmonic in nature. Comparing it will $A = -\omega^2 x$

We get $\quad \omega^2 = \dfrac{kQq}{m(r^2+x^2)^{3/2}}$

In this case $x << r$

$$\therefore \quad \omega^2 = \frac{kQq}{mr^3}$$

$$\Rightarrow \quad \omega = \sqrt{\frac{kQq}{mr^3}}$$

$$\therefore \quad \frac{2\pi}{T} = \sqrt{\frac{kQq}{mr^3}}$$

$$T = 2\pi\sqrt{\frac{mr^3}{kQq}}$$

$$T = 2 \times 3.14\left[\frac{0.9\times10^{-3}\times1^3}{9\times10^9\times10^{-5}\times10^{-6}}\right]^{1/2}$$

$$= 6.28\,[0.01]^{1/2} = 6.28\,[0.1]$$
$$T = \textbf{0.628 sec} \approx \textbf{0.6 sec}$$

13. 4

Consider a small element of length $d\ell$ of the wire with centre at O, as shown in Fig. The charge on this element is

$$dq = \frac{q\,d\ell}{\pi R} = \frac{q\times(R\,d\theta)}{\pi R} = \frac{q\,d\theta}{\pi}$$

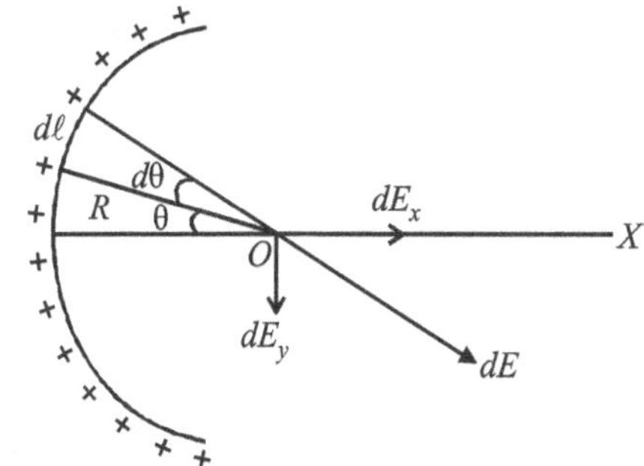

The electric field due to the current element at O is

$$dE = \frac{1}{4\pi\,\epsilon_0}\cdot\frac{dq}{R^2}$$

From symmetry, net field at O is

$$E = \int dE_x$$

(Since the net electric field along y-axis vanishes as each current element nulify the effect due to diametrically opposite similar current element)

$$= \int \frac{1}{4\pi\,\epsilon_0}\frac{dq\,\cos\theta}{R^2} = \frac{1}{4\pi\,\epsilon_0}\int\limits_{-\pi/2}^{+\pi/2}\frac{q\,\cos\theta\,d\theta}{\pi R^2}$$

$$= \frac{1\times q}{4\pi^2\,\epsilon_0\,R^2}(\sin\theta)_{-\pi/2}^{\pi/2}$$

$$E = \frac{2q}{4\pi^2\,\epsilon_0\,R^2} = \frac{2\times7\times10^{-10}\times9\times10^9}{\frac{22}{7}(0.2)^2}$$

$$E = \textbf{100 V/m}$$

14. (b) Electric field in region $y < L$

$$\vec{E} = 4\pi\sigma\hat{y}$$

Hence, electric force on the electron is given as

$$\vec{F} = -(e)\vec{E} = -4\pi e\sigma\hat{y}$$

From Newton's second law, we get

$$a_x = \frac{d^2x}{dt^2} = 0$$

$$a_y = \frac{d^2y}{dt^2} = \frac{-4\pi e\sigma}{m_e} = \text{constant}$$

15. (a) $\therefore$ Trajectory of the electron is that of a projectile in a homogeneous gravitational field.

Hence, $v_x(0) = v_0\sin\alpha = -\sqrt{\dfrac{2K_0}{m_e}}\sin\alpha$

$$v_y(0) = v_0\cos\alpha = \sqrt{\frac{2K_0}{m_e}}\cos\alpha$$

and $\quad x(0) = y(0) = 0$

Thus, by integrating (for $L > L_0$), we get

$$x(t) = \sqrt{\frac{2K_0}{m_e}}\,t\sin\alpha$$

$$y(t) = \sqrt{\frac{2K_0}{m_e}}\,t\cos\alpha - \left(\frac{2\pi e\sigma}{m_e}\right)t^2$$

Eliminating t we get :

$$y = -\frac{\pi e\sigma}{K_0\sin^2\alpha}x^2 + x\cot\alpha$$

Hence, the trajectory of the electron is parabolic.

16. (d) For the spherical shell
$E_{in} = 0$ for $x < R$
and for solid non conducting sphere

$$E_{in} = \frac{KQx}{R^3}\,0 \le x \le R$$

17. (a) For circular ring

$$E = k\frac{Qx}{\left(R^2+x^2\right)^{3/2}}$$

For E_{max}, at $x = \pm\dfrac{R}{\sqrt{2}}\left[\text{use }\dfrac{dE}{dx} = 0\right]$

$$E_{max}{}^m = \frac{Q}{6\sqrt{3}\pi\varepsilon_0 R^2}$$

18. **(b)** E_{disc} (at $x = R$) is

$$\frac{2kQ}{R^2}\left(1 - \frac{R}{\sqrt{R^2 + R^2}}\right) = \frac{2KQ}{R^2}\left(1 - \frac{1}{\sqrt{2}}\right)$$

$E_{spherical\ shell}$ (at $x = R$) i.e., at the surface

$$= \frac{kQ}{R^2}$$

$E_{solid\ non\ conducting\ sphere}$ (at $x = R$) i.e., at the surface $= \dfrac{kQ}{R^2}$

19. $(A) \to q$, $(B) \to p$, $(C) \to r$, $(D) \to s$

20. A-p, s; B-p, r; C-p, s; D-q, s

(A) Due to q_1 distribution of charge on inner surface of conductor is uniform. Due to q_2 distribution of charge on outer surface of conductor is non-uniform.

(B) Due to q_1 distribution of charge on inner surface of conductor is uniform. Due to q_2 distribution of charge on outer surface of conductor is uniform.

(C) Due to q_1 distribution of charge on inner surface of conductor is uniform. Due to q_2 distribution of charge on outer surface of conductor is non-uniform.

(D) If the inside charge is displaced by small amount from centre then symmetry will be distorted hence distribution due to q_1 will not be uniform.

1. **(b)** $E = -\nabla\phi = -\phi_0 2[x\hat{i} + y\hat{i} + z\hat{x}]$

$= \varepsilon_0 \nabla.E = -2\varepsilon_0\phi_0 \nabla.(x\hat{i} + y\hat{i} + z\hat{x})$

$n = -6\phi_0\varepsilon_0$

2. **(d)** Fundamental frequency, $f = \dfrac{1}{2L}\sqrt{\dfrac{T}{\mu}}$

T = force on dielectric slab.

To calculate force on slab consider capacitor as combination of two capacitors one with slab and one with air.

$$F = -\dfrac{dU}{dx} \; ; \; U = \dfrac{1}{2}\left[\dfrac{k \in_0 bx}{d} + \dfrac{\in_0 b(b-x)}{d}\right]V^2$$

$$\dfrac{dU}{dx} = \dfrac{1}{2}\left[\dfrac{k \in_0 b}{d} - \dfrac{\in_0 b}{d}\right]V^2 = \dfrac{1}{2}\dfrac{\in_0 bV^2}{d}(k-1)$$

Thus, $f = \dfrac{1}{2L}\sqrt{\dfrac{\in_0 bV^2(k-1)}{2d\mu}}$

3. **(c)** The charge q_1 of the sphere can be determined from the formula

$q_1 = 4\pi\varepsilon_0 V_1 r_1$

After the connection of the sphere to the envelope, the entire charge q_1 will flow from the sphere to the envelope, and will be distributed uniformly over its surface. Its potential V_2 (coinciding with the new value of the potential of the sphere) will be

$$V_2 = \dfrac{q_1}{4\pi\varepsilon_0 r_2} = V_1\dfrac{r_1}{r_2}$$

4. **(b)** At the centre of the square net force on the charge is zero. However, in this position the charge is in unstable equilibrium

5. **(c)** When key is on the position BD, the situation is shown in the figure.

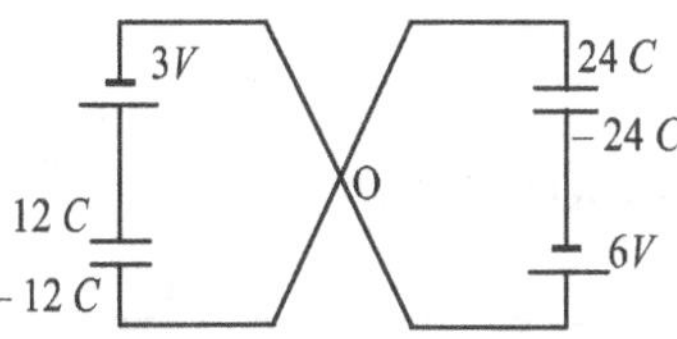

When key is on the position AD, the situation is shown in the figure.

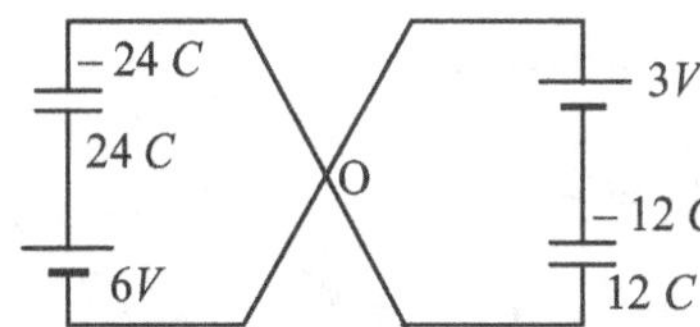

The charge flows to each capacitor is 36 μC, and so total charge flows through point O is 72 μC.

6. **(a)** 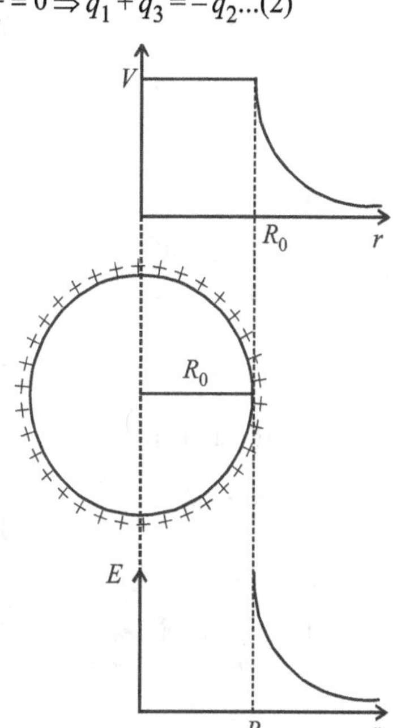

Charge on C_1 is $q_1 = \left[\left(\dfrac{12}{4+12}\right)\times 8\right]\times 4 = 24\mu c$

The voltage across C_P is $V_P = \dfrac{4}{4+12}\times 8 = 2v$

∴ Voltage across $9\mu F$ is also 2V

∴ Charge on $9\mu F$ capacitor $= 9\times 2 = 18\mu C$

∴ Total charge on 4 μF and $9\mu F = 42\mu c$

$$\therefore E = \dfrac{KQ}{r^2} = 9\times 10^9 \times \dfrac{42\times 10^{-6}}{30\times 30} = 420\,Nc^{-1}$$

7. **(b,d)** $V = \dfrac{1}{4\pi \in_0}\left[\dfrac{q}{R} - \dfrac{q}{R}\right] = 0$

and $E = 2\times\dfrac{1}{4\pi \in_0}\dfrac{q}{R^2}\left(\dfrac{\sin \pi/2}{\pi/2}\right) = \dfrac{q}{\pi^2 \in_0 R^2}.$

8. **(b,d)**

9. **(a,b,c)** Potential on innermost shell is zero

$$\dfrac{q_1}{r} + \dfrac{q_2}{2r} + \dfrac{q_3}{3r} = 0$$

$$\Rightarrow 6q_1 + 3q_2 + 2q_3 = 0 \;\;....(1)$$

Potential on outermost shell is zero

$$\dfrac{q_1}{3r} + \dfrac{q_2}{3r} + \dfrac{q_3}{3r} = 0 \Rightarrow q_1 + q_3 = -q_2...(2)$$

10. **(a,b,d)**

(a) The whole charge Q will be enclosed in a sphere of diameter $2R_0$.

(b) Electric field $E =$ zero inside the sphere. Hence electric field is discontinued at $r = R_0$.

(c) Changes in V and E are continuously present for $r > R_0$. Option (c) is incorrect.

(d) For $r < R_0$, the potential V is constant and the electric intensity is zero. Obviously, the electrostatic energy is zero for $r < R_0$.

11.   **5**

The adjacent figure is a case of parallel plate capacitor. The combined capacitance will be

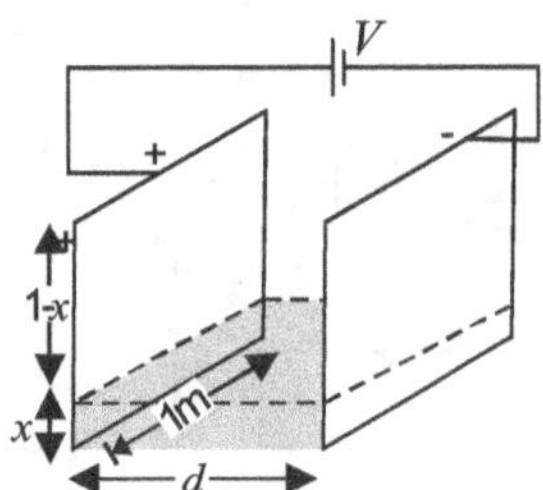

$$C = C_1 + C_2$$

$$= \frac{k\varepsilon_0(x \times 1)}{d} + \frac{\varepsilon_0[(1-x) \times 1]}{d}$$

$$C = \frac{\varepsilon_0}{d}[dx + 1 - x] \qquad \qquad \text{...(i)}$$

After time dt, the dielectric rises by dx. The new equivalent capacitance will be

$$C + dC = C_1' + C_2'$$

$$= \frac{\varepsilon_0}{d}[(x+dx) \times 1] + \frac{\varepsilon_0[(1-x-dx) \times 1]}{d}$$

$$= \frac{\varepsilon_0}{d}[kx + kdx + 1 - x - dx] \qquad \text{...(ii)}$$

Charge of capacitance in time dt

$$dC = \frac{\varepsilon_0}{d}[kx + kdx + 1 - x - dx - kx - 1 + x]$$

$$= \frac{\varepsilon_0}{d}(k-1)\,dx$$

$$\frac{dC}{dt} = \frac{\varepsilon_0}{d}(k-1)\frac{dx}{dt} = \frac{\varepsilon_0}{d}(k-1)v \qquad \text{...(iii)}$$

where $v = \dfrac{dx}{dt}$

We know that $q = CV$

$$\frac{dq}{dt} = V\frac{dC}{dt} \qquad \qquad \text{...(iv)}$$

$$\Rightarrow \quad I = V\frac{\varepsilon_0}{d}(k-1)v$$

From (i) and (ii)

$$I = \frac{564 \times 8.85 \times 10^{12}}{0.01}(11-1) \times 0.001 \cong 5 \times 10^{-9}\,\text{A}$$

12.   **4**

Here, $r_1 = 10$ cm, $r_2 = 15$ cm

$V_1 = 150\,\text{V}, V_2 = 100\,\text{V}$

Common potential

$$V = \frac{C_1 V_1 + C_2 V_2}{C_1 + C_2} = \frac{4\pi \in_0 (r_1 V_1 + r_2 V_2)}{4\pi \in_0 (r_1 + r_2)} = 120 \text{ volt.}$$

$$q_1 = C_1 V = 4\pi\in_0 r_1 V = \frac{12}{9 \times 10^9}C$$

$$= \frac{12}{9 \times 10^9} \times 3 \times 10^9 \text{ esu} = \mathbf{4\,esu}$$

13.   **2**   The equivalent system of capacitors is shown in figure.

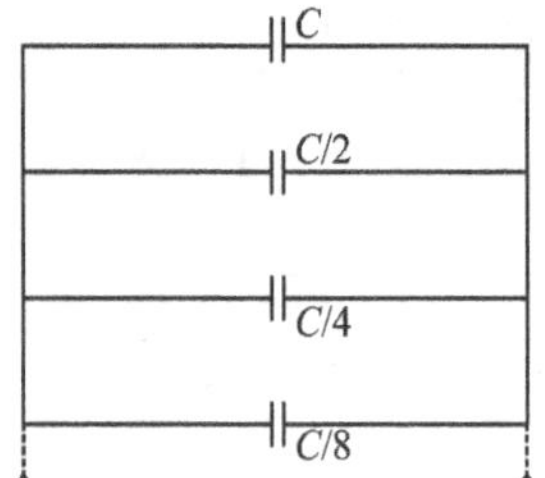

If C' is the equivalent capacitance, then

$$C' = C + \frac{C}{2} + \frac{C}{4} + \frac{C}{8} + \cdots$$

$$= C\left[\frac{1}{1 - \frac{1}{2}}\right] = 2C = 2\mu F$$

14.   **2**

When battery is replaced by another uncharged capacitor

then $C' = 2C$ and $V_{C'} = \dfrac{V}{2};\ U_{\text{initial}} = \dfrac{1}{2}CV^2,$

$$U_{\text{final}} = \frac{1}{2}(2C)\left(\frac{V}{2}\right)^2$$

$$U_{\text{final}} = \frac{1}{2}\,U_{\text{initial}} \text{ i.e., total electrostatic energy of resulting}$$

system decreased by a factor of 2.

15.   **(c)**   **16.**   **(a)**

17.   **(a)** $C_1 = \dfrac{\varepsilon_0 kA}{t}, C_2 = \dfrac{\varepsilon_0 A}{d-t}$

Two capacitors are in series

$$\therefore \frac{1}{C} = \frac{1}{C_1} + \frac{1}{C_2} = \frac{t}{\varepsilon_0 kA} + \frac{d-t}{\varepsilon_0 A}$$

$$C = \frac{\varepsilon_0 A}{d - (t/2)}$$

18.   **(a)** $C_{eq} = \dfrac{3}{2}C_{air}$

$$C_{eq}\frac{\varepsilon_0 A}{d-(t/2)} = \frac{3}{2}\frac{\varepsilon_0 A}{d} \Rightarrow \frac{t}{d} = \frac{2}{3}$$

19. **A – r :** $E = \dfrac{1}{4\pi \epsilon_0} \dfrac{Q}{z^2} = \dfrac{KQ}{4}$

B – s : $V = \dfrac{1}{4\pi \epsilon_0}\left[\dfrac{Q}{2} - \dfrac{Q}{3}\right]$

$\qquad = \dfrac{1}{4\pi \epsilon_0} \dfrac{Q}{6} = \dfrac{KQ}{6}$.

C – P : $V = \dfrac{Q}{4\pi \epsilon_0} - 0 = \dfrac{Q}{4\pi \epsilon_0} = kQ$

D – q : $E \times 2\pi r = \dfrac{1}{\epsilon_0}(q_{in})$

$\qquad\qquad = 0$

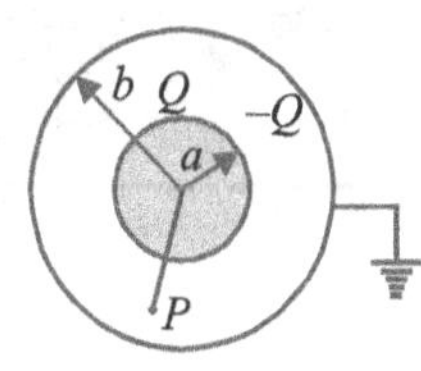

20. **A-s; B-q, r; C-p, r; D-q**

(A) At constant voltage removal of dielectric decreases capacity,

$\therefore$ Charge decreases. $V = Ed$, E remains constant.

(B) Insertion of dielectric increases capacity hence charge and energy increases at constant voltage. $V = Ed$, E remain constant

(C) At constant Q removal of dielectric decreases capacity hence voltage increases, and hence energy increases.

(D) Insertion increases capacity.

1. **(d)** Reading of potentiometer is accurate because during taking reading it does not draw any current from the circuit.

2. **(a)** It follows from symmetry considerations that the initial circuit can be replaced by an equivalent one (figure).

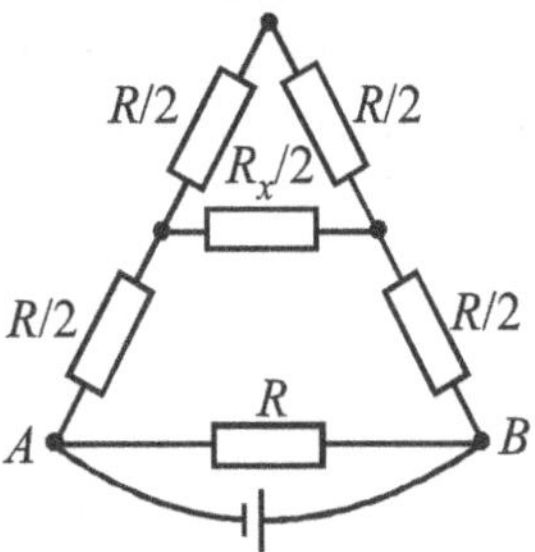

We replace the "inner" triangle consisting of an infinite number of elements by a resistor of resistance $R_{AB}/2$, where the resistance R_{AB} is such that $R_{AB} = R_x$ and $R_{AB} = a\rho$. After simplification, the circuit becomes a system of series and parallel connected conductors. In order to find R_x, we write the equation

$$R_x = R\left(R + \frac{RR_x/2}{R+R_x/2}\right)\left(R + R + \frac{RR_x/2}{R+R_x/2}\right)^{-1}$$

Solving this equation, we obtain

$$R_{AB} = R_x = \frac{R(\sqrt{7}-1)}{3} = \frac{a\rho(\sqrt{7}-1)}{3}$$

3. **(b)** Let R be the resistance of wire.

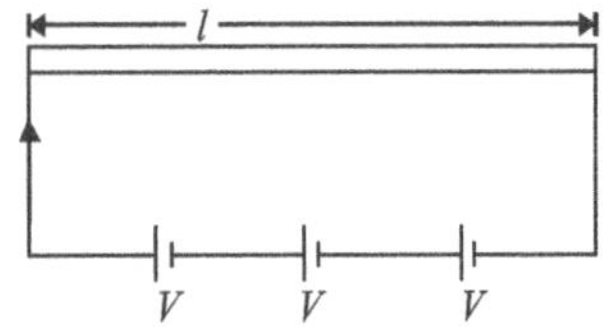

Energy released in t second $= \frac{(3V)^2}{R} \times t$

$$\therefore \quad Q = \frac{9V^2}{R} \times t \quad \text{But } Q = mc\Delta T \text{ (where } m = \text{mass of wire)}$$

$$\therefore \quad mc\Delta T = \frac{9V^2}{R} \times t \qquad \text{.... (i)}$$

Let R' be the resistance of the second wire

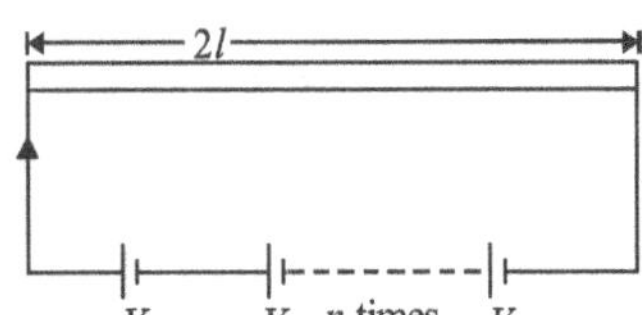

$$\Rightarrow \quad R' = 2R \qquad (\because \text{ length is twice})$$

$$\therefore \quad \text{Energy released in t-seconds} = \frac{(NV)^2}{2R} \times t$$

Also $Q' = m'c\Delta T = (2m)\,C\Delta T$

$$2\,mc\Delta T = \frac{N^2V^2}{2R} \times t \qquad \text{.... (ii)}$$

Dividing (i) by (ii)

$$\frac{mc\Delta T}{2mc\Delta T} = \frac{9V^2 \times t/R}{N^2V^2 t/2R} \quad \text{or,} \quad \frac{1}{2} = \frac{9\times 2}{N^2}$$

or, $\qquad N^2 = 18 \times 2 \quad \therefore \quad N = 6$

4. **(c)** $R_A' = R_A(1+\alpha_A \Delta T)$

$R_B' = R_B(1+\alpha_B \Delta T)$

$R' = R_A(1+\alpha_A \Delta T) + R_B(1+\alpha_B \Delta T)$

From given condition,

$R_A(1+\alpha_A \Delta T) + R_B(1+\alpha_B \Delta T) = R_A + R_B$

$$\frac{\rho_A \ell_A}{A_A}\alpha_A + \frac{\rho_B \ell_B}{A_B}\alpha_B = 0 \Rightarrow \frac{\ell_A}{\ell_B} = \frac{3}{10}$$

5. **(c)** $J = \dfrac{I}{2\pi r\ell} = \dfrac{dV/dR}{2\pi r\ell} \qquad …(i)$

$$dR = \rho\frac{dr}{2\pi r\ell} = \frac{1}{\sigma}\times\frac{dr}{2\pi r\ell} \qquad …(ii)$$

Now $E = -\dfrac{dV}{dr}$

$$\therefore \quad dV = -Edr = -\frac{\lambda}{2\pi \in r}dr \qquad …(iii)$$

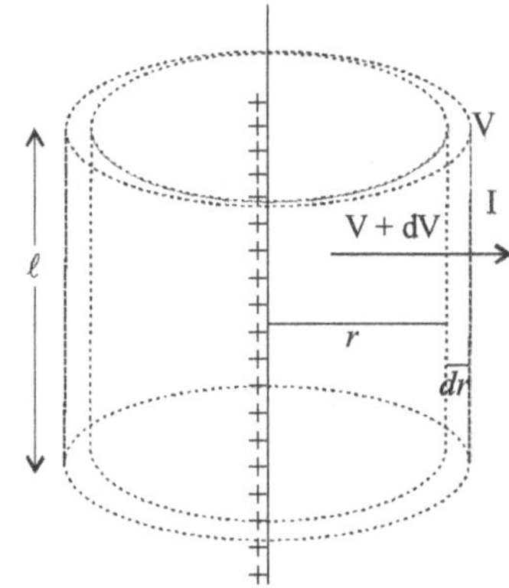

From (i), (ii), and (iii)

$$J = \frac{1}{2\pi r\ell}\left[\frac{\lambda dr}{2\lambda \in r}\times\frac{\sigma 2\pi r\ell}{dr}\right] = \frac{\lambda\sigma}{2\pi \in r} \qquad …(iv)$$

Also $I = \dfrac{dV}{dR} = \dfrac{-\lambda}{2\pi \in r}dr \times \dfrac{\sigma \times 2\pi r\ell}{dr} = \dfrac{-\lambda\sigma\ell}{\in} \qquad …(v)$

Here negative sign signifies that the current is decreasing

But $I = \dfrac{d(q)}{dt} = \dfrac{d(\lambda\ell)}{dt} = \ell\dfrac{d\lambda}{dt} \qquad …(vi)$

From (v) and (vi)

$$\ell \frac{d\lambda}{dt} = -\frac{\lambda \sigma \ell}{\epsilon} \Rightarrow \frac{d\lambda}{\lambda} = \frac{-\sigma}{c\,\ell} dt$$

On integrating

$$\int_{\lambda_0}^{\lambda} \frac{d\lambda}{\lambda} = -\frac{\sigma}{\epsilon} \int_0^t dt$$

$$\therefore \log_e \frac{\lambda}{\lambda_0} = -\frac{\sigma t}{\epsilon} \quad \therefore \lambda = \lambda_0 e^{-\frac{\sigma}{\epsilon} t}$$

Substituting this value in (iv) we get

$$J = \frac{\sigma \lambda_0}{2\pi \in r} e^{-\frac{\sigma}{\epsilon} t}$$

6. **(a, b)**

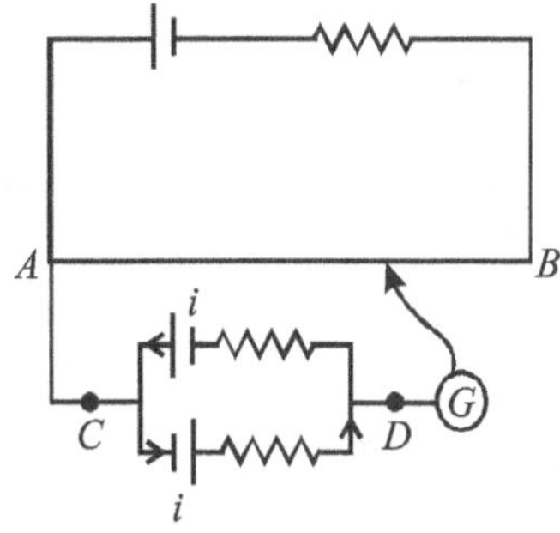

For null point current flow in the loop CD only.

$$i = \frac{3V}{2\Omega + 1\Omega} = 1A$$
$$V_{CD} = 1V - 1\,(1) = 0$$
∴ option (a) is correct.

When Jockey touches to B current flow from A to B to increase the P.D. across the secondary circuit.
∴ option (b) is correct.

7. **(c, d)** With the use of filament and the evaporation involved, the filament will become thinner thereby decreasing the area of cross-section and increasing the resistance. Therefore the filament will consume less power towards the end of life. As the evaporation is non-uniform, the area of cross-section will be different at different cross-section. Therefore temperature distribution will be non-uniform. The filament will break at the point where the temperature is maximum.

When the filament temperature is higher $\left(\lambda_n \propto \dfrac{1}{T} \right)$, it emits light of lower wavelength or higher band of frequencies.

8. **(a, c)**

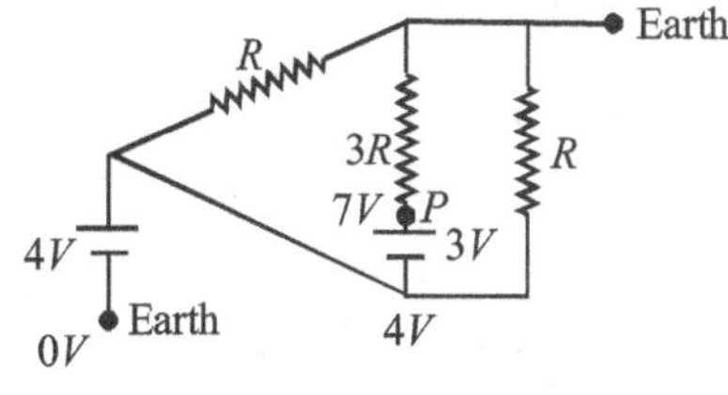

$$\therefore \; V_P = 7V \; ; \; i = \frac{7-0}{3R} = \frac{7}{3R}$$

9. **(a, d)**

Initial $PD = \dfrac{Q}{4\pi \in_0 r} - \dfrac{Q}{8\pi \in_0 r} = \dfrac{Q}{8\pi \in_0 r}$

$$\therefore \; \text{Initial current} = PD = \frac{Q}{8\pi \in_0 rR}$$

Current reduces to half in time , RC_{eq} ln 2
(Using $i = i_0 e^{-t/RC}$)

$$C_{eq} = \frac{8\pi \in_0 r}{3} \; \text{(Both spherical capacitor are in series)}$$

10. **3** The equivalent resistance of the circuit

$$R = 2\frac{10 \times 5}{10 + 5} = 6.67\,\Omega$$

The heat evolved in 10 minute,

$$H = i^2 Rt = 10^2 \times 6.67 \times (10 \times 60)$$
$$= 4 \times 10^5 \text{ J.} = 95238 \text{ Cal.}$$

The amount of ice required

$$m = \frac{H}{L} = \frac{95238}{80} = 1.2 \text{ kg}$$

11. **5** The resistance of the heater is

$$R = \frac{V^2}{P} = \frac{100 \times 100}{100} = 10\,\Omega$$

The power on which it operates is $62.5\ W$

$$\therefore \quad V = \sqrt{R \times P'} = \sqrt{10 \times 62.5} = \sqrt{625} = 25$$

$$\therefore \quad \text{The current in } AB = I = \frac{V}{R} = \frac{75}{10} = 7.5\,A$$

This current divides into two parts. Let I_1 be the current that passes through the heater. Therefore
$25 = I_1 \times 10$
$\Rightarrow \quad I_1 = 2.5$ A
$\Rightarrow \quad$ Curent through R in 5A.

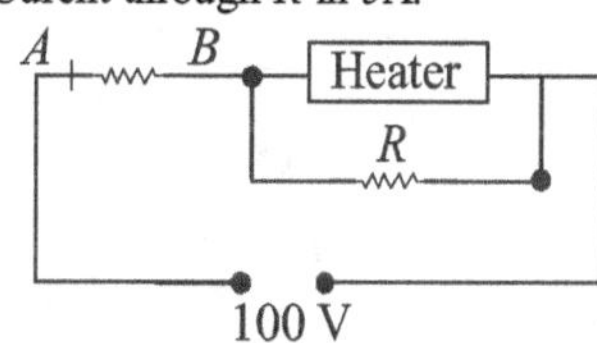

Applying Ohm's law across R, we get
$25 = 5 \times R \Rightarrow R = \mathbf{5\,\Omega}$

12. **4** We know that, charge

$$q = \int_0^t i\,dt = \int_0^{10} (20 + 4t)\,dt = \left| 20t + \frac{4t^2}{2} \right|_0^{10} = 400 \text{ C}$$

13. **8**

Applying Kirchoff's first law at junction M, we get the current $i_1 = 3A$

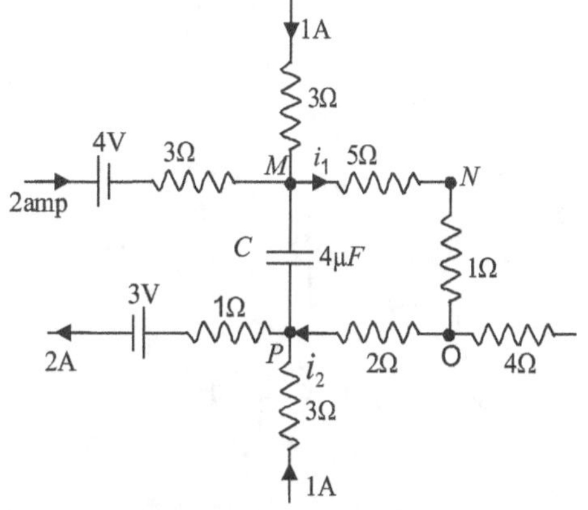

Applying Kirchoff's first law at junction P, we get current
$i_2 = 1A$
Moving the loopfrom MNO to P
$\therefore \quad V_M - 5 \times i_1 - 1 \times i_1 - 2 \times i_2 = V_P$
$\therefore \quad V_M - V_P = 6i_1 + 2i_2 = 6 \times 3 + 2 \times 1 = 20 \text{ V}$
Energy stored in the capacitor

$$= \frac{1}{2}CV^2 = \frac{1}{2} \times 4 \times 10^{-6} \times 20 \times 20 = 8 \times 10^{-4} \text{ J} = \textbf{0.8 mJ}$$

14. (a) Let j be the current density.

Then $\quad j \times 2\pi r^2 = I \Rightarrow j = \dfrac{I}{2\pi r^2}$

$\therefore \quad E = \rho j = \dfrac{\rho I}{2\pi r^2}$

Now, $\Delta V'_{BC} = -\displaystyle\int_{a+b}^{a} \vec{E}.\,\overline{dr} = -\int_{a+b}^{a} \dfrac{\rho I}{2\pi r^2}dr$

$= -\dfrac{\rho I}{2\pi}\left[-\dfrac{1}{r}\right]_{a+b}^{a} = \dfrac{\rho I}{2\pi a} - \dfrac{\rho I}{2\pi\,(a+b)}$

On applying superposition as mentioned we get

$$\Delta V_{BC} = 2 \times \Delta V'_{BC} = \dfrac{\rho I}{\pi a} - \dfrac{\rho I}{\pi(a+b)}$$

15. (c) $E = \dfrac{\rho I}{2\pi r^2}$ [As explained above]

16. (b) 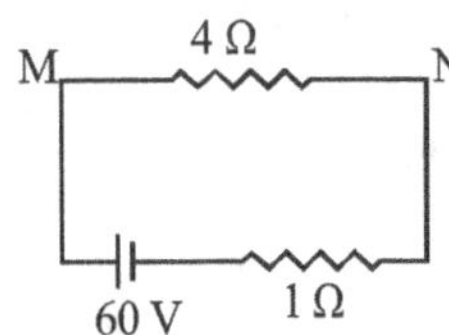

$r + \dfrac{r}{3} = \dfrac{4r}{3} = \dfrac{4 \times 3}{3} = 4\Omega$
Now if battery of emf 60 V and resistance 1 Ω is connected

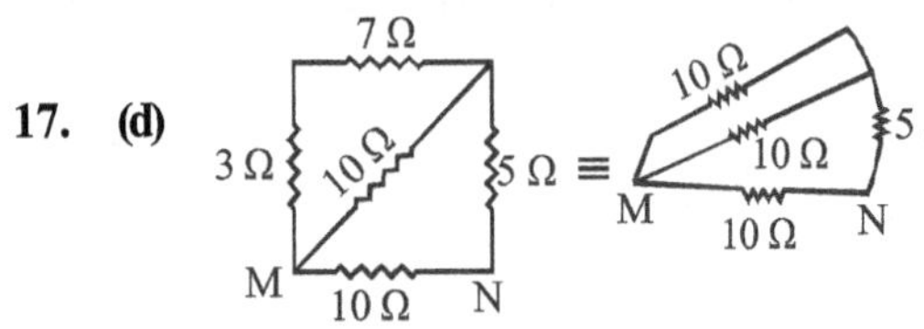

$$I = \dfrac{60}{4+1} = 12 \text{ A}$$

17. (d) 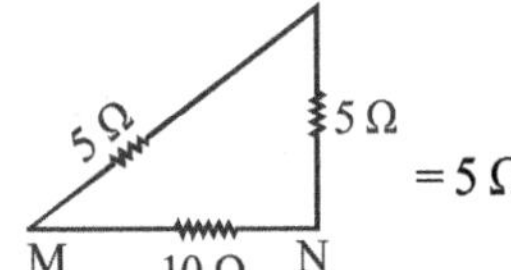

So current $I = \dfrac{60}{5+1} = 10A$

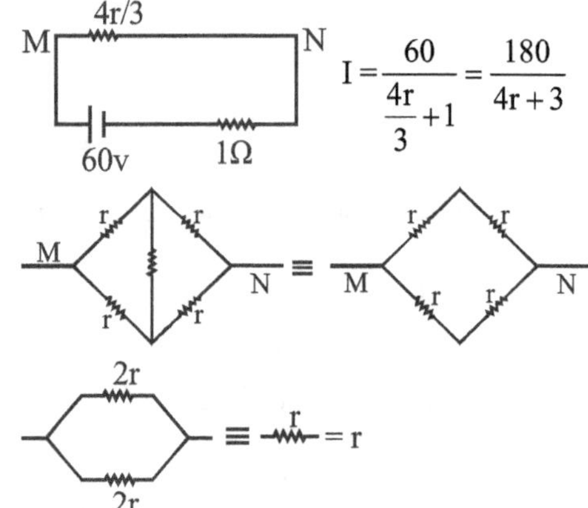

$$\equiv \dfrac{6 \times 3}{6+3} = 2\Omega$$

So current $I = \dfrac{60}{2+1} = 20A$

18. (d)

$\equiv r + \dfrac{r}{3} = \dfrac{4r}{3}$
Now if battery of emf 60v and resistance 1Ω is connected across M and N. Then

$$I = \dfrac{60}{\dfrac{4r}{3}+1} = \dfrac{180}{4r+3}$$

$$\equiv \;-\!\!\!\text{www}\!\!\!- = r$$

Now if battery is connected then $\quad I = \dfrac{60}{r+1}$

19. $A \rightarrow q, s; \; B \rightarrow q, s; \; C \rightarrow r, s; \; D \rightarrow s$

$T \uparrow \rho \uparrow R \uparrow n \uparrow ; \ell \uparrow R \uparrow n \uparrow ; \; A \uparrow R \downarrow n \uparrow$
Volume $\uparrow n \uparrow$ (Volume $\uparrow$ may be due to

$A \uparrow \ell \uparrow$ or $A \downarrow \ell \uparrow$ or $A \uparrow \ell \downarrow$, so variation in
resistance is not certain)

20. $A \rightarrow r ; B \rightarrow q ; C \rightarrow p ; D \rightarrow s$

A-r : $R_{AC} = R$

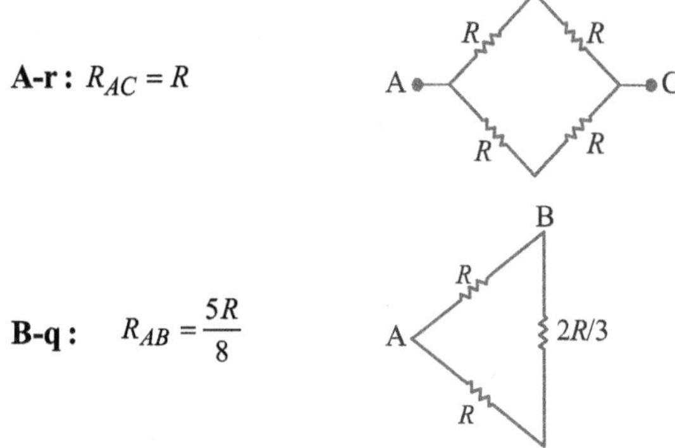

B-q : $R_{AB} = \dfrac{5R}{8}$

C-p : It is the balance bridge and so $V_B = V_D$.

D-s : $V_B \neq V_D$.

1. **(b)** Case (a):

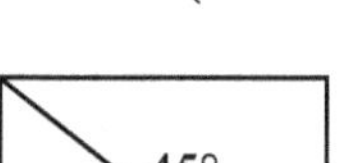

$$B_A = \frac{\mu_0}{4\pi} \frac{I}{R} \times 2\pi = \frac{\mu_0}{4\pi} \frac{I}{\ell/2\pi} \times 2\pi \qquad (2\pi R = \ell)$$

$$= \frac{\mu_0}{4\pi} \frac{I}{\ell} \times (2\pi)^2$$

Case (b):

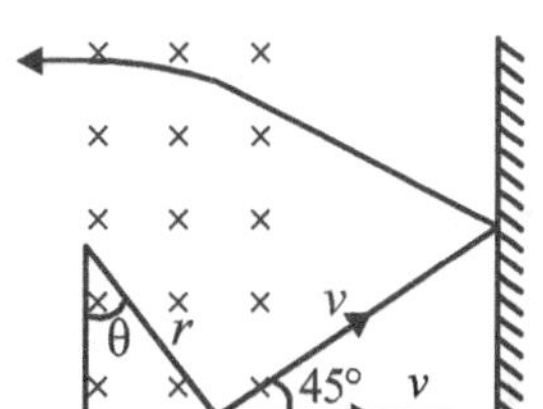

$$B_B = 4 \times \frac{\mu_0}{4\pi} \frac{I}{a/2} [\sin 45° + \sin 45°]$$

$$= 4 \times \frac{\mu_0}{4\pi} \times \frac{I}{\ell/8} \times \frac{2}{\sqrt{2}} = \frac{\mu_0}{4\pi} \frac{I}{\ell} \times 32\sqrt{2} \qquad [4a = 1]$$

2. **(a)** $r = \dfrac{mv}{qB}$

$$\sin\theta = \frac{x}{r}$$

$$= \frac{\dfrac{mv}{\sqrt{2}qB}}{\dfrac{mv}{qB}} = \frac{1}{\sqrt{2}}$$

or $\qquad \theta = \dfrac{\pi}{4}$

Time to complete the circle (2π), $T = \dfrac{2\pi m}{qB}$

$\therefore$ time taken to traverses $\dfrac{\pi}{4}$, $t = \dfrac{\pi m}{4qB}$

Time taken to travel horizontal distance

$$t_1 = \frac{\dfrac{mv}{\sqrt{2}qB}}{\dfrac{v}{\sqrt{2}}} = \frac{m}{qB}$$

Total time taken $= 2t + 2t_1$

$$= \frac{m}{2qB}(\pi + 4)$$

3. **(b)** A charged particle projected perpendicular to the direction of a magnetic field moves along a circular path, while one projected at an angle with the magnetic field moves along a helical path with a uniform pitch.

4. **(d)** Magnetic field at the centre of

the shell $= 2\dfrac{\mu_0 i_1}{\pi^2 r}$

Force per unit length of the wire

$$F = Bi_2 \times 1$$

$$= \left[2\frac{\mu_0 i_1 i_2}{\pi^2 r}\right]$$

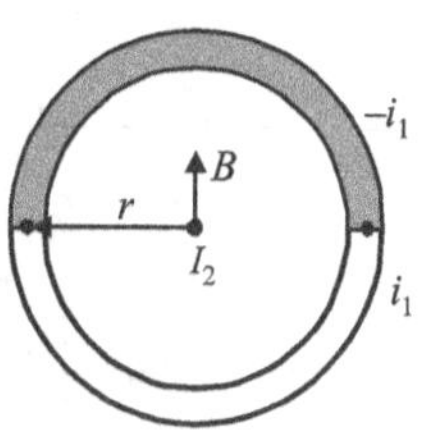

5. **(d)** $\vec{I}\vec{\omega} = 0 = -\int \tau \, dt \hat{k} = -\int \dfrac{1}{2\pi R} \dfrac{d\phi}{dt} \times QR \, dt \hat{k} z$

$$= -\lambda R \int d\phi = -B\lambda \pi a^2 R \hat{k}$$

$$\vec{\omega} = \frac{-B\pi a^2 \lambda}{mR}\vec{k}$$

6. **(c, d)** The magnetic field inside the inner solenoid is zero if,

$$B_{outer} = B_{inner}$$
or $\qquad \mu_0 n_1 i_1 = \mu_0 n_2 i_2$
or $\qquad n_1 i_1 = n_2 i_2$

Also if $i_1 = i_2$, then $n_1 = n_2$.

7. **(a, d)** On x-axis two conductors produce equal and opposite fields, so net field becomes zero.

8. **(b, d)** Current flowing per unit length $= \sigma \dfrac{dx}{dt} = \sigma v$

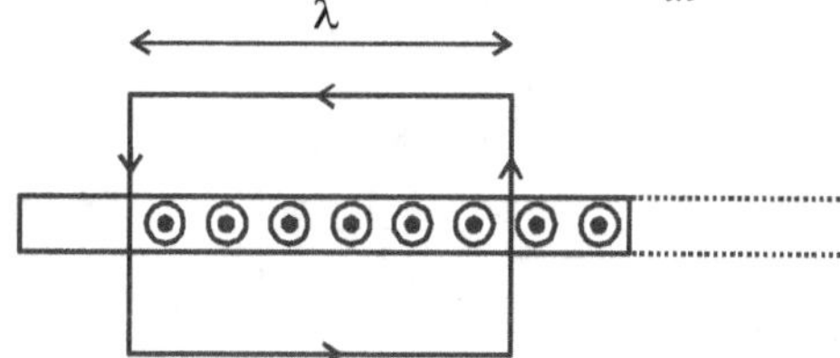

By Ampere's law

$$B\ell + B\ell = \mu_0 \sigma v \ell \Rightarrow B = \frac{\mu_0 \sigma v}{2}$$

9. **(a, c)** Net force on the loop :

Force on AB : The magnetic field due to current I_1 is along AB.

$$dF = I\,(d\ell \times B \times \sin 0°) = 0$$

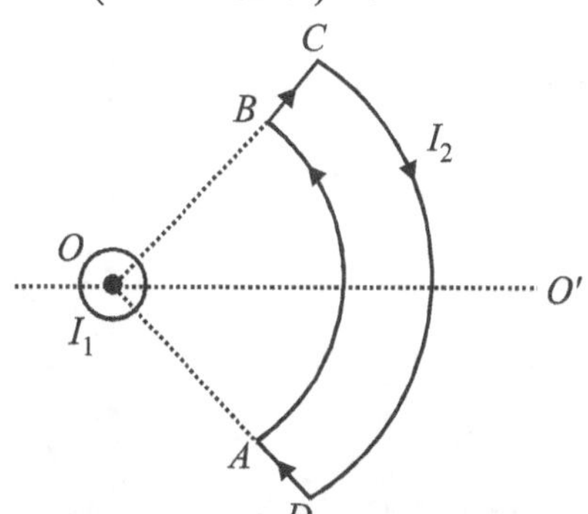

Force on CD : Similarly the magnetic field due to current I_1 is along DC. Because $\theta = 180°$ here, therefore force on DC is zero.

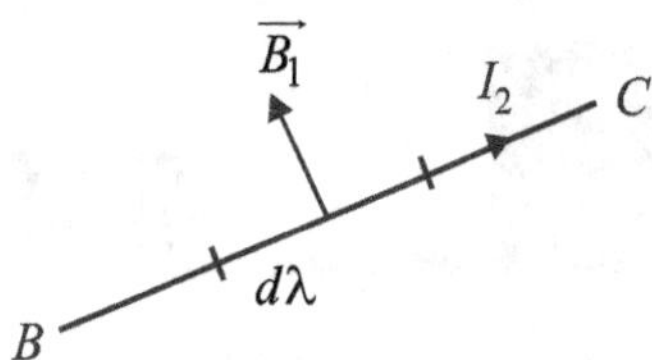

Force on BC : Consider a small element $d\ell$.

$$dF = I_2\, d\ell\, B_1 \sin 90° \Rightarrow dF = I_2\, d\ell\, B_1$$

By Fleming's left hand rule, the direction of this force is perpendicular to the plane of the paper directed outwards.

Force on AD : $dF = I_2\, d\ell\, B_1 \sin 90° = I_2\, d\ell\, B_1$

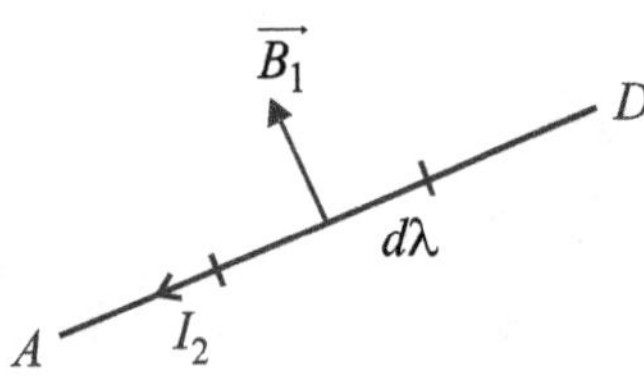

By Fleming's left hand rule, the direction of this force is perpendicular to the plane of paper directed inwards. Since the current elements are located symmetrical to current I_1, therefore force on BC will cancel out the effect of force on AD.

$\Rightarrow$ Net force on loop $ABCD$ is zero.

Net Torque on the loop : The force on BC and AD will create a torque on $ABCD$ in clockwise direction about OO' as seen by the observer at O.

10. 4 The inner radius is

$$r_i = 0.15m, \text{ so}$$
$$\text{outer radius} = (0.15 + 0.05)\text{m}$$

11. 5

Let us resolve the velocity to rectangular component v_1 $(= v\cos\theta)$ and v_2 $(v\sin 60°)$, v_1 component of velocity is responsible to move the charged particle in the direction of the magnetic field whereas v_2 component is responsible for rotating the charged particle in circular motion. The overall path is helical. The condition for the charged particle to strike S with minimum value of B is

Pitch of Helix $= GS$

$$T \times v_1 = GS \Rightarrow \frac{2\pi m}{qB} \times v\cos 60° = 0.1 \quad \frac{1}{2}mv^2 = E$$

$$\Rightarrow \quad v = \sqrt{\frac{2E}{m}}$$

$$B = \frac{2\pi\, mv\cos 60°}{q \times 0.1}$$

$$\Rightarrow \quad B = \frac{2\pi m}{q \times 0.1} \times \sqrt{\frac{2E}{m}} \times \cos 60°$$

$$= \frac{2\pi}{q \times 0.1} \times \sqrt{2mE} \times \cos 60°$$

$$= \frac{2 \times 3.14}{1.6 \times 10^{-19} \times 0.1}$$

$$= \sqrt{2 \times 9.1 \times 10^{-31} \times 2 \times 10^3 \times 1.6 \times 10^{-19}} \times \frac{1}{2}$$

$$= \frac{149.8}{10^{-19}} \times 0.316 \times 10^{-23} \cong 5\,\text{mT}$$

12. 3 $\quad R = \dfrac{mv}{qB}$

$$\frac{R_1}{R_2} = \frac{B_2}{B_1} \qquad [\because m, q, v \text{ are the same}]$$

$$\frac{R_1}{R_2} = \frac{\dfrac{\mu_0}{4\pi} \times 2I \left[\dfrac{1}{X_1} + \dfrac{1}{X_0 - X_1}\right]}{\dfrac{\mu_0}{4\pi} \times 2I \left[\dfrac{1}{X_1} - \dfrac{1}{X_0 - X_1}\right]}$$

$$= \frac{X_0 - X_1 + X_1}{X_0 - X_1 - X_1} = \frac{X_0}{X_0 - 2X_1}$$

$$\therefore \quad \frac{R_1}{R_2} = \frac{\dfrac{X_0}{X_1}}{\dfrac{X_0}{X_1} - 2} = \frac{3}{3-2} = 3$$

13. 5 Current density $J = \dfrac{\text{current}}{\text{area}} = \dfrac{I}{\pi(2a)^2} = \dfrac{I'}{\left(\pi a^2\right)}$

$$\Rightarrow \quad I' = \frac{I}{4}$$

Let us consider the cavity to have current I' flowing in both the directions.

The magnetic field at P due to the current flowing through the cylinder

$$B_1 = \frac{\mu_0}{4\pi} \frac{2I}{a}$$

The magnetic field at P due to the current (I') flowing in opposite direction is

$$B_2 = \frac{\mu_0}{4\pi} \frac{3I'}{3a/2} = \frac{\mu_0}{4\pi} \frac{2(I/4)}{3a/2} = \frac{\mu_0}{4\pi} \frac{I}{3a}$$

$\therefore$ The net magnetic field is

$$B = B_1 - B_2 = \frac{\mu_0}{4\pi} \frac{I}{a}\left[2 - \frac{1}{3}\right] = \frac{\mu_0}{4\pi} \frac{I}{a} \times \frac{5}{3}$$

$$\therefore \quad B = \frac{\mu_0}{4\pi} \frac{J\pi a^2}{a} \times \frac{5}{3} = \mu_0 \frac{5Ja}{12}$$

14. (c) Inside the cylinder

$$B.2\pi r = \mu_0 \frac{I}{\pi R^2}\, \pi r^2$$

$$\Rightarrow B = \frac{\mu_0 I}{2\pi R^2}.r \quad \text{.......(1)}$$

Outside the cylinder

$$B.2\pi r = \mu_0 I$$

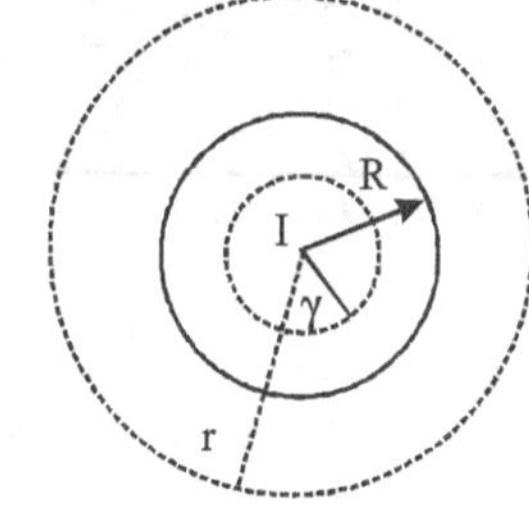

$$\therefore \quad B = \frac{\mu_0 I}{2\pi r} \quad \text{......(2)}$$

Inside the cylinder $B \propto r$ and outside $B \propto \dfrac{1}{r}$

So from surface nature of magnetic field changes.

Hence it is clear from the graph that wire 'c' has greatest radius.

15. (a) $B = \dfrac{\mu_0}{2\pi}.\dfrac{I}{R^2}r \Rightarrow \dfrac{dB}{dr} = \dfrac{\mu_0}{2\pi}.\dfrac{I}{R^2}$

i.e. slope $\propto \dfrac{I}{\pi R^2} \propto$ current density

It can be seen that slope of curve for wire a is greater than wire c.

16. (c) $\overrightarrow{ST} = 2\,OS \cos \angle OST$

$$= 2 \times \frac{mv \cos 45°}{qB}$$

$$= 2 \times \frac{mv}{qB} \times \frac{1}{\sqrt{2}}$$

$$= \sqrt{2} \times \frac{mv}{qB}$$

17. (b) $\angle OST = \angle OTS = 45°$

So, $\angle SOT = 90°$

Arc length $\widehat{ST}$

$$= \frac{3}{4} \times 2\pi\,OS$$

$$= \frac{3}{4} \times 2 \times \frac{22}{7} \times \frac{mv}{qB}$$

$$= \frac{33}{7}.\frac{mv}{qB}$$

18. (d) For the combination,

(a) III (i) R

$$\overline{ST} = 2 \times r = 2 \times \frac{mv}{2qB} = \frac{mv}{qB}$$

(b) IV (ii) Q

$$\text{Arc } \widehat{ST} = \frac{1}{2} \times 2\pi r = \frac{1}{2} \times 2 \times \frac{22}{7} \times \frac{mv}{2qB}$$

$$= \frac{11\,mv}{7\,qB}$$

(c) III (i) Q

Same as explained above.

19. $A \rightarrow r, s; B \rightarrow r, s; C \rightarrow p, s; D \rightarrow p, s$

20. $A \rightarrow r, s; B \rightarrow r, s; C \rightarrow q, r; D \rightarrow p, r$

(A) Because the magnetic field is parallel to x-axis, the force on wire parallel to x-axis is zero. The force on each wire parallel to y-axis is $B_0 \dfrac{I}{2}\ell$. Hence net force on loop is $B_0 I\ell$, $\perp$ to loop plane (downward). Since force on each wire parallel to y-axis passes through centre of the loop net torque about centre of the loop is zero.

(B) Because the magnetic field is parallel to y-axis, the force on wire parallel to y-axis is zero. The force on each wire parallel to x-axis is $B_0 \dfrac{I}{2}\ell$. Hence net force on loop is $B_0 I\ell$, $\perp$ to loop plane (upward). Since force on each wire parallel to x-axis passes through centre of the loop, net torque about centre of the loop is zero.

(C) Since net displacement of current from entry point in the loop to exit point in the loop is along the diagonal of the loop. The direction of external uniform magnetic field is also along the same diagonal. Hence net force on the loop is zero. Since force on each wire on the loop passes through centre of the loop net torque about centre of the loop is zero.

(D) The net displacement of current from entry point in the loop to exit point in the loop is along the diagonal (of length $\sqrt{2}\ell$) of the loop. The direction of external uniform magnetic field is also perpendicular to the same diagonal. Hence magnitude of net force on the loop is $B_0 I\sqrt{2}\ell$. Since force on each wire on the loop passes through centre of the loop net torque about centre of the loop is zero.

1. **(c)**

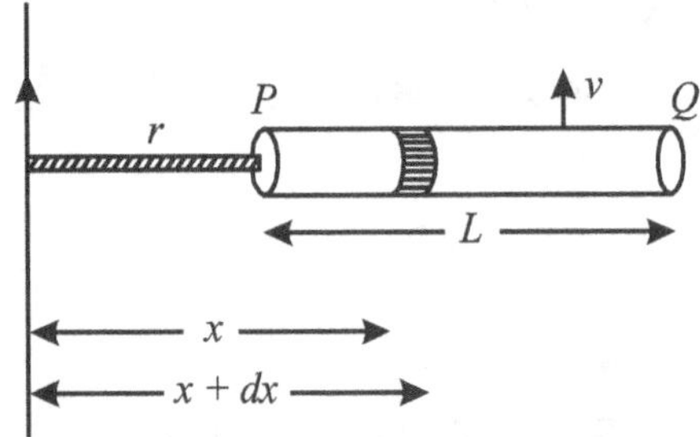

Figure shows a rod PQ of length L which moves with a uniform velocity v parallel to a long straight wire carrying a current i. Here a magnetic field is produced by the current carrying wire and the rod moves in this field. Consider a small element of length dx of the rod at a distance x and $(x + dx)$ from the wire.
The emf induced across the element

$$de = B\,v\,dx \qquad \text{..(i)}$$

We know that magnetic field B at a distance x from a wire carrying a current i is given by

$$B = \frac{\mu_0}{2\pi}\cdot\frac{i}{x} \qquad \text{...(ii)}$$

From eqs. (i) and (ii),

$$de = \frac{\mu_0 i}{2\pi x}v\,dx \qquad \text{...(iii)}$$

The emf e induced in the entire length of the rod PQ is given by

$$e = \int de = \int_P^Q \frac{\mu_0}{2\pi}\frac{i}{x}v\,dx = \int_r^{r+L} \frac{\mu_0}{2\pi}\frac{i}{x}v\,dx$$

$$= \frac{\mu_0}{2\pi}iv\int_r^{r+L}\frac{dx}{x} = \frac{\mu_0 iv}{2x}[\log_e x]_r^{r+L}$$

$$= \frac{\mu_0 iv}{2\pi}[\log_e(r+L)-\log_e r] = \frac{\mu_0 iv}{2\pi}\log_e\left(\frac{r+L}{r}\right)$$

2. **(c)** The induced emf across the ends B and F due to motion of the loop,
$e_1 = Bv(BF) = 5 \times 1 \times 2 \sin 60° = 5\sqrt{3}\ V$.
The induced emf across the loop due to change in magnetic field

$$e_2 = A\frac{dB}{dt} = \frac{\pi R^2}{3}\left(\frac{dB}{dt}\right)$$

$$= \frac{\pi(1)^2}{3}\times 2 = \frac{2\pi}{3}\ V.$$

So $e = e_1 + e_2 = \left(5\sqrt{3}+\frac{2\pi}{3}\right)\ V$.

3. **(b)** The magnetic field at the centre of the coil
$B(t) = \mu_0 n I_1$.

As the current increases, B will also increase with time till it reaches a maximum value (when the current becomes steady).
The induced emf in the ring

$$e = -\frac{d\phi}{dt} = -\frac{d}{dt}(\vec{B}.\vec{A}) = -A\frac{d}{dt}(\mu_0 n I_1)$$

$\therefore$ The induced current in the ring

$$I_2(t) = \frac{|e|}{R} = \frac{\mu_0 nA}{R}\frac{dI_1}{dt}$$

[**NOTE :** $\dfrac{dI_1}{dt}$ decreases with time and hence I_2 also decreases with time.]
Where $I_1 = I_{max}(1 - e^{-t/\tau})$
The relevant graphs are

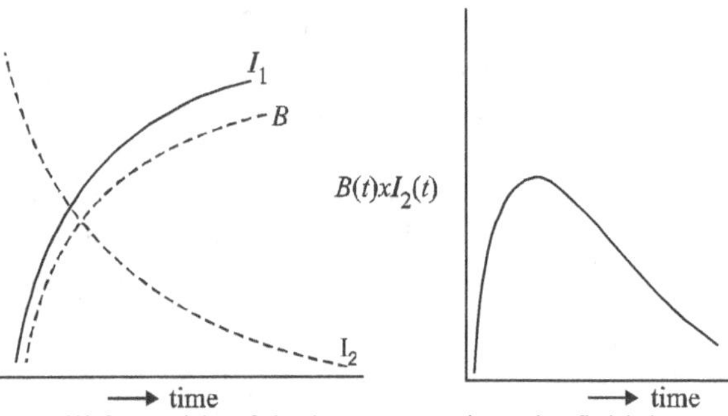

4. **(b)** Till front side of the loop moves into the field the emf induced $e = Bv\ell$ across it. When rear side comes in the field, the emf is induced across it.

5. **(d)** $e = -\dfrac{d\phi}{dt} = -A\dfrac{dB}{dt} = -\pi r^2\dfrac{d}{dt}(B_0 e^{-t})$

$$= \pi r^2 B_0 e^{-t}$$

At $t = 0$, $e = \pi r^2 B_0$.

Power developed, $P = \dfrac{e^2}{R} = \dfrac{(\pi r^2 B_0)^2}{R} = \dfrac{\pi^2 r^4 B_0^2}{R}$

6. **(a)** Induced emf $= \displaystyle\int_a^b Bvdx = \int_a^b \frac{\mu_0 I}{2\pi x}vdx$

$$\Rightarrow \quad \text{Induced emf} = \frac{\mu_0 Iv}{2\pi}\ln\left(\frac{b}{a}\right)$$

$$\Rightarrow \quad \text{Power dissipated} = \frac{E^2}{R}$$

Also, power $= F.\,v \Rightarrow F = \dfrac{E^2}{vR}$

$$\Rightarrow F = \frac{1}{vR}\left[\frac{\mu_0 Iv}{2\pi}\ln\left(\frac{b}{a}\right)\right]^2$$

7. **(b,d)**

Magnitude of induced electric field due to change in magnetic flux is given by

$$\oint \vec{E}.d\vec{\ell} = \frac{d\phi}{dt} = A\frac{dB}{dt} \quad (\because N = 1 \text{ and } \cos\theta = 1)$$

or $E.\ell = \pi R^2 (2B_0 t) \quad \left(\frac{dB}{dt} = 2B_0 t\right)$

Here, E = induced electric field due to change in magnetic flux

$E(2\pi R) = 2\pi R^2 B_0 t$

or $E = B_0 R t$

Hence, $F = QE = B_0 QRt$

This force is tangential to ring. Ring starts rotating when torque of this force is greater than the torque due to maximum friction $(f_{max} = \mu mg)$

or when $\tau_F \geq \tau_{f_{max}}$

Taking the limiting case, $\tau_F = \tau_{f_{max}}$ or

$F.R = (\mu mg) R$

It is given that ring starts rotating after 2 seconds.

So, putting $t = 2$ seconds, we get $\mu = \dfrac{2B_0 RQ}{mg}$

8. **(b,d)** Use Lenz's law to get the answer.

9. **(a, b, c, d)** $I = \dfrac{\varepsilon}{\frac{2R}{3}} = \dfrac{3\varepsilon}{2R}$

$= \dfrac{3}{2R} \times \dfrac{1}{2} B\omega l^2 = \dfrac{3B\omega l^2}{4R}$

Magnetic force $F = \dfrac{3B\omega l^2}{4R} \times l \times B$

$= \dfrac{3B^2\omega l^3}{4R}$

$\tau = \dfrac{3B^2\omega l^3}{4R} \times \dfrac{l}{2} = \dfrac{3B^2\omega l^4}{8R}$

$\therefore$ Force to be applied at the end $= \dfrac{3B^2\omega l^3}{8R}$.

10. **(a, c)**

The emf induced in each of the vertical sides of frame P will be $E_1 = B(\ell) 2v$, with upper point at a lower potential, while the emf induced in each of the vertical sides of frame Q will be $E_2 = B(2\ell) v$, with upper point at a higher potential. The emf induced are as shown

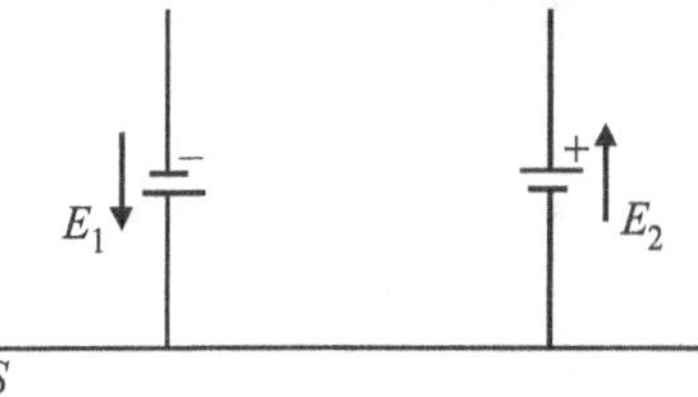

11. **5** $|e_s| = N_s \dfrac{d\phi_s}{dt}$ and $|e_s| = M \dfrac{di_p}{dt}$;

$\therefore \quad N_s \dfrac{d\phi_s}{dt} = M \dfrac{di_p}{dt}$

or $M = N_s \dfrac{d\phi_s}{di_p} = \dfrac{200(2.5\times10^{-4} - 0)}{(2-0)} = 2.5\times10^{-2} = \textbf{25mH}$

12. **4** For $0 = 2\sin t^2 \Rightarrow t = 0$

and $2 = 2\sin^2 t \Rightarrow t^2 = \dfrac{\pi}{2}, \quad \therefore t = \sqrt{\dfrac{\pi}{2}}$

The energy spent, $E = \dfrac{1}{2}Li^2 = \dfrac{1}{2}L(2\sin t^2)^2$

$= 2L\sin^2 t = 2\times 2\sin^2 \pi/2 = 4J.$

13. **3** The induced emf, $|e| = A\left(\dfrac{\Delta B}{\Delta t}\right)$

$= (\pi R)^2 \mu_0 n\left(\dfrac{\Delta i}{\Delta t}\right)$

$= \pi(1.8\times10^{-2})^2 \times (4\pi\times10^{-7}) \times 220\times10^2 \times \left(\dfrac{1.5}{25\times10^{-3}}\right) = 68.6\,\text{mV}$

Current, $i = \dfrac{e}{R} = 30$ mA

14. **7** The magnetic field due to current carrying wire at the location of square loop is

$$B = \dfrac{\mu_0}{4\pi} \dfrac{2\pi i R^2}{(R^2 + 3R^2)^{3/2}} = \dfrac{\mu_0 i}{16R}$$

The mutual induction

$$M = \dfrac{N\phi}{i} = \dfrac{2}{i}\left[\dfrac{\mu_0 i}{16R} \times a^2 \cos 45°\right]$$

$\therefore \quad M = \dfrac{\mu_0 a^2}{2^{\frac{7}{2}} R}$

15. **(a)** In 'P'

$\phi = B \times A \times \cos\theta° = BA(\text{max})$

16. **(b)** $t_{restoring} = -mg\ell\sin\theta = -mg\ell\theta$

$\alpha = \dfrac{\vec{\tau}}{I} = -\dfrac{mg\ell}{m\ell^2}\theta = -\left(\dfrac{g}{\ell}\right)\theta$

$T = 2\pi\sqrt{\dfrac{\ell}{g}}, \omega = \sqrt{\dfrac{g}{\ell}} = \sqrt{\dfrac{10}{2}} = \sqrt{5}\,\text{rad/sec}$

$\theta = \theta_0 \sin\omega t \qquad ...(1)$

Now, $e = -\dfrac{d\phi}{dt} = -\dfrac{d}{dt}(BA)\cos\theta = BA\omega\sin\theta$

$e = BA\,\omega\sin(\omega t)$

$e = BA.\left(\dfrac{d\theta}{dt}\right).\sin\omega t$

$e = BA\,(\theta_0\,\omega\cos\omega t)\sin\omega t \qquad \text{from (1)}$

$= BA\,(\theta_0\,\omega\cos\omega t)\,(\theta_0\sin\omega t)$ taking $(\sin\theta = \theta)$

$e = \dfrac{BA.\theta_0^2\omega.\sin 2\omega t}{2}$

$e = \dfrac{1\times 4\times10^{-4} \times \omega \times \sin(2\sqrt{5}t)}{2} \times \dfrac{10^{-4}}{4}$

$$= \frac{2\sqrt{5}}{2}\sin(2\sqrt{5}t)\times10^{-8}$$

$$= 5\sqrt{5}\sin(2\sqrt{5}t)\times10^{-9} \text{ volt.}$$

17. (a) For simplicity we can take the moment when side EF of he loop is at $y = 0$, so

$$B_1 = 0 \,; \, e_1 = 0$$

and at $y = a$, $B_2 = \dfrac{B_0 \times a}{a} = B_0$; $e_2 = B_0 v a$.

The induced emf $e = e_1 + e_2 = B_0 v_a$.

Thus induced current, $i = \dfrac{e}{R} = \dfrac{B_0 v a}{R}$, anticlockwise.

18. (a) For ternminal speed (constant speed), net force on the loop is zero, and so

$$mg = \frac{B_0^{\,2} v a^2}{R}$$

or $v = \dfrac{mgR}{B_0^{\,2}a^2}$.

19. (A) $\rightarrow$ p; (B) $\rightarrow$ r; (C) $\rightarrow$ s; (D) $\rightarrow$ q

20. (A)$\rightarrow$p, r; (B)$\rightarrow$q; (C)$\rightarrow$s; (D)$\rightarrow$p, r

$e = -\dfrac{d\phi}{dt}$. In case (A), flux changes wrt time in case (B), flux is constant.

In case (C), $e = Bv\ell$, $q = CBv\ell$,

$\dfrac{dq}{dt} = CB\ell\dfrac{dv}{dt} = +ve \ const.$

In Case D, Angle between $\vec{B}$ and $\vec{A}$ changes with time hence i changes with time.

1. **(a)** At resonance

$$I_R = \frac{E_0}{R} \Rightarrow \frac{I_R}{\sqrt{2}} = \frac{E_0}{\sqrt{2}R} = \frac{E_0}{\sqrt{R^2 + \left(\omega L - \dfrac{1}{\omega C}\right)^2}}$$

$$\Rightarrow \omega_1 L - \frac{1}{\omega_1 C} = -R \text{ and } \omega_2 L - \frac{1}{\omega_2 C} = +R$$

$$\Rightarrow L(\omega_1 + \omega_2) = \left(\frac{\omega_1 + \omega_2}{\omega_1 \omega_2}\right)\frac{1}{C} \Rightarrow \omega_1 \omega_2 = \frac{1}{LC}$$

and $L(\omega_2 - \omega_1) + \left(\dfrac{\omega_2 - \omega_1}{\omega_1 \omega_2}\right)\dfrac{1}{C} = 2R$

Putting value of $\omega_1 \, \omega_2$ we get

$$\omega_2 - \omega_1 = \frac{R}{L} \Rightarrow f_2 - f_1 = \frac{R}{2\pi L}$$

2. **(c)** If $Z_L = Z_C$ current will be same,

So, $V_{Z_L} = V_{Z_C}$;

$$\therefore \quad V_L = 1 \times 2\pi \times 30 \times \frac{1}{\pi} = 60 \text{ Volt}$$

$$V_R = 80 \times 1 = 80 \text{ Volt};$$

$$V = \sqrt{V_L^2 + V_R^2} = \sqrt{(80)^2 + (60)^2} = 100 \text{ Volt}$$

3. **(a)**

$$\frac{i_{R_0}}{\sqrt{(i_{R_0})^2 + (i_{c_0} - i_{L_0})^2}} = \frac{1}{2}$$

$$\Rightarrow \frac{\varepsilon_0 / R}{\sqrt{(\varepsilon_0 / R^2) + \left(\varepsilon_0 \omega C - \dfrac{\varepsilon_0}{\omega L}\right)^2}} = \frac{1}{2}$$

$$\Rightarrow R = \frac{\sqrt{3}}{\left(\omega C - \dfrac{1}{\omega L}\right)}$$

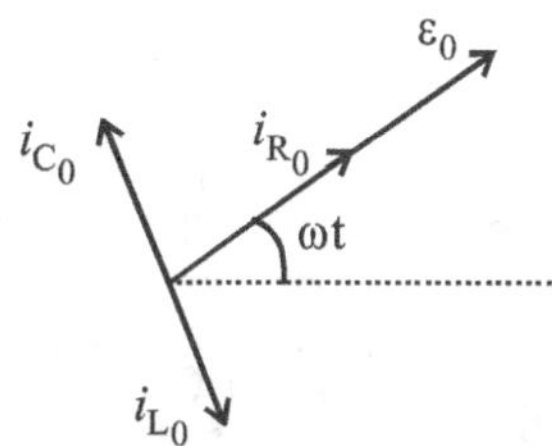

4. **(c)** For capacitor circuit, $i = i_0 e^{-t/RC}$

For inductor circuit, $i = i_0 \left(1 - e^{-\dfrac{Rt}{L}}\right)$

Hence graph (c) correctly depicts i versus t graph.

5. **(d)** Impedance (Z) of the series LCR circuit is

$$Z = \sqrt{R^2 + (X_L - X_C)^2}$$

At resonance, $X_L = X_C$

Therefore, $Z_{minimum} = R$

6. **(a,c)** We know that $Z = \sqrt{R^2 + \left(\dfrac{1}{WC}\right)^2}$

The capacitance in case B is four times the capacitance in case A

$\therefore$ Impedance in case B is less then that of case A $(Z_B < Z_A)$

Now $I = \dfrac{V}{Z}$

$\therefore I_R^A < I_R^B$. option (a) is correct.

$\therefore V_R^A < V_R^B.$

$\Rightarrow V_C^A > V_C^B$

[$\because$ If V is the applied potential difference access

series R-C circuit then $V = \sqrt{V_R^2 + V_C^2}$]

$\therefore$ (c) is the correct option.

7. **(a,b,c)**

It is apparent from the graph that emf attains its maximum value before the current does, therefore current lags behind emf in the circuit. Nature of the circuit is inductive.

Value of power factor $\cos\phi$ increases by either deceasing L of increasing C.

8. **(a, b, c, d)**

Since there is no current through BD therefore points B and D are at the same potential

$$V_B = V_D$$

Potential difference, $V_{AB} = V_{AD}$

$$L_1 \frac{di_1}{dt} + i_1 R_1 = L_2 \frac{di_2}{dt} + i_2 R_2 \quad \text{.......(1)}$$

Similarly, $V_{BC} = V_{DC}$

$$i_1 R_3 = i_2 R_4 \quad \text{.......(2)}$$

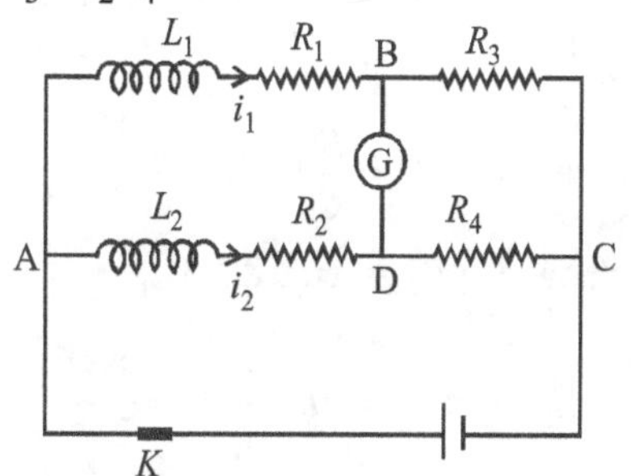

From equations (1) and (2),

$$\frac{di_1}{dt}R_3 = \frac{di_2}{dt}R_4$$

or $\dfrac{di_1}{dt} = \dfrac{R_4}{R_3}\dfrac{di_2}{dt}$ and $i_1 = i_2\dfrac{R_4}{R_3}$

$$L_1\frac{R_4}{R_3}\frac{di_2}{dt} + i_2\frac{R_1R_4}{R_3} = L_2\frac{di_2}{dt} + i_2R_2$$

$$\left(L_1\frac{R_4}{R_3} - L_2\right)\frac{di_2}{dt} = i_2\left[R_2 - \frac{R_1R_4}{R_3}\right] \quad .... (3)$$

At $t = 0$, $i_2 = 0$

$\therefore \quad L_1\dfrac{R_4}{R_3} - L_2 = 0$ as $\dfrac{di_2}{dt} \neq 0$

$\therefore \quad \dfrac{L_1}{L_2} = \dfrac{R_3}{R_4} \quad\quad\quad .... (4)$

At $t = \infty$, $\dfrac{di_2}{dt} = 0$, $i_2 = \left(\dfrac{E}{R_2 + R_4}\right) = $ constant

$\Rightarrow R_2 - \dfrac{R_4R_1}{R_3} = 0 \therefore \dfrac{R_1}{R_2} = \dfrac{R_3}{R_4} \quad .... (5)$

From equations (4) and (5), $\dfrac{L_1}{L_2} = \dfrac{R_1}{R_2} = \dfrac{R_3}{R_4}$

9.   **(a, b, c)**

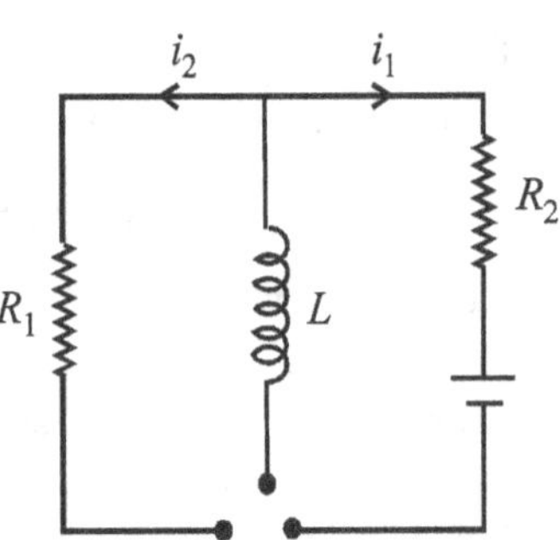

At time t, $i_1 = \dfrac{E}{R_2}\left(1 - E^{-\frac{t}{L}R_2}\right)$

So, $i_1 = i_2 = i_{2\,max}$; $i_2(t) = i_1 e^{-\frac{(t')}{L}R_1}$

Now for power become half $i_2(t) = \dfrac{i_1}{\sqrt{2}}$

$\Rightarrow \dfrac{i_1}{\sqrt{2}} = i_1\left[e^{-\frac{(t')}{L}R_1}\right]$ (don't depend on t)

When $t = \infty$, $i_1 = \dfrac{E}{R_2}$

So power in R_2 generated

$$\frac{1}{2}L\,[i_1(t=\infty)]^2 = \frac{1}{2}L\left(\frac{E}{R_2}\right)^2 = \frac{L}{2}\frac{E^2}{R_2^2}$$

10. **7**   For the maximum current,

$$X_C = X_L \quad \text{or} \quad \frac{1}{\omega C} = \omega L$$

$$\therefore \quad C = \frac{1}{\omega^2 L} = \frac{1}{(2\pi f)^2 L}$$

$$= \frac{1}{(2\pi \times 2 \times 10^3)^2 \times 100 \times 10^{-3}} = 63 \times 10^{-9}\,F$$

11. **4** $\tan\dfrac{\pi}{6} = \dfrac{X_L}{R} = \dfrac{1}{\sqrt{3}}$

$R = 3\,\Omega$

$\tan\theta = \dfrac{X_C}{R} = 1\,\Omega$

$\phi = \dfrac{\pi}{4}$

12. **4** $X_L = \omega L = (2\pi \times 500) \times 8.1 = 25.4\,\Omega$

and $X_C = \dfrac{1}{\omega C} = \dfrac{1}{(2\pi \times 500) \times (12.5 \times 10^{-6})} = 25.4\,\Omega$

As $X_L = X_C$, so resonance will occur and $V_R = 100V$.

13. **5**   The impedance, $z = \dfrac{Vrms}{i} = \dfrac{160}{2} = 80\,\Omega$

We know that, Power,

$$P = \frac{V_{rms}^2 R}{Z^2} \quad \text{or} \quad 200 = \frac{160^2 \times R}{80^2}$$

$\therefore \quad R = 50\,\Omega$

We know that, $Z = \sqrt{R^2 + X_L^2}$

or $80 = \sqrt{50^2 + X_L^2} \quad \therefore \quad X_L = 62.5\,\Omega$

The back emf, $V_L = iX_L = 2 \times 62.5 = 125\,V.$

14. **(a)**

15. **(b)**

16. **(b)**

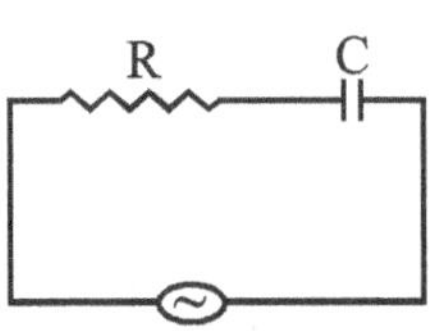

For a C-R series circuit

$$Z = \sqrt{R^2 + \frac{1}{\omega^2 C^2}}$$

So, $I = \dfrac{E}{Z} = \dfrac{E}{\sqrt{R^2 + \dfrac{1}{\omega^2 C^2}}}$, $\left(\text{here, } X_C = \dfrac{1}{\omega C}\right)$

Voltage across capacitor $= I \times X_C$

$$= \frac{E}{\sqrt{R^2 + \dfrac{1}{\omega^2 C^2}}} \times \frac{1}{\omega C}$$

$$= \frac{E}{\sqrt{R^2\omega^2 C^2 + 1}} \quad \text{or} \quad V_C = \frac{E}{\sqrt{(XY\omega)^2 + 1}}$$

17. (b) For L-R series circuit,

$$Z = \sqrt{R^2 + \omega^2 L^2}$$

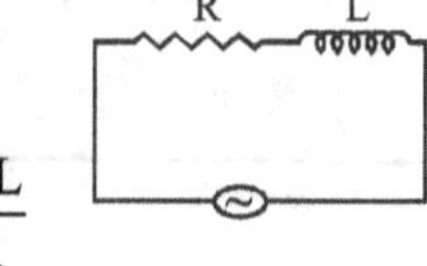

Phase difference $\phi = \tan^{-1}\dfrac{\omega L}{R}$

and voltage is leading.

18. (c)

19. $A \rightarrow q;\ B \rightarrow r, p;\ C \rightarrow r, s;\ D \rightarrow q, r$

Resonant frequency is $\omega_c^2 = \dfrac{1}{LC}$.

(i) if $\omega < \omega_c$, capacitor dominates

(ii) if $\omega > \omega_c$, inductor property dominates

20. $A \rightarrow p;\ B \rightarrow q;\ C \rightarrow p;\ D \rightarrow s$

A: $i_{rms} = \dfrac{V_R}{R} = \dfrac{40}{4} = 10A$; $i_0 = \sqrt{2}\,i_{rms} = 10\sqrt{2}\ A$

B: $\therefore\ V_{rms} = iZ = 10 \times 5 = 50V$; $V_0 = \sqrt{2}\,V_{rms} = 50\sqrt{2}\ V$

C: $i_{rms} = \dfrac{V_R}{R} = \dfrac{40}{4} = 10A$; $i_0 = \sqrt{2}\,i_{rms} = 10\sqrt{2}\ A$

D: Now $V^2 = V_R^2 + (V_L - V_C)^2$

or $50^2 = 40^2 + (40 - V_C)^2$

$\therefore\ V_C = 10V$,

and $X_C = \dfrac{V_C}{i} = \dfrac{10}{10} = 1\Omega$

1. **(d)** $\dfrac{1}{2}\varepsilon_0 E_0^2$ is electric energy density.

$\dfrac{B^2}{2\mu_0}$ is magnetic energy density.

So, total energy $= \dfrac{1}{2}\varepsilon_0 E_0^2 + \dfrac{B_0^2}{2\mu_0}$

2. **(a)** Direction of energy progration of EM-waves is given by

$$\vec{D} = K(\vec{E} \times \vec{B}) \qquad \text{or} \qquad -\hat{k} = K(E\,\hat{j} \times \vec{B})$$

3. **(b)** Wavelength of monochromatic green light
$= 5.5 \times 10^{-5}$ cm

$$\text{Intensity } I = \dfrac{\text{Power}}{\text{Area}}$$

$$= \dfrac{100 \times (3/100)}{4\pi (5)^2} = \dfrac{3}{100\pi}\,\text{Wm}^{-2}$$

Now, half of this intensity (I) belongs to electric field and half of that to magnetic field, therefore,

$$\dfrac{I}{2} = \dfrac{1}{4}\varepsilon_0 E_0^2 C \quad \text{or} \quad E_0 = \sqrt{\dfrac{2I}{\varepsilon_0 C}}$$

$$= \sqrt{\dfrac{2 \times \left(\dfrac{3}{100}\pi\right)}{\left(\dfrac{1}{4\pi \times 9 \times 10^9}\right) \times \left(3 \times 10^8\right)}} = \sqrt{7.2}$$

$$\therefore \quad E_0 = 2.68 \text{ V} / \text{m}$$

4. **(a)** $\dfrac{E_0}{B_0} = c$. also $k = \dfrac{2\pi}{\lambda}$ and $\omega = 2\pi v$

These relation gives $E_0 k = B_0 \omega$

5. **(c)** **Given:** Amplitude of electric field,
$E_0 = 4$ v/m
Absolute permitivity,
$\varepsilon_0 = 8.8 \times 10^{-12}$ c^2/N-m^2
Average energy density $u_E = ?$
Applying formula,

Average energy density $u_E = \dfrac{1}{4}\varepsilon_0 E^2$

$$\Rightarrow \quad u_E = \dfrac{1}{4} \times 8.8 \times 10^{-12} \times (4)^2$$

$$= 35.2 \times 10^{-12} \text{ J/m}^3$$

6. **(a)** $\mathbf{E} = \dfrac{\lambda \hat{\mathbf{e}}_s}{2\pi \varepsilon_o a}\hat{\mathbf{j}}$

$$\mathbf{B} = \dfrac{\mu_o i}{2\pi a}\hat{\mathbf{i}} = \dfrac{\mu_o \lambda v}{2\pi a}\hat{\mathbf{i}}$$

$$\mathbf{S} = \dfrac{1}{\mu_o}(\mathbf{E} \times \mathbf{B}) = \dfrac{1}{\mu_o}\left(\dfrac{\lambda \hat{\mathbf{j}}_s}{2\pi\varepsilon_o a}\hat{\mathbf{j}} \times \dfrac{\mu_o \lambda v}{2\pi a}\hat{\mathbf{i}}\right)$$

$$= \dfrac{-\lambda^2 v}{4\pi^2 \varepsilon_o a^2}\hat{\mathbf{k}}$$

7. **(a, d)** $\lambda_{\text{micro}} > \lambda_{\text{infrared}} > \lambda_{\text{ultraviolet}} > \lambda_{\text{gamma}}$

8. **(a, c)** Momentum per unit time per unit area

$$= \dfrac{\text{intensity}}{\text{speed of wave}} = \dfrac{I}{c}$$

Change in momentum per unit time per unit area
$= \Delta I/c =$ radiation pressure (P), *i.e.* $P = \Delta I/c$.
Momentum of incident wave per unit time per unit area $= I/c$
When wave is fully absorbed by the surface, the momentum of the reflected wave per unit time per unit area $= 0$
Radiation pressure $(P) =$ change in momentum per unit time per unit area $= \dfrac{\Delta I}{c} = \dfrac{I}{c} - 0 = \dfrac{I}{c}$

When wave is totally reflected, then mommentum of the reflected wave per unit time per unit area $= -\, I/c$.

Radiation pressure $(P) = \dfrac{I}{c} - \left(-\dfrac{I}{c}\right) = \dfrac{2I}{c}$

Here, P lies between $\dfrac{I}{c}$ and $\dfrac{2I}{c}$.

9. **(a,b)**

10. **(a, b, c, d)** Velocity of electromagnetic wave

$$c = \dfrac{1}{\sqrt{\mu_0 \varepsilon_0}} = 3 \times 10^8 \ m \ s^{-1}$$

It is independent of amplitude, frequency and wavelength of electromagnetic wave.

11. **2** On comparing the given equation to

$$\vec{E} = a_0\hat{i}\cos(\omega t - kz)$$
$$\omega = 6 \times 10^{8z},$$

$$k = \dfrac{2\pi}{r} = \dfrac{\omega}{c}$$

$$k = \dfrac{\omega}{c} = \dfrac{6 \times 10^8}{3 \times 10^8} = 2\,\text{m}^{-1}$$

12. **6** As we know,

$$v = \dfrac{C}{\lambda}$$

or $\qquad \lambda = \dfrac{C}{v} = \dfrac{3 \times 10^8}{2 \times 10^6} = 150\text{m} = 25 \times 6\,\text{m}$

13. **3** $E_0 = 300\,\text{V/m}$, $\therefore\ B_0 = \dfrac{E_0}{C} = \dfrac{300}{3\times10^8} = 1\times10^{-6}\ \text{N/A-m}$

The maximum electric force,

$$F_0 = E_0 q = 300 \times 1.6 \times 10^{-19}$$
$$= 4.8 \times 10^{-7}\,\text{N}.$$

The maximum magnetic force,

$$F_b = qvB = (1.6\times10^{-19}) \times (2\times10^7) \times (1\times10^{-6})$$
$$= 3.2 \times 10^{-18}\,\text{N}.$$

$$\frac{F_0}{F_b} = \frac{4.8\times10^{-7}}{3.2\times10^{-18}} = 15 \times 10^{10}$$

14. **9**   The intensity is given by

$$I = \frac{1}{2}\,\epsilon_0\,E^2 C$$

or $2.5\times10^{14} = \dfrac{1}{2} \times (8.86\times10^{-12}) \times E_0^2 \times (3\times10^8)$

$\therefore$ $E_0 = 4.3\times10^8\ \text{V/m}$

and $B_0 = \dfrac{E_0}{C} = 1.44\,\text{T}$

15. **(c)**   We know that, $i_d = \epsilon_0\,A\left(\dfrac{dE}{dt}\right)$

$\therefore\ \left(\dfrac{dE}{dt}\right) = \dfrac{i_d}{\epsilon_0\,A} = \dfrac{2}{8.86\times10^{-12}\times1^2} \approx 2.3\times10^{11}\,\text{V/m.}$

16. **(b)** $\oint \vec{B}.d\vec{\ell} = \mu_0 i_{in}$

$= 4\,\pi \times 10^{-7} \times (2 \times 0.5^2) = 0.63 \times 10^{-6}\,\text{T-m}$

17. **(a)**   Comparing the given equation with

$$B_y = B_0 \sin\left[2\pi\left(\frac{x}{\lambda} + \frac{t}{T}\right)\right]$$

We get, $\lambda = \dfrac{2\pi}{0.5\times10^3}\,\text{m} = 1.26\ \text{cm}$

and $\dfrac{1}{T} = v = (1.5\times10^{11})\,/\,2\pi = 23.9\ \text{GHz}$

18. **(b)** $E_0 = B_0 c = 2 \times 10^{-7}\,\text{T} \times 3 \times 10^8\,\text{m/s} = 6 \times 10^1\,\text{V/m}$

The electric field component is perpendicular to the direction of propagation and the direction of magnetic field. Therefore, the electric field component along the z-axis is obtained as

$E_z = 60 \sin(0.5 \times 10^3 x + 1.5 \times 10^{11}\,t)\ \text{V/m}$

19. **(A) $\to$ (q); (B) $\to$ (p); (C) $\to$ (s); (D) $\to$ (r)**

Wavelength emitted by atomic hydrogen in interstellar space - Part of short radio wave of electromagnetic spectrum.

Doublet of sodium - visible radiation.

20. **(A) $\to$ (p); (B) $\to$ (q); (C) $\to$ (r); (D) $\to$ (s)**

Vibration of atoms and molecules 700 nm to 1 mm

Radioactive decay of the nucleus $< 10^{-3}$ nm

Magnetron valve 1 mm to 0.1 m

1. **(b)** By Lens maker's formula for convex lens

$$\frac{1}{f} = \left(\frac{\mu}{\mu_L} - 1\right)\left(\frac{2}{R}\right)$$

for, $\mu_{L_1} = \frac{4}{3}, f_1 = 4R$

for $\mu_{L_2} = \frac{5}{3}, f_2 = -5R$

$$\Rightarrow f_2 = (-)\text{ve}$$

2. **(b)** Velocity of light in medium

$$V_{med} = \frac{3\,cm}{0.2\,ns} = \frac{3 \times 10^{-2}\,m}{0.2 \times 10^{-9}\,s} = 1.5\,m/s$$

Refractive index of the medium

$$\mu = \frac{V_{air}}{V_{med}} = \frac{3 \times 10^8}{1.5} = 2\,m/s$$

As $\mu = \frac{1}{\sin C}$ $\therefore$ $\sin C = \frac{1}{\mu} = \frac{1}{2} = 30°$

Condition of TIR is angle of incidence i must be greater than critical angle. Hence ray will suffer TIR in case of (B) (i = 40° > 30°) only.

3. **(a)** Let refractive index of glass be μ.

Let after first refraction, image distance be v then

$$\frac{\mu}{v} - \frac{1}{\infty} = \frac{\mu - 1}{R} \Rightarrow v = \frac{\mu R}{\mu - 1}$$

Now second refraction will take place.
So distance of first image from O is

$$u_1 = \frac{\mu R}{\mu - 1} - R = \frac{R}{\mu - 1}$$

and image is formed at R

$$\therefore \frac{1}{R} - \frac{\mu\,(\mu - 1)}{R} = \frac{2\,(1 - \mu)}{R}$$

$$\Rightarrow \mu^2 - 3\mu + 1 = 0 \text{ So, } \mu = \frac{3 + \sqrt{5}}{2}$$

4. **(a)** $\vec{v}_{obj,\,mirror} = 4\hat{i} + 9\hat{j}$

$$\frac{dx}{dt} = 4, \frac{dy}{dt} = 9 \quad ; \qquad u = -x$$

$$-\frac{1}{10} = \frac{1}{V} + \frac{1}{-x} \; ; \; V = \frac{-10x}{x - 10}$$

$$v_{1x} = \frac{dV}{dt} = \left(\frac{10}{x - 10}\right)^2 \left(\frac{dx}{dt}\right) \; ; v_{1x} = -16$$

$$m = -\frac{V}{-x} = \frac{-10}{x - 10} = \frac{y_1^0}{y}$$

$$v_{1y} = -\left(\frac{10}{x - 10}\right)\frac{dy}{dt} \; ; v_{1y} = -18$$

$$\vec{v}_{image,\,mirror} = -16\hat{i} - 18\hat{j} \; ; \; \vec{v}_{image} = -12\hat{i} - 16\hat{j}$$

$$|v| = 20\,cm/s$$

5. **(b)** Refraction at convex lens
$v_1 = 20\,cm$
Refraction at concave lens $u = -10\,cm$

$$\frac{1}{v} - \frac{1}{-10} = -\frac{1}{-10} \Rightarrow v = -5\,cm$$

$$\Rightarrow \text{height} = \frac{5mm}{2} = 2.5\,mm = 0.25\,cm$$

Hence co-ordinate of the final image
$$= (25\,cm, 0.25\,cm)$$

6. **(a, d)**

For lens

$$\frac{1}{v} - \frac{1}{u} = \frac{1}{f} \Rightarrow \frac{1}{v} - \frac{1}{-30} = \frac{1}{f}$$

Also $m = \frac{v}{u} \Rightarrow -2 = \frac{v}{u}$

On solving we get $f = +20$ cm and $v = 60$ cm.
For reflection

$$\frac{1}{v} + \frac{1}{u} = \frac{1}{f} = \frac{2}{R} \Rightarrow \frac{1}{10} + \frac{1}{-30} = \frac{2}{R} \Rightarrow R = 30\,cm$$

The image formed by convex side is faint erect and virtual.
By lens maker formula

$$\frac{1}{f} = \left(\frac{n_l}{n_s} - 1\right)\left(\frac{1}{R_1} - \frac{1}{R_2}\right)$$

$$\therefore \frac{1}{20} = \left(\frac{n_l}{1} - 1\right)\left(\frac{1}{30}\right) \therefore n_l = 2.5$$

7. **(a, b, c, d)**

Here, $u = -8$ cm, $f = +12$ cm

$$\frac{1}{v} - \frac{1}{u} = \frac{1}{f} \Rightarrow v = -24\,cm$$

$$m = \frac{v}{u} = 3, \; H_2 = 3H_1 = 6\,cm$$

Image formed is erect.

8. **(a, c)** Let us first neglect the size of the pupil, assuming that it is point-like. Obviously, only those of the beams passing through the lens will get into the eye which have passed through point B before they fall on the lens (figure). This point is conjugate to the point at which the pupil is located.

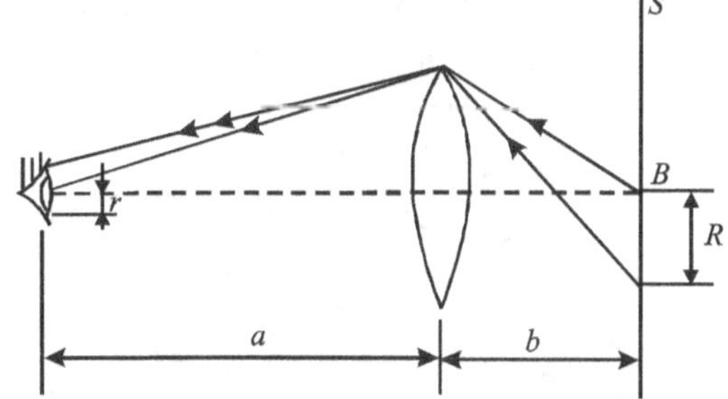

The distance b from the lens to point B can be calculated by using the formula for a thin lens :

$$\frac{1}{F} = \frac{1}{a} + \frac{1}{b}, \quad b = \frac{aF}{a-F} = 12\,\text{cm}.$$

It is clear now that the screen must coincide with the real image of the pupil in the plane S, figure shows that the minimum radius of the screen is

$$R = \frac{b}{a}\,r \simeq 0.5\,\text{mm},$$ and the screen must be placed

in the plane S with its centre at point B.

9. **(a, b, c, d)** In case of an astronomical telescope the distance between the objective lens and eyepiece lens
$$= f_0 + f_e = 16 + 0.02 = 16.02\,\text{m}$$

The angular magnification $= -\dfrac{f_{\text{objective}}}{f_{\text{eye piece}}} = \dfrac{-16}{0.02} = -800$

The image seen by the astronomical telescope is inverted. Also the objective lens is larger than eye piece lens.

10. **5**
This silvered concavo-convex lens behaves like a mirror whose focal length can be calculated by the formula

$$\frac{1}{f} = \frac{2}{f_1} + \frac{1}{f_2}$$

f_1 = focal length of concave surface.
f_2 = focal length of concave mirror

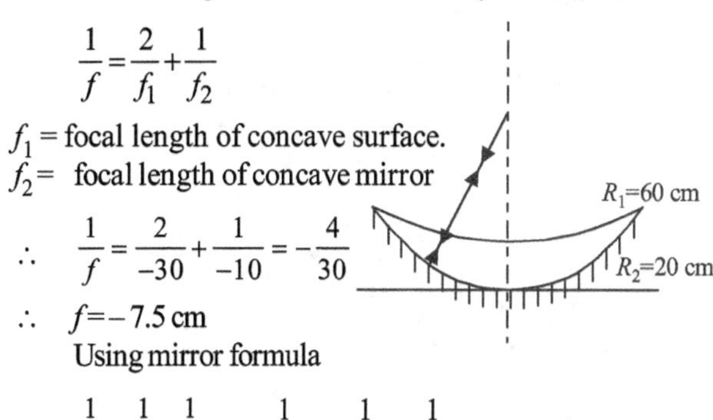

$$\therefore \quad \frac{1}{f} = \frac{2}{-30} + \frac{1}{-10} = -\frac{4}{30}$$

$\therefore \quad f = -7.5\,\text{cm}$
Using mirror formula

$$\frac{1}{f} = \frac{1}{v} + \frac{1}{u} \Rightarrow \frac{1}{-7.5} = \frac{1}{-x} + \frac{1}{-x} \Rightarrow x = \mathbf{15\ cm}$$

Alternatively :

$$-\frac{\mu_1}{u} + \frac{\mu_2}{v} = \frac{\mu_2 - \mu_1}{R}$$

$$\Rightarrow \quad -\frac{1}{-x} + \frac{1.5}{-20} = \frac{1.5 - 1}{-60} \quad \Rightarrow \quad x = \mathbf{15\ cm}$$

11. **6**
Let θ is the angle of incidence and C_1 is the critical angle, then

$$\sin\theta > \sin C,$$

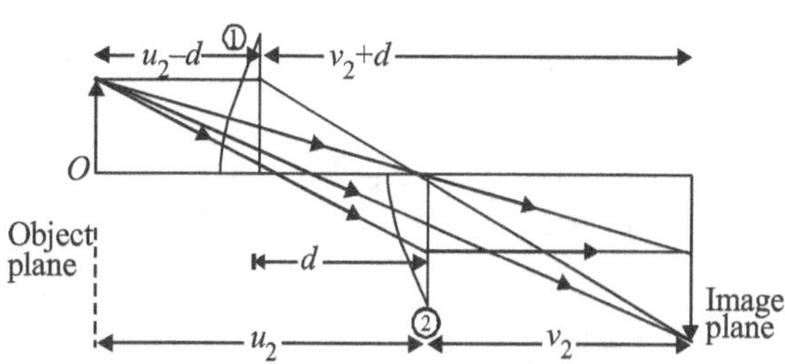

$$> \frac{\mu_1}{\mu_2}$$

$$> \frac{\sqrt{2}}{2}$$

$$\therefore \quad \theta > 45°.$$

For total internal reflection at the face CD

$$\sin\theta > \sin C_2$$

$$> \frac{\mu_3}{\mu_2}$$

$$> \frac{\sqrt{3}}{2} \qquad \therefore \theta > 60°$$

For total internal reflection at both the surfaces

$$\theta_{\min} = 60°.$$

12. **2**

Given $\quad u_2 + v_2 = 1.8\,\text{m}$ ... (i)
The magnification of lens (i) is 2

$$\therefore \quad 2 = \frac{v_2 + d}{u_2 - d} \qquad \text{...(ii)}$$

$$\Rightarrow \quad 2 = \frac{1.8 - u_2 + d}{u_2 - d} \Rightarrow 2u_2 - 2d = 1.8 - u_2 + d$$

$$\Rightarrow \quad 3u_2 = 1.8 + 3d$$
$$\Rightarrow \quad u_2 = 0.6 + d$$
$$\Rightarrow \quad v_2 = 1.8 - 0.6 - d$$
$$v_2 = 1.2 - d$$

Applying lens formula for lens (1)

$$\frac{1}{v_2 + d} + \frac{1}{u_2 - d} = \frac{1}{f} \qquad \text{.... (iii)} \quad \text{for lens (2)}$$

$$\frac{1}{v_2} + \frac{1}{u_2} = \frac{1}{f} \qquad \text{... (iv)}$$

From (iii) and (iv)

$$\frac{1}{v_2+d}+\frac{1}{u_2-d}=\frac{1}{v_2}+\frac{1}{u_2}$$

$$\Rightarrow \frac{1}{1.2-d+d}+\frac{1}{0.6+d-d}=\frac{1}{1.2-d}+\frac{1}{0.6+d}$$

$$\Rightarrow \frac{1}{1.2}+\frac{1}{0.6}=\frac{0.6+d+1.2-d}{(1.2-d)(0.6+d)}$$

$$\Rightarrow \frac{3}{1.2}=\frac{1.8}{(1.2-d)(0.6+d)}$$

$$\Rightarrow (1.2-d)(0.6+d)=0.6\times1.2$$

$$\Rightarrow (1.2\times0.6+1.2d-0.6d-d^2=0.6\times12)$$

$$\Rightarrow d(d-0.6)=0 \Rightarrow d=0.6\,\text{m}$$

Substituting this value in (iv)

$$\frac{1}{1.2-0.6}+\frac{1}{0.6+0.6}=\frac{1}{f}$$

$$\Rightarrow \frac{1}{0.6}+\frac{1}{1.2}=\frac{1}{f}=\frac{1.2+0.6}{0.6\times1.2}=\frac{1.8}{0.6\times1.2}$$

$$\Rightarrow f=\frac{0.6\times1.2}{1.8}=0.4\,\text{m}=\frac{4}{10}=\frac{2}{5}\text{m}$$

13. 6

$$f_0=+50\,\text{cm}; f_e=+5\,\text{cm}; \qquad D=25\,\text{cm}; u_1=-200\,\text{cm}$$

For objective lens

$$\frac{1}{v_0}=\frac{1}{f_0}+\frac{1}{u_0}=\frac{1}{50}-\frac{1}{200}=\frac{4-1}{200}=\frac{3}{200}$$

$$\Rightarrow v_0=\frac{200}{3}e$$

For eyepiece lens

$$\frac{1}{u_e}=\frac{1}{v_e}-\frac{1}{f_e}=\frac{1}{-25}-\frac{1}{5}=-\frac{6}{25}$$

$$\Rightarrow u_e=\frac{25}{6}\text{cm}$$

$[v_e$ is take negative because the image is virtual]

$\therefore$ Separation between objective and eyepiece

$$=|v_0|+|u_e|$$

$$=\frac{200}{3}+\frac{25}{6}=\frac{400+25}{6}=\frac{425}{6}$$

14. (a) $\dfrac{h_i}{h_0}=\dfrac{-v}{u}=\dfrac{r_i}{r_0}=\dfrac{-v}{u}=\dfrac{-\dfrac{uf}{u-f}}{u}=\dfrac{-f}{u-f}$

So only dimension of image changes and not the shape. (v is same for every part)

15. (b) $\dfrac{r_i}{r_0}=\dfrac{-v}{u}\Rightarrow r_i=-r_0\dfrac{v}{u}=-\dfrac{r_0 f}{u-f}=1.2\,\text{cm}.$

$\therefore$ Area of image $=\pi r_i^2=\pi(1.2)^2=1.44\,\pi\,\text{cm}^2$

16. (a) focal length of each part = f

focal length of each part = f^1

$$\frac{1}{f}=\frac{1}{f^1}+\frac{1}{f^1}\Rightarrow\frac{1}{f}=\frac{2}{f^1}\Rightarrow f^1=2f$$

17. (a) or

$$\frac{1}{f}=\frac{1}{2f}+\frac{1}{2f}=\frac{1}{f}$$

$$\Rightarrow F=f=10$$

18. (d) For,

$$\frac{1}{F}=\frac{1}{f}+\frac{1}{f}=\frac{2}{f}\Rightarrow F=\frac{f}{2},\; P=\frac{2}{f}$$

also for,

$$\frac{1}{F}=\frac{1}{+f}+\frac{1}{-f}=0\Rightarrow F=\infty,\; P=0$$

19. A–s; B–q; C–r; D–p

$$\frac{1}{f}=\left(\frac{\mu_2}{\mu_1}-1\right)\left(\frac{1}{R_1}+\frac{1}{R_2}\right).$$

20. A–s; B–p; C–q; D–r

1. **(c)** Given $D = 1.0$ m, wavelength of monochromatic light $\lambda = 600$ nm.

$$d : D\theta = 1 \times \frac{\pi}{180} \times \frac{1}{60}$$

$$d_0 = 2 \times 10^{-3} = 2 \text{ mm}$$

2. **(d)** According to malus law, intensity of emerging beam is given by,
$$I = I_0 \cos^2\theta$$
Now, $I_{A'} = I_A \cos^2 30°$

$$I_{B'} = I_B \cos^2 60°$$

As $I_{A'} = I_{B'}$

$$\Rightarrow \quad I_A \times \frac{3}{4} = I_B \times \frac{1}{4} \quad \therefore \quad \frac{I_A}{I_B} = \frac{1}{3}$$

3. **(d)** Due to reflection virtual source will be formed at distance D from mirror.

The effective distance of the screen $= 2D + 2D = 4D$

$$\therefore \text{ Fringe width} = \frac{4D\lambda}{d}$$

4. **(c)** In absence of film or for $m = 0$ intensity is maximum at screen. As the value of m is increased, intensity shall decrease and then increase alternately. Hence the correct variation is.

5. **(b)** Constructive interference happens when

$2t = (m - 1/2)\lambda$. The minimum value for $m =$ is $m = 1$, the maximum value is the integer portion of

$$\frac{2d}{\lambda} + \frac{1}{2} = \frac{2 \times 0.034 \times 10^{-3}}{680 \times 10^{-9}} + \frac{1}{2} = 100.5$$

$$m_{max} = 100$$

6. **(c)**

7. **(a, c, d)** $I_{max} = (\sqrt{I_1} + \sqrt{I_2})^2 = \left(\sqrt{I_1} + \sqrt{\frac{I}{2}}\right)^2 < 4I$

$$I_{min} = \left(\sqrt{I_1} - \sqrt{\frac{I}{2}}\right)^2 > 0$$

8. **(a, b, c, d)**
For maxima $d = n\lambda$.
For minima $d = (n + 1/2)\lambda$

For intensity $\frac{3}{4}$ th of maximum $d = \left(n \pm \frac{1}{3}\right)\frac{\lambda}{2}$

9. **(b, d)** $\dfrac{I_{max}}{I_{min}} = \dfrac{\left(\sqrt{I_1} + \sqrt{I_2}\right)^2}{\left(\sqrt{I_1} - \sqrt{I_2}\right)^2} = \dfrac{9}{1}$

$$\therefore \quad \frac{I_1}{I_2} = 4 = \frac{a^2}{b^2} \Rightarrow \frac{a}{b} = 2$$

10. **(a, c)** Fringe width, $\beta = \dfrac{D\lambda}{d}$, and so with the increase in D, fringe width will increase. As angular fringe width $\alpha = \dfrac{\lambda}{d}$, and so it is independent of D.

11. **7** **For Red Light**

The shifts of fringes due to glass plate $= \dfrac{Dt(\mu - 1)}{d}$

where t is the thickness of the plate.
This shift is equal to 5ω where ω is the fringe width

$$\frac{Dt(\mu - 1)}{d} = 5\omega \Rightarrow \frac{Dt(\mu - 1)}{d} = \frac{5\lambda_R D}{d}$$

$$t = \frac{5\lambda}{(\mu - 1)} = \frac{5 \times 7 \times 10^{-7}}{1.5 - 1} = 7 \times 10^{-6} \text{ m} = 7\mu\text{m}$$

12. **2** The total intensity at point P will be
$$= I_A + I_B + I_C$$

$$I_A = \frac{(\text{Illuminating power}) \times \cos\theta}{4\pi r^2} = \frac{90 \times \cos 0}{4\pi \times 3^2}$$

$$= \frac{10}{4\pi} \text{ watt} / \text{m}^2$$

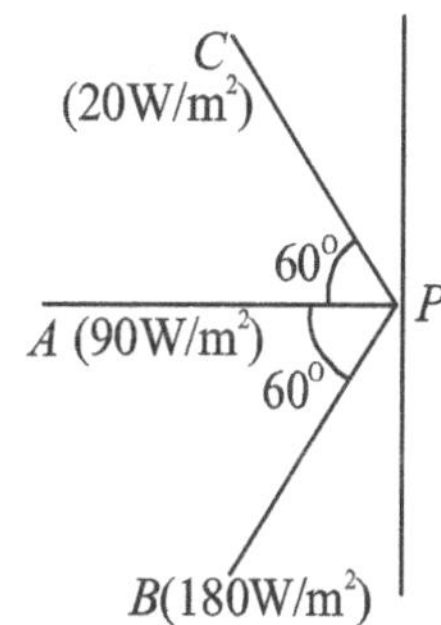

$$I_B = \frac{180 \times \cos 60°}{4\pi \times (1.5)^2} = \frac{10}{\pi} \text{watt} / \text{m}^2$$

$$I_C = 20 \cos 60° = 10$$

$$\therefore \quad I_p = \frac{10}{4\pi} + \frac{10}{\pi} + 10 \approx 14 \text{ W} / \text{m}^2$$

13. **2** At the place where maxima for both the wavelengths coincide, y will be same for both the maxima, i.e.,

$$\frac{n_1 \lambda_1 D}{d} = \frac{n_2 \lambda_2 D}{d} \Rightarrow \frac{n_1}{n_2} = \frac{\lambda_2}{\lambda_1} = \frac{700}{500} = \frac{7}{5}$$

$\therefore$ Minimum distance of maxima of the two wavelengths from central fringe is

$$= 5 \times 700 \times 10^{-9} \times 10^3 = \frac{7}{2} \text{ mm}.$$

14. **3** For maxima
Path defference $= m\lambda$
$$\therefore \quad S_2 A - S_1 A = m\lambda$$

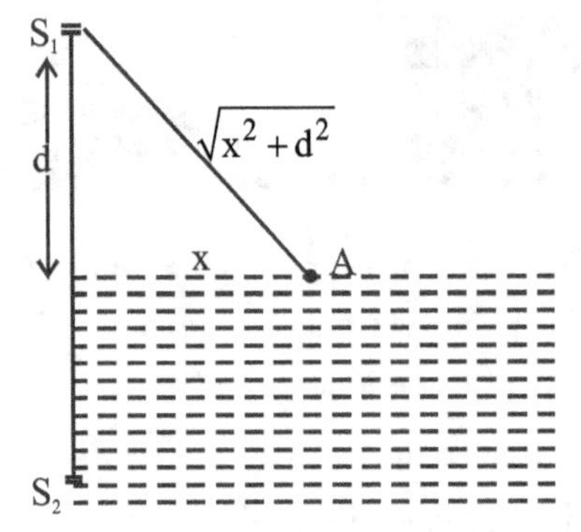

$$\therefore \quad \left[(n-1)\sqrt{d^2+x^2} + \sqrt{d^2+x^2}\right] - \sqrt{d^2-x^2} = m\lambda$$

$$\therefore \quad (n-1)\sqrt{(d^2+x^2)} = m\lambda$$

$$\therefore \quad \left(\frac{4}{3}-1\right)\sqrt{d^2+x^2} = m\lambda$$

$$\therefore \quad \sqrt{d^2+x^2} = 3m\lambda$$
$$\therefore \quad d^2+x^2 = 9m^2\lambda^2$$
$$\therefore \quad x^2 = 9m^2\lambda^2 - d^2$$
$$\therefore \quad p^2 = 9 \quad \Rightarrow \quad p = 3$$

15. (a) $S_1P - S_2P = \dfrac{dy}{D}$

$$\Delta x = (n_0 + kt)\frac{dy}{D} - d\sin\phi = 0$$

For central maxima.

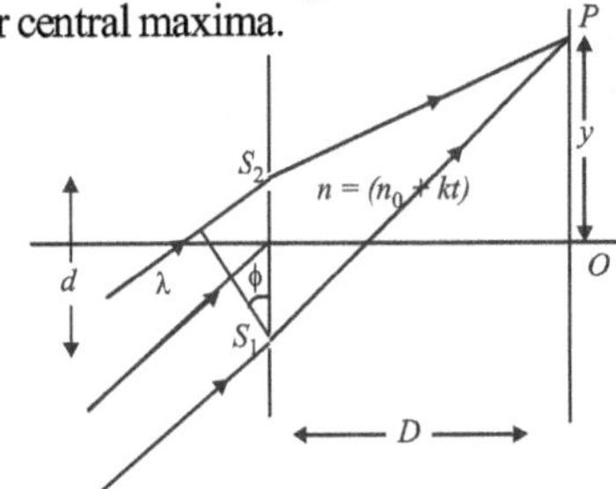

$$\therefore y = \frac{D\sin\phi}{n_0 + kt} \ (\text{y-coordinate of central maximum}).$$

16. (b) $\dfrac{dy}{dt} = \dfrac{-kD\sin\phi}{(n_0+kt)^2} = $ velocity of central maximum.

17. (a) For plane wave fronts the beam of light is parallel.

18. (c) Since points c and d are on the same wavefront, therefore $\phi_d = \phi_c$
Similarly, $\phi_e = \phi_f$ $\therefore \phi_d - \phi_f = \phi_c - \phi_f$

19. A-s; B-r; C-q; D-p

20. A-p, q; B-r, C-s, D-p

(A) $\sqrt{D^2+(2\lambda)^2} - D = \Delta x$
For maximas $\Delta x = n\lambda$
$D^2+(2\lambda)^2 = (D+n\lambda)^2$, $\quad 4\lambda^2 = n^2\lambda^2 + 2Dn\lambda$
Only two possible values of n, $\quad n = 1$,
$$D = \frac{3\lambda}{2} \ ; \ n = 2, \ D = 0$$
Similarly, for minimas, $\Delta x = (2n-1)\dfrac{\lambda}{2}$

(B) For maxima, $\Delta x = n\lambda$
$\cos\theta = n$,
Possible values of $n = 0, 1$
$\cos\theta = 0, \Rightarrow \theta = 90°, 270°$
$\cos\theta = 1, \Rightarrow \theta = 0°, 360°$
$\therefore$ Number of maximas $= 4$
Similarly for minimas, $\Delta x = (2n-1)\dfrac{\lambda}{2}$

(C) Virtual image of S will act as another source
$\Delta x = d\sin\theta$, $d = 2\lambda$
For maximas, $n\lambda = 2\lambda\sin\theta \Rightarrow \sin\theta = \dfrac{n}{2}$
$n = 0, 1, 2,$
$\theta = 0, 30°, 90°, 150°$
Total maximas possible $= 7$ (centre $+$ 3 up $+$ 3 down)

(D) $\Delta x = 2\lambda\cos\theta$; $\theta \le 60°$
For maximas, $\Delta x = n\lambda \Rightarrow \cos\theta = \dfrac{n}{2}$; $n = 0, 1, 2, \theta \neq 90°$,
$\theta = 60°, \theta = 0°$

Total maximas two, For minima, $\Delta x = (2n-1)\dfrac{\lambda}{2}$;
$$\cos\theta = \frac{2n-1}{4}$$
$n = 1, \ \cos\theta = \dfrac{1}{4}$; $\theta > 60°$; $n = 2,$
$\cos\theta = \dfrac{3}{4}$; $\theta < 60°$; No. of possible minimas $= 1$.

1. **(c)** $h\nu_0^2 - h\nu_0 = \dfrac{1}{2}mv^2$

$\therefore \dfrac{4}{3}h\nu_0 - h\nu_0 = \dfrac{1}{2}mv'^2$

$\therefore \dfrac{v'^2}{v^2} = \dfrac{\dfrac{4}{3}v - v_0}{v - v_0}$ $\qquad \therefore v' = v\sqrt{\dfrac{\dfrac{4}{3}v - v_0}{v - v_0}}$

$\therefore v' > v\sqrt{\dfrac{4}{3}}$

2. **(a)** Final speed of α-particle will be less than the initial speed therefore,

$$\left(\dfrac{h}{\lambda_f}\right) < \left(\dfrac{h}{\lambda_i}\right) \text{ or } \lambda_f > \lambda_i$$

3. **(a)** $\lambda_{min} = \dfrac{hc}{ev_0}$

$\lambda_1 = \dfrac{hc}{ev_1}$; $\lambda_2 = \dfrac{hc}{ev_2}$

$\dfrac{\lambda_2}{\lambda_1} = \dfrac{v_1}{v_2} \Rightarrow \dfrac{3}{4} = \dfrac{v_1}{v_2}$

$\dfrac{v_2}{v_1} = \dfrac{4}{3} \Rightarrow \left(\dfrac{v_2 - v_1}{v_1}\right) \times 100 = \dfrac{100}{3}$

Hence, P.D. must be increased by $\dfrac{100}{3}\%$.

4. **(c)** The energy of incident photons is given by

$h\nu = eV_s + \phi_0 = 2 + 5 = 7\,eV$

(V_s is stopping potential and ϕ_0 is work function)

Saturation current $= 10^{-5}\,A$

$= \dfrac{\eta P}{h\nu}e = \dfrac{10^{-5}P}{7 \times e}e$ (η is photon emission efficiency)

$\therefore \quad P = 7W$

5. **(c)** $\lambda_{min} = \dfrac{hc}{eV}$

and $\lambda_{\text{de-Broglie}} = \dfrac{h}{\rho} = \dfrac{h}{\sqrt{2meV}}$.

6. **(d)** $\omega_{max} = 3 \times 3 \times 10^{15}$;

$\nu_{max} = \dfrac{3 \times 3 \times 10^{15}}{2\pi}$ Hz

$K.E_{max} = h\nu_{max} - W = 4\,eV$

7. **(b, c)** $\phi = h\nu - k_{max}$
and $k_{max} = |eV_s|$

8. **(a, b, c)**

9. **(a, c)** $\phi_1 : \phi_2 : \phi_3 = eV_{0_1} : eV_{0_2} : eV_{0_3}$

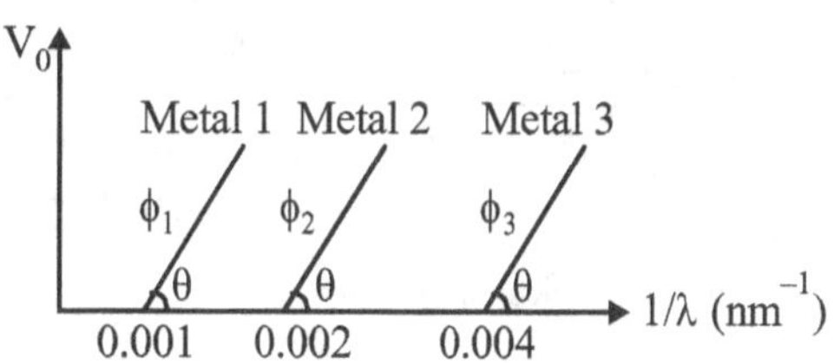

$= V = V_{0_1} : V_{0_2} : V_{03} = 0.001 : 0.002 : 0.004 = 1 : 2 : 4$

Therefore option (a) is correct

By Einstein's photoelectric equation. $\dfrac{hc}{\lambda} - \phi = eV$

$\Rightarrow \quad V = \dfrac{hc}{e\lambda} - \dfrac{\phi}{e}$ $\qquad$ ...(i)

Comparing equation (i) by $y = mx + c$, we get the slope of the line

$m = \dfrac{hc}{e} = \tan\theta$

$\Rightarrow \quad$ Option (c) is correct.

From the graph it is clear than,

$\dfrac{1}{\lambda_{0_1}} = 0.001\,\text{nm}^{-1} \Rightarrow \lambda_{0_1} = \dfrac{1}{0.001} = 1000\,\text{mn}$

Also $\dfrac{1}{\lambda_{0_2}} = 0.002\,\text{nm}^{-1} \Rightarrow \lambda_{0_2} = 500\,\text{nm}$ and

$\lambda_{0_2} = 250\,\text{nm}$

Violet colour light will have wavelength less than 400 nm. Therefore this light will be unable to show photo electric effect on plate, $3 \Rightarrow$ Option (d) is wrong.

10. **(a, b, c)**

11. **7**

Stopping potential $= \dfrac{1}{e}\left[\dfrac{hc}{\lambda} - \phi\right]$ where hc $= 1240\,eV$ –nm

$= \dfrac{1}{e}\left[\dfrac{1240}{200} - 4.7\right] = \dfrac{1}{e}[6.2 - 4.7 \quad]$

$= \dfrac{1}{e} \times 1.5\,eV = 1.5V$

But $V = \dfrac{1}{4\pi\varepsilon_0}\dfrac{q}{r} = \dfrac{1}{4\pi\varepsilon_0}\dfrac{ne}{r}$

$\therefore n = \dfrac{Vr(4\pi\varepsilon_0)}{e} = \dfrac{1.5 \times 10^{-2}}{9 \times 10^9 \times 1.6 \times 10^{-19}}$

$\therefore n = 1.04 \times 10^7$

Comparing it with $A \times 10^z$ we get, $z = 7$

12. **1** For photoelectric effect

$\dfrac{h\nu}{e} - \dfrac{\phi_0}{e} = V_0$

The slope is

$\tan\theta = \dfrac{h}{e} = \text{constant}$

$\therefore$ The ratio will be 1.

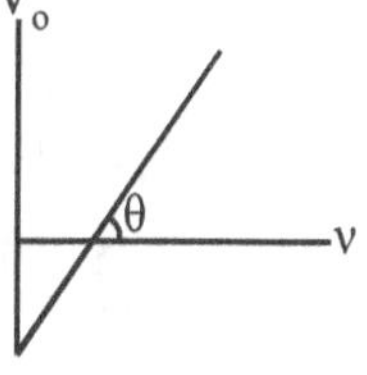

13. **2**

Work funciton $W_0 = h\nu_0 = 6.6 \times 10^{-34} \times 1.6 \times 10^{15}$

$$= 1.056 \times 10^{-18} \text{ J} = 6.6 \text{ eV}$$

From $E = W_0 + K_{max} \Rightarrow K_{max} = E - W_0 = 2$ eV

14. **4**

If E is the energy of each photon, then

$$nE = P$$

$$\therefore \quad E = \frac{P}{n} = \frac{200}{4 \times 10^{20}} = 50 \times 10^{-20} J$$

If λ is the wavelength of light, then

$$E = \frac{hc}{\lambda}$$

$$\therefore \quad \lambda = \frac{hc}{E} = \frac{(6.63 \times 10^{-34}) \times (3 \times 10^8)}{500 \times 10^{-20}} = 400 \text{ nm}$$

15. **(b)** The current $= 2.566 - 2.55 = 0.016$

$$\therefore \text{ No. of } e^- = \frac{0.016}{1.6 \times 10^{-19}} = 10^{17} e^-$$

for every 100 $e^-(s)$ 1 photon is produced

$$\Rightarrow \text{ No. of X-ray photons} = \frac{10^{17}}{100} = 10^{15}$$

16. **(d)** Power available from X-ray tube is :

$$P = VI = 50000 \times 0.016$$

$$P = 800 \text{ Watt}$$

Since efficiency of X-rays production is 1% therefore 99% of available power is converted into heat

$$P_{heat} = 0.99 \times 800 \text{ W} = 99 \times 8 \text{ W}$$

$$P_{heat} = 792 \text{ W}$$

17. **(a)** $\Delta E = W_0 + E$; $(E_k) = \Delta E - W_0$

For maximum value of (E_k), W_0 should be minimum

W_0 for lithium $= 2.3$ eV

$$\therefore \quad (E_k) = 2.75 - 2.3 = 0.45 \text{ eV}$$

18. **(c)** The maximum magnitude of stopping potential will be for metal of least work function.

$\therefore$ required stopping potential is

$$V_s = \frac{h\nu - \phi_0}{e} = 0.45 \text{ volt.}$$

19. A→p, r; B→q, s; C→s; D→p, r

20. A → p, B → r, C → q, D → s

1. **(a)** $-\dfrac{dU}{dr} = F$ (conservative force field)

$\Rightarrow \quad F = \dfrac{-K}{r}$ provides the centrifugal force for circular motion of electron.

$\dfrac{mv^2}{r} = \dfrac{K}{r} \Rightarrow r = \dfrac{nh}{2\pi\sqrt{mK}}$

K.E. of electron $= \dfrac{1}{2}mv^2 = \dfrac{1}{2}K$

P.E. of electron $= K \ln r$

$E(n)$ = Total energy = K.E. + P.E.

$= \dfrac{1}{2}K + K \ln r = \dfrac{K}{2}\left[1 + \log\dfrac{n^2 h^2}{4\pi^3 mk}\right]$

Required ratio $= \dfrac{E(2) - E(1)}{E(4) - E(2)} = 1$

2. **(d)** Radius of nth orbit $r_n \propto n^2$, graph between r_n and n is a

parabola. Also, $\dfrac{r_n}{r_1} = \left(\dfrac{n}{1}\right)^2 \Rightarrow \log_e\left(\dfrac{r_n}{r_1}\right) = 2\log_e(n)$

Comparing this equation with $y = mx + c$,

Graph between $\log_e\left(\dfrac{r_n}{r_1}\right)$ and $\log_e(n)$ will be a straight

line, passing from origin.

Similarly it can be proved that graph between

$\log_e\left(\dfrac{f_n}{f_1}\right)$ and $\log_e n$ is a straight line. But with

negative slops.

3. **(b)** 10 emission lines

$\Rightarrow$ final state n = 5

If the initial state were not $n = 4$, in the emission spectrum some lines with energies less than that of absorbed radiation would have been observed.

$\therefore$ initial state $n = 4$.

$$\begin{array}{l} \underline{\qquad\qquad\qquad\qquad} \; n = 5 \\ \underline{\qquad\qquad\qquad\qquad} \; n = 4 \\ \underline{\qquad\qquad\qquad\qquad} \; n = 3 \\ \underline{\qquad\qquad\qquad\qquad} \; n = 2 \\ \underline{\qquad\qquad\qquad\qquad} \; n = 1 \end{array}$$

4. **(d)** The energy of the system of two atoms of diatomic

molecule $E = \dfrac{1}{2}I\omega^2$

where I = moment of inertia

ω = Angular velocity $= \dfrac{L}{I}$,

L = Angular momentum

$I = \dfrac{1}{2}(m_1 r_1^2 + m^2 r_2^2)$

Thus, $E = \dfrac{1}{2}(m_1 r_1^2 + m_2 r_2^2)\omega^2$ ...(i)

$E = \dfrac{1}{2}(m_1 r_1^2 + m_2 r_2^2)\dfrac{L^2}{I^2}$

$L = n\dfrac{nh}{2n}$ (According Bohr's Hypothesis)

$E = \dfrac{1}{2}(m_1 r_1^2 + m_2 r_2^2)\dfrac{L^2}{(m_1 r_1^2 + m_2 r_2^2)^2}$

$E = \dfrac{1}{2}\dfrac{L^2}{(m_1 r_1^2 + m_2 r_2^2)} = \dfrac{n^2 h^2}{8\pi^2(m_1 r_1^2 + m_2 r_2^2)}$

$E = \dfrac{(m_1 + m_2)n^2 h^2}{8\pi^2 r^2 m_1 m_2} \left[\because r_1 = \dfrac{m_2 r}{m_1 + m_2}; r_2 = \dfrac{m_2 r}{m_1 + m_2}\right]$

5. **(c)** In the nth orbit, let r_n be the radius and v_n be the speed of electron.

Time period, $T_n = \dfrac{2\pi r_n}{v_n} \propto \dfrac{r_n}{v_n}$

Now $r_n \propto n^2$; $v_n \propto \dfrac{1}{n} \quad \therefore \dfrac{r_n v_n}{v_n} \propto n^3$ or $T_n \propto n^3$

Here $8 = \left(\dfrac{n_1}{n_2}\right)^3$ or $\dfrac{n_1}{n_2} = 2$ i.e., $n_1 = 2n_2$

6. **(a, b)** $|F| = \dfrac{dU}{dr} = \dfrac{Ke^2}{r^4}$ .... (1)

$\dfrac{Ke^2}{r^4} = \dfrac{mv^2}{r}$ .... (2)

and $mvr = \dfrac{nh}{2\pi}$ .... (3)

By (2) and (3),

$r = \dfrac{Ke^2 4\pi^2}{h^2}\dfrac{m}{n^2} = K_1\dfrac{m}{n^2}$ .... (4)

Total energy $= \dfrac{1}{2}$ (potential energy)

$= \dfrac{Ke^2}{6r^3} = \dfrac{-Ke^2}{6\left(\dfrac{K_1 m}{n^2}\right)^3} = \dfrac{-Ke^2 n^6}{6K_1^3 m^3}$

Total energy $\propto n^6$

Totan energy $\propto m^{-3}$

7. **(a,b,d).**

$$\because \; r_n = n^2 r_1$$

$$\ln\left(\frac{A_n}{A_1}\right) = \ln\left(\frac{\pi r_n^2}{\pi r_1^2}\right)$$

$$= \ln n^4 = 4\ln(n)$$

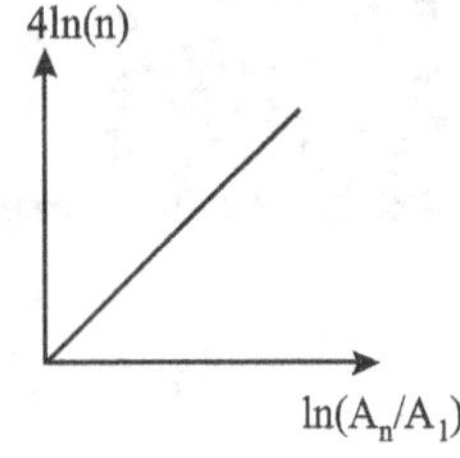

8. **(a, b, d)**

We know that $r = r_0 \dfrac{n^2}{z}$, $E_n = -\dfrac{13.6 Z^2}{n^2}$, $L_n = \dfrac{nh}{2\pi}$

Relative change in the radii of two consecutive orbitals

$$\frac{r_n - r_{n-1}}{r_n} = 1 - \frac{r_{n-1}}{r_n} = 1 - \frac{(n-1)^2}{n^2} \text{ does not depend on Z}$$

$$= \frac{2n-1}{n^2} \approx \frac{2}{n} \quad (\because \; n >> 1)$$

Relative change in the energy of two consecutive orbitals

$$\frac{E_n - E_{n-1}}{E_n} = 1 - \frac{E_{n-1}}{E_n} = 1 - \frac{n^2}{(n-1)^2} = \frac{-2n+1}{(n-1)^2} \approx \frac{-2}{n}$$

$$\frac{L_n - L_{n-1}}{L_n} = 1 - \frac{L_{n-1}}{L_n} = 1 - \frac{(n-1)}{n} = \frac{1}{n}$$

9. **(a, c)** Angular momentum $= \dfrac{nh}{2\pi} = \dfrac{3h}{2\pi}$. Therefore n = 3.

Also $r_n = \dfrac{a_0 n^2}{z} = 4.5 a_0$

$$\therefore \; \frac{n^2}{z} = 4.5 \qquad \Rightarrow \frac{9}{z} = 4.5 \Rightarrow z = 2$$

we know that

$$\frac{1}{\lambda} = R z^2 \left[\frac{1}{n_1^2} - \frac{1}{n_2^2}\right] = \frac{1}{\lambda} = 4R\left[\frac{1}{n_1^2} - \frac{1}{n_2^2}\right]$$

For $n_2 = 3$, $n_1 = 1$ we get $\lambda = \dfrac{9}{8 \times 4R} = \dfrac{9}{32R}$

For $n_2 = 3$, $n_1 = 2$ we get $\lambda = \dfrac{36}{5 \times 4R} = \dfrac{9}{5R}$

For $n_2 = 2$, $n_1 = 1$ we get $\lambda = \dfrac{4}{3 \times 4R} = \dfrac{1}{3R}$

(a), (c) are correct options

10. **6**

For hydrogen like atoms

$$E_n = -\frac{13.6}{n^2} Z^2 \text{ eV/atom}$$

Given $E_n - E_2 = 10.2 + 17 = 27.2$ eV   ..(i)

$E_n - E_3 = 4.24 + 5.95 = 10.2$ eV

$\therefore E_3 - E_2 = 17$

But $E_3 - E_2 = -\dfrac{13.6}{9} Z^2 - \left(-\dfrac{13.6}{4} Z^2\right)$

$$= -13.6 Z^2 \left[\frac{1}{9} - \frac{1}{4}\right]$$

$$= -13.6 Z^2 \left[\frac{4-9}{36}\right] = \frac{13.6 \times 5}{36} Z^2$$

$$\therefore \frac{13.6 \times 5}{36} Z^2 = 17 \Rightarrow Z = 3$$

$$E_n - E_2 = -\frac{13.6}{n_2} \times 3^2 - \left[-\frac{13.6}{2^2} \times 3^2\right]$$

$$= -13.6\left[\frac{9}{n^2} - \frac{9}{4}\right] = -13.6 \times 9\left[\frac{4-n^2}{4n^2}\right] \qquad ...(ii)$$

From eq. (i) and (ii)

$$-13.6 \times 9\left[\frac{4-n^2}{4n^2}\right] = 27.2$$

$$\Rightarrow -122.4\,(4 - n^2) = 108.8 n^2 \Rightarrow n^2 = \frac{489.6}{13.6} = 36 \Rightarrow n = 6$$

11. **8**

Let e^- in hydrogen atom is excited to n^{th} level.

$$\therefore \quad E_{KE(n-1)} = 8\,|\,E_{P.E.(n)}\,|$$

$$\therefore \quad 13.6 eV = 8\,|\,2 \times \frac{13.6}{n^2} eV\,| \quad \Rightarrow n = 4$$

$$\therefore \quad \Delta E = 13.6\left(1 - \frac{1}{16}\right) = \frac{15}{16} \times 13.6 eV = 12.75 eV$$

Using conservation of linear momentum

$$mv = mv_1 + mv_2 \qquad ...(1)$$

$$\left(v_2 - v_1 = \frac{1}{2} v\right) \qquad ...(2)$$

$$\therefore v_1 = \frac{v}{4}, v_2 = \frac{3v}{4} \qquad ....(3)$$

By energy conservation

$$\therefore \frac{1}{2} mv^2 = \frac{1}{2} mv_1^2 + \frac{1}{2} mv_2^2 + \Delta E$$

$$\Rightarrow \frac{1}{2} mv^2 \left(1 - \frac{1}{16} - \frac{9}{16}\right) = \Delta E$$

$$\Rightarrow \frac{1}{2} mv^2 = \frac{16}{6} \Delta E = \frac{8}{3} \times 12.75 eV = 32 \text{ eV}$$

12. **3**

If x is the difference in quantum number of the states than $^{x+1}C_2 = 6 \Rightarrow x = 3$

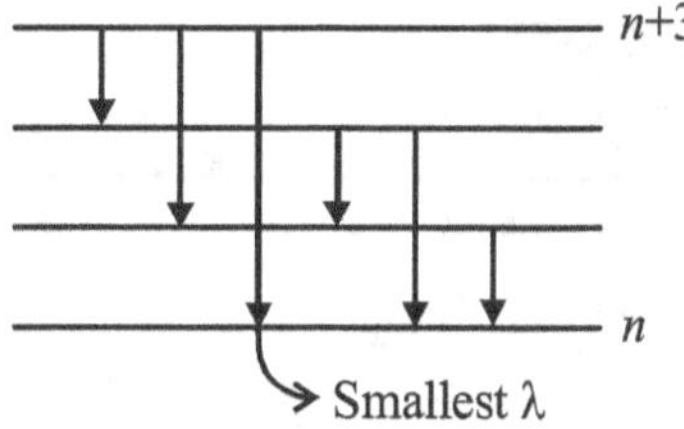

Now, we have $\dfrac{-Z^2(13.6\,\text{eV})}{n^2} = -0.85\,\text{eV}$ ...(i)

and $\dfrac{-Z^2(13.6\,\text{eV})}{(n+3)^2} = -0.544\,\text{eV}$ ...(ii)

Solving (i) and (ii), we get $Z = \mathbf{3}$.

13. **2**

For hydrogen like atom energy of the nth orbit is

$$E_n = -\frac{13.6}{n^2}Z^2 \ \text{eV/atom}$$

For transition from $n = 5$ to $n = 4$,

$$h\nu = 13.6 \times 9\left[\frac{1}{16}-\frac{1}{25}\right] = \frac{13.6 \times 9 \times 9}{16 \times 25} = 2.754\,\text{eV}$$

For transition from $n = 4$ to $n = 3$,

$$h\nu' = 13.6 \times 9\left[\frac{1}{9}-\frac{1}{16}\right] = \frac{13.6 \times 9 \times 7}{9 \times 16} = 5.95\,\text{eV}$$

For transition $n = 4$ to $n = 3$, the frequency is high and hence wavelength is short.

For photoelectric effect, $h\nu' - W = eV_0$, where W = work function

$5.95 \times 1.6 \times 10^{-19} - W = 1.6 \times 10^{-19} \times 3.95$

$\Rightarrow W = 2 \times 1.6 \times 10^{-19} = 2\,\text{eV}$

14. **(a)**   **15.** **(c)**

$$F = -\frac{dU}{dr} = \frac{mv_n^2}{r_n} \qquad m\alpha^2 r_n = \frac{mv_n^2}{r_n} \qquad ...\ (i)$$

and $mv_{n'}r_n = \dfrac{nh}{2\pi}$ ... (ii)

Solving equations (i) and (ii)

$$r_n = \left(\frac{nh}{2\pi m\alpha}\right)^{1/2}$$

and $\text{KE} = \dfrac{1}{2}mv_n^2 = \dfrac{nh\alpha}{4\pi}$

Total energy, $E = U + KE = -\dfrac{1}{2}m\alpha^2 r_n^2 + \dfrac{1}{2}mv_n^2 = 0.$

16. **(a)**   Current developed due to motion of an electron in n^{th} Bohr's orbit = $I_0\dfrac{Z^2}{n^3}$ (unit ampere) here in column III

option (r) $C_0\dfrac{Z^2}{n^3}$, for $z = 3$ and $n = 3$, $I = C_0 \times \dfrac{3^2}{3^3} = \dfrac{C_0}{3}$

17. **(b)** $\omega_n = \omega_0 \dfrac{z^2}{n^3}\ \text{sec}^{-1}$, $I_n = I_0\dfrac{Z^2}{n^3}\ \text{A}$,

$V_n = V_0\dfrac{Z}{n}\ \text{m/s}$, $E_n = E_0\dfrac{Z^2}{n^2}\ \text{J}$

18. **(d)**   Ionization energy, $E_n = E_0\dfrac{Z^2}{n^2}$

19.   (A) $\to$ q; (B) $\to$ r; (C) $\to$ p; (D) $\to$ s

20.   **(A) $\to$ p, r; (B) $\to$ q, s; (C) $\to$ q; (D) $\to$ q, s**

(A) $B = \dfrac{\mu_0 i}{2\pi r}$ where $i_{eq} = \dfrac{q}{T} = \dfrac{e}{2\pi r/v}$

$\Rightarrow B = \dfrac{\mu_0 e}{4\pi^2}\dfrac{v}{r^2} \propto \dfrac{v}{r^2} \propto \dfrac{(Z/n)}{(n^2/Z^2)} \propto \dfrac{Z^3}{n^5}$

(B)   Magnetic moment,

$$M = iA = \left(\frac{q}{T}\right)(\pi r^2) = \frac{e}{2\pi r/v}\pi r^2 \propto rv \propto \left(\frac{n^2}{Z}\right)\left(\frac{Z}{n}\right)$$

(C) $\lambda = \dfrac{h}{mv} \propto \dfrac{1}{Z/n} \propto \dfrac{n}{Z}$

(D)   Areal velocity = $\dfrac{L}{2m} = \dfrac{nh/2\pi}{2\pi} \propto n$

1. (a)

Sample S–1
Activity 5 μCi
No. of nuclei $N_1 = 2N$

$$-\left(\frac{dN}{dt}\right)_1 = \lambda_1 N_1$$

$$\Rightarrow -5 = \lambda_1 \times 2N \,...(i)$$

From (i) and (ii)

Sample S – 2
10 μCi
$N_2 = N$

$$-\left(\frac{dN}{dt}\right)_2 = \lambda_2 N_2$$

$$-10 = \lambda_2 \times N \qquad ...(ii)$$

$$\frac{5}{10} = \frac{\lambda_1 \times 2N}{\lambda_2 \times N} \quad \Rightarrow \quad \frac{\lambda_1}{\lambda_2} = \frac{1}{4}$$

$$\Rightarrow \frac{(T_{1/2})_2}{(T_{1/2})_1} = \frac{1}{4} \quad \left[\because \lambda \propto \frac{1}{T_{1/2}}\right]$$

2. (c) Energy is released when stability increases. This will happen when binding energy per nucleon increases.

	Reactant	Product
Reaction (a)	$60 \times 8.5\,\text{MeV} = 510\,\text{MeV}$	$2 \times 30 \times 5 = 300$ MeV
Reaction (b)	$120 \times 7.5 = 900$ MeV	$(90 \times 8 + 30 \times 5) = 870$ MeV
Reaction (c)	$120 \times 7.5 = 900$ MeV	$2 \times 60 \times 8.5 = 1020$ MeV
Reaction (d)	$90 \times 8 = 720$ MeV	$(60 \times 8.5 + 30 \times 5) = 600$ MeV

3. (c) $N = N_0 e^{-\lambda/t} = 10^6 e^{-\left[\frac{\ln 2}{20} \times 10\right]}$

$$= 10^6 e^{-\ln\sqrt{2}} = \frac{10^6}{\sqrt{2}} = \approx 7.07 \times 10^5$$

4. (c) $3Q \to P + \text{energy}(e)$
$e = E_P - 3E_Q$

5. (a) Let $t = $ time for the potential of metal sphere to rise by one volt.

Now β – particles emitted in this time

$$= (6.25 \times 10^{11}) \times t$$

Number of β -particles escaped in this time

$$= (80/100) \times (6.25 \times 10^{10})t = 5 \times 10^{10} t$$

∴ Charge acquired by the sphere in t sec.

$$Q = (5 \times 10^{10} t) \times (1.6 \times 10^{-19})$$

$$= 8 \times 10^{-19} t \text{ coulomb} \qquad ...(i)$$

(∵ emission of β -particle lends to a charge e on metal sphere)

The capacitance C of a metal sphere is given by

$$C = 4\pi\varepsilon_0 \times r$$

$$= \left(\frac{1}{9 \times 10^9}\right) \times \left(\frac{10^{-3}}{2}\right) = \frac{10^{-12}}{18} \text{ farad} ...(ii)$$

we know that $Q = C \times V$ {Here $V = 1$ volt}

$$\therefore \quad (8 \times 10^{-9})t = \left(\frac{10^{-12}}{18}\right) \times 1$$

Solving it for t, we get $t = 6.95$ μsec.

6. (d) Given : $T_{1/2} = 20$ min

decay constant, $\lambda = \dfrac{0.693}{T_{1/2}} = \dfrac{0.693}{20} = 0.0345/\text{minute}.$

we have $N = N_0 e^{-\lambda t}$

Case-I: (When 33% disintegrated)

$$N_1 = N_0 - \frac{33}{100}N_0 = \frac{67}{100}N_0$$

$$\therefore \quad \frac{67}{100}N_0 = N_0 e^{-\lambda t_1} \qquad\qquad ....(1)$$

$$\frac{67}{100}e^{-\lambda t_1} \quad \text{or} \quad 0.67 = e^{-\lambda t_1}$$

$$t_1 = \frac{2.303}{\lambda}(\log 0.67) = 11.60 \text{ min}.$$

Case-II: (when 67% disintegrated)

$$N_2 = N_0 - \frac{67}{100}N_0 = \frac{33}{100}N_0$$

$$\therefore \quad \frac{33}{100} = e^{-\lambda t_2} \qquad\qquad ......(2)$$

or $0.33 = e^{-\lambda t_2}$

or $t_2 = \dfrac{2.303}{\lambda} \log(0.33) = 32.14$ min.

Difference between time $= t_2 - t_1 = 20$ min.

7. (b, c, d) $^{236}_{92}\text{U} \to\, ^{140}_{54}\text{Xe} +\, ^{94}_{38}\text{Sr} + x + y$

The number of proton in reactants is equal to the products (leaving x and y) and mass number of product (leaving x and y) is two less than reactants
∴ $x = p$, $y = e^-$ is ruled out [B] is incorrect
and $x = p$, $y = n$ is ruled out [C] is incorrect
Total energy loss $= (236 \times 7.5) - [140 \times 8.5 + 94 \times 8.5]$
$= 219$ MeV
The energies of kx and ky together is 4MeV
The energy remain is distributed by Sr and Xe which is equal to $219 - 4 = 215$ MeV
∴ A is the correct option
Also momentum is conserved

$$\therefore K.E. \propto \frac{1}{m} . \text{ Therefore K.E}_{sr} > \text{K.E}_{xe}$$

The energies of kx and ky together is 4MeV
The energy remain is distributed by Sr and Xe which is equal to $219 - 4 = 215$ MeV
∴ A is the correct option
Also momentum is conserved
. Therefore K.E$_{sr}$ > K.E$_{xe}$

8. **(c, d)** In the case of hydrogen, atomic number = mass number
In the other atoms, atomic number < mass number.

9. **(a, b)** The mass number decreases by 32 hence 8 α-particles and 6 β-particles are produced.

$$_{92}U^{238} \longrightarrow {}_{82}Pb^{206} + 8\ {}_2He^4 + 6\ {}_{-1}\beta^0$$

10. **(a, b)** Let q be the charge on the capacitor after a time t.

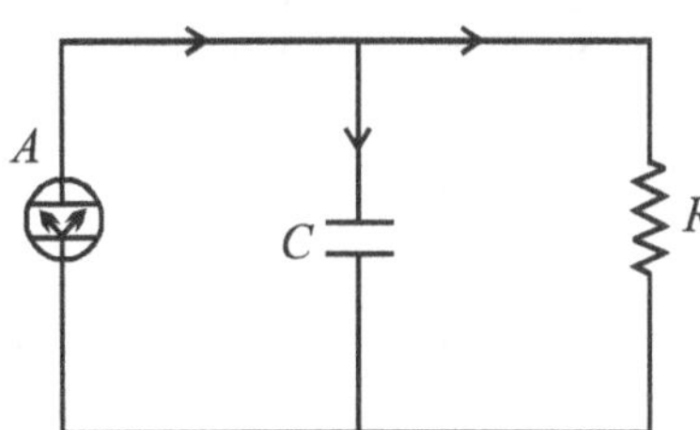

Then, we can write

$$\left(\frac{dq}{dt}\right) + \frac{1}{R}\left(\frac{q}{C}\right) = i(t) \qquad ......(1)$$

where $i(t)$

$$= (\lambda N_0 e^{-\lambda t})\,2e.f = (2e.f\lambda N_0)\,e^{-\lambda t} = i_0 e^{-\lambda t} .. (2)$$

Solving eq. (1), we get

$$q = \frac{i_0 e^{-\lambda t}}{\dfrac{1}{RC} - \lambda} + C_1 e^{-\frac{1}{RC}},$$

where C_1 is an arbitrary constant.
Using the initial condition, we get,

$$q(t) = -\left(\frac{i_0}{\dfrac{1}{RC} - \lambda} + q_0\right) e^{-\frac{1}{RC}} + \frac{i_0}{\dfrac{1}{RC} - \lambda} e^{-\lambda t}$$

$$= -q_1 e^{-\frac{t}{RC}} + q_2 e^{-\lambda t}$$

The total charge on the capacitor becomes zero at a time
$t = \tau$, where $q(\tau) = 0$

$$0 = -q_1 e^{-\frac{\tau}{RC}} + q_2 e^{-\lambda t} \text{ or } \tau = \frac{1}{\dfrac{1}{RC} - \lambda}\ln\left(\frac{q_1}{q_2}\right)$$

11. **8** We know that $N = N_0 e^{-\lambda t}$

$$\therefore \frac{dN}{dt} = N_0 e^{-\lambda t}(-\lambda) = -N_0 \lambda\, e^{-\lambda t}$$

Taking log on both sides

$$\log_e \frac{dN}{dt} = \log_e(-N_0\lambda) - \lambda t$$

Comparing it with the graph line,

we get $\lambda = \dfrac{1}{2}\,\text{yr}^{-1}$ $\qquad \left[\dfrac{AC}{BC} = \dfrac{1}{2}\right]$

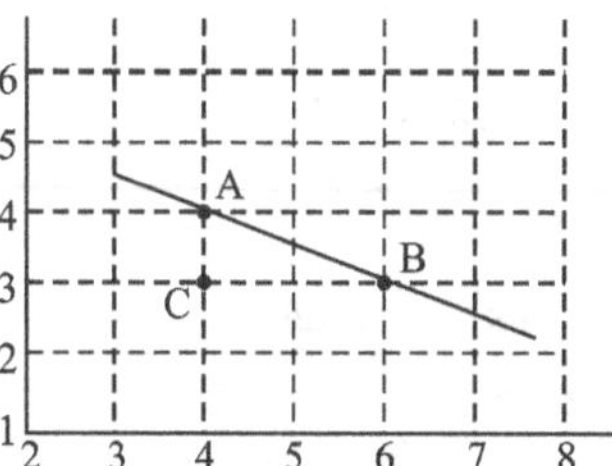

$$\backslash T_{1/2} = \frac{0.693}{\lambda} = 0.693 \times 2 = 1.386 \text{ years}$$

Now $\dfrac{N}{N_0} = \left(\dfrac{1}{2}\right)^{\frac{t}{T_{1/2}}} \Rightarrow \dfrac{1}{p} = \left(\dfrac{1}{2}\right)^{\frac{4.16}{1.386}} = \dfrac{1}{8}$

12. **4** We have $K_\alpha = \dfrac{m_y}{m_y + m_\alpha}.Q$

$$\Rightarrow K_\alpha = \frac{A-4}{A}.Q \Rightarrow 48 = \frac{A-4}{A}.50 \Rightarrow A = 100$$

13. **1** Let $\lambda_A = \lambda \ \therefore\ \lambda_B = 2\lambda$
If N_0 is total no. of atoms in A and B at $t = 0$, then initial rate of disintegration of $A = \lambda N_0$, and initial rate of disintegration of $B = 2\lambda N_0$

As $\lambda_B = 2\lambda_A \ \therefore\ T_B = \dfrac{1}{2}T_A$

i.e. half life of B is half the half life of A.
After one half life of A.

$$\left(-\frac{dN}{dt}\right)_A = \frac{\lambda N_0}{2}$$

Equivalently, after two half lives of B

$$\left(-\frac{dN}{dt}\right)_B = \frac{2\lambda N_0}{4} = \frac{\lambda N_0}{2}$$

Clearly, $\left(-\dfrac{dN}{dt}\right)_A = -\left(\dfrac{dN}{dt}\right)_B$

after n = 1, i.e., one half life of A.

14. **5** The formula for η of power will be

$$\eta = \frac{P_{our}}{P_{in}}$$

$$\therefore P_{in} = \frac{P_{out}}{\eta} = \frac{1000 \times 10^6}{0.1} = 10^{10}\ \text{W}$$

Energy required for this power is given by

$$P = \frac{E}{t}$$

$\therefore E = P \times t = 1010 \times 86,400 \times 365 \times 10 = 3.1536 \times 10^{18}\ \text{J}$
$200 \times 1.6 \times 10^{-13}$ J of energy is released by 1 fission
$= 3.1536 \times 10^{18}$ J of energy is released by

$$\frac{3.1536 \times 10^{18}}{200 \times 1.6 \times 10^{-13}} = 0.9855 \times 10^{29} \text{ fission}$$

$$= 0.985 \times 10^{29} \, U^{235} \text{ atoms.}$$

$$\therefore 0.9855 \times 10^{29} \text{ atoms of Uranium has}$$

$$\frac{235 \times 0.9855 \times 10^{29}}{6.023 \times 10^{23}} \cong 40 \times 10^{6} g$$

15. (a) $X \longrightarrow Y \longrightarrow Z$

$$A_0 = \lambda_X N_X(0) = \lambda_Y N_Y(0)$$

where $\lambda_X = \dfrac{\ln 2}{2}, \lambda_Y = \dfrac{\ln 2}{1}$

Putting these values in the given equation for N_Y, we get, (at $t = 0$).

$$C_1 = -\frac{A_0}{2}$$

16. (a) From equation (i) given in the passage.

$$N_Y = \frac{1}{\lambda_Y - \lambda_X}\left[A_0 e^{-\lambda_X t} - \frac{A_0}{2} e^{-\lambda_Y t} \right]$$

17. (d) Total energy released from $Au^{198} \to Hg^{198}$ in ground

state $= (\Delta m_{loss}) c^2 = (197.9682 - 197.9662)(930) = 1.86$ MeV

Energy released from ^{198}Hg in first excited state $\to Hg$ in ground state $= (-1.6) - (-2) \, MeV$

$$= 0.4 \, MeV$$

$\Rightarrow$ Energy released from $Ag^{198} \to Hg^{198}$ second excited state

$= 1.86 - 0.4 = 1.46 \, MeV = \max K.E. \text{ of } \beta_2 \text{ particle.}$

18. (a)

19. (A) $\to$ r (B) $\to$ s (C) $\to$ p (D) $\to$ q

20. (A) $\to$ p, q, s; (B) $\to$ q; (C) $\to$ r; (D) $\to$ r

(p) When an uncharged capacitor is connected to a battery, it becomes charged and energy is stored in the capacitor. (A) is the correct option.

(q) When a gas in an adiabatic container fitted with an adiabatic piston is compressed by pushing the piston

(i) the internal energy of the system increases

$$\Delta U = Q - W = 0 - (-PdV) = +PdV$$

(ii) Mechanical energy is proceeded to the piston which is converted into kinetic energy of the gas molecules.

(r) When a heavy nucleus initially at rest splits into two nuclei of nearly equal masses and some neutrons are emitted then

(i) Internal energy of the system is converted into mechanical energy (precisely speaking kinetic energy) and

(ii) Mass of the system decreases which converts into energy.

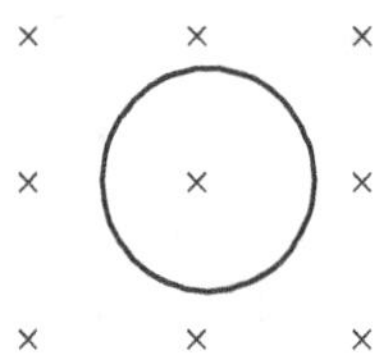

(s) When a resistive wire loops is placed in a time varying magnetic field perpendicular to its palne.

(i) Induced current shows in the loop due to which the energy of system is increased.

Mock Test Full Syllabus Physics

Paper - 1

SECTION – I – Multiple Correct Choice Type

This section contains 7 multiple choice quesitons. Each question has 4 choices (a), (b), (c) and (d) for its answer, out of which ONE OR MORE is/are correct.

1. Figure shows the variation of frequency of a characteristic X-ray and atomic number.

   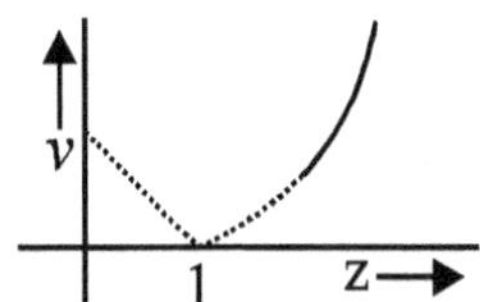

   (a) The characteristic X-ray is K_β
   (b) The characteristic X-ray is K_α
   (c) The energy of photon emitted when this X-ray is emitted by a metal having $Z = 101$ is 204 keV.
   (d) The energy of photon emitted when this X-ray is emitted by a metal having $Z = 101$ is 102 keV.

2. Graph shows a hypothetical speed distribution for a sample

   of N gas particle (for $v > v_0$; $\dfrac{dN}{dv} = 0$)

   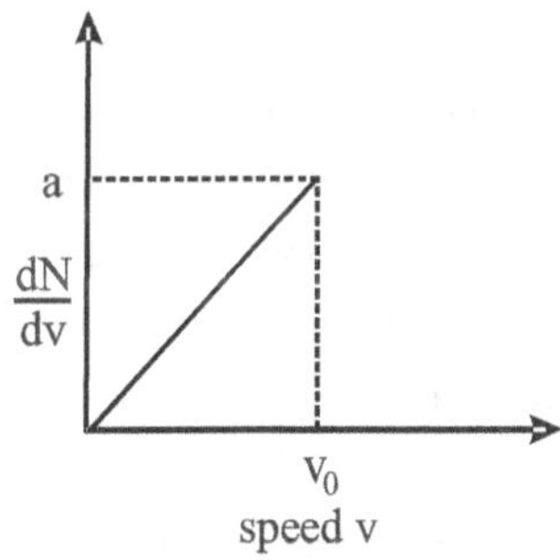

   (a) The value of (av_0) is 2N

   (b) The ratio v_{avg}/v_0 is equal to 2/3

   (c) The ratio v_{rms}/v_0 is equal to $1/\sqrt{2}$

   (d) Three fourth of the total particle has a speed between $0.5v_0$ and v_0.

3. Standing waves are produced on a stretched string of length L with fixed ends . When there is a node at a distance L/3 from one end, then :
   (a) minimum and next higher number of nodes excluding the ends are 2, 5 respectively
   (b) minimum and next higher number of nodes excluding the ends are 2, 4 respectively
   (c) frequency produced may be V/3L
   (d) frequency produced may be 3V/2L
   [V = Velocity of waves in the string]

4. From a cylinder of radius R, a cylinder of radius R/2 is removed, as shown.

   Current flowing in the remaining cylinder is I. Magnetic field strength is

   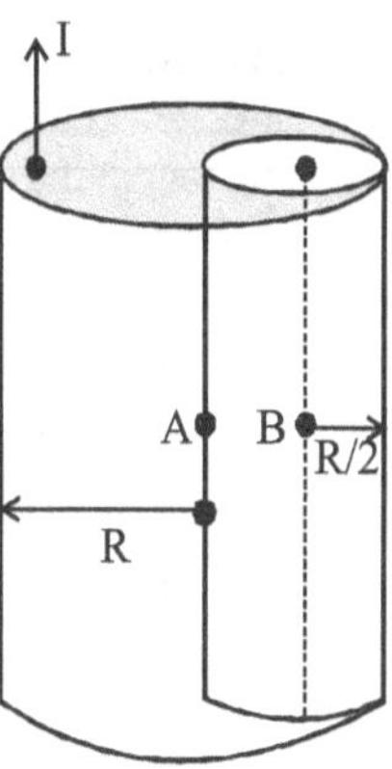

   (a) Zero at point A
   (b) Zero at point B
   (c) $\dfrac{\mu_0 I}{3\pi R}$ at point A
   (d) $\dfrac{\mu_0 I}{3\pi R}$ at point B

5. The magnitudes of the gravitational field at distance r_1 and r_2 from the centre of a uniform sphere of radius R and mass m are F_1 and F_2 respectively. Then:

   (a) $\dfrac{F_1}{F_2} = \dfrac{r_1}{r_2}$ if $r_1 < R$ and $r_2 < R$

   (b) $\dfrac{F_1}{F_2} = \dfrac{r_2^2}{r_1^2}$ if $r_1 > R$ and $r_2 > R$

   (c) $\dfrac{F_1}{F_2} = \dfrac{r_1}{r_2}$ if $r_1 > R$ and $r_2 > R$

   (d) $\dfrac{F_1}{F_2} = \dfrac{r_1^2}{r_2^2}$ if $r_1 < R$ and $r_2 < R$

6. An ideal monoatomic gas is confined in a horizontal cylinder by a spring loaded piston (as shown in the figure). Initially the gas is at temperature T_1, pressure P_1 and volume V_1 and the spring is in its relaxed state. The gas is then heated very slowly to temperature T_2, pressure P_2 and volume V_2. During this process the piston moves out by a distance x. Ignoring the friction between the piston and the cylinder, the correct statement(s) is (are)

   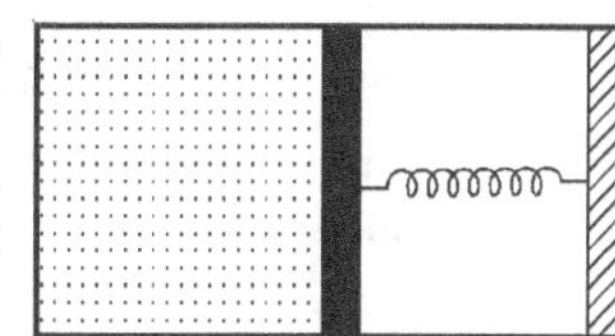

   (a) If $V_2 = 2V_1$ and $T_2 = 3T_1$, then the energy stored in the spring is $\dfrac{1}{4} P_1 V_1$

   (b) If $V_2 = 2V_1$ and $T_2 = 3T_1$, then the change in internal energy is $3P_1V_1$

   (c) If $V_2 = 3V_1$ and $T_2 = 4T_1$, then the work done by the gas is $\dfrac{7}{3} P_1 V_1$

   (d) If $V_2 = 3V_1$ and $T_2 = 4T_1$, then the heat supplied to the gas is $\dfrac{17}{6} P_1 V_1$

7. A parallel plate capacitor has a dielectric slab of dielectric constant K between its plates that covers 1/3 of the area of its plates, as shown in the figure. The total capacitance of the capacitor is C while that of the portion with dielectric in between is C_1. When the capacitor is charged, the plate area covered by the dielectric gets charge Q_1 and the rest of the area gets charge Q_2. The electric field in the dielectric is E_1 and that in the other portion is E_2. Choose the correct option/options, ignoring edge effects.

(a) $\dfrac{E_1}{E_2} = 1$

(b) $\dfrac{E_1}{E_2} = \dfrac{1}{K}$

(c) $\dfrac{Q_1}{Q_2} = \dfrac{3}{K}$

(d) $\dfrac{C}{C_1} = \dfrac{2+K}{K}$

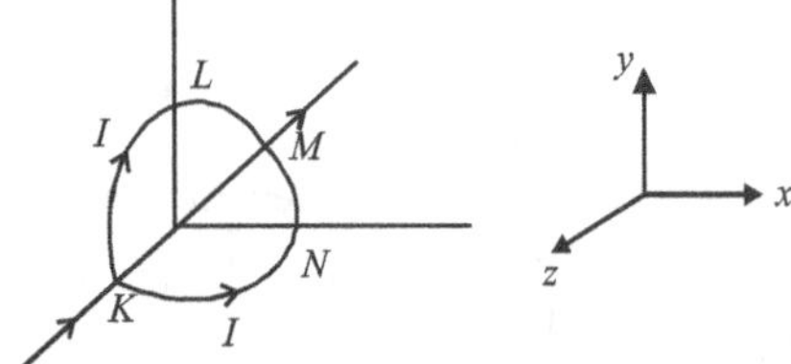

SECTION – II - Integer Answer Type

This section contains 5 questions. The answer to each of the questions is a single-digit integer, ranging from 0 to 9. The appropriate bubbles below the respective question numbers in the ORS have to be darkened. For example, if the correct answers to question numbers X, Y, Z and W (say) are 6, 0, 9 and 2, respectively, then the correct darkening of bubbles will look like the following:

X	Y	Z	W
⓪	⓪	⓪	⓪
①	①	①	①
②	②	②	②
③	③	③	③
④	④	④	④
⑤	⑤	⑤	⑤
⑥	⑥	⑥	⑥
⑦	⑦	⑦	⑦
⑧	⑧	⑧	⑧
⑨	⑨	⑨	⑨

8. Find the self inductance (in henry) of a coil in which an e.m.f. of 10 V is induced when the current in the circuit changes uniformly from 1 A to 0.5 A in 0.2 sec.

9. A circular loop of radius R is bent along a diameter and given a shape as shown in the figure. One of the semicircles (KNM) lies in the x-z plane and the other one (KLM) in the y-z plane with their centres at the origin. Current I is flowing through each of the semi-circles as shown in figure.

A particle of charge q is released at the origin with a velocity $\vec{v} = -v_0\hat{i}$. Find the magnitude of instantaneous force $\vec{F}$ on the particle if $\mu_0 q v_0 I = 8$ R. Assume that space is gravity free.

10. Consider a parallel plate capacitor of capacity 10 μF with air filled in the gap between the plates. Now one half of the space between the plates is filled with a dielectric of dielectric constant K = 4 as shown in figure. If the new capacitance of the capacitor (in μF) is 5^x, find the value of x?

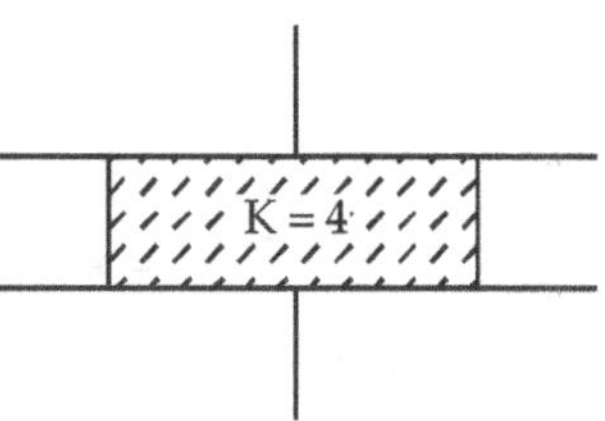

11. 0.05 kg steam at 373 K and 0.45 kg of ice at 253K are mixed in an insulated vessel. Find the equilibrium temperature (in degree celcius) of the mixture. Given, L_{fusion} = 80 cal/g = 336 J/g, $L_{vaporization}$ = 540 cal/g = 2268 J/g, S_{ice} = 2100 J/kg K = 0.5 cal/gK and S_{water} = 4200 J/kg K = 1 cal/gK

12. In a resonance tube experiment to determine speed of sound, air column in the pipe is made to resonate with a given tuning fork of frequency 480 Hz. The diameter of the pipe is 5 cm and it is open at one end. The smallest resonating length is observed to be 16 cm. The speed of sound in m/s from the given experimental data is found to be $(330 + z)$. Find the value of z.

SECTION – III - Matching Type

This section contains 6 questions of Matching Type, contains two tables each having 3 columns and 4 rows. Based on each table, there are three questions. Each question has four options (a), (b), (c) and (d) ONLY ONE of these four options is correct.

(Qs. 13-15): By appropriately matching the information given in the three columns of the following table, give the answer of the question that follows.

When a body performed translatory as well as rotatory motion we say it is rolling motion. Figure in column I shows the different types of motion while column II and III gives the corresponding velocity of topmost point P and contact point O of the sphere respectively.

	Column I		Column II		Column III
I.	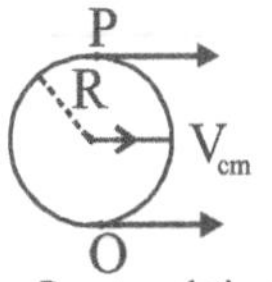 Pure translational	(i)	$V_p = V_{cm} + \omega R$	(P)	$V_0 \neq O$
II.	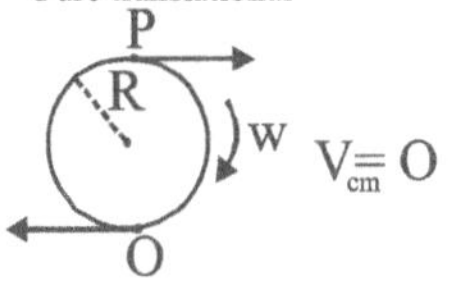 Pure rotational	(ii)	$V_p \neq 2\omega R$	(Q)	$V_0 = O$
III.	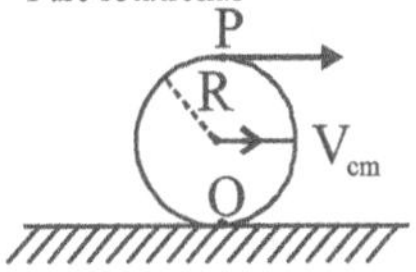 Rolling without slipping	(iii)	$V_p = V_{cm}$	(R)	$V_0 = -R\omega$
IV.	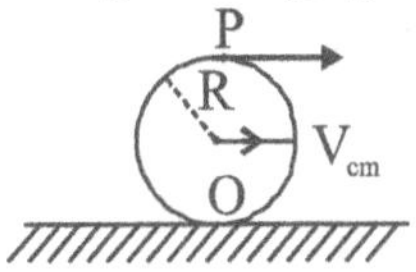 Rolling with slipping	(iv)	$V_p = R\omega$	(S)	$V_0 = V_{cm}$

13. If $\omega = 2 sec^{-1}$, R = 4cm, then the velocity of point P and velocity of contact point O for the sphere in pure rotational motion are equal in magnitude but opposite in direction. The correct matching for pure rotational motion is :

(a) II (iii) Q (b) II (iv) R (c) IV (i) Q (d) II (ii) Q

14. Which of the following is the correct matching for the body rolling without slipping?

(a) III (i) Q (b) I (iii) P (c) III (iv) S (d) III (iii) R

15. Which of the following is incorrect matching?

(a) I (iii) S (b) II (iv) R (c) IV (iii) Q (d) IV (ii) P

(Qs. 16-18): By appropriately matching the information given in the three columns of the following table, give the answer of the question that follows.

Time period of spring-mass system executing S.H.M is given by $T = 2\pi\sqrt{\frac{M}{K_{eff}}}$ Column I shows the spring-mass system executing S.H.M. column II shows the force constant (spring constant) of the combination, while column III represents the time period of the oscillation.

	Column I		Column II		Column III
I.	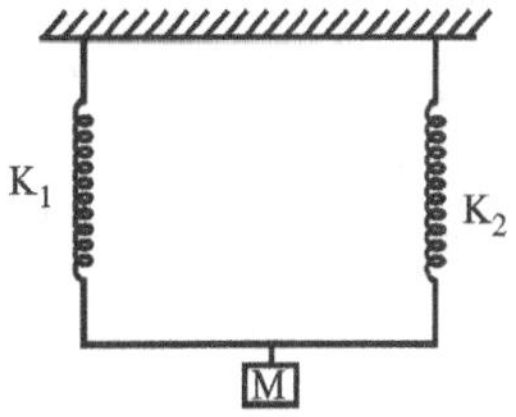	(i)	$K = K_1 + K_2$	(P)	$T = 2\pi[M/K_1 + K_2]^{1/2}$
II.	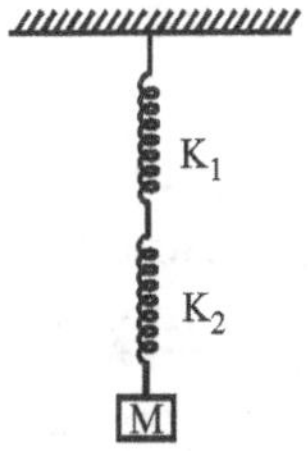	(ii)	$K = K_1 + 2K_2$	(Q)	$T = 2\pi[M(K_1 + K_2)/K_1K_2]^{1/2}$
III.	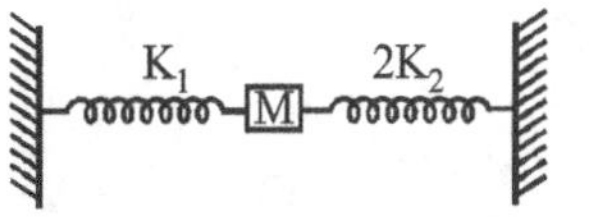	(iii)	$K = \frac{K_1K_2}{K_1 + K_2}$	(R)	$T = 2\pi[M(2K_1 + K_2)/2K_1K_2]^{1/2}$

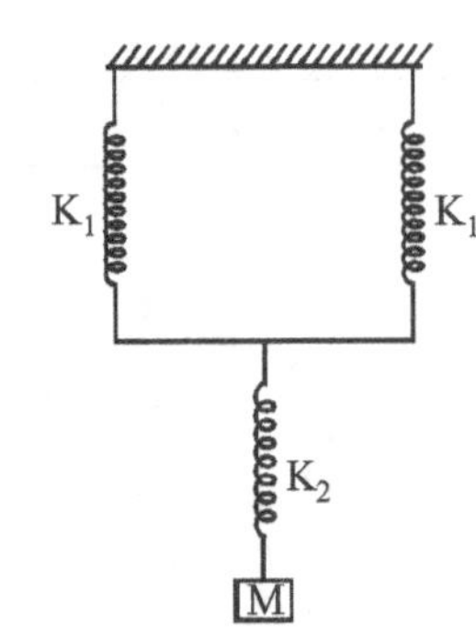

IV.

(iv) $K = \dfrac{2K_1 K_2}{2K_1 + K_2}$

(S) $T = 2\pi\left[M/K_1 + 2K_2\right]^{1/2}$

---

16. If the time period of the combination of spring-mass system shown in column I (III) [if $K_1 = K_2 = K^1$] is $2\pi\sqrt{M/3K^1}$. The correct matching for the system is:

(a) III (i) P   (b) III (ii) S   (c) III (iv) R   (d) IV (iii) Q

17. The spring constant for the combination shown in the column I (II) becomes twice if K_1 and K_2 becomes twice. Then correct matching shown for this spring-mass system is

(a) II (iii) Q   (b) I (ii) S   (c) II (i) P   (d) II (iv) R

18. Which of the following shows the wrong matching?

(a) I (i) P (b)   II (iii) Q   (c) III (ii) R   (d) IV (iv) R

Paper - 2

SECTION – I - Single Correct Choice Type

This section contains 7 multiple choice questions. Each question has 4 choices (a), (b), (c) and (d) for its answer, out of which ONLY ONE is correct.

---

1. As shown in arrangement, waves with identical wavelengths and amplitudes that are initially in phase travel through different media, ray 1 travels through air and ray 2 through a transparent medium for equal length L, in four different situations. In each situation the two rays reach a common point on the screen.

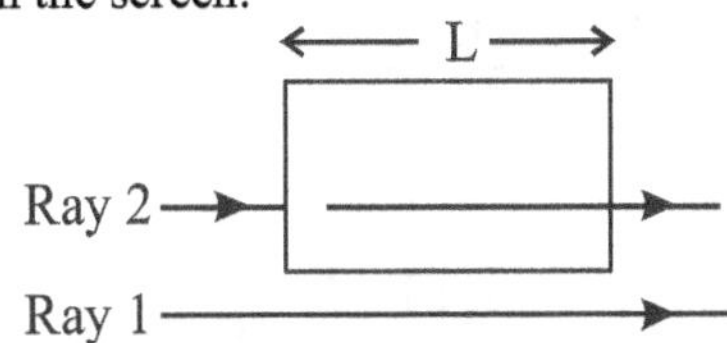

The number of wavelengths in length L is N_2 for ray 2 and N_1 for ray 1. In the following table, values of N_1 and N_2 are given for all four situations. The order of the situations according to the intensity of the light at the common point in descending order is

Situations	1	2	3	4
N_1	2.25	1.80	3.00	3.25
N_2	2.75	2.80	3.25	4.00

(a) $I_3 = I_4 > I_2 > I_1$ (b) $I_1 > I_3 = I_4 > I_2$

(c) $I_1 > I_2 > I_3 > I_4$ (d) $I_2 > I_3 = I_4 > I_1$

2. If the magnetic field at P can be written as $K \tan(\alpha/2)$ then K is

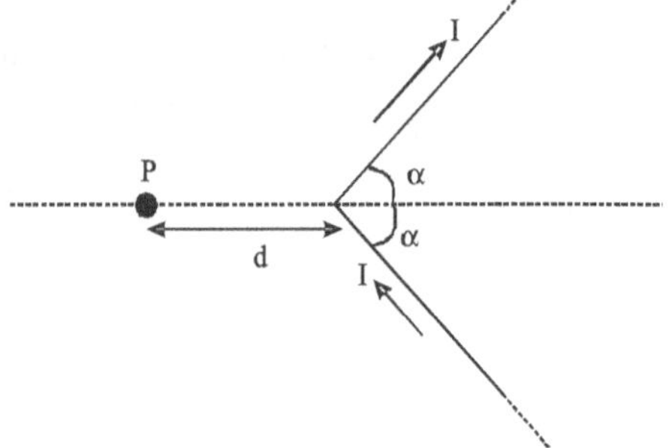

(a) $\dfrac{\mu_0 I}{4\pi d}$ (b) $\dfrac{\mu_0 I}{2\pi d}$

(c) $\dfrac{\mu_0 I}{\pi d}$ (d) $\dfrac{2\mu_0 I}{\pi d}$

3. The molar heat capacity C for an ideal gas going through a given process is given by $C = a/T$, where 'a' is a constant. If $\gamma = C_P/C_V$, the work done by one mole of gas during heating from T_0 to ηT_0 through the given process will be

(a) $\dfrac{1}{a}\ln\eta$ (b) $a\ln\eta - \left(\dfrac{\eta-1}{\gamma-1}\right)RT_0$

(c) $a\ln\eta - (\gamma-1)RT_0$ (d) none of these

4. Let $y = \ell^2 - \dfrac{\ell^3}{z}$ where $\ell = 2.0 \pm 0.1$, $z = 1.0 \pm 0.1$ then the value of y is given by

(a) $+2 \pm 0.8$ (b) -4 ± 1.6

(c) -4 ± 0.8 (d) None of these

5. An electric field is given by $E_x = -2x^3$ kN/C. The value of the potential at the point $(1, -2)$, if potential of the point $(2, 4)$ is taken as zero, is

(a) 7.5×10^3 V   (b) 2.5×10^3 V

(c) 15×10^3 V   (d) 5×10^3 V

6. A wall is moving with velocity u and a source of sound moves with velocity u/2 in the same direction as shown in the figure. Assuming that the sound travels with velocity 10u, the ratio of incident sound wavelength on the wall to the reflected sound wavelength by the wall, is equal to

(a) $9:11$

(b) $11:9$

(c) $4:5$

(d) $5:4$

7. Which of the following statement(s) is/are correct ?

(a) A particle has initial velocity $\vec{u} = 2\hat{i} + 3\hat{j}$ and acceleration $\vec{a} = 3\hat{i} - 2\hat{j}$ always. It's resultant path will be a circle.

(b) The potential energy of a particle moving along x-axis in a conservative force field is $U = 2x^2 - 5x + 1$ in S.I. units. No other forces are acting on it. It performs SHM.

(c) A standing wave pattern is formed on a string. The power transfer through a point (other than node and antinode) is zero always.

(d) None of these

SECTION – II - Multiple Correct Choice Type

This section contains 7 multiple choice questions. Each question has 4 choices (a), (b), (c) and (d) for its answer, out of which ONE OR MORE is/are correct.

---

8. Suppose the potential energy between electron and proton at a distance r is given by $-\dfrac{Ke^2}{3r^3}$. Application of Bohr's theory to hydrogen atom in this case shows that

(a) energy in the nth orbit is proportional to n^6

(b) energy is proportional to m^{-3} (m : mass of electron)

(c) energy in the nth orbit is proportional to n^{-2}

(d) energy is proportional to m^3 (m = mass of electron)

9. Which of the following is/are conservative force(s) ?

(a) $\vec{F} = 2r^3\hat{r}$

(b) $\vec{F} = -\dfrac{5}{r}\hat{r}$

(c) $\vec{F} = \dfrac{3(x\hat{i} + y\hat{j})}{(x^2 + y^2)^{3/2}}$

(d) $\vec{F} = \dfrac{3(y\hat{i} + x\hat{j})}{(x^2 + y^2)^{3/2}}$

10. Relation between current in conductor and time is shown in figure then correct options are

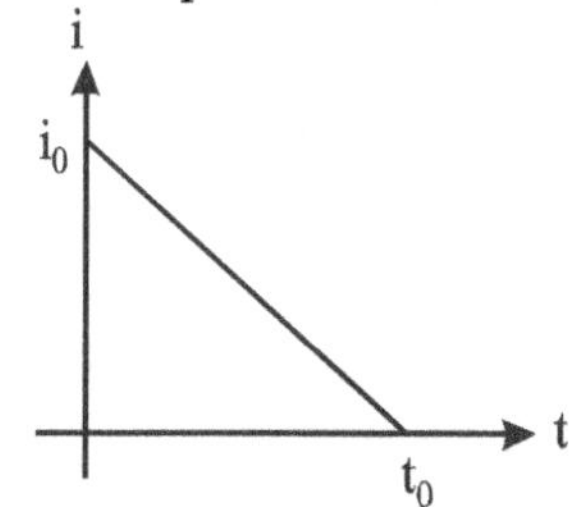

(a) Total charge flow through the conductor is $\dfrac{1}{2}i_0 t_0$

(b) Expression of current in terms of time is $i_0\left(1 - \dfrac{t}{t_0}\right)$

(c) If resistance of conductor is R then total heat dissipated across resistance R is $\dfrac{Rt_0 i_0^2}{3}$

(d) If resistance of conductor is R then total heat dissipated across resistance R is $\dfrac{2Rt_0 i_0^2}{3}$

11. In the circuit shown, resistance R = 100Ω, inductance $L = \dfrac{2}{\pi}$ H and capacitance $C = \dfrac{8}{\pi}\,\mu F$ are connected in series with an ac source of 200 volt and frequency f. If the readings of the hot wire voltmeters V_1 and V_2 are same then

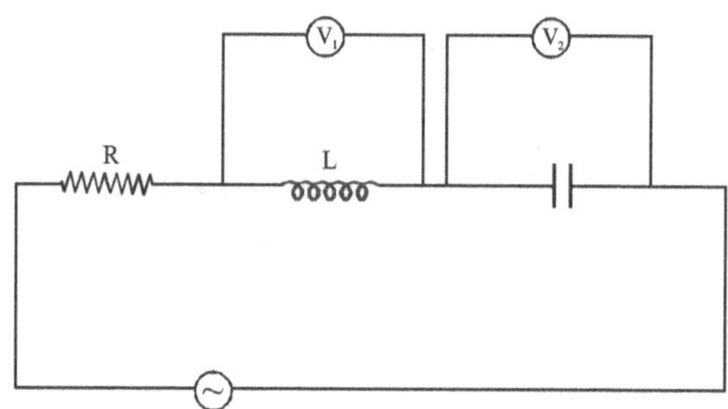

(a) $f = 250\,\pi$ Hz

(b) $f = 125$ Hz

(c) current through R is 2A

(d) $V_1 = V_2 = 1000$ volt

12. The dimensions of energy per unit volume are the same as those of

(a) work

(b) stress

(c) pressure

(d) modulus of elasticity

13. A parallel plate capacitor having plates of area S and plate separation d, has capacitance C_1 in air. When two dielectrics of different relative primitivities ($\varepsilon_1 = 2$ and $\varepsilon_2 = 4$) are introduced between the two plates as shown in the figure, the capacitance becomes C_2. Which is not the correct ratio of C_2/C_1 :-

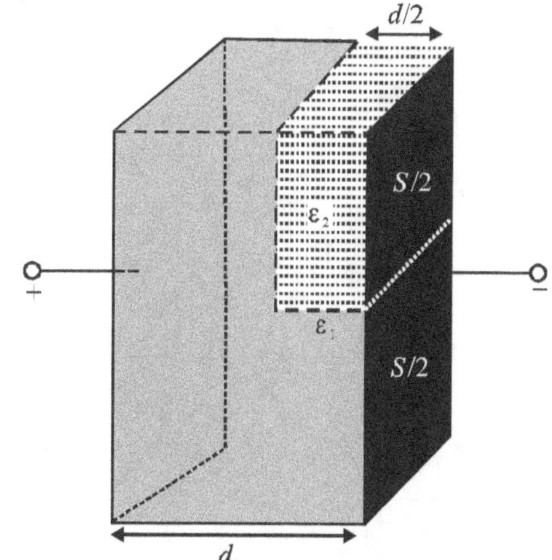

(a) 6/5 (b) 5/3
(c) 7/5 (d) 7/3

14. Two spheres P and Q of equal radii have densities ρ_1 and ρ_2, respectively. The spheres are connected by a massless string and placed in liquids L_1 and L_2 of densities σ_1 and σ_2 and viscosities η_1 and η_2, respectively. They float in equilibrium with the sphere P in L_1 and sphere Q in L_2 and the string being taut (see figure). If sphere P alone in L_2 has terminal velocity $\vec{V}_P$ and Q alone in L_1 has terminal velocity $\vec{V}_Q$, then

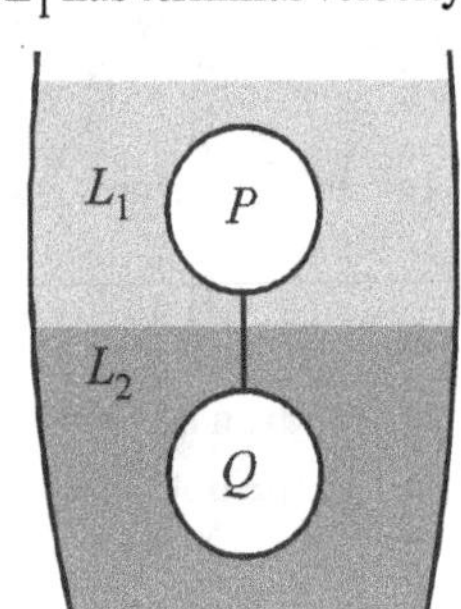

(a) $\dfrac{\left|\vec{V}_P\right|}{\left|\vec{V}_Q\right|} = \dfrac{\eta_1}{\eta_2}$

(b) $\dfrac{\left|\vec{V}_P\right|}{\left|\vec{V}_Q\right|} = \dfrac{\eta_2}{\eta_1}$

(c) $\vec{V}_P \cdot \vec{V}_Q > 0$

(d) $\vec{V}_P \cdot \vec{V}_Q < 0$

SECTION – III - Comprehension Type

This section contains 2 paragraphs. Each paragraph has 2 multiple choice questions based on a paragraph. Each question has 4 choices (a), (b), (c) and (d) for its answer, out of which ONLY ONE is correct.

PARAGRAPH - 1

If the current flowing through the coil is i and the flux linked with each turn is ϕ, then the total flux linkage is $N\phi$.

$$N\phi \propto i \text{ or } N\phi = Li$$

where L is a constant called the 'coefficient of self-induction' or 'self-inductance' of the coil. By the above equation, we have $L = N\phi/i$.

In this equation, if $i = 1$, then $L = N\phi$. Hence the coefficient of self-induction of a coil is equal to the number of flux-linkages in the coil when unit current is flowing in the coil.

Alternatively, the coefficient of self inductance can be defined as twice of the work done in establishing a flow of one ampere current in the circuit. This energy is stored in the magnetic field of the inductor.

15. A long coaxial cable consists of two concentric cylinders of radii a and b. The central conductor of the cable carries a steady current i and the outer conductor provides the return path of the current. The self inductance of this length l of the cable is

(a) $\dfrac{\mu_0 \ell}{2\pi} \log_e\left(\dfrac{b}{a}\right)$

(b) $\dfrac{\mu_0 \ell}{\pi} \log_e\left(\dfrac{b}{a}\right)$

(c) $\dfrac{\mu_0 \ell}{2\pi} \log_e\left(\dfrac{a}{b}\right)$

(d) $\dfrac{\mu_0 \ell}{\pi} \log_e\left(\dfrac{a}{b}\right)$

16. Calculate the self inductance per unit length of a current loop formed by joining the ends of two long parallel wires of radius r separated by a distance d between their axes, neglecting the end effects and magnetic flux within the wires.

(a) $\dfrac{\mu_0}{2\pi} \log_e \dfrac{d-r}{r}$

(b) $\dfrac{\mu_0}{2\pi} \log_e \dfrac{d+r}{r}$

(c) $\dfrac{\mu_0}{\pi} \log_e \dfrac{d-r}{r}$

(d) None of these

PARAGRAPH - 2

If the container filled with liquid gets accelerated horizontally or vertically, pressure in liquids gets changed. In case of horizontally accelerated liquid (a_x), the free surface has the slope $\dfrac{a_x}{g}$. In case of vertically accelerated liquid (a_y) for calculation of pressure, effective g is used. A closed box with horizontal base 6m by 6m and a height 2m is half filled with liquid. It is given a constant horizontal acceleration g/2 and vertical downward acceleration g 2.

17. The angle of the free surface with the horizontal is equal to

(a) $30°$ (b) $\tan^{-1}(2/3)$
(c) $\tan^{-1}(1/3)$ (d) $45°$

18. Length of exposed portion of top of box is equal to

(a) 2m (b) 3m
(c) 4m (d) 2.5m

SOLUTIONS

<table>
<tr><td colspan="8" align="center">ANSWER KEY - PAPER 1</td></tr>
<tr><td>1</td><td>(b, d)</td><td>6</td><td>(a, b, c)</td><td>11</td><td>0</td><td>16</td><td>(b)</td></tr>
<tr><td>2</td><td>(a, b, c, d)</td><td>7</td><td>(a, d)</td><td>12</td><td>6</td><td>17</td><td>(a)</td></tr>
<tr><td>3</td><td>(a, d)</td><td>8</td><td>4</td><td>13</td><td>(b)</td><td>18</td><td>(c)</td></tr>
<tr><td>4</td><td>(c, d)</td><td>9</td><td>2</td><td>14</td><td>(a)</td><td></td><td></td></tr>
<tr><td>5</td><td>(a, b)</td><td>10</td><td>2</td><td>15</td><td>(c)</td><td></td><td></td></tr>
<tr><td colspan="8" align="center">ANSWER KEY - PAPER 2</td></tr>
<tr><td>1</td><td>(d)</td><td>6</td><td>(a)</td><td>11</td><td>(b, c, d)</td><td>16</td><td>(c)</td></tr>
<tr><td>2</td><td>(b)</td><td>7</td><td>(b)</td><td>12</td><td>(b, c, d)</td><td>17</td><td>(d)</td></tr>
<tr><td>3</td><td>(b)</td><td>8</td><td>(a, b)</td><td>13</td><td>(a, b, c)</td><td>18</td><td>(c)</td></tr>
<tr><td>4</td><td>(b)</td><td>9</td><td>(a, b, c)</td><td>14</td><td>(a, d)</td><td></td><td></td></tr>
<tr><td>5</td><td>(a)</td><td>10</td><td>(a, b, c)</td><td>15</td><td>(a)</td><td></td><td></td></tr>
</table>

EXPLANATORY NOTES

Paper -1

1. (b, d)

From Moseley's law $\sqrt{v} = a(Z-b)$

$v = 0$ at $Z = b$ — From graph $v = 0$ at $Z = 1$

$\therefore b = 1$ — $\therefore K_\alpha$

For K_α, $\sqrt{v} = \sqrt{\dfrac{3RC}{4}}\,(Z-1)$

Put $Z = 101 \Rightarrow \sqrt{v} = \sqrt{\dfrac{3RC}{4}}\,100$

Photon energy $= hv$

$= \dfrac{3}{4}hRC\,100^2 = \dfrac{3}{4} \times (13.6\,\text{eV}) \times 100^2 = 102\,\text{keV}$

2. (a, b, c, d)

Area under the curve is equal to number of molecules of the gas sample.

Hence $N = \dfrac{1}{2}av_0 \Rightarrow av_0 = 2N$

Also, $\dfrac{dN}{v\,dv} = \dfrac{a}{v_0}$

$v_{avg} = \dfrac{\displaystyle\int_0^{v_0} v\,dN}{N} = \dfrac{1}{N}\int_0^{v_0} \dfrac{v^2 a}{v_0}\,dv = \dfrac{2}{3}v_0$ (using $av_0 = 2N$)

$\Rightarrow \dfrac{v_{avg}}{v_0} = \dfrac{2}{3}$

$v_{rms}^2 = \dfrac{1}{N}\int_0^{v} v^2\,dN = \dfrac{1}{N}\int_0^{v_0} v^2\,\dfrac{a}{v_0}\,v\,dv = \dfrac{v_0^2}{2}$

$\Rightarrow \dfrac{v_{rms}}{v_0} = \dfrac{1}{\sqrt{2}}$

Area under the curve from $0.5\,v_0$ to v_0 is $\dfrac{3}{4}$ of total area.

3. (a, d) $\dfrac{3\lambda}{2} = L$

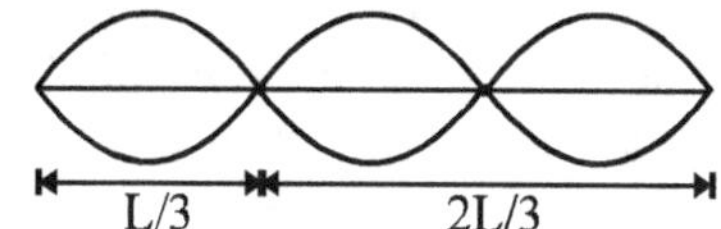

Minimum nodes $= 2$, Fundamental $v = \dfrac{3}{2L}\,V$

(excluding ends)

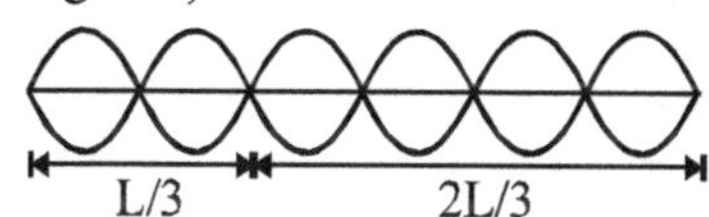

Next higher nodes $= 5$

4. (c, d)

For cylinder :

$B = \dfrac{\mu_0 I r}{2\pi R^2}$; $\qquad r < a$

$B = \dfrac{\mu_0 I}{2\pi r}$; $\qquad r \geq a$

$\vec{B}_{\text{due to remaining portion}} = \vec{B}_{\text{due to whole cylinder}} - \vec{B}_{\text{due to removed portion}}$

Current that can be consider in whole cylinder $= 4I/3$ and in removed part $= I/3$.

At point A : $B = 0 - \dfrac{\mu_0(I/3)}{2\pi\,(R/2)} = -\dfrac{\mu_0 I}{3\pi R}$

At point B : $B = \dfrac{\mu_0}{2}\left(\dfrac{4I/3}{\pi R^2}\right)\left(\dfrac{R}{2}\right) - 0 = \dfrac{\mu_0 I}{3\pi R}$

5. (a, b) For $r > R$, the gravitational field is $F = \dfrac{GM}{r^2}$

$\therefore \quad F_1 = \dfrac{GM}{r_1^2}$ and $F_2 = \dfrac{GM}{r_2^2} \Rightarrow \dfrac{F_1}{F_2} = \dfrac{r_2^2}{r_1^2}$

For $r < R$, the gravitational field is $F = \dfrac{GM}{R^3} \times r$

$\therefore \quad F_1 = \dfrac{GM}{R^3} \times r_1 \quad$ and $\quad F_2 = \dfrac{GM}{R^3} \times r_2$

$\Rightarrow \quad \dfrac{F_1}{F_2} = \dfrac{r_1}{r_2}$

6.   (a, b, c)

Applying combined gas law

$$\dfrac{P_1 V_1}{T_1} = \dfrac{P_2 V_2}{T_2}$$

If $V_2 = 2\,V_1$ and $T_2 = 3T_1$ then

$$\dfrac{P_1 V_1}{T_1} = \dfrac{P_2 \times 2V_1}{3T_1} \Rightarrow P_1 = \dfrac{2}{3} P_2$$

Now change in internal energy

$$\Delta U = \dfrac{f}{2}\, [nR\,(T_2 - T_1)] = \dfrac{f}{2}\,[P_2 V_2 - P_1 V_1]$$

For monoatomic gas $f = 3$

$$\Delta U = \dfrac{3}{2}\left[\dfrac{3}{2}\,P_1 \times 2V_1 - P_1 V_1\right] = 3P_1 V_1$$

$\therefore$ (b) is the correct option.

Now assuming that the pressure on the piston on the right hand side (not considering the affect of spring) remains the same throughout the motion of the piston then,

Pressure of gas $= P_1 + \dfrac{kx}{A} \Rightarrow P_2 = P_1 + \dfrac{kx}{A}$

where k is spring constant and A = area of piston

Energy stored $= \dfrac{1}{2}kx^2$

$$P_2 = P_1 + \dfrac{kx}{A} \Rightarrow \dfrac{3}{2}P_1 = P_1 + \dfrac{kx}{A}$$

$$\dfrac{P_1}{2} = \dfrac{kx}{A}$$

$\therefore \quad kx = \dfrac{P_1 A}{2}$

Also,

$V_2 = V_1 + Ax$

$V_1 = Ax$

$\therefore \quad x = \dfrac{V_1}{A}$

$\therefore \quad$ Energy $= \dfrac{1}{2}\dfrac{P_1 A}{2} \times \dfrac{V_1}{A} = \dfrac{1}{4}P_1 V_1$

$\therefore$ A is correct

Now

$$W = \int P\,dV = \int\left(P_1 + \dfrac{kx}{A}\right)dV = \int P_1\,dV + \int \dfrac{kx}{A}\,dV$$

$\therefore \quad W = \int P_1\,dV + \int \dfrac{kx}{A} \times (dx)\,A$

$\therefore \quad W = P_1\,(V_2 - V_1) + \dfrac{kx^2}{2}$

$$\left[\text{Here on applying } \dfrac{P_1 V_1}{T_1} = \dfrac{P_2 V_2}{T_2} \text{ we get } P_2 = \dfrac{4P_1}{3} \right.$$
$$\left. \text{and } V_2 = V_1 + Ax \Rightarrow x = \dfrac{2V_1}{A}\,[\because V_2 = 3V_1] \right]$$

$\therefore \; W = 2P_1 V_1 + \dfrac{1}{2} \times \dfrac{P_1 A}{3} \times \dfrac{2V_1}{A} = \dfrac{7}{3} P_1 V_1$

C is correct option

Heat supplied

$Q = W + \Delta U$

$\quad = \dfrac{7\,P_1 V_1}{3} + \dfrac{3}{2}\,(P_2 V_2 - P_1 V_1)$

$\quad = \dfrac{7P_1 V_1}{3} + \dfrac{3}{2}\left[\dfrac{4}{3}P_1\,3V_1 - P_1 V_1\right] = \dfrac{41}{6}P_1 V_1$

7.   (a, d)

This is a combination of two capacitors in parallel. Therefore

$C = C_1 + C_2$ $\qquad\qquad \therefore\; C_2 = C - C_1$

where $C_1 = \dfrac{kA}{3\epsilon_0 d}$ and $C - C_1 = \dfrac{2A}{3\epsilon_0 d}$

$\therefore\; \dfrac{C - C_1}{C_1} = \dfrac{2}{k}$ $\qquad \therefore\; \dfrac{C}{C_1} - 1 = \dfrac{2}{k}$

$\therefore\; \dfrac{C}{C_1} = \dfrac{2}{k} + 1$

$\dfrac{C}{C_1} = \dfrac{2}{k} + 1$

$\therefore$ (d) is a correct option.

Now, $Q_1 = C_1 V = \dfrac{kA}{3\epsilon_0 d} \times V$

and $Q_2 = (C - C_1)V = \dfrac{2A}{3\epsilon_0 d} \times V$

$\therefore\; \dfrac{Q_1}{Q_2} = \dfrac{k}{2}$ $\qquad\qquad \therefore$ (c) is incorrect

Also $V = E \times d$

$\therefore\; E = \dfrac{V}{d} = E_1 = E_2$ $\qquad \therefore$ (a) is a correct option

8.   4

Given : $e = 10$ V and $\dfrac{dI}{dt} = \dfrac{1 - 0.5}{0.2} = \dfrac{0.5}{0.2} = 2.5$ A/s

Self inductance of coil $\quad L = \dfrac{e}{dI/dt} = \dfrac{10}{2.5} = \mathbf{4\,H}$

9. **2**

Magnetic field $(\vec{B})$ at the origin = Magnetic field due to semicircle KLM + Magnetic field due to other semicircle KNM.

Therefore, $\vec{B} = \dfrac{\mu_0 I}{4R}(-\hat{i}) + \dfrac{\mu_0 I}{4R}(\hat{j})$

$\Rightarrow \quad \vec{B} = -\dfrac{\mu_0 I}{4R}\hat{i} + \dfrac{\mu_0 I}{4R}\hat{j} = \dfrac{\mu_0 I}{4R}(-\hat{i} + \hat{j})$

$[\vec{B}$ due to a circular current carrying loop is $\dfrac{\mu_0 I}{2R}$

$\therefore$ For semicircle it is half]

Therefore, magnetic force acting on the particle,

$\vec{F} = q(\vec{v} \times \vec{B}) = q\left\{(-v_0\hat{i}) \times (-\hat{i} + \hat{j}) \times \dfrac{\mu_0 I}{4R}\right\}$

$= \dfrac{-\mu_0 q v_0 I}{4R}\hat{k}$

$\therefore \quad |\vec{F}| = \dfrac{\mu_0 q v_0 I}{4R} = \dfrac{8R}{4R} = \textbf{2 units}$

10. **2**

The arrangement is equivalent to three capacitors in parallel

$C_1 = \dfrac{\varepsilon_o A/4}{d} = \dfrac{10}{4} = 2.5\,\mu\text{F}$;

$C_2 = \dfrac{K\varepsilon_o A/2}{d} = 4 \times \dfrac{10}{2} = 20\,\mu\text{F}$;

$C_3 = \dfrac{\varepsilon_o A/4}{d} = \dfrac{10}{2} = 2.5\,\mu\text{F}$

$\therefore \quad C_p = C_1 + C_2 + C_3 + = 2.5 + 20 + 2.5 = 25\,\mu\text{F} = 5^2\,\mu\text{F}$

$\therefore \quad \boldsymbol{x = 2}$

11. **0**

(1) Heat lost by steam at 100°C to change to 100°C water
$mL_{vap} = 0.05 \times 2268 \times 1000 = 1,13,400\,\text{J}$

(2) Heat lost by 100°C water to change to 0°C water
$= 0.05 \times 4200 \times 100 = 21,000\,\text{J}$

(3) Heat required by 0.45 kg of ice to change its temperature from 253 K to 273 K $= m \times S_{ice} \times \Delta T = 0.45 \times 2100 \times 20 = 18,900\,\text{J}$

(4) Heat required by 0.45 kg ice at 273 K to convert into 0.45 kg water at 273 K $= mL_{fusion} = 0.45 \times 336 \times 1000 = 151,200\,\text{J}$

From the above data it is clear that the amount of heat required by 0.45 kg of ice at 253 K to convert into 0.45 kg of water at 273 K (1,70,100 J) cannot be provided by heat lost by 0.05 kg of steam at 273 K to convert into water at 273 K. Therefore, the final temperature will be 273 K or **0°C.**

12. **6**

The smallest resonating length ℓ_1, corresponds to the fundamental mode. The diameter D, of the pipe is not very small compared to the resonating length ℓ_1. So one should account for the end correction which is generally taken to be in the range of 0.29 D to D/3. Taking the end correction to be 0.3 D.

$\ell_1 + 0.3D = \dfrac{\lambda}{4}$; where λ is the wavelength of the

fundamental mode.

Then $\lambda = 70$ cm and the velocity of sound $= 336$ m/s $= 330 + 6$

$\therefore \quad z = \textbf{6}$

13. **(b)** For pure rotational motion
$V_p = R\omega = 8\,\text{cm sec}^{-1}$ and $V_o = -R\omega = -8\,\text{cm sec}^{-1}$

14. **(a)** For body rolling without slipping
$V_p = V_{cm} + \omega R$ and $V_o = 0$

15. **(c)** For body in pure rotational motion
$V_p = V_o = V_{cm}$
For body rolling with slipping
$V_p \neq 2\omega R$ and $V_o \neq 0$

16. **(b)**

$K = K_1 + 2K_2 = K^1 + 2K^1 = 3K^1$

$\Rightarrow T = 2\pi\sqrt{M/3K^1}$

17. **(a)**

$K = \dfrac{K_1 K_2}{K_1 + K_2}$ but condition given as K_1 and K_2 becomes twice so

$K = \dfrac{2K_1 \times 2K_2}{2K_1 + 2K_2} = \dfrac{2K_1 K_2}{K_1 + K_2}$

18. **(c)** in case III, K_1 and $2K_2$ are parallel so $K = K_1 + 2K_2$,
$T = 2\pi\sqrt{M/K_1 + 2K_2}$

Paper -2

1. **(d)** In cases 1, 2, 3, 4 the path difference are respectively

$\dfrac{\lambda}{2}, \lambda, \dfrac{\lambda}{4}$ and $\dfrac{3\lambda}{4}$

$\Rightarrow$ phase difference are respectively

$\pi, 2\pi, \pi/2, 3\pi/2$ and $I = I_0 \cos^2\left(\dfrac{\phi}{2}\right)$

$\therefore$ the intensity in the four cases are $0, I_0, \dfrac{I_0}{2}, \dfrac{I_0}{2}$ respectively.

2. **(b)** Let us compute the magnetic field due to any one segment :

$B = \dfrac{\mu_0 I}{4\pi\,(d\sin\alpha)}(\cos 0° + \cos(180° - \alpha))$

$= \dfrac{\mu_0 I}{4\pi\,(d\sin\alpha)}(1 - \cos\alpha) = \dfrac{\mu_0 I}{4\pi d}\tan\dfrac{\alpha}{2}$

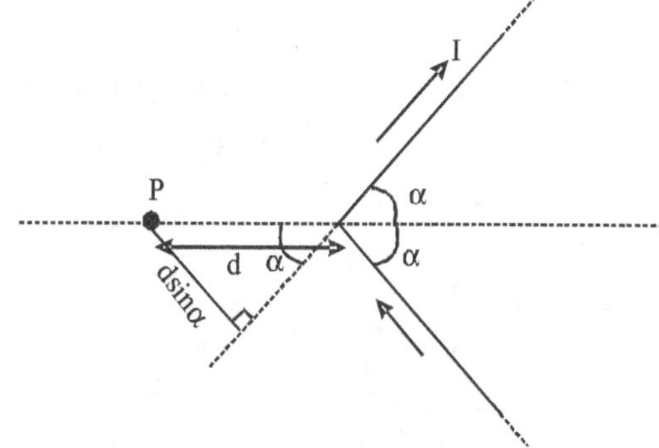

Resultant field will be

$$B_{net} = 2B = \frac{\mu_0 I}{2\pi d}\tan\frac{\alpha}{2} \Rightarrow K = \frac{\mu_0 I}{2\pi d}$$

3. (b)

$$Q = \int_{T_0}^{\eta T_0} C\,dT = a\ln\frac{\eta T_0}{T_0} = a\ln\eta$$

$$\Delta U = C_V\Delta T = \frac{R}{\gamma - 1}(\eta - 1)T_0$$

$$W = Q - \Delta U = a\ln\eta - \left[\frac{\eta - 1}{\gamma - 1}\right]RT_0$$

4. (b)

$$y = \ell^2 - \frac{\ell^3}{z}$$

$$dy = 2\ell d\ell - \left(\frac{z.3\ell^2 d\ell - \ell^3 dz}{z^2}\right) = \left(2\ell - \frac{3\ell^2}{z}\right)d\ell + \frac{\ell^3}{z^2}dz$$

$$= \left(2\times 2 - \frac{3\times 2^2}{1}\right)(\pm 0.1) + \frac{8}{1}(\pm 0.1)$$

$$= -8\,(\pm 0.1) + 8\,(\pm 0.1) = \pm 1.6$$

$$y = \ell^2 - \frac{\ell^3}{Z} = 2^2 - \frac{2^3}{1} = 4 - 8 = -4$$

$$\therefore\ y = -4 \pm 1.6$$

5. (a)

$$dV = -\vec{E}d\vec{r} = -(-2x^3\hat{i}).(dx\hat{i} + dy\hat{j} + dz\hat{k}) = 2x^3\,dx$$

$$\Rightarrow \int_0^V dV = \int_2^1 (2x^3)\times 10^3\,dx \Rightarrow V = -7.5\times 10^3\,V$$

6. (a) λ_i = wavelength of the incident sound

$$= \frac{10u - (u/2)}{f} = \frac{19u}{2f}$$

f_i = frequency of the incident sound

$$= \frac{10u - u}{10u - (u/2)}f = \frac{18}{19}f = f_r$$

= frequency of the reflected sound

λ_r = wavelength of the reflected sound

$$= \frac{10u + u}{f_r} = \frac{11u}{18f}\times 19 = \frac{11\times 19}{18}\cdot\frac{u}{f}$$

$$\frac{\lambda_i}{\lambda_r} = \frac{19u}{2f}\times\frac{18f}{11\times 19u} = \frac{9}{11}$$

7. (b) (i) $\because \vec{a}$ = constant and $\theta \neq 0, 180°$

$\therefore$ resultant path is parabola

(ii) $F = -\dfrac{dU}{dx} = -4x + 5$ $\therefore$ SHM

(iii) At node $v = 0$, at antinode tension $\perp$ to velocity

$\therefore$ at these points power = 0 $(P = \vec{F}.\vec{v})$

At other points $P \neq 0$

8. (a, b)

$$|F| = \frac{dU}{dr} = \frac{Ke^2}{r^4} \qquad \ldots\ldots\ldots\ldots(1)$$

$$\frac{Ke^2}{r^4} = \frac{mv^2}{r} \qquad \ldots\ldots\ldots\ldots(2)$$

and $mvr = \dfrac{nh}{2\pi}$ $\qquad \ldots\ldots\ldots\ldots(3)$

By (2) and (3),

$$r = \frac{Ke^2 4\pi^2}{h^2}\frac{m}{n^2} = K_1\frac{m}{n^2} \qquad \ldots\ldots\ldots\ldots(4)$$

From (2) $KE = \dfrac{1}{2}mv^2 = \dfrac{1}{2}\dfrac{Ke^2}{r^3}$

Total energy $= KE + PE = \dfrac{Ke^2}{2r^3} - \dfrac{Ke^2}{3r^3}$

$$= \frac{Ke^2}{6r^3} = \frac{Ke^2}{6\left(\dfrac{K_1 m}{n^2}\right)^3} = \frac{Ke^2 n^6}{6K_1^3 m^3}$$

Total energy $\propto n^6$

Total energy $\propto m^{-3}$

9. (a, b, c)

Since, $W = \int\vec{F}.d\vec{r}$

Clearly for forces (A) and (B) the integration do not require any information of the path taken.

For (C): $W_c = \displaystyle\int\frac{3(x\hat{i} + y\hat{j})}{(x^2 + y^2)^{3/2}}(dx\hat{i} + dy\hat{j}) = 3\int\frac{xdx + ydy}{(x^2 + y^2)^{3/2}}$

Taking : $x^2 + y^2 = t$

$$2x\,dx + 2y\,dy = dt \Rightarrow x\,dx + y\,dy = \frac{dt}{2}$$

$$\Rightarrow W_c = 3\int\frac{dt/2}{t^{3/2}} = \frac{3}{2}\int\frac{dt}{t^{3/2}} \text{ which is solvable}$$

Hence (a), (b) and (c) are conservative forces.
But (d) requires some more information on path. Hence non-conservative.

10. (a, b, c)

(a) $q = \displaystyle\int i\,dt$ = area of given curve $q = \dfrac{1}{2}i_0 t_0$

(b) $\dfrac{i}{i_0} + \dfrac{t}{t_0} = 1 \Rightarrow i = i_0\left(1 - \dfrac{t}{t_0}\right)$

(c) Heat $= \displaystyle\int i^2 R\,dt = \int_0^{t_0} i_0^2 R\left(1 - \frac{t}{t_0}\right)^2 dt\ ;\ H = \frac{Rt_0 i_0^2}{3}$

11. (b, c, d)

$$V_1 = V_2 \Rightarrow X_L = X_C \Rightarrow f = \frac{1}{2\pi\sqrt{LC}} = 125\text{ Hz}$$

$$I_0 = \frac{V_0}{R} = \frac{200}{100}\ (X = 0\ \because Z = R) = 2A$$

$\because V_1 = V_2 = IX_L = I.(\omega L) = 2\times 2\pi\times 125\times 2/\pi = 1000$ volt

12. (b, c, d)

Dimensions of energy per unit volume are
= dimensions of energy/dimensions of volume
$ML^2 T^{-2}/L^3 = ML^{-1}T^{-2}$.
Stress, pressure and modulus of elasticity all have the dimensions of $ML^{-1}T^{-2}$. The dimensions of work are $ML^2 T^{-2}$.

13. **(a, b, c)**

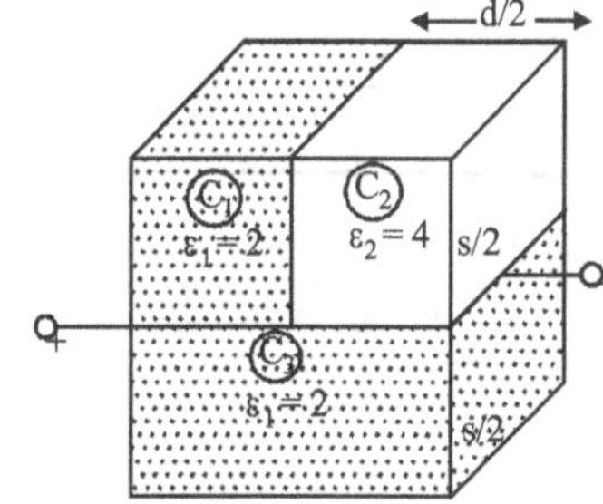

$$C_1 = \frac{2\,\varepsilon_0\, s/2}{d/2} \qquad C_2 = \frac{4\,\varepsilon_0\, s/2}{d/2}$$

$$C_3 = \frac{2\,\varepsilon_0\, s/2}{d} = \frac{\varepsilon_0 s}{d}$$

$$C_{eq} = \frac{C_1 \times C_2}{C_1 + C_2} + C_3 = \frac{\dfrac{2\varepsilon_0 s}{d} \times \dfrac{4\,\varepsilon_0 s}{d}}{\dfrac{6\varepsilon_0 s}{d}} + \frac{\varepsilon_0 s}{d}$$

$$= \frac{4}{3}\frac{\varepsilon_0 s}{d} + \frac{\varepsilon_0 s}{d}$$

$$\therefore \quad C_{eq} = \frac{7}{3}\frac{\varepsilon_0 s}{d} = \frac{7}{3}C_1 \qquad \left[\because C_1 = \frac{\varepsilon_0 s}{d}\right]$$

14. **(a, d)** From the figure it is clear that
    (a) $\sigma_2 > \sigma_1$
    (b) $\rho_2 > \sigma_2$ [As the string is taut]
    (c) $\rho_1 < \sigma_1$ [As the string is taut]
    $\therefore$ $\rho_1 < \sigma_1 < \sigma_2 < \rho_2$
When P alone is in L$_2$

$$V_P = \frac{2\pi r^2\,(\rho_1 - \sigma_2)g}{9\eta_2} \quad \text{is negative as } \rho_1 < \sigma_2$$

Where r is radius of sphere.
When Q alone is in L$_1$

$$V_Q = \frac{2\pi r^2\,(\rho_2 - \sigma_1)g}{9\eta_1} \quad \text{is positive as } \rho_2 > \sigma_1$$

Therefore $\vec{V}_P . \vec{V}_Q < O$ option (d) is correct

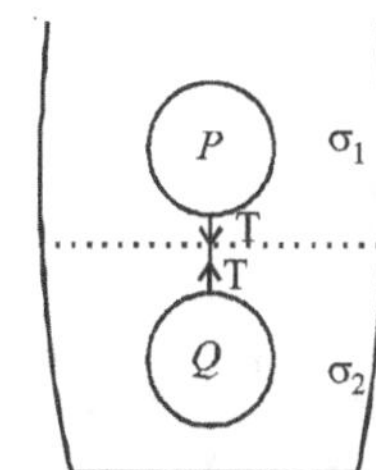

Also $\dfrac{V_P}{V_Q} = \dfrac{\rho_1 - \sigma_2}{\rho_2 - \sigma_1} \times \dfrac{\eta_1}{\eta_2}$ ...(i)

For equilibrium of Q

$$T + \frac{4}{3}\pi r^3\,\sigma_2 g = \frac{4}{3}\pi r^3\,\rho_2 g \qquad \text{...(ii)}$$

For equilibrium of P

$$T + \frac{4}{3}\pi r^3\,\rho_1 g = \frac{4}{3}\pi r^3\,\sigma_1 g \qquad \text{...(iii)}$$

(iii) − (ii) gives
$$\rho_1 - \sigma_2 = \sigma_1 - \rho_2 \qquad \text{...(iv)}$$
From (i) and (iv)

$$\frac{V_P}{V_Q} = -\frac{\eta_1}{\eta_2} \qquad \therefore \qquad \frac{|V_P|}{|V_Q|} = \frac{\eta_1}{\eta_2}$$

$\therefore$ A is also a correct option

15. **(a)**   The magnetic field B in the space between the two conductors is given by

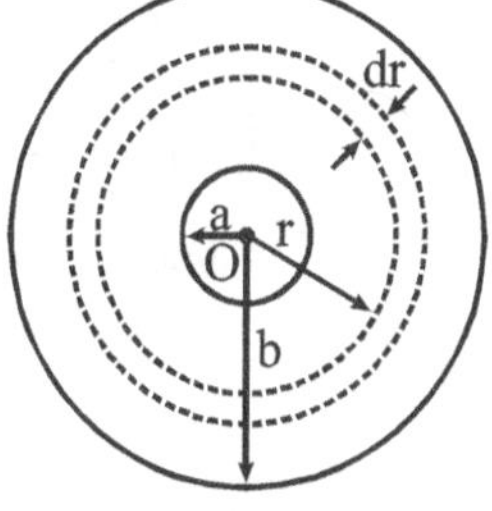

$$B = \frac{\mu_0 i}{2\pi r} \qquad \text{...(i)}$$

where, i = current in either of two conductors
r = distance of the point from the axis.

Because $\oint \vec{B}.d\vec{\ell} = \mu_0 \times$ current enclosed by the path
(Ampere's law)
or $B.2\pi r = \mu_0 i$
The energy density in the space between the conductors

$$u = \frac{B^2}{2\mu_0} = \frac{1}{2\mu_0}\left[\frac{\mu_0 i}{2\pi r}\right]^2 = \frac{\mu_0 i^2}{8\pi^2 r^2}\,\frac{\text{joule}}{\text{metre}^3}$$

Consider a volume element dV in the form of a cylindrical shell of radii r and (r + dr) as shown in the figure.

$$\text{Energy } dW = u\,dV = \frac{\mu_0 i^2}{8\pi^2 r^2} \times 2\pi r\,\ell dr = \frac{\mu_0 i^2 \ell}{4\pi}\left(\frac{dr}{r}\right)$$

Total magnetic energy can be obtained by integrating this expression between the limits r = a to r = b. Hence,

$$W = \int dW = \frac{\mu_0 i^2 \ell}{4\pi} \int_a^b \left(\frac{dr}{r}\right) = \frac{\mu_0 i^2 \ell}{4\pi}\log_e\left(\frac{b}{a}\right)$$

If L be the self inductance of length ℓ of the cable, then the energy in magnetic field will be $(1/2)Li^2$. Hence

$$\frac{1}{2}Li^2 = \frac{\mu_0 i^2 \ell}{4\pi}\log_e\left(\frac{b}{a}\right) \;;\; L = \frac{\mu_0 \ell}{2\pi}\log_e\left(\frac{b}{a}\right)$$

16. **(c)**   Let A and B are the two long parallel wires as shown which are formed to form a current loop. The two wires would obviously be carrying equal currents in opposite direction. Consider a space length ℓ and thickness dx as shown in figure.
The magnetic flux through the area ℓdx due to the currents in the two wires is $d\phi = B\ell dx$ where B is the intensity of magnetic field due to current carrying wires at a distance x from A.

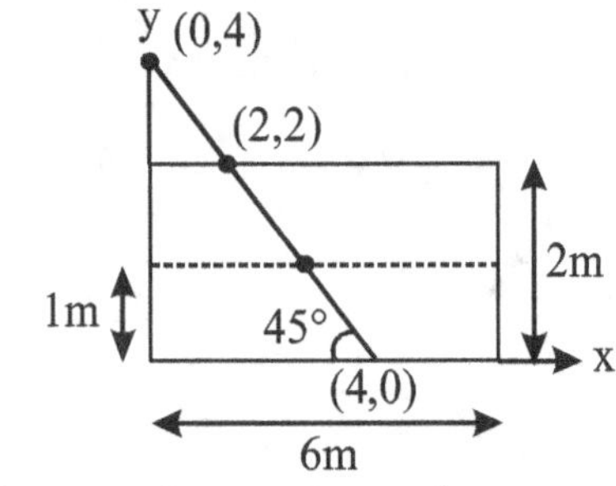

$$B = \frac{\mu_0}{2\pi}\frac{i}{x} + \frac{\mu_0}{2\pi}\cdot\frac{i}{d-x}$$

$$d\phi = B\ell dx = \frac{\mu_0 i}{2\pi}\left(\frac{1}{x} + \frac{1}{d-x}\right)\ell dx$$

$$\therefore \; \phi = \int_{r}^{d-r} \frac{\mu_0 i}{2\pi}\left(\frac{1}{x} + \frac{1}{d-x}\right)\ell dx$$

$$\frac{\mu_0 i\ell}{2\pi}[\log_e x - \log_e(d-x)]_r^{d-r} = \frac{\mu_0 i\ell}{\pi}\log_e\frac{d-r}{r}$$

Magnetic flux linked with unit length of the loop

$$\phi = \frac{\mu_0 i}{\pi}\log_e\frac{d-r}{r}$$

But $\phi = Li$ where L is self-inductance.

$$\therefore \; L = \frac{\mu_0}{\pi}\log_e\frac{d-r}{r}$$

17. (d) $$\frac{dy}{dx} = \frac{a_x}{a_y + g} = \frac{g/2}{-g/2 + g} = 1$$

(effective g will be $g - a = g/2$]
$\theta = 45°$

18. (c)

As the slope of free surface is 45°. Thus free surfaces passes through centre of box and having co-ordinates (2, 2) at top of box. Thus length of exposed top part $= 6 - 2 = 4m$.

www.ingramcontent.com/pod-product-compliance
Lightning Source LLC
LaVergne TN
LVHW080058160726
843469LV00047B/1840